DIGITAL DNA

Digital DNA

DISRUPTION AND THE CHALLENGES
FOR GLOBAL GOVERNANCE

Peter F. Cowhey and Jonathan D. Aronson

OXFORD
UNIVERSITY PRESS

OXFORD
UNIVERSITY PRESS

Oxford University Press is a department of the University of Oxford. It furthers
the University's objective of excellence in research, scholarship, and education
by publishing worldwide. Oxford is a registered trade mark of Oxford University
Press in the UK and certain other countries.

Published in the United States of America by Oxford University Press
198 Madison Avenue, New York, NY 10016, United States of America.

Library of Congress Cataloging-in-Publication Data
author. | Cowhey, Peter F., 1948– author.
Title: Digital DNA : disruption and the challenges for global governance /
Peter F. Cowhey, Jonathan D. Aronson.
Description: New York, NY : Oxford University Press, 2017.
Identifiers: LCCN 2016047342 | ISBN 9780190657932 (hardback) | ISBN 9780190657949 (updf) |
ISBN 9780190657956 (epub)
Subjects: LCSH: Telecommunication policy. | Internet governance. | Economic policy. | Disruptive
technologies. | Internet—Security measures.
Classification: LCC HE7645.A76 2017 | DDC 658.4/038—dc23
LC record available at https://lccn.loc.gov/2016047342

9 8 7 6 5 4 3 2

Printed by Sheridan Books, Inc., United States of America

As always,
for Margaret and Haruka
and for Joan, Adam, and Zachary

Contents

Prologue

REGIONAL INNOVATION CLUSTERS AND GLOBAL ECONOMIC GOVERNANCE

DIGITAL TECHNOLOGIES ARE becoming critical to every facet of the world economy. These digital technologies are the "digital DNA" that unleashes dazzling changes in the information, communication, and production capabilities that are transforming how the world works. We call this the information and production disruption (IPD). The IPD is rapidly altering the dynamics of firms, how markets perform, and the potential for stronger economic growth and social prosperity. Government policy makers with an eye to the future are searching for policies to leverage the best potential of these disruptions, but have yet to determine how to reconcile seemingly contradictory policy challenges. We offer recommendations for global economic governance that provide a new foundation for problem solving to cope with messy problems that inevitably accompany large-scale change. Despite the current political headwinds, we show how trade policy can be the key platform for enabling an extensive complementary set of regulatory and nongovernmental actions to govern the IPD productively.

Scholars, government officials, and corporate executives from around the Pacific Rim have frankly acknowledged to us that the disruption is occurring but that it is difficult to grasp because it is so multifaceted. This diffuseness makes it hard to distill the first priorities necessary for governance reform. We respond to this challenge by clarifying the fundamentals on how the IPD is altering national and global patterns of innovation. We choose this leverage point because economists agree that innovation—which we define as the commercialization of new knowledge—is central to global growth and prosperity. We further distill our inquiry by probing how the IPD alters the dynamics of regional innovation clusters.

We call the emerging regional patterns "digital platform clusters." These clusters extend the dynamics associated with digital platforms (often associated with giant information companies like Google and Microsoft)[1] to smaller specialized technology firms and, as important, to firms rooted in more traditional industries. The sustainable success of industries close to the heart of the economic agenda of the Trump Administration, such as autos and other heavy manufacturing markets, depends heavily on how the IPD evolves on a global scale.

The digital DNA of the new innovation model entails distinctively global forces. Global interactions allow information feedback cycles to speed the production of initial designs and constantly refine them. As a result, the prospects for digital platform clusters depend in part on sound global economic governance. The governance choices include traditional issues of market access and competition, but they also require choices about how to build a trusted digital environment that covers cybersecurity and digital privacy. Getting the governance of the IPD right is critical to capturing the growth opportunities afforded by this new model of innovation. Getting it wrong could slow the world economy in the coming decades. Even worse, bad governance choices could breed widespread social and political mistrust because of the cynicism that surrounds the use of digital technologies.

We explain how national policy responses intersect and potentially conflict with choices about global economic governance. In an interconnected world, the intersection of national and international choices alters the vector of technological and economic change. Hence, we propose a strategy for updating global governance that better reconciles the diversity of national preferences with the need for common global understandings about market governance. The necessary changes are too vast for a single book. Instead, we test our strategy against a series of "hard cases" that are critical to getting the governance of digital DNA right.

The specific catalyst for this effort is a reflection on a failed project. In 2009–2010, shortly after Cowhey exited from his senior trade policy role in the Obama administration, we agreed to become policy officers for an ambitious project of the Aspen Institute to chart ground rules for digital innovation in the world economy. The International Digital Economy Agreement, modestly called the IDEA project, had a talented, experienced leader on technology policy (Reed Hundt, a former chairman of the Federal Communications Commission), a strong professional management cast with deep policy experience (Gary Epstein, Don Abelson, and Charlie

Firestone), significant funding from foundations, and excellent participants from industry, civil society, and government. Yet, no consensus on first principles could be reached.

There were several reasons for the impasse at Aspen.[2] First, many participants doubted that the scope of the changes in information and communication technology (ICT) markets was so vast that significant updating of their traditional policy preferences was required. They favored nips and tucks over significant rethinking.

Second, IDEA covered too much ground in an integrated package. Everything was on the table: trade in digital technology and services, intellectual property, net neutrality, and freedom and speech rights on the Internet. Aggregation led to paralysis when we attempted to craft enlightened compromises.

Third, participants kept wondering how to make progress on an international agreement without the representation of the major emerging economies. What constituted a necessary core to get started globally?

Fourth, in an effort to bridge gaps and broker compromises, the project staff recommended going beyond status quo policy recommendations to embrace a significant new approach about how to manage global governance. The most controversial recommendation was a proposal to build a system of multistakeholder organizations (MSOs), joining together governments, industry, and civil society to undertake a larger share of the decision making about governance of the global digital economy. We saw no way to make the key policies binding without embedding them in a new treaty structure. Thus, we put forward an elaborate plan that proposed divisions of labor among MSOs and treaty-style obligations linking them to government policies. Our plan left participants, particularly those from the Obama Administration, wondering whether our approach would set the wrong precedent for discussions about how to restructure Internet governance. (Many of the government participants were focused on the challenges surrounding the "privatization" of the Internet Corporation for Assigned Names and Numbers.)[3] This time, we will show that existing treaty arrangements could be the anchor if countries wish to build on them.

We learned several lessons from the IDEA experience that ground this book. We want to be bolder, but also pragmatic. Hence, our process this time was different. We started by brainstorming with a few close colleagues with intimate knowledge of the changing dynamics of technology and markets. Along the way, we consulted with and interviewed senior government, private-sector, and nongovernmental organization stakeholders from various countries, as well as our fellow scholars. Responsibility for the recommendations, however, is ours alone.

Like the Internet, the IPD's future will be influenced by such threats as hackers, cyberattacks, limits on the global flow of data, and worries about the emergence of a world of digital haves and have-nots.[4] Nonetheless, we still believe that the best way forward involves pragmatic cooperation and compromise among public, private, and civic stakeholders coming together to work within MSOs. The MSO process itself is in vogue, but making it work requires a clear understanding of the respective roles of government and civil society. Our challenge is to persuade the stakeholders that progress and compromise are essential to innovation, job growth, and prosperity everywhere. We are encouraged that some leaders are urging initial steps toward embracing the challenge and taking the first steps toward international progress on cooperative solutions.[5] Our argument is a probe of where the first steps could ultimately lead. It unfolds in four parts.

The first step, in Part I, is to define the scale, character, and urgency of the challenge that is raised by digital DNA. Nongovernmental organizations, corporate executives, and policy officials can churn out memos and issue a profusion of white papers, but unless the issue at hand is of major importance and is time sensitive, neither senior government officials nor high-level business executives will devote enough of their scarce time and attention to solving the challenge.

We argue that the IPD is changing how societies innovate and is an important driver of global economic growth. We compare this emerging digital platform cluster model to the dominant innovation model of the past thirty years that was symbolized by the vast successes of Silicon Valley. Our discussions with senior business executives showed a far more widespread appreciation than in 2010 that the IPD is a big deal. Specialized government technocrats have also grasped the point. But, although top political leaders praise entrepreneurship and innovation, they are more preoccupied by debates over slow economic growth, job creation, and the complex links between globalization and economic inequality.[6] Layered on top of these concerns are worries about unfair trade and investment policies, a fear emphasized in the Presidential campaign of Donald Trump. And, although some of these complaints (such as Chinese industrial policy in digital industries) deserve serious attention and targeted policy responses, they also divert attention from the importance of IPD dynamics of such grassroot concerns as manufacturing and farming. Unless we get the global governance of the IPD right, it will be difficult to create the better jobs and higher productivity growth needed to fuel long-term economic progress. We synthesize the central dynamics of the changes to chart a path to making wise choices about the IPD's governance.

We build on several insightful studies of ongoing disruptive change that focus on individual management choices, particular economic consequences, or specific policy issues.[7] However, our concern is different. We seek a path toward an integrated approach to global economic governance that deals with ongoing disruptions, requiring a fresh approach to the synthesis of regulatory convergence, civic society engagement, and aspects of trade policy.[8] Part I highlights the critical importance of the IPD challenge, explores its links to the emergence of digital platform clusters, and lays out the pattern of governance choices.

We begin this assessment by analyzing today's dominant patterns of advanced technology innovation in the United States and elsewhere. Next, we examine the profound changes spurred by the IPD that are sweeping across firms and markets and the links between these changes and several major policy debates, especially competition in digital markets and the creation of a trusted digital environment. We conclude that the fate of a changed system of regional innovation and digital platform clusters will depend in important ways on choices about global economic governance. We sharpen our case by honing in on how two major firms in two distinct sectors, Monsanto and Qualcomm, are innovating in response to the IPD. Their strategies illuminate how governance and innovation policies must evolve.

Part II adds the next piece of the argument. We lay out a strategy and a design for governing the disruptions that relies on a mix of international agreements and the partial convergence of national policies that builds on our personal experience and the existing scholarship related to global governance and MSOs. Our focus is on governance instead of policy because private innovations by industry and civil society must complement government decisions and rules.

An international strategy that addresses the changing context of 21st-century global negotiations is needed for governance to evolve productively. Part II first considers who must be at the table and why. We take as a given that global economic power is dispersing and that governance preferences among actors are widening. Although more vigorous advocacy of particular national economic interests may influence specific advantages in global markets, the governance of the IPD will be more successful if there is some alignment of emerging national strategies. To build this foundation of collaboration will require bargaining, and therefore compromises among some cadre of countries. Therefore, we identify what would entail a "credible club," a core group of reasonably like-minded countries with sufficient influence to alter the world market through their choices. Over time, this club could add supporters and help forge important international governance innovations that eventually could win larger adherence. We also show why technocratic efficiency and political reality require that "civil society" play a larger role in any governance strategy.

Our strategy focuses on building from small groups of like-minded countries to larger coalitions because it creates greater credibility for new rules faster. But the Trump Administration seems likely to favor bilateral "deals." That does not doom a "club" strategy; the United States has mixed bilateral and plurilateral strategies in the past. But we urge careful thought on how to use bilateral pacts as templates for subsequent group negotiations.

Our approach also emphasizes the advantages of using trade as a platform for complementary regulatory and nongovernmental undertakings. Although recent political dynamics have diminished political support for trade policy, we remain convinced that it is still the simplest and sturdiest beginning point. Our discussion of cybersecurity demonstrates that various forms of cross-national regulatory collaboration can substitute for a trade foundation, but in the end such collaborations will repackage many of the features of trade pacts in new regulatory language. Therefore, we focus on trade as the beginning point of understanding which policies are needed for success. We also believe that trade and regulatory policies to enable the IPD globally are consistent with economic growth producing better jobs.

The IPD also requires that two different sets of bargaining challenges be addressed. First, there are "coordination" problems. Solutions to these types of problems include agreements on globally applied technical standards and national air traffic control systems with compatible practices for international flights. But coordination problems can slip into a second dynamic that scholars characterize as "cooperation" problems. Cooperation emerges from rough-and-tumble bargaining over negotiating challenges that seem to be the early focus of the Trump Administration. In cooperation situations, major actors may find that the best feasible solution is the second-best outcome from their individual perspective. Therein lies the challenge. Even the second-best solution may elude us because each player pursuing its best outcome may lead to collective failure. Actors also may not choose to focus on cooperation solutions. The successful resolutions of coordination and cooperation challenges often are linked. We propose a strategy to link coordination and cooperation mechanisms.

To decide how to proceed, we first must determine how much uniformity is necessary or politically possible among global policies. The trick is to embrace a strategy that helps sort out the minimum necessary degree of coordination. In some cases, convergence is less critical, as when the European Union (EU) and the United States are moving in close policy lock step. What is more important is the removal of certain risks created by the diversity of their policy rules. In other cases, more harmonization on a single policy is vital. It depends on the nature of the interdependence. To support our case, we compare and contrast the level of necessary harmonization needed to improve the security of digital e-commerce payments with what is needed to safeguard cross-border financial payments among banks.

In addition, in developing a design strategy, we repeatedly stress the importance of achieving an appropriate minimum baseline of authoritative international agreement. This baseline can mix "soft" rules that commit governments to create certain types of policy and governance capabilities and "hard" rules that command or forbid specific forms of behavior. For example, both types of rules are binding in trade agreements, but the right mix of hard and soft facilitates partial convergence of national governance approaches and still allows for national diversity in the policy mix.

The baseline also should pave the way for complementary governance mechanisms. We believe that, deployed appropriately, MSOs allow a more flexible, experimental, and expert way to link a policy framework to implementation schemes that can better respond to dynamic technological environments.[9] MSOs also can make it easier to nudge political–economic coalitions across national boundaries toward more compatible understandings of their interests.[10] We conclude that it is counterproductive to seek a neatly architected scheme of interrelated MSOs to respond to major issues. Ad hoc specialization and problem solving through many different kinds of institutions will prove superior to a grand scheme. But MSOs can only be fully effective if governments set clear baselines for policy and hold MSOs accountable. The use of international agreements that permit a greater role for MSOs in governance is an important building block for the management of the IPD.

Part III provides a detailed examination of three representative issues that are critical to the dynamics of digital platform clusters—cloud computing, cybersecurity, and privacy. These three issues, which the IPD brings to the fore, must be disaggregated and addressed to avoid paralysis.[11] We test our preferred governance strategy against these hard problems for global governance raised by the IPD. Other important issues remain, but these three case studies illustrate the particular policy challenges created by the IPD.

The first case covers governance for cloud computing and its related services (a foundational capability for the IPD). It focuses on the international commercial rules governing the emerging cloud architecture for computing, information-enabled services, and the associated issue of the transborder movement of data. Significant competition and market access issues loom in the growth of an inherently global information infrastructure. Trade negotiators have tackled part of the governance challenge, but we point out how civil society innovations are changing the "facts on the ground" while negotiators groped for consensus on some formal trade rules. We conclude that rules governing cloud computing and data flows will be effective only if they are linked to ways to forge a trusted digital environment.

The second case concentrates on international issues pertaining to cybersecurity. Creating a trusted digital environment requires strengthening cybersecurity and data privacy, not a comprehensive framework. We explore the governance of cybersecurity using cases from the finance sector.

The third case considers challenges about the balance between the economic gains from Big Data and the protection of personal privacy. We examine the privacy of data based on a comparison of the contrasting U.S. and EU approaches as a springboard for our analysis. This negotiation permits a better balancing of the costs and benefits of different forms of regulation, a key concern of conservative economic analysts.

Cybersecurity and privacy are "hard cases" for global economic governance because, until recently, they largely were outside the frameworks of binding international agreements. Instead, they relied on consensus statements of normative expectations and endorsements of best practices. We argue that our strategy for governance creates more productive governance options.

The three issue areas are interlinked. Thus, it is hard to imagine a productive governance regime for the cloud ecosystem that exists separate from some common international understandings about cybersecurity and digital privacy. At the same time, we show that tidy grand bargains are unnecessary to make progress on these linked issues.

Finally, in the concluding chapter we suggest linking, or nesting, international agreements to advance a trusted digital environment into annexes of a new digital economy agreement to address gaps in trade policy related to the IPD's impact on the functioning of world markets. We argue that such linkage is synergistic because it will strengthen the pacts on the trusted digital environment and reduce risks that rules on privacy and security will become excuses for protectionist strategies. There are several ways to anchor these policy arrangements to binding international agreements, but trade is the simplest conceptual and practical fit, so we focus on it in our proposal.

The most antitrade U.S. presidential campaign in memory has now concluded. The short and medium-term future of trade policy and agreements under the Trump Administration will diverge sharply in parts from past trade approaches. During the campaign Donald Trump and Hillary Clinton both opposed ratification of the Trans-Pacific Partnership (TPP) in its present form and followed through on this campaign promise on the Monday after his inauguration. Donald Trump also advocated tearing up the North American Free Trade Agreement. On the other side of the Atlantic, the consequences of Britain's vote on June 23, 2016, to exit the EU and the defeat of the Italian Constitutional Referendum on December 4, 2016, which could undermine the Euro, continue to unfold as this volume moves towards publication. The ultimate consequences of the Brexit shock, and the defeat of the Renzi reforms in Italy, and the election of Emmanuel Macron in the French presidential election in May of 2017 are unknown.

The current divisive controversies raise proper concerns over the political will to rely on trade agreements to address crucial governance choices. Although we believe that, as a whole, we are far better off because of trade agreements, we also recognize that they have not delivered the unmitigated benefits that they promised and Congress has failed to provide and pay for adjustment mechanisms for those injured by trade. The funding for trade adjustment assistance to retrain and reemploy workers displaced by trade agreements and the IPD was wholly inadequate.[12] Further, the TPP and Transatlantic Trade and Investment Partnership (TTIP, the TPP's more European counterpart) are so ambitious in scope that their specific provisions on the IPD are lost in other controversies involving the pacts. Even assuming the TTIP follows the TPP in succumbing to current political passions, the provisions tied to the IPD may emerge in new packaging, and with important enhancements, as a new generation of political leadership recognizes that the proper global governance will remove impediments to the economic future they champion.

Preparing for a moment that is "riper" for negotiating and reaching an agreement, we explore the template of a trade agreement for a stand-alone pact on the digital economy. Our purpose is to show what could be done. Experienced negotiators would make adjustments as necessary. We argue that starting with a trade template provides a governance infrastructure of established principles (such as nondiscrimination) that simplify the creation of specific governance frameworks on issues such as improved market access for providers of the cloud infrastructure and its digital ecosystem of services and goods. Many who are not trade policy devotees may be surprised that trade agreements also can strengthen national commitments to create governing capabilities that could advance digital privacy and security. They could provide principles and norms needed to underpin a converged, coordinated international baseline of soft and hard rules, including significant privacy principles. (We believe that we are the first to propose a way to incorporate privacy protection systematically into trade policy.) At the same time, the negotiating process allows for a closer coordinated review of the costs and benefits of various governance choices, all of which are important to getting the proper balance of growth and safeguards of civil liberties right.

Along with many critics of trade agreements, we conclude that traditional trade agreements alone will fail as a governance response. Our approach allows ample room for variance in national policies and for extensive reliance on civil society innovations. We also rely on coordination among national regulators and MSOs to produce workable governance arrangements. We believe that, in a time of profound economic and technological transition, the philosophy of economic governance must emphasize the virtues of experimentation and learning, two tricks that are difficult to fold into traditional governance arrangements. But if trade agreements turn out to be a political "bridge too far," other ways exist to package international agreements to achieve many of the same purposes.

Ultimately, this book is an extended thought experiment or plausibility probe. We do not know whether every part of our argument is correct (although we are prepared to defend each part vigorously). But the architecture of the argument shows how to integrate the digital DNA driving the IPD into a more ambitious line of policy development. Comments, criticisms, and corrections of our errors and omissions will, we hope, refine the end-game solution as we move forward. We think that we have a better "IDEA" than our last engagement on this challenge, but we also recognize that it is imperfect.

The authors take full responsibility for the errors, distortions, and misunderstandings in the book that follows. But we also owe a tremendous debt to our friends and colleagues. We are especially grateful to Don Abelson, Sam Bozzette, Dan Breznitz, Tai Ming Cheung, Bob Friedman, David Hytha, Al Pisano, John Richards, and Stefan Savage for brainstorming with us. We also thank Manuel Castells, Todd Coleman, Stefan Haggard, Pramod Khargonekar, Nahoi Koo, James Lambright, Noëlle Lenoir, Margaret Levi, Nathalie Marechal, David Michael, Robert Pepper, Camille Saucier, David Victor, and Yiru Zhou for useful comments. Peter Cowhey was in residence at Sciences Po in Paris for part of 2014. He learned much that shaped the book's argument. We also are grateful to Parul Agarwal, Galen Berkowitz, Nahoi Koo, Peter Larson, Mingda Qiu, Nick Sramek, and Heran Wang for research assistance.

Notes

1. For example, see Nicholas Carr, *The Big Switch: Rewiring the World, from Edison to Google* (New York: Norton, 2008).

2. These are the authors' conclusions. Others may differ. The final report of the IDEA project is Aspen Institute, "Project on International Digital Economy Accords, toward a Single Global Digital Economy," April 24, 2012, http://csreports.aspeninstitute.org/documents/IDEA_Project_Toward_a_Single_Global_Digital_Economy.pdf.

3. The proposal submitted to the U.S. government for the future structure of ICANN operations in 2106 was derived from an MSO model, https://www.icann.org/en/system/files/files/iana-stewardship-transition-proposal-10mar16-en.pdf.

4. Global Commission on Internet Governance, "One Internet," final report by the Centre for International Governance and the Royal Institute for International Affairs, 2016 (hereafter the Bildt Commission), http://ourinternet.org/report#chapter--preface.

5. Others are weighing in on the creation of a global digital marketplace. One especially insightful suggestion is in a report co-chaired by two leaders in the Atlantic community, Carl Bildt and William Kennard: "Building a Transatlantic Digital Marketplace: Twenty Steps toward 2020," the Lisbon Council, April 4, 2016, http://www.lisboncouncil.net/news-a-events/688-building-a-transatlantic-digital-marketplace-twenty-steps-to-2020.html. More briefly, see "Bildt and Kennard: Obama and Merkel: A Chance to Make History in Hanover," Atlantic Council, April 23, 2016, http://www.politico.eu/article/barak-obama-and-angela-merkel-a-chance-to-make-history-in-hannover/.

6. Chapter 2 explicitly discusses how our approach to the IPD relates to the growth and inequality debates.

7. Works that probe the IPD include Larry Downes and Paul Nunnes, *Big Bang Disruption* (New York: Portfolio/Penguin, 2014); Gautam Shroff, *The Intelligent Web: Search, Smart Algorithms, and Big Data* (New York: Oxford University Press, 2014); Erik Brynjolfsson and Andrew McAfee, *The Second Machine Age: Work, Progress, and Prosperity in a Time of Brilliant Technologies* (New York: Norton, 2014), and Joshua Gans, *The Disruption Dilemma*, (Cambridge, MA: MIT Press, 2016).

8. Excellent examples of traditional trade analysis are found in the works of William Cline, Gary Clyde Hufbauer, Marcus Noland, Jeffrey Schott, and others issued by the Peterson Institute on International Economics, http://www.iie.com/. A more sweeping approach to governance is found in Robert D. Atkinson and Stephen J. Ezell, *Innovation Economics: The Race for Global Advantage* (New Haven, CT: Yale University Press, 2012).

9. Ian Brown and Christopher T. Marsden, in *Regulating Code: Good Governance and Better Regulation in the Information Age* (Cambridge, MA: MIT Press, 2014), provide a complementary line of arguments.

10. Even profit-maximizing multinationals calculate their interests differently depending on the national context or, more precisely, the institutional channels through which they frame their policy choices. Cornelia Woll, *The Power of Inaction: Bank Bailouts in Comparison* (Ithaca, NY: Cornell University Press, 2014).

11. The case against broadly synoptic policy schemes was brilliantly laid out almost four decades ago. See Charles Lindblom, *Politics and Markets* (New York: Basic Books, 1977), and Aaron Wildavsky, *Speaking Truth to Power: The Art and Craft of Policy Analysis* (New York: Little, Brown, 1979).

12. David H. Autor, David Dorn, and Gordon H. Hanson, "The China Syndrome: Local Labor Market Effects of Import Competition in the United States," *American Economic Review*, 103, no. 6 (2013): 2121–2168.

I The Evolution of Innovation Systems and of Information and Production Disruption

1 National Innovation Systems

THE WORLD'S SYSTEM for innovation is facing disruptive changes. This is significant because innovation is a major driver of long-term economic growth and per capita income.[1] Although individual innovations can dramatically impact economies and societies, they are also a product of a system of innovation in a national economy. This book explores how disruptive changes that emanate from information and communications technologies (ICT) and production technologies are changing national innovation systems and the implications of these changes for global economic governance. We think of this as the digital DNA of the evolving world economy.

Technological disruption has three broad effects. The first-order consequences are changes in the organization and business models that dominate specific markets. New mixes of winners and losers pave the way for new political economic coalitions that can influence policy dynamics. The second-order consequences are changes in the dynamics of national innovation systems that respond to changing marketplaces. Innovation is more than the product of inspired individuals or ambitious firms; it is part of a system of complementary functions that emerge in national economies. These innovation systems evolve over time and impact how societies grow and operate. The third-order consequences are the emergence of potential gains and complementary risks that require management. Governance is important for charting the path of change because it is an instrument for managing the opportunities and risks created by innovation and the disruption that confronts major stakeholders.

Moreover, the type of governance bends the path for the disrupted innovation system.[2]

Chapter 1 defines a national innovation system, discusses how disruptions can change innovation systems over time, and examines the implications of these systems for the world economy. Chapters 2 and 3 elaborate on how the disruptions will alter markets and governance issues. We conclude that the disruptions will transform traditional manufacturing and service markets, as well as "high-technology" markets. Some pundits dub this phenomenon the "third industrial revolution," but this term is too narrow. The information and production disruption (IPD) of digital DNA will alter how national innovation systems work.

A clearer picture of the challenges and opportunities confronting global governance choices emerges from our examination of the link between the disruptions and the pattern of governance choice. We identify the problem that must be solved to update and improve public policy and governance. Government intervention will be necessary, but where should policy makers begin and how far should they venture?

Our discussion of national innovation systems focuses on the United States, the world leader in high technology since 1945, because its innovation model influenced practices and policies elsewhere. During the past seven decades, America saw at least two dominant models of innovation. To illustrate how national innovation systems may vary among capitalist economies, we also briefly compare the American and Korean systems. South Korea often employed strong government intervention to support export-led industrialization and was a pioneering leader in technological upgrading and rapid economic growth in East Asia. Hence, South Korea provides a contrast to the U.S. approach to markets and illuminates the path followed by many emerging economic powers. South Korea also is representative of how national governments often benchmark their national innovations systems against the U.S. system.

1.1. Defining Innovation and Innovation Systems

Economists acknowledge the benefits of technological innovation for growth, but more thorough economic analysis of the dynamics of innovation is needed.[3] In line with Schumpeter's classic approach, we define innovation as the commercialization of new knowledge.[4]

We think of innovation as the product of a system where the relationships among inputs, the environment, and planned output mesh in typical patterns of interaction. Performance trade-offs exist for every organizational form. Indeed, as the American experience since 1945 shows, every system of innovation contains trade-offs and is vulnerable to disruption. Hence, the way in which innovation is organized changes periodically as the environment for innovation evolves and the characteristics of the technological possibilities shift. Still, all national innovation systems have the same five building blocks.[5]

1. *Social networks and dynamic labor markets*: Innovation thrives where there are clusters of entrepreneurs, scientists, engineers, and experts who interact in unpredictable ways to facilitate the generation and diffusion of ideas while continuing to protect crucial intellectual property.

2. *Shared assets that lower costs for innovative companies*: Innovation typically draws on complementary assets beyond the boundaries of the firm. These assets include universities, research facilities, and new social infrastructure, such as broadband, that lower the cost of production and distribution. Regional technology clusters and social networks often play an important role in creating such shared assets.[6]

3. *Flexible business models*: Many innovations fail because firms do not develop new business models to capture their potential. The iPod business model, for example, turned the prevailing wisdom of the day—that content was more lucrative than hardware—upside down.

4. *Financial models to support innovation*: Innovation requires that innovative ideas can secure funding and move from concept into production and the market, whether they involve banks, capital markets, or venture capital.

5. *Appropriate government policies*: Appropriate policies are needed, but may range from research and development (R&D) support to corporate governance to policies related to foreign trade and investment.[7]

Innovation takes several forms, and countries excel in different types of innovation at various times. For example, most discussions of innovation highlight novel breakthrough developments that fostered game-changing American technology and generated enormous economic benefits.[8] Think of this first category as *novel-product innovation*. Examples include lasers and the modern web search engine. A second category encompasses a larger stream of *incremental and process innovation*, including incremental product innovations. Examples of incremental innovations include continual improvements in automobile transmissions or the German machine tool industry, together with innovations in production processes. Since the 1980s, globalization of design, production, sophisticated manufacturing, and distribution transformed incremental and process innovation. A third innovation variant is *architectural product innovation*, which could grow in importance. In 1990, Rebecca Henderson and Kim Clark noted, "There is growing evidence that there are numerous technical innovations that involve apparently modest changes to the existing technology but that have quite dramatic competitive consequences."[9] As the iPad demonstrated, the essence of architectural innovation is the reconfiguration of well-established technological capabilities in important new ways. For years, Korea specialized in incremental and process innovation and has now moved strongly into architectural innovation. China is following a similar path.

1.2. Changing National Innovation Systems: The American and Korean Experiences

To show how innovation systems can change, we focus on the evolution of the U.S. innovation system as a baseline, because for decades the United States was the leader in high-end (novel-product and architectural) innovation. We concentrate on higher-end innovations, but recognize the long history of regional clusters and national systems that focus on incremental and process innovation.[10] Changes in the U.S. innovation system had wider ramifications because they swept across the global competitive landscape. The systems of Korea, Germany, and other important innovators diverge in important respects from the U.S. system, but these countries explicitly or implicitly use the U.S. system as a benchmark for their own national progress. Hence, global impacts arose. To underscore how innovation systems may vary, we will suggest how the Korean system is distinctive.[11]

1.2.1. The Vertically Integrated Firm Model: The First Wave of Innovation after 1945

Two dominant but overlapping U.S. innovation systems thrived since World War II. The first relied heavily on the efforts of vertically integrated firms. The second is now thought of as the Silicon Valley model of startup-driven innovation.

After 1945, U.S. research spending and technology production were centered in large enterprises conducting novel, as well as incremental and process innovation in house. Typically, first-wave innovators were vertically integrated (from production to final sales) and many had substantial product diversification. Many enterprises worked in both defense and civilian markets. These firms had production and design know-how and basic research talent that could be shared within the firm as new ideas for commercialization emerged. For individual business divisions, the management talent guiding production capacity represented a shared asset that could be tapped for new product lines. These firms also possessed enormous financial and human capital resources. They internalized many of the financial risk management functions for innovation, including pools of "patient capital" that could be invested in novel products without the expectation of rapid returns. In many cases, U.S. government defense and infrastructure programs provided early pilot funding and resources to scale up through government procurement.

These companies internalized social networking among specialist groups in different phases of design and production. For example, AT&T's Bell Labs designed its facilities with long halls, forcing researchers to walk past other labs, creating opportunities for conversation and unforeseen collaboration.[12] In addition, these firms took advantage of their scale and scope to roll out large innovations in novel business packages. IBM's leasing arrangements for its pathbreaking "bet the company" IBM System/360 mainframe computer departed sharply from traditional sales models. Similarly, Boeing recognized that global sales of jet aircraft required the company to create an informal "foreign aid" group to provide technical assistance for other countries to upgrade their airports, air traffic, and aviation safety systems. This assistance helped persuade many countries to buy their planes from Boeing.[13]

U.S. government policies were especially helpful in this era. They continued World War II mobilization in Cold War trappings. The government spent massively to support firms, universities, and national labs on basic R&D.[14] Defense and related civilian technology efforts, from DARPA to NASA to health, provided large-scale purchasing power that fueled commercial innovation. To fill a human capital gap, the government also recruited the best German scientific talent after 1945. Furthermore, the Great Depression prompted regulatory innovations for financial markets (such as generally accepted accounting principles) that made large-scale capitalization easier and less expensive by fostering greater transparency in financial markets.

This first-wave innovation model receded after American corporations were battered by the Japanese economic challenges beginning in the 1970s. Japanese firms had studied the American innovation model and significantly refined the approaches of American firms. The "Toyota way" embodied the essence of the Japanese challenge in incremental process innovation. Japanese firms made quality improvement innovations that lowered production costs. The Japanese challenge also spilled over into microelectronics and other novel product fields. Japanese government industrial policy further bolstered the challenge by deflecting foreign competition in the Japanese home market. This was important because Japan was still in a period of high growth "takeoff" and maintained high prices at home, which generated significant corporate profits in strategic markets.

In response, by the 1980s, giant American firms began corporate restructurings that focused narrowly on their "core competencies," where they enjoyed sustainable advantages and could continuously renovate cost and product structures. These reforms reduced product diversification and allowed the firms to prune support for general R&D groups, thus aligning research more closely with anticipated commercial needs.[15] These firms also shifted their finances as financial markets began to "monitor" publicly traded firms by emphasizing quarterly financial returns and investment. Executive compensation was tied closely to these metrics. Ultimately, this incentive system perversely affected long-term investments by firms because the pressures of quarterly benchmarks often induced caution about long-term investments.[16] Although firms such as Intel in high-value-added industries with larger profit margins showed that massive spending on capital-intensive investments with long-term paybacks was still possible, the strategy faced a steeper threshold for approval under this approach.

Korea translated this first-wave model into the chaebol, its own distinctive variation of a multidivisional firm.[17] The Korean experience, since its takeoff in the 1960s and 1970s, was built around large, integrated groups that were initially the heart of economic growth. At first, chaebols were driven by strong investment in physical and human capital and successful technological borrowing from abroad. They became adept at manufacturing and the incremental development of production technologies. These groups were more diversified than their American counterparts, operating in virtually every major product market. Chaebols leveraged complementarities among nominally independent firms and invested heavily in R&D and other shared assets. The movement of managers and engineers within chaebols supported innovation. Funding came from the state-owned banking system and from financial transactions among group companies. The government supported industrial policies, including select barriers meant to hamper entry by foreign competitors in important industries. Korean policy relied less on university or government research centers than that in the United States.

The Korean model rested on successful technological borrowing from abroad, coupled with small incremental innovations in production technologies. Over time, Korean firms mastered complex manufacturing processes and developed cutting-edge production technologies in steel, shipbuilding, automobiles, integrated circuits, and other goods. More recently, larger Korean consumer electronics firms moved from global export production bases for software and hardware to commercially viable innovations and standards. Since the 1997–1998 Asian financial crisis, Korea significantly opened its market to foreign competitors.[18]

1.2.2. The Rise of the Silicon Valley Model: The Second Wave

The second wave of innovation—ascendant in the United States since the 1980s—was dominated by a technology cluster system built around startup firms and venture capital (VC). One or more research universities usually served as the anchor for second-wave regional clusters.[19] For example, Silicon Valley and Boston's Route 128 dominated information technology (IT), with Seattle a close third. Biotech innovation clustered in San Francisco, Boston, and San Diego. Communications technology, once the stronghold of the East Coast, mostly migrated to California, with technology for terrestrial networks concentrated in the north and that for wireless networks in the south. Content leadership was centered in Los Angeles and New York.

The new firms evolved rapidly. Their business models shifted as they grew more central as suppliers of key inputs to established suppliers such as Intel, Microsoft, IBM, Cisco, and Lucent. The new firms resembled many of the specialized suppliers found in the supply chain of global automobile makers. Unlike first-wave suppliers, however, these second-wave firms quickly claimed increasing shares of the value chain and often defined the leading edge of innovation for the entire market. Rapid scaling of novel, specialized solutions was at the core of the startup models. Frequently, this entailed significant innovations in business models in a manner unimaginable in the machine shops in Michigan and Ohio. Google's emphasis on free search, and later on software monetized by ads, disrupted the Microsoft model. (Earlier, Microsoft had disrupted the vertically integrated IBM business.)

Another feature of the second wave was widespread vertical disintegration, a process that ultimately forced changes in first-wave firms. Startups ruthlessly specialized, which allowed them to capture value by defining standards and reaping returns from product design and brand management. Expertise in managing complex international production networks—mostly manufacturing in Asia—also emerged as a core competence.

Clusters were built on components of national innovation systems. Successful innovation clusters require deep social and informational networking. Strong social networks, abetted by formal and informal institutions, are essential to the circulation of knowledge and people and for building the trust that makes for successful clusters.[20] In addition, cluster leaders acknowledge that people are the most important asset for ambitious innovation industries. Clusters provide a social institutional response to the narrowness of the human networks in highly specialized firms. They also develop informal normative and formal legal mechanisms to protect important intellectual property while people and ideas circulate.

Anchor universities became critical both for the underlying R&D for startups and for the training and networking of their employees. This occurred because flows of people take place in the context of a technological innovation pattern that depends more on science and engineering research than on incremental processes of trial and error.[21] However, the flow of knowledge depends at least as much on informal networks of people as on formal technology transfer from universities to companies. Among the companies in a cluster, the flows of people that matter may be either scientific personnel or skilled managers. For example, funders often push clusters located some distance from their Silicon Valley base to hire experienced managers. Otherwise, the VCs worry that they will be unable to personally watch their more distant startup investments as closely as they can those located nearby. This effort may explain why clusters, like those in San Diego, see strong interaction between managers and researchers in their large research universities. The university is a common gathering point for two types of scarce talent.[22]

The second-wave system matured in the context of common assets (some public, some private). Common assets in the private sector emerged for production (through networks of contract manufacturers), quality testing, and knowledge creation. Sometimes, as for measurement technology for semiconductors, these assets were a product of the combined investments by industry and government. Other assets depended on regional sharing arrangements, for instance, when time was rented on electron microscopes from research universities.[23]

New systems of finance were part of the digital DNA of the second wave. When academic researchers were not part of internal corporate innovation systems, startups raised funds by courting venture and angel investors attuned to the region and to promoting incubators and, later, startup boot camps, which lowered costs and identified prospective investors. New laws and regulations that allowed and incentivized the creation of novel financial vehicles were essential to this model. VC and the creation of markets such as NASDAQ rapidly generated large financial gains. In addition, major financial business strategy innovations emerged from the flexible American organization of financial markets. Starting in late 1984, Goldman Sachs helped the system of initial public offerings scale enormously by placing them with large institutional investors, rather than individual retail customers.[24]

Although the U.S. government periodically resorted to VC-style funds to support the Central Intelligence Agency, e-Energy, and other projects, the heart of the U.S. VC system is in the private sector. This divorce from government was critical to the system's success. Innovation often arises from the unexpected, not from the consensus views that too frequently guide the funding path of more risk-averse, government-related VC funds.[25]

Finally, both national and local policies undergirded these regional clusters. These policies funded basic and applied R&D, promoting the training of researchers and engineers. Several important changes altered how universities related to government and the private sector. The 1980 Bayh–Dole Act allowed universities, small businesses, and nonprofit institutions to commercially license the results from federally funded research. Securities and Exchange Commission rules also introduced changes in how pension funds could invest, allowing such entities to invest with VCs.[26] There also was considerable experimentation with intellectual property law because firms sought to strengthen intellectual property protection while allowing the knowledge sharing that second-wave innovators depended on. The U.S. government also opted to use "light-hand" regulation in technologically dynamic markets. For example, the government largely refrained from selecting mandatory technology standards and initially adopted a "green field" view of e-commerce markets to remove it from traditional regulatory frameworks.[27]

Significantly, federal competition policy initiatives, especially the breakup of AT&T in the early 1980s, opened many markets for new technological entrants. America's continental market and the major regional economic clusters within it are ever-present factors that strongly influence the political economy of the United States. They are reinforced by the constitutional reliance on federalism and the specific makeup of the U.S. Senate, which gives equal weight to every state, regardless of the size of its population. As a result, regional rivalries reinforced normal industry disputes, giving momentum to the push for vigorous competition policy.[28] Competition policy usually seeks to reinforce the right of competitive entry into markets. Thus, a series of ICT-related antitrust cases from the 1950s to the 1990s established policies that favored "modularity" in the design of systems. Modularity created standardized, easy-to-use interconnections between the systems of dominant suppliers. Hence, the offerings of dominant competitors were publicly disclosed and relatively easily accessed, providing critical policy support for the emerging technology startup system.

As U.S. partisan politics intensified, regional anchors and supporting federal measures made the second-wave model politically viable in both Democrat- and Republican-dominated states.[29] These commitments could strengthen the innovation environment, helping to promote a virtuous circle. For example, "research environment" is an important criterion for scoring National Institute of Health applicants. A high score can bolster a region's competitiveness.[30] This measurement encouraged efforts to improve common research assets (such as electron microscope sharing) because they were fed into the scoring system for National Institute of Health grants.

The emergence of the second wave did not altogether displace first-wave innovators, but most of them needed to retool to respond to the rise of new domestic business models and rising competition from abroad, particularly from Asia. Many of today's U.S. corporate giants began as second-wave startups. The thirty firms that make up the Dow Jones index include venerable first-wave companies such as 3M, IBM, Boeing, and Coca-Cola, oil giants such as Chevron and ExxonMobil, and financial behemoths like Goldman Sachs, JPMorgan, and Visa. It also includes firms that participated in the second-wave model: Apple, Cisco, Intel, Microsoft, and retail firms such as Home Depot, McDonald's, and Nike that share some characteristics with the restructured giants of the first wave.

The most successful of these giants gravitated to platform economic models. Like any form of market organization, however, platforms can vary significantly in their scope and scale. In the second wave, some companies emerged to become powerful players in specialized markets and technological niches. They owned pieces of specialized technological expertise used by many other players.[31] In this context, ownership means that they commanded the core know-how more fully than their rivals, successfully scaled global supply and service support, and used intellectual property to reinforce their position. The technology often was highly specialized in its role in larger product spaces. Qualcomm and Cisco are examples of such companies. A second group successfully created general-purpose platforms—a technical competence that is foundational to a vast scope of complementary products and markets. General platforms can be unusually stable because they are "sticky" and have penetrated so many dissimilar markets.[32] These firms, which included Microsoft in the 1990s, supplied something akin to a general-purpose technology, like electricity, for many critical functions that are important to various applications. Once others invested in the platform, they were reluctant to leave it because a huge array of complementary assets depended on the platform.

1.2.3. Benchmarking Korea's Second Wave

Korean firms reaped advantages but also faced challenges with the rise of the second wave.[33] In sectors such as automobiles and shipbuilding, the first-wave chaebol form was well suited to continuing incremental product innovation and moving up the value chain, even as they struggled against global competitors. In other sectors, particularly consumer electronics, Korea became skilled in incremental and even architectural innovations and developed its own production networks in Asia and beyond.

Yet as Korea transitioned to an advanced industrial state, its ability to continue to grow on the back of an input-driven model declined. Korea's presence in the Asia-Pacific provides advantages, but also challenges as it navigates a path between rising regional competitors and the continuing ability of the United States, Japan, and Europe to push the technological frontier. As then president Park Geun-hye's innovation initiative in 2014 calling for a "creative economy" acknowledged, sustained growth will increasingly rely on continued innovation and creativity, in services as well as manufacturing, among suppliers, small and medium-size enterprises (SMEs), new startups, and the largest chaebols.[34] A new Ministry of Science, ICT, and Future Planning was established to promote the creative economy.[35]

How did Korea's innovation system change in ways that aligned with and differed from the United States along the dimensions just outlined? First, with respect to business strategies, the chaebol form persisted, but with a much greater share of total economic activity occurring within individual chaebols than was the case for evolving first-wave and particularly second-wave American companies. Chaebols developed networks of dedicated onshore and offshore suppliers, which increased skills and capacity. But so far, strong innovation in the Korean SME sector from startups and established suppliers has lagged. Strengthening the SME sector was a central focus of President Park's innovation strategy.

A second feature of the overall Korean business environment is the weak performance of the service sector. Services account for about half of the Korean gross domestic product and 6% of employment, but they contribute little to overall productivity growth, except for some Internet services. A major challenge for Korea is to incentivize a more dynamic service economy through increased foreign investment and other methods.[36]

Labor immobility was one reason why the new clustering strategy failed to fully take root. Chaebols still effectively guide the movement of personnel. They can hire talent from SMEs, limiting their growth. But the reverse is not true. Youth unemployment and job security concerns, the prestige associated with chaebol employment (often reinforced by parental pressure to choose a prestigious job), and group loyalty limit the flow of personnel from large firms to smaller entrepreneurial firms. Moreover, at least in anecdotal accounts from Korean executives, the Korean labor market has yet to value the human capital benefits that are learned from entrepreneurial failure. This is in sharp contrast to the U.S. startup market.

With respect to shared assets and the related phenomenon of clustering, linkages between the large and small private-sector firms, universities, and government research institutes remain suboptimal. Universities have yet to embrace the full range of reforms and experiments that facilitate such integration, including organizational norms that reward links with the private sector.[37] Government research institutes also face challenges to define a role between basic research and a more commercial approach that would deepen linkages to both larger and smaller firms. Foreign firms are closely watching the new experiment with the Institute for Basic Science in Daejeon and efforts to establish regional technology transfer centers and techno parks such as the Pangyo Techno Valley and the Gwanggyo BT Valley.[38]

In the wake of the financial crisis, Korea initiated experiments in government-led venture financing and also rolled out extensive incentives for startup companies. Yet, its VC model still lags. Moreover, the existing startup ecosystem in Korea still relies on government cues. For example, government research institutes are overweighted compared with universities, and startups rely heavily on cues from the chaebols.[39] Our interviews in Korea suggest that adequate capital is available for startups, but the risk–reward balance is flawed. One noted investor explained to us that failed

Korean startups lose as much money as quickly as American ones, but successful Korean startups provide much less upside because Korean firms have a smaller home market, must compete against established chaebols, and still find global markets difficult territory.

Three issues stand out with respect to government policy. First, although Korea often adopted best practices from abroad, each new administration brings in a new set of ideas. They restructure past innovation efforts and create new bodies, often including ministries. This inconsistency fans uncertainty about the durability of policy. Second, the American innovation system is built on decentralization. New clusters often emerge when local actors and governments actively compete against other regions. By contrast, in Korea a relatively centralized political system may limit local initiative. For example, President Park's "creative economy plan" called for a centrally planned distribution of features across preselected regions, some of which would be coordinated by chaebols. Third, Korean competition policy focuses on the abuse of a dominant market position, which is in line with competition law in most advanced economies even if its interpretation of the doctrine is controversial. Distinctively, however, Korean policy also focuses on "fair behavior" by nondominant firms. The disruption of an existing business model by a startup likely will shake up established practices in ways that raise cries about fairness.

1.3. Trouble in Paradise?

It is worthwhile to continuously reexamine success stories in search of potential weaknesses. For example, U.S. entrepreneurs complain that cumbersome government regulations restrict innovative opportunities. In segments such as alternative energy, government policies flip too frequently to generate a consistent business case. The high-tech industry constantly complains that America's lagging primary and secondary schools do not produce the skilled workforce they require and despairs about restrictive immigration policies that hamper their access to global talent pools. These issues are important, but other problems may be even more fundamental for the second-wave model.

One problem is that, for all of its virtues, the cluster model is difficult to consistently replicate successfully. In the United States, the Silicon Valley, Boston, North Carolina Research Triangle, Seattle, San Diego, and Los Angeles clusters usually dominate the list of successes. Smaller clusters in Austin, Chicago, and Pittsburgh also scored gains, but for all of the talk of cluster dynamics, cities such as Atlanta and New York were not big winners under the cluster model.[40] This picture is not limited to the United States. Higher-value-added innovation tends to cluster in most countries.[41] To illustrate this point, Figure 1.1 depicts this clustering of innovative

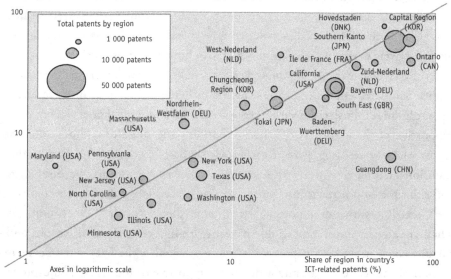

FIGURE 1.1: Innovation hot spots in information and communications technologies, biotechnologies, and nanotechnologies, 2006–2008.

hotspots in ICT, biotechnology, and nanotechnology. Many of the leading firms in these knowledge-intensive industries emerged in only a few regions, which appear to be fertilized by particularly conducive conditions for business innovation.

Relying on patent data to measure innovation, Figure 1.1 shows how clustered innovation remains in leading economies. Although patent grants have drawbacks as a measurement of innovation, they are the most consistent cross-national data. The size of the circle indicates the number of patents filed between 2006 and 2008 in these fields. The *X*-axis shows the percentage share of regional patents in a country's ICT-related patents, whereas the *Y*-axis shows the percentage share of regional patents in biotechnology- and nanotechnology-related patents.

Why did this cluster pattern evolve? One reason was that second-wave clusters typically add high value, are nurtured in deeply technological market environments, and favor volatile business models. Although many efforts at innovation ended modestly, the goal always was for novel product or major architectural product innovation. (Clusters were not identified with traditional industrial agglomerations focused on incremental and process innovations like automobiles and machine tools.) In this specialized environment, success was built on the expert density level. In successful ICT and biotech clusters, for example, there were huge talent clusters and local geographic mobility. Atlanta, by contrast, is spread out and lacks easy transportation from place to place. Second, the cost of ramping up startups based on other forms of regional expertise was high. For example, New York's Silicon Alley in the 1990s boasted extraordinary cultural, content, and media talent, but failed to attract sufficient numbers of IT engineers because living expenses were so high. Google and other Silicon Valley stalwarts now face this problem as well and are acting proactively to retain their talent as Bay Area housing prices soar.

A third challenge for the second wave in the United States was the struggle among traditional incremental and process clusters in fiercely globalized markets such as the automotive industry. For various reasons, the second-wave model was not overly supportive of these clusters.[42] When faced with the surge of competition from China, there was a deep, permanent displacement of a considerable part of these traditional cluster activities.[43] This was important because as wage increases lagged and full-time employment in traditional middle-class jobs fitfully recovered from the Great Recession, an important structural challenge for the U.S. economy was whether and how innovation could revive growth in sectors where these jobs traditionally concentrated.[44] Chapter 2 will examine whether the IPD and an evolving version of the second wave might be more supportive of incremental and process innovations vital to strengthening older industrial clusters.

Another looming issue for the second-wave model is that overall federal support for the underlying basic research and training missions of anchor universities seems to be declining over time by most key metrics.[45] Universities are scrambling to find alternative revenues, for example, from institutes funded by for-profit entities. This will influence a vital "shared asset" for innovation changes.[46]

The VC model itself has vulnerabilities. In some respects, VC investment is still healthy. In 2014, it accounted for $52.1 billion of the $87 billion invested globally (60%, but down from 70% the previous eight years). However, a geographic focus is extremely narrow. Four U.S. regions were among the top five: Silicon Valley dominated, followed distantly by New York, New England, and Southern California.[47] The second-wave VCs had a great deal of money chasing a relatively narrow range of opportunities. This occurs because the VC model thrives by investing in companies that offer potential financial returns within five years of a hundred or more times the amount invested. VCs invest in a large portfolio of companies to find a few winners. Only a handful of industries can deliver this potential, and their activity typically is concentrated in a handful of industries as well. The sectors receiving more than $ 2.5 billion in VC investments in the United States for 2015, according to the National Venture Capital Association, were software ($23.60 billion), biotech ($7.41 billion), consumer products and services ($4.8 billion), media and entertainment ($4.75 billion), industrial/energy ($3.16 billion), IT services ($3.86 billion), financial services ($3.05 billion), and medical devices and equipment ($2.73 billion).[48] Hence, a great deal of money is chasing closely related ideas. This relatively concentrated portfolio sometimes leads to declining returns. In the past ten years, as the number of big hits declined in proportion to the growing pool of VC capital, many VC firms opted for a more conservative approach. To reduce losses, they declined to invest in the earliest stages of innovation.[49] Today, they often track crowdsourcing efforts on Kickstarter and other online funders to test the waters and get a sense of whether the market might embrace a new idea. Perhaps even more troubling, the VC industry remains male dominated and geographically concentrated, possibly because of the perceived need to do close personal monitoring of client companies.[50]

On the flip side, from the viewpoint of upwardly mobile countries like Korea, there is the question of whether the traditional funding model for startups, backed by VCs, is adequate to fully meet their needs.[51] Finding ways to drive down startup costs so that success within their home market provides higher profits may be a crucial step forward.

Finally, globalization of higher-value-added expertise through the diffusion of global engineering and scientific talent is a competitive risk for U.S. leadership in innovation. Over time, this talent pool outside of the United States is becoming more commercially adept as entrepreneurs, which means that implicit assumptions about the superiority of U.S. clusters will come into question more frequently. At a minimum, the added competition suggests that early innovating in the United States and early commercialization of products in the United States and Europe will likely face competition from Asia and other parts of the world.

Notes

1. Erik Brynjolfsson and Adam Saunders, *Wired for Innovation: How Information Technology Is Reshaping the Economy* (Cambridge, MA: MIT Press, 2009), explains how and why innovation capacity matters for long-term relative economic health and growth.

2. Atkinson and Ezell, *Innovation Economics*, 2012; Dan Breznitz and John Zysman (eds.), *The Third Globalization: Can Wealthy Nations Stay Rich in the Twenty-First Century?* (New York: Oxford University Press, 2013).

3. Atkinson and Ezell, *Innovation Economics*, 2012.

4. This chapter draws on Dan Breznitz and Peter Cowhey, "America's Two Systems of Innovation: Innovation for Production in Fostering U.S. Growth," *Innovations*, 7, no. 3 (Summer 2012): 127–154. On the economics of innovation and clusters, see Gerald Carlino and William R. Kerr, "Agglomeration and Innovation," Research Department, Federal Reserve Bank of Philadelphia, Working Paper 14–26, August 2014.

5. This synthesis draws on the literature review by Breznitz and Cowhey and on Tai Ming Cheung and Bates Gill, "Trade versus Security: How Countries Balance Technology Transfers with China," *Journal of East Asian Studies*, 13, no. 3 (September–December 2013): 457–482. The literature on regional clusters is rooted in the economics of agglomeration. "Marshall . . . highlighted three distinct drivers of agglomeration: input–output linkages, labor market pooling, and knowledge spillovers. . . . Over time, an extensive literature has broadened the set of

agglomeration drivers, including local demand conditions, specialized institutions, the organizational structure of regional business, and social networks." Mercedes Delgado, Michael E. Porter, and Scott Stern, "Defining Clusters of Related Industries," NBER Working Paper 20375, August 2014, http://www.nber.org/papers/w20375.

6. They may pool resources to provide the capability collectively or evolve a system for using a third party's asset on their behalf.

7. A complete analysis would include "environmental factors" related to governance, such as transparency, corruption, or independence of courts, all of which influence market dynamics.

8. Mikko Packalen and Jay Bhattacharya, "New Ideas in Invention," National Bureau of Economic Research, Working Paper 20922, January 2012, http://www.nber.org/papers/w20922.

9. "Architectural innovation is often triggered by a change in a component—size or some other subsidiary parameter of its design—that creates new interactions and new linkages with other components in the established product. The core design concept behind each component—and the associated scientific and engineering knowledge—remains the same." Rebecca M. Henderson and Kim Clark, "Architectural Innovation: The Reconfiguration of Existing Technologies and the Failure of Established Firms," *Administrative Science Quarterly*, 35, no. 1 (March 1990): 9–30, http://links.jstor.org/sici?sici=0001-8392%281990003%2935%3A1%3C9%3AAITROE%3E2.0.CO%3B2-U.

10. Steven Klepper, *Experimental Capitalism: The Nanoeconomics of American High-Tech Industries* (Princeton, NJ: Princeton University Press, 2015), points out that industries like autos were once novel-product innovations that led to clustering.

11. Our discussion of Korea draws liberally from Peter F. Cowhey and Stephan Haggard, "The Information and Production Disruption: Implications for Innovation Policy," U.S.–Korea Business Council, 2014, http://www.uskoreacouncil.org/wp-content/uploads/2014/12/Innovation_WhitePaper_English_FINAL.pdf.

12. Similarly, according to Walter Isaacson, "When Steve Jobs designed a new headquarters for Pixar, he obsessed over ways to structure the atrium, and even where to locate the bathrooms, so that serendipitous personal encounters would occur," http://www.entrepreneur.com/article/238433.

13. James Fallows, *China Airborne* (New York: Random House, 2012). In addition, in many years the U.S. Export–Import Bank extended a significant majority of their loan guarantees to the aircraft and avionics industry. *Export–Import Bank of the United States, 2014 Annual Report*, accessed January 21, 2015, http://www.exim.gov/sites/default/files/reports/annual/EXIM-2014-AR.pdf.

14. Beth-Anne Scheulke-Leech, "Volatility of Federal Funding of Energy R&D," *Energy Policy*, 67 (April 2014): 943–950. Also David Hart, *Forged Consensus: Science, Technology and Economic Policy the United States, 1921–1953* (Princeton, NJ: Princeton University Press, 1998).

15. Shared assets of internal capital markets in first-wave firms often functioned inefficiently because of internal "rent seeking" by divisions. See David S. Scharfstein and Jeremy C. Stein, "The Dark Side of Internal Capital Markets: Division Rent-Seeking and Inefficient Investment," *Journal of Finance*, 55, no. 6 (December 2000): 2537–2564. On the weaknesses of centralized R&D labs, see Josh Lerner, *The Architecture of Innovation* (Boston: Harvard Business Review Press, 2012).

16. John R. Graham, Campbell R. Harvey, and Shiva Rajgopal, "The Economic Implications of Corporate Financial Reporting," *Journal of Accounting and Economics*, 40, nos. 1–3 (2005): 3–73.

17. Korean chaebols resemble, but also are quite different from, keiretsus, the Japanese variant on multidivisional firms. Keiretsus are informal business groups of firms with interlocking business shareholdings and relationships. The member companies cross-invest in each other's shares. Unlike the chaebols, keiretsus are generally organized around a core bank that helps insulate them from takeover attempts and fluctuations in their stock prices, so they can concentrate on long-term planning and innovation.

18. Disputes still abound, such as the complaints by the U.S. auto industry about the Korean market. The U.S.–Korea Trade Agreement in 2011 somewhat eased these tensions. See International Trade Administration, "The U.S.–Korea Trade Agreement: Opportunities for the U.S. Automotive Sector," April 2011, accessed January 22, 2015, http://www.trade.gov/mas/ian/build/groups/public/@tg_ian/documents/webcontent/tg_ian_002590.pdf.

19. Mary Lindenstein Walshok and Abraham J. Shragge, *Invention and Reinvention: The Evolution of San Diego's Innovation Economy* (Palo Alto, CA: Stanford University Press, 2013).

20. The classic analysis of why the Silicon Valley cluster became dominant stresses the stronger social network emerging among the flatter startup structures of California firms. See AnnaLee Saxenian, *Regional Advantage: Culture and Competition in Silicon Valley and Route 128* (Cambridge, MA: Harvard University Press, 1994). On clusters and anchor research universities, see Martin Kenney and David C. Mowery (eds.), *Public Universities and Regional Growth: Insights from the University of California* (Palo Alto, CA: Stanford University Press, 2014).

21. Kenney and Mowery, *Public Universities*, 2014.

22. Steven Casper found that the San Francisco biotech cluster relied more on science networks, whereas San Diego's cluster evolved with more reliance on managerial networking. Each one relied on major universities and institutes for basic research. VCs disproportionately invest in nearby firms because they want to maintain extensive personal monitoring. San Diego had a weak local VC system, so Silicon Valley funds prized firms organized by proven executives. Steve Casper, "The University of California and the Evolution of the Biotechnology Industry in San Diego and the San Francisco Bay Area," in Kenney and Mowery, pp. 66–96; Lerner on local bias of VCs, p. 68.

23. On measurement technology, see Atkinson and Ezell, *Innovation Economics*, 2012, p. 147. In an interview in 2013 with a member of Shanghai's Science and Technology Commission, we learned that the sharing of equipment in regional technology clusters in China was difficult because the central government's agencies controlled much of the equipment and were difficult to engage with in a simple, transparent manner.

24. In 2013 dollars, U.S. initial public offerings totaled $1.3 billion in 1980 but reached $150 billion in 2013. Quoted in 2013 dollars in Leslie Picker, "Meet the Father of the Modern IPO," *Bloomberg Business Weekly*, May 15, 2014. Lerner, pp. 65–75. For an insider's account of the early days of VC funding, see William H. Janeway, *Doing Capitalism in the Innovation Economy* (Cambridge: Cambridge University Press, 2012), pp. 81–84. For a broader history of Silicon Valley, see Arun Rao, *A History of Silicon Valley*, 2nd ed. (Palo Alto, CA: Omniware Group, Kindle eBooks, 2013).

25. The legendary successes of DARPA, the military's hybrid of an R&D fund and angel investment through government contracts, often succeeded because DARPA is mission driven to create long-term capabilities relevant to the military. This drove the effort to create what became the Internet. A DARPA agenda does not crowd out the private venture space.

26. Speech by commissioner Luis A. Aguilar, "Evaluating Pension Fund Investments through the Lens of Good Corporate Governance," June 27, 2014, http://www.sec.gov/News/Speech/Detail/Speech/1370542193403#.VMGiBy7F-7U.

27. Peter F. Cowhey and Jonathan D. Aronson, *Transforming Global Information and Communications Markets* (Cambridge, MA: MIT Press, 2009).

28. For a fuller analysis, see Cowhey and Aronson, *Transforming Global Information*, 2009.

29. Jonathan Sallet, Ed Paisley, and Justin Masterman, *The Geography of Innovation: The Federal Government and the Growth of Regional Innovation Clusters* (Washington, D.C.: Science Progress, 2009).

30. We thank Sam Bozzette for this observation.

31. Wesley M. Cohen, Richard R. Nelson, and John P. Walsh, "Protecting Their Intellectual Assets: Appropriability Conditions and Why U.S. Manufacturing Firms Patent (or Not)," NBER Working Paper 7552, February 2000, notes that these ICT technologies are complementary assets that are suited for cooperative arrangements among specialists, http://www.nber.org/papers/w7552.

32. Chapter 2 discusses the economic logic of platforms more fully. Briefly, a technology platform enables complementary technologies and easier user access and interaction with this ecosystem. An example illustrates the difference between niche and general platforms. Although now being challenged, Cisco long dominated routers. For a time, as it assembled products like cameras and videoconferencing, it contemplated whether its software ecosystem for networking was a "secret sauce" that could be powerfully embedded in all of its offerings and become a compelling platform for all its associated markets. This did not occur, partly because Internet protocols and the operating systems of end terminals crowded out its middleware's significance. Howard A. Shelanski, "Information, Innovation, and Competition Policy for the Internet," *University of Pennsylvania Law Review*, 161 (2012): 1664–1706, provides a sophisticated survey of platform economics. Also see Martin Kenney and John Zysman, "The Rise of the Platform Economy," *Issues in Science and Technology*, 32, no. 3 (Spring 2016), http://issues.org/32-3/the-rise-of-the-platform-economy/.

33. We thank Nahoi Koo for suggestions on this section.

34. Asia-Pacific Global Research Group, "South Korea's "Creative Economy"—6 Strategies," February 12, 2014, http://asiapacificglobal.com/2014/02/south-koreas-creative-economy-primer-6-strategies/.

35. http://english.msip.go.kr/english/msipContents/contents.do?mId=Mjc5. President Park was impeached in March 2017, so her initiatives could be revisited.

36. This is especially striking since U.S. and Korean per capita data usage is roughly equivalent—about 65 gigabytes of data per month in 2014. The EU average (and that of Germany) is less than a third of that per capita. If the use of consumer video is omitted, the gap shrinks, but German use is still less than half that of America. Today, about 20% of the Korean economy is largely Internet based—content, ICT, and finance. The Internet of Things likely will open the other 80%. But Korea still lags. See Paul Hofheinz and Michael Mandel, "Bridging the Data Gap," Progressive Policy Institute, No. 15, 2014, http://www.progressivepolicy.org/wp-content/uploads/2014/04/LISBON_COUNCIL_PPI_Bridging_the_Data_Gap.pdf.

37. During the second wave in the United States, government research institutes were led by technology transfer offices that were later expanded to other models, including approaches to vest some rights with inventors, while maintaining some university ownership (so-called "free agency" models).

38. Yeon Choul-Woong, "The "Next Pangyo Techno Valley" Gateway for Global Companies," *Korea IT Times*, December 15, 2015, http://www.koreaittimes.com/story/56546/%E2%80%9Cnext-pangyo-techno-valley%E2%80%9D-gateway-global-companies. A comparison of these two initiatives is Wonil Lee and Jong-in Choi, "Industry–Academia Cooperation in Creative Innovation Clusters: A Comparison of Two Clusters in Korea," *Academy of Entrepreneurial Journal*, August 2013, https://www.questia.com/library/journal/1P3-3325216641/industry-academia-cooperation-in-creative-innovation.

39. U.S. VC investments totaled $58.8 billion in 2015, more than that of all other countries combined. Korea was hardly a blip on the radar. National Venture Capital Association, "$58.8 Billion in Venture Capital Invested across U.S. in 2015, According to the Money Tree Report," http://nvca.org/pressreleases/58-8-billion-in-venture-capital-invested-across-u-s-in-2015-according-to-the-moneytree-report-2/. It is striking, however, that the percentage of mobile-related patents as a percentage of total patents increased from 4% in 2000 to 20% in 2013 in both countries. Cowhey discussions with Korean officials, November 6, 2014.

40. Breznitz and Cowhey, "America's Two Systems," 2012. Recently, New York finally succeeded in attracting significant amounts of tech VC funds, North Carolina has lost some of its allure, and Atlanta has yet to attract much VC funding. Richard Florida, "The Global Cities Where Tech Venture Capital Is Concentrated," *The Atlantic*, January 26, 2016, http://www.theatlantic.com/technology/archive/2016/01/global-startup-cities-venture-capital/429255/.

41. Richard Florida, "The World's Leading Startup Cities" (2015), identifies seven of the top twenty startup locations as American. Silicon Valley remains number one. http://www.citylab.com/tech/2015/07/the-worlds-leading-startup-cities/399623/?utm_source=nl__link1_072715.

42. Susan Helper, Timothy Krueger, and Howard Wial, *Locating American Manufacturing: Trends in the Geography of Production* (Washington, D.C.: Brookings Institution, 2012).

43. Autor, Dorn, and Hanson; Daron Acemoglu, David Autor, David Dorn, Gordon H. Hanson, and Brendan Price, "Return of the Solow Paradox? IT, Productivity and Employment in U.S. Manufacturing," *American Economic Review*, Papers and Proceedings, 104, no. 5 (2014): 394–399.

44. "Briefing: The Future of Jobs," *The Economist*, January 18, 2014, pp. 24–28, notes, "Previous technological innovation has always delivered more long-run employment, not less. But things can change."

45. Funding medical research that could lead to new cures for disease is much more appealing to Congress than funding basic research. The 2016 National Institutes of Health budget ($32.31 billion) was more than four times greater than the 2016 National Science Foundation budget ($7.46 billion). https://nexus.od.nih.gov/all/2016/01/27/nih-budget-highlights-for-2016/ and http://www.sciencemag.org/news/2015/12/updated-budget-agreement-boosts-us-science.

46. The benchmark statement is Committee on Science, Engineering, and Public Policy, *Rising above the Gathering Storm* (Washington, D.C.: National Academies Press, 2007).

47. The next five largest magnets for venture capital in 2014 were China ($15.5 billion), Europe ($10.6 billion), India ($5.2 billion), Israel ($1.9 billion), and Canada ($1.4 billion). Peter Vanham, "Top Countries for Total Venture Capital Invested," World Economic Forum, July 28, 2015, https://www.weforum.org/agenda/2015/07/which-countries-have-the-most-venture-capital-investments/; Steve Case, the founder of AOL, notes that in 2014, 75% of VC funding went to just three states (California, Massachusetts, and New York), yet three-quarters of the Fortune

500 companies were based in the other forty-seven states. Steve Case, "Get Ready, the Internet Is about to Change Again. Here's How," *The Washington Post*, May 30, 2015.

48. Quandl, National Venture Capital Association Data, "Venture Capital Investments by Industry," January 28, 2016, https://www.quandl.com/data/NVCA/VENTURE_3_10-Venture-Capital-Investments-By-Industry.

49. Robert E. Litan and Carl J. Schramm, *Better Capitalism: Renewing the Entrepreneurial Strength of the American Economy* (New Haven, CT: Yale University Press, 2012).

50. Ethan Mollick, "It's Not Just the Experts: Crowds Can Pick a Winner, Too," 2014, http://knowledge.wharton.upenn.edu/article/just-experts-crowds-can-pick-winner/.

51. Korea is a huge investor in R&D but still lags in VC investments, although it is trying to catch up. The Korean Venture Capital Association Korea calculated that VC funding in the service sector has increased significantly from 2014 to 2015. "New investments by venture capital in 2014 reached 1,639 billion won, up 18.4%" from 2013 (about $1.5 billion). Korea Venture Capital Association, "Korean Venture Capital Statistics 2014," Yearbook 2015 KVCA. This would place it higher in the rankings than the figures cited in Note 47.

2 Information and Production Disruptions
THE DIGITAL PLATFORM CLUSTER SYSTEM?

THE SECOND-WAVE INNOVATION system in the United States is being disrupted. Similar changes are showing up worldwide. The cause is clear. Digital technology helped enable a rapidly expanding range of transformational economic and social processes. Ideas (enshrined in intellectual property), networked information (software), the collection and analysis of Big Data, and services are all growing rapidly as a share of value added in many products, including traditional manufactured products and commodities.[1] New production techniques are reinforcing the impact of this change.

This digitally enabled phenomenon is the *digital DNA* that disrupts the way in which industries and regional innovation clusters are organized. The far-reaching transformation that is underway gives special meaning to the concept of "glocal"—the relationship between the local and the global. Digital DNA has operational implications that drive changes in the models organizing local innovation clusters, but its digital drivers are inherently global. Thus, the impact of digital DNA depends on whether renovated global governance frameworks deliver maximum economic benefits while they address proliferating public-interest concerns.

Our analysis separates the implications of digital DNA into two interrelated bundles of economic drivers that we call the *information disruption* and the *production disruption*. First, as the "cheap revolution," modularity, and ubiquitous broadband alter the models for innovation, the information value of commercial products is increasing radically, even in traditional product markets. Second, a new generation of digitally enabled production technologies is transforming the global system for producing goods and services.

Chapter 1 noted that elements of first-wave innovation models and practices remained significant in the second wave. Similarly, the second wave will remain an important part of the innovation ecosystem going forward. But here we focus on the implications of an emerging third wave powered by *"digital platform clusters."* Digital platforms are more than purely digital services. The IPD has so intensively reshaped the value-added proposition that even traditional goods often come to resemble the business models and innovation dynamics of pure digital plays.

The emergence of digital platform clusters and the continuing impact of the IPD on the mix of economic opportunities also spawn new operational risks. As these risks alter the benefits of different types of business model "structures," significant experimentation and innovation in the organization of markets will occur.[2] Many of the innovations in market organization and governance will develop from business and civil society,[3] but there also will be challenges and, we hope, innovations in public policies to address these shifts. These intersections of government, business, and civil society are the focus of our discussions of "economic governance."

This chapter and the next analyze the forces that enable digital platform clusters and probe their consequences. We gauge the directional tendencies of change emanating from digital DNA. We will err in many details, but if we get the vector basically right, then the parameters for important governance priorities become clearer.

Any effort to predict directional vectors will encounter major surprises, such as the unexpected explosion of social media and smartphones or significant errors about their specific effects.[4] Consider the impact of digital technology on content companies. Chris Anderson shrewdly foresaw that the digital disruption would drive the decline of the CD market and that the cloud would radically change the downloaded music market and the movie industry. E-commerce for music, for example, gutted part of the traditional revenue for music companies and music stars, leading to a rapid series of changes in how music is supplied (single hit songs more than albums) and delivered (including streaming services). But, the "long tail" of markets for specialized musicians was less buoyant than once predicted.[5]

Another fundamental reason why the specific technological path is indeterminant is that governance responses evolve, thereby altering the trajectories of technological disruptions. This was driven home to us when touring the Rungis International Market outside Paris, the largest fresh food wholesale market in the world (with about 12,000 employees and an annual turnover of more than 7 billion Euros).[6] It is striking that at the huge Rungis wholesale fish market, slips of papers remain the basis of sales transactions. Walk to the meat wholesale market and sales transactions are entirely electronic. Why the difference? The answer is that the "mad cow" disease emergency led to health-reporting rules requiring animals to be tracked at every step, from where they were raised to the final retailer. The solution was to use electronic radiofrequency identification (RFID) tracking tags for all of the meat. Once that system was electronic, the financial transaction piece soon followed suit.[7]

Pinpoint forecasting is impossible, but we can show why the innovation system is in flux and sketch out the resulting challenges for economic governance. In a true glocal situation, where grassroots innovation clusters will be sensitive to emerging patterns of global economic governance, governance will emerge in piecemeal experiments in civil society and in formal government policies. Some governance efforts will fail, but understanding the basic vectors and principles can better steer the priorities of governance entrepreneurs.

To establish these vectors and principles, we first describe the broader economic context of the IPD and consider several uncertainties that could impact its economic trajectory. We then address the information and the production disruptions. This leads to our projections about digital platform clusters that allow us to sketch out some implications for economic governance. Chapter 3 then offers two mini case studies to probe deeper into the dynamics of the IPD and lay out additional governance guidelines that flow from them.

2.1. Larger Economic Forces and Questions

Before examining the evolving innovation system, we acknowledge three limits to our analysis. First, innovation is critical to increasing productivity, a fundamental driver of growth and income levels.[8] However, debate continues regarding whether the boost for economic growth from innovation is currently waxing or waning.[9] Our methodology cannot settle the debate. Instead, we describe how the IPD changes the ways that we innovate. Whatever the overall level of innovation, changes in how we innovate and how major markets respond are crucial to economic governance.

Second, technology talent, entrepreneurial experience, and national wealth are distributed more broadly than thirty years ago. Today, digital data flows across borders may rival the value of global trade in goods.[10] As the centers of market demand shift, Organization for Economic Co-operation and Development (OECD) start-ups can and should master globalization more quickly than their predecessors.[11] Further, the increase in non-OECD capabilities means that firms from those countries can now move more rapidly up the value chain as exporters into global supply chains anchored in rich countries. Thus, because outcomes are more volatile, assessing how disruption will alter the fate of individual national systems is more difficult.

Third, substantial uncertainties about the impact of the IPD on employment remain. Changing production technologies reinforced by information technology (IT) may seem to offer a shimmering promise to enthusiastic promoters of a boom in U.S. manufacturing employment. However, the IPD will play out in a world where large forces are variable, and national policies will influence its configuration and consequences.[12] Declining U.S. costs for secure energy may further reduce U.S. manufacturing costs. These factors may make "near sourcing" sufficiently cost competitive to permit U.S.-based production and seize the collateral benefits afforded by a shorter supply lead time and smaller required inventory reserves. However, manufacturing locations also depend on such factors as labor costs in China and Vietnam and on transport costs from China to its industrial trading partners.[13] These disruptions are unfolding as the "trade in tasks" makes the value added in all products and services subject to more mobile, specialized inputs.[14]

Even if U.S. manufacturing volumes increase markedly, this may only slow the loss of manufacturing jobs, although the jobs that remain may be higher skilled and better paid. Meanwhile, panic is increasing that robots will displace many assembly-line workers. The unresolved, politically charged issue is whether the related pools of professional service jobs will be boosted or depressed.[15] Automation and new forms of outsourcing could promote or discourage the emergence of a new "craft economy" that mixes customized services and products in novel ways that bolster employment.[16] If social welfare policies can be adapted to make them work better in an economy where more workers combine their efforts (e.g., contract service tasks like Uber), a productive upside is far more likely to be forged from the labor market changes.[17] More darkly, recall that the seminal apocalyptic novel of the information age, Neal Stephenson's *Snow Crash*, envisioned a stratified America that was only preeminent in software and pizza delivery, and pizza was an information-intensive industry in its distribution system.[18]

Even given these caveats, something major is reshaping global economic developments. In the words of Buffalo Springfield's classic rock song, "There's something happening here. What it is ain't exactly clear." These changes have consequences that should be high on the attention agenda of anyone concerned with economic governance.[19]

2.2. The Information and Production Disruptions

The IPD drives the disruption of the established innovation system. We probe the IPD's underpinnings to gain deeper insight into the vector of digital platform clusters.

2.2.1. The Information Disruption

The information disruption has five drivers. First, the "cheap revolution" adds to information value because networked IT is nearly everywhere and incredibly cheap, even compared to 2000.[20] Cloud computing and ubiquitous (especially mobile) broadband are crucial. The predicted end of the stunning price/performance progress for semiconductors embodied in Moore's law may eventually materialize, but other forms of improved performance in IT are already taking hold.[21] Second, the rise of the Internet of Things reinforces this trend. The Internet of Things is the interrelated system of observational capabilities (e.g., sensors), networked information, big data analysis, and the infusion of information technology functions into an expanding range of terminals that will vastly outnumber computers and smartphones. Although not commonly recognized, the evolution of drones is creating an inexpensive general-purpose platform for easily customized sensing and observation systems tied to novel analytic applications ranging from environmental monitoring and natural resource management to infrastructure maintenance. The third driver is the growth of Big Data accelerated by the explosion of machine learning (whereby machines improve their analytic algorithms on their own) and the conversion of this learning into applications abetted by elements of artificial intelligence programs.[22] The fourth driver is the continued rise of "modular" (standardized, easy to use) IT interfaces that facilitate the "mix and match" of digital building blocks and the spread of information with value added.[23] A fifth, complementary, driver is the expansion of open-source software codes that startups can fold into their own IT creations, which lower the cost and increase the speed of innovation.[24] For example, it is estimated that ICT startup costs (hardware, software, and personnel) dropped by 70% to 80% between 2000 and 2012, making it easier to aggregate and organize capital using alternative models.[25]

Technology enabled the cheap revolution, but governance also played an important role. The emphasis on ICT modularity benefited from a steady dose of U.S. competition policy that ranged from the early antitrust cases that required AT&T and IBM to open their systems, to complementary products of competitors (such as telephone handsets and software), to the epic 1990's Microsoft antitrust case. Policy makers insisted that modular interfaces be incorporated into ongoing systems design. In 2012 the Federal Trade Commission compelled Google to open its Application Program Interfaces for advertising to allow consumers greater ease in switching to rival ad platforms. The Federal Trade Commission also ruled that Intel chips could not be designed to block users from choosing a competitive chip for graphics processing.[26] Modularity represented a policy design choice to use competition policy to enhance market entry and choice by making interoperability easier. Significantly, it did so without government mandating specific technologies or technology standards to try to make competitive entry easier. Such mandates can limit competition among competing technology designs, an inhibitor of innovation in the long term.

The obvious immediate impact of the IPD was on digital services. The rise of search and online advertising, social networking, and the app stores of platforms like Apple and Google were dramatic changes. Equally important was the increase in upstream basic and applied research. For example, biological science is changing because of "quantitative and systems biology" that combines big data analysis of biological processes with crossover insights from fields like physics and engineering. Every major university is racing to create new tools derived from improved observational and computational capabilities that cover virtually every facet of scholarship. These changes in academe, in turn, will feed the problem-solving frames of enterprises. For example, advances in machine learning and visualization techniques are creating the field of "contextual robotics," with the goal of empowering robots to function in highly unstructured environments for tasks such as disaster response.

The information disruption is reducing barriers to entry for small enterprises because they can scale IT resources proportionate to the business opportunity.[27] For example, FerroKin, a biopharma startup, uses IT to slash management overhead costs and speed research processes by rapidly circulating important data. The use of Skype and other tools helped new enterprises reduce office space needs and use flexible contractors, even for highly skilled core tasks. The United Kingdom Science Park Association observes that the firms in their parks average fewer than fifty employees. They still gather in clusters, but the clusters are smaller because they rely more on networked forms to "catalyze, communicate, collaborate, and create business."[28] For the same reasons, these firms globalize more easily than earlier startups. For example, Estonia, with a population of 1.3 million, is a global player in Internet security and other aspects of IT because of a talent pool nurtured by its ambitious deployment of a national information infrastructure. Pathbreaking innovators including Skype and Kazaa (an early file-sharing network), as well as cybersecurity ventures, started in Estonia but grew as they built global networks of specialized collaborators at low cost.[29] Combinations of startups from Israel, Korea, and Estonia with California firms are becoming common.[30] Many intriguing wireless health device and services startups maintain headquarters in both Europe and California.

Further, the process begins again as each "Next Big Thing" emerges. For example, speculation abounds that voice may be the next big thing because of the rise of Big Data, the cloud, machine learning, and other innovations.[31]

2.2.2. *The Production Disruption*

The production disruption complements the information disruption and shares some overlapping drivers of digital technology. The major drivers are additive manufacturing (popularly called 3D printing), robotics, and new "smart" materials combined with sensors. Collectively, these changes are sometimes described as "advanced manufacturing," which will alter the speed and cost of product development and scale economies.[32] Germany and China, for example, launched major programs to anchor innovation around these capabilities.[33]

Today, *3D* "printers" and other new production tools change the dynamics of specialized products. Making new product prototypes and producing specialized orders with short production runs is now common and is becoming routine. Striking examples are NASA's ability to email a wrench to the international space station, where it was printed on a 3D computer,[34] and the efforts of a Danish company to print a forty-nine-foot bridge in one shot instead of printing it in prefabricated sections and assembling it later.[35] 3D printers already are producing biological products, including prototypes of artificial livers.[36] Moreover, additive manufacturing is improving rapidly enough to customize parts of traditional manufactured products.[37] Feetz, a startup shoe manufacturer in Tennessee, started selling customized shoes in 2016. Customers snap three photos of their feet on a white sheet of paper, from which Feetz generates a 3D model of the foot. Add a dash of biometric data (height and weight), select shoe type and color, and press the buy button. The customized pair of shoes is printed on a 3D printer and shipped to the buyer.[38]

Yet, additive manufacturing is more than small-scale production. For example, GE uses additive manufacturing to produce jet nozzles for a new line of engines for smaller jets, like the Boeing 737. It does so because advanced manufacturing prioritizes the combination of multiple components into a single manufactured piece ("parts consolidation"). Traditional manufacturing techniques required multiple parts to form the shape of a nozzle; a 3D printer could produce the nozzle as a single piece, thereby saving on both materials and labor costs. The role of printers should further expand because technology advances involving lasers will allow the printers to use an expanding array of metal oxides.[39]

As robots become smaller, cheaper, smarter, and more mobile, robotics increasingly reinforces disruptive production possibilities for large economies of scale[40] and now for smaller "batch" operations.[41] Robotic-assisted, minimally invasive surgery also is spreading. In the future, doctors (or technicians) may assist the robots, rather than vice versa.[42] Moreover, robots are evolving to become platforms where multiple specialized applications and manipulators, from independent firms, can be performed by the same robot.

Also transforming production is the synthesis of new materials in response to product design goals, including whole new classes of synthetic materials such as bioengineered silk.[43] "Smart materials," such as piezocomposite materials used in actuators and sensors, are already the basis for the sensors that activate automobile airbags in a crash.[44] Many new materials will include networked monitoring sensors to report, for example, deficiencies in the manufacturing process. Eventually, "printed" sheets of sensors will permit greater observational and monitoring capabilities for sensitive products, such as "smart" packaging for fresh meat.[45] Similarly, self-regulating ("homeostatic") nano materials and nano robots may have the capacity to regulate glucose or carbon dioxide levels in the bloodstream.[46] The growth of "epidermal electronics" employs "tattoos" attached to the skin that are laden with networked sensors to allow both the gathering of medical data and an entire new class of specialized user interfaces with digital systems. To take advantage of these possibilities, both traditional electronics firms and medical device companies are investing in this space.[47]

Production innovations also are changing commercial scientific innovation processes to sometimes resemble contract-manufacturing systems. For example, Emerald Therapeutics and Transcriptic use networked robots to operate laboratory-testing equipment and integrate them with their own software operating systems. This allows them to offer sophisticated lab testing to new biopharma firms at low cost, with rapid turnaround, and with high accuracy. These labs can design and monitor experiments that use a web interface that lower the amount of high-end equipment and laboratory personnel needed for a biopharma startup.[48] The next logical steps will be to move from the lab bench to the production of end products.

The impact of the combined IPD is giving rise to digital platform clusters that cut across traditional divides between high-tech and traditional goods and services.[49] Next, we lay out the characteristics of these clusters.

2.3. The Dynamics of Digital Platform Clusters

Digital platform clusters are beginning to emerge, propelled by the innovations unleashed by the IPD. Platforms provide "a gateway between consumers and many diverse applications well beyond the specific product or service that constitutes the platform itself."[50] Underlying the platform are digital tools (such as a software operating system) and common capabilities provided to diverse pools of customers, audiences, and related product suppliers that vary in their complexity and cost to duplicate. The tools can be continuously updated because they are digitally intensive and rely on user feedback and other information drivers that are part of the information disruption. The "store" is one such tool. It serves as a digital transaction facility that requires a complex digital infrastructure, which evolved on the basis of significant experimentation.[51] The store opens new ways to organize global markets for both specialized information applications and physical goods, such as a German platform for global trading in German steel products. Production tools complement the digital information array. For example, "shared facilities incubators" that popped up ubiquitously are created by production workshops ("maker spaces"). Their infrastructure ranges from 3D printers to robotics, as part of new "design districts" for entrepreneurs experimenting with the full range of IPD capabilities. Training courses and business "incubators" are often part of the workshop array.

These emerging clusters have six major dynamics.

First, digital platform clusters rely on ICT and services to a broader array of markets than second-wave clusters. In short, ICT enables the automation and network organization of many traditional production tasks. For example, minuteKEY is the first company to create a self-service, fully automated machine kiosk that duplicates keys. Traditionally, most keys were duplicated in hardware stores using a machine/service combination. MinuteKEY replaces the human role by adding a smarter ICT component and robotics, changing key making into an automated kiosk service. Reliability also improved; the system reduced the failed key-making rate from the normal 10–15% to 0.4% and network-enabled diagnostics allow the kiosks to solve most customer service issues remotely. Its last building block is an automated credit card system for payment. In 2014–2015, minuteKEY's revenues climbed by about a third, to $35 million.[52]

Second, the network economics of digital platforms make technology more valuable as the number of users climbs and an "ecosystem" of co-suppliers grows around it. The platform and its anchor products grow more valuable as more co-suppliers offer complementary offerings, as Apple's success attests. (Most platforms never achieve market dominance. Part III examines selected issues about dominance.)

A collateral benefit of digital platforms is that they also increase the significance of "user interaction," including user co-invention. The ongoing, networked interaction of product suppliers and users allows continual re-invention of the product/ business model, an important differentiator of digital-driven innovation. The implication of co-invention for startups is striking. More and more startups, especially for consumer products, substitute an experimentation and discovery model for the traditional development and marketing model.[53] From the start, they use IT platforms to interact with potential and, ultimately, actual users to refine product designs and marketing.[54] Co-invention also is central to growing numbers of large market incumbents.[55] Together, these changes permit greater customization of products to the tastes of specific groups of consumers and allow more cost-effective alteration of product specifications, even in larger-scale production. However, as explained in Part III, inappropriate privacy and cybersecurity policies could blunt this dynamic.

The third characteristic of digital platforms is that even manufactured goods have started to rely on ICT and services with networked effects to maintain market shares and to drastically redefine or create new end markets.[56] This is a variant on a well-worn strategy—Gillette makes money on razor blades, not razors.[57] In this spirit, a major supplier of climate control equipment for large commercial buildings partnered with IBM to create real-time sensor and data analysis systems to offer optimal use of the equipment installed in buildings. GE is investing heavily in its Predix platform for the industrial Internet of Things. GE believes that sensors and big data analysis will allow them to predict problems in equipment infrastructures, thus creating a market for services that reduce maintenance costs and optimize the use of its capital assets.[58]

Significantly, platform strategies are open to smaller specialist firms as well as to giant ones. Biotech equipment is one example. The head of a prominent producer of sophisticated medical equipment and a West Coast venture capitalist in biotech separately told us that since 2000, business cycles shortened and funders grew obsessed with updating features as networked information became more central for competitiveness. This raised concerns about "tipping," especially because information about product features spread instantly in social media. This happened first in genetic sequencing systems (like the high-end leader, Illumina) and is spreading to other medical technologies. For example, the combination of synthetic genetics and big data analytics may introduce diagnostic platforms that could display tipping dynamics reminiscent of the software industry. Detailed measurements and big data analytics open new ways to analyze individual biomes and suggest new treatment alternatives. Moreover, users are appropriating biomedical device platforms to devise their own diagnostic and intervention solutions that are akin to "off-patent" uses of prescription medicines.[59]

The intersection of software and hardware also was critical to *Dropcam*, which sells systems of video cameras. Initially, its founders intended to provide inexpensive home security. Dropcam became a leader in the nearly ubiquitous consumer devices that observe homes and offices. In January 2013, Greg Duffy, the co-founder of Dropcam, claimed that more video data was uploaded from Dropcam than from YouTube.[60] Dropcam was built on a software app that was spliced into standardized software embedded in digital cameras' chips. The system was refined using inexpensive, virtual simulation runs without commissioning a specialized chip for their app. Dropcam then resold the cameras into an observation system backed with cloud storage capacity. As Dropcam grew, it lowered costs and dropped prices and accelerated its rollout to the mass market by building its own cameras. This was possible because 3D prototyping allowed faster and cheaper design. The founders estimate that development of the system from inception through their prototype cost a tenth of what would have been needed a few years earlier. Only when Dropcam transitioned to mass production, where replicable, high-quality scale economies mattered, did they finally outsource manufacturing to China. In the future, evolving production technology and adept cluster policies may again lead to revision of their production strategy.

The larger lesson of Dropcam is that the hardware facilitated the software solution. Dropcam's advantage was that its software accounted for the bulk of the value.[61] The increasing importance of user interaction and the major role services play as a building block of innovation suggest that Dropcam now uses data analytics to refine visual recognition to send specific, focused, automatic activity alerts to users. Perhaps the ultimate testament to the software factor came in June 2014 when Google's Nest Lab announced that it would buy Dropcam. (Nest Labs embodies the use of IT to transform a traditional market.)[62] This purchase gave Google the leading product in the thermostat, security system, and smoke and fire alarm market and made it a major force in the fast-growing "residential Internet of Things market."[63] Fear rippled through boardrooms as competitors worried that Google's control of huge data troves from Nest Labs/Dropcam on household and small-office life could be translated into a huge competitive advantage. But, remember, disruption is not automatically sustainable. Alphabet (the successor holding company for Google's enterprises) faced challenges in managing Nest.[64]

The integration of sophisticated physical goods with analytics also opens the expansion of once small new markets, such as medical monitoring. For example, X2 offers a new biomedical diagnostic technology system to monitor concussions and head injuries, mainly in football and other contact sports. X2 charges $120 per monitoring device. Each user also is charged a fee of $1 per month and provides a dependable, long-term stream of data.[65] Thus, its long-term advantage is built on its data-monitoring and predictive modeling service for risk management.

A further extension of the logic of redefining markets is the rise of the "sharing economy." A more recent variant is the "gig economy" featuring workers as "independent contractors" on short-term engagements.[66] Sharing as it relates to economic models occurs when "individuals are able to borrow or rent assets owned by someone else. The sharing economy model is most likely to be used when the price of a particular asset is high and the asset is not fully utilized all the time."[67] IT unlocks the ability to create these operations and their business models. We will return to the sharing economy in the next section.

A fourth feature of digital platform dynamics follows from this case. Information derived from products can generate a collateral revenue stream and analytic learning because firms rely on "data uses [that] are non-rivalrous."[68] Once information is used, it is available for infinite reuse.[69] Search engines track patterns of aggregate use to target and auction ads presented as part of individual search results. The Big Data collected as part of the primary consumer products can be reused flexibly to improve products and processes (or, as with Google's Nest, to produce information on consumer behavior that leads to better targeting of online ads). Big Data also can spin off additional products or be sold to third parties who want to combine it with other data. This drives firms, even those that offer only specialized products, to emphasize investments in platform tools. For example, one firm, which is trying to "disintermediate" the market for SMEs purchasing business insurance, spent heavily to make it possible for its clients—large insurance companies or SMEs—to easily analyze their data on liability and cost patterns to help them recalibrate their business strategies.

Fifth, the IPD spurred various financial experiments that are opening new financial alternatives for funding innovation in a broader geographic array of applications. This development was compounded by the evolution of the VC funding model. As a leading venture capitalist explained to us, three- to five-year time frames for returns now thoroughly dominate the major firms. Although some firms go public to huge returns, many VCs also now lean heavily on sales to established market leaders, thus avoiding many of the complexities and risks of going public. And VCs now shy away from excessively risky bets for all but small slivers of their portfolios. Indeed, VCs now value a complementary ecosystem of very-early-stage investors, so-called "angels." Angel investing ranges from the "billionaire bets" of people like Elon Musk and Jeff Bezos on new space launch systems through the more common pooling of smaller sums in the hundreds of thousands to a few million dollars from affluent investors willing to take on some higher-risk, higher-return investments as part of their personal or family wealth management portfolios.[70] (Some of this is channeled through specialized investment houses such as the one that funded minuteKEY.) The VC gladly pays a premium to the early investors for successful forays because the VC's risk factor is lower and the time to market is shorter.

The changes in the VC market mean that both VCs and a wide range of startups see a need for supplemental financial mechanisms. To illustrate the funding arrays, Table 2.1 compares the amount of VC investment in the United States and China in two newer categories, angel investment and equity-based crowdfunding. It is striking that the gap between VC and angel funding is less than expected. A third alternative, crowdsourcing, is a direct product of the IPD. It is still novel, but is growing rapidly.

Crowdsourcing required networking and transaction costs to fall. Crowdsourced funding of projects is less geographically biased than traditional VC funding, but before 2015, no project ever raised more than a few million dollars.[71] Crowdfunding

TABLE 2.1

A Comparison of Innovation Funding in 2014

Innovation funding	United States	China
Angel investment	$24.1 billion	Estimates vary from $640 million to $4.5 billion
Venture capital investment	$49.3 billion	$15.5 billion
Equity-based crowdfunding	$870 million (September 2014 to September 2015)	Renminbi 384.4 million ($58.4 million)

Source: Peter Larson and Mingda Qiu, "Innovation Funding in the US and China," Memo to Experts Group on Innovation, Strategic and Economic Dialogue, February 2016. (Available from Peter Cowhey on request.) The Center for Venture Research at the University of New Hampshire estimated the U.S. angel market. "The Angel Investor Market in 2014: A Market Correction in Deal Size," https://paulcollege.unh.edu/sites/paulcollege.unh.edu/files/webform/2014%20Analysis%20Report.pdf.

also interacts with features such as the growth of online experimentation and co-invention with "early adopters" to create options for early-stage capital and market brand building. Early successes lead to later equity investments, as exemplified by Moov, an activity-monitoring device that combines sensors and artificial intelligence to guide conditioning. Early on, Moov relied on crowdfunding, coupled with a presales campaign to garner feedback on design and build brand awareness. Then it turned to Banyan Capital for series A financing.[72]

Sixth, digital platform clusters also facilitate changes in the size and geographic focus of clusters. Core geographic clusters of talent for advanced technology likely will persist because commercializing innovation involves betting on people. Clusters thrive on a larger talent pool and typically develop informal ways to measure reputations, beyond resumes, that may be vital for commercializing knowledge.[73] However, as IPD platform dynamics become more accessible, they drive more markets, including traditional markets not commonly associated with ICT. Hence, the platform cluster model will create more specialized innovation clusters than the second wave, which mainly adhered around ICT and biotech. Further, specialized clusters will rely more on local and global network dynamics. Traditional industries will be restructured in a world of IPD-enabled digital platform clusters. Technologically infused clusters can be built around "craft" knowledge.[74] They can build on virtual ICT platforms, such as the cloud and its ecosystem of services, or on specialized batch production. This occurred in New York City, where Silicon Alley was widely hailed during the 1990s. Yet, despite New York's strength as a content creator, it was never a big ICT star. Today, New York is becoming a major application content innovator because there no longer is a need for a Manhattan-based

ICT platform with bulky equipment, large rental spaces, and swarms of ICT engineers. FinTech, which builds on new ICT approaches for financial transactions, also blooms in New York among startups and giants embracing ICT-enabled business models.[75]

Significantly, supplementing ICT with new production technology opens paths to growth that rely on traditional clusters built on incremental and process innovation. Traditional knowledge experts like farmers now are reorganizing as global information service providers, as we show in Chapter 3. Similarly, Germany's Fraunhoefer Institute is advocating "Industrie 4.0" as the German manufacturing Mittelstand's formula for embracing this change.[76]

2.4. Synergies in Disruption

It is one thing to discuss individual products or pure digital offerings, such as Facebook, that are enabled by the IPD. But how would digital platform clusters influence large, capital-intensive industries?[77] We explore this question by examining two industries where past capital investment and their human organizational systems made radical change difficult. In the automotive and electric utility industries, digital platform innovations are forcing a reconceptualization of their strategy and structure. Both the business models and the technology underpinnings of these industries are changing significantly despite the inertia of large, capital-intensive industries.

2.4.1. Transformation of the Automotive Industry

A renowned computer scientist with deep industry connections told us after touring the Tesla operation, "They think and organize more like a computer company." We mentioned this remark to senior executives of one of the world's largest, most innovative automotive component suppliers. They completely agreed; Tesla is a truly different automotive company.[78] What makes it different? IT drives Tesla's design and production process. They think of the vehicle as a system problem, so they were the only electric car company to design the vehicle around the battery, not just to treat the battery as an awkward component to be crammed into a traditional car.[79] Tesla also embraced a remarkable modular approach to car systems to make it simpler to envision dual use of key components. Tesla plans to build on its car battery technology to launch home-energy storage units that extend the practicality of solar power by storing energy each night.[80] In addition, fully grasping the way that IT drives performance, Tesla designed its entire software system from the ground up, thus vastly simplifying updates of many key features of the car remotely. One test of the impact on production is this: Tesla used new computer-assisted design systems and the latest generation of robots for its design and production process. This approach significantly reduced the time from model conception to commercial production. Tesla improved on the previous industry best time from design to market by one-third. In a capital-intensive industry, time is money, and Tesla predicts vastly improved further production efficiencies on a two-year cycle.[81] Tesla also produced a user experience that won enthusiastic devotees, at least until it stumbled in its handling of a fatal crash involving its autopilot system.[82] And, Tesla hinted that it would further redefine its innovative business model when it opened a gigantic battery factory in a co-venture with Panasonic whose products would serve Tesla cars and as energy storage devices for renewable energy systems. As one investment executive explained the move to us, Tesla was transforming the car into simply one more appliance in a radically redefined notion of an electric energy system. It remains an open question whether these gambits will propel Tesla to long-term success, but they show that even the most traditional industrial processes and organizations can be transformed significantly.

Tesla shows what can occur when the IPD impacts traditional manufacturing systems and their products. But an even larger change is unfolding as the IPD takes hold and digital platform clusters emerge: a revolution in organizing the use of, and therefore the business model for, automotive vehicles. Autonomous driving by a computer system failed in its first DARPA road test in 2004, but by 2012 Google successfully tested a self-driving vehicle that employed big data analytics, lots of computing power, and sophisticated sensor systems. "Semiautonomous vehicles" with IT-enabled braking and steering assists were widely available by 2015. Cars are getting "smarter." In 2014, a luxury auto had 300 million lines of software code, compared to 8 million in a jet fighter.[83] The information value added in the vehicle is now its most expensive input.[84] Depending on law and infrastructure investments (such as sensors in the road that interact with cars), fully autonomous vehicles could be available in the 2020s. Essentially, the car melds IT, robotics, and transport. The robotic elements include sophisticated sensors, internal networking in the car and with surrounding cars, and decision-making programs to guide the car when rapid responses are needed.

By 2015, the connectivity of cars brought the sharing economy of services like Uber and Lyft to transportation, which unleashed revolutions in their business utilization models. In addition to using IT to coordinate drivers and vehicles, these services rely on GPS services to guide drivers, online rating systems to weed out unacceptable drivers and passengers, and networked payment systems. The business models of the largest auto manufacturers are flirting with significant change. Investments by General Motors and Toyota, for example, appear to be in direct response to the rise of the Uber/Lyft revolution, the emergence of driverless cars, and the need for competence in artificial intelligence.[85] Even in personal vehicles, the business model of auto manufacturers will evolve in parallel with their vehicles to be personal transportation systems where both drivers and passengers are treated like commuters.[86]

The automotive story points to a broader tension over the business models tied to digital platforms. Many investors hope to use the IPD to disaggregate the value propositions of an expanding range of industries. Uber, Airbnb, and the sharing economy are the most prominent symbols of this movement.[87] But the "sharing economy" is only part of the story.[88] As a prominent investor told us, the factors in the IPD allow businesses to revolutionize specific processes (and their value added) in traditional industries and then turn them into high-growth companies whose capital requirements are far lower than was the case traditionally. Fast growth, capital-"lite" investment models, strong margins, and demonstrable advantages on performance over traditional methods make for high valuation models. Thus, Google's story in autos takes on a larger significance if viewed as a probe to see whether the IPD disruption can repurpose and stimulate technology functionalities in a car as a business separate from the control of auto companies and their traditional suppliers.[89] As noted in Chapter 6, defenders of European and other innovation systems that are more married to traditional industries with capital-intensive strategies are fighting back. They want to use the IPD to revitalize old industries, not disrupt them.

Further, with regard to autos, privacy and security policies will shape how information can be reused and combined. Beyond immediate profits from the resale of Big Data, many "big data" benefits come from experimenting with its use in previously unimagined ways. The IPD gnaws away at traditional market and sectoral distinctions. Yet, many regulations lock down data and restrict deeper innovation by those who want to hive off one piece of value added in capital-lite strategies. We argue that, as with the choices on government policies about modularity, the question is not whether there is a role for governance oversight, but what form it should take. Part III considers the political economy of these tensions and its implication for digital platforms.

2.4.2. The Energy Grid

The efforts to transform electric energy systems provide another glimpse into the unpredictable transformation of digital platform dynamics. Despite the impression created by the bankruptcy of Solyndra, the failed solar company backed by the Obama administration, the Obama energy investments worked reasonably well to lower the cost structure for renewables. Yet, they missed the largest supply-side development that transformed the American energy landscape after 2008—expanded fracking and the explosion in U.S. shale oil production. Similarly, savvy private investors sometimes stumble, as shown by those VCs that lost significant sums on alternative energy after guessing incorrectly about whether their business models would succeed. Their mistakes help explain the interaction of production and information technologies in driving change.

When the VC industry embraced clean tech, especially alternative energy, it bet that it would unleash major network effects and huge economies of scale. Investors presumed that they would earn large returns and that the sector's dynamics would resemble that of software or semiconductors.[90] In addition, they wrongly assumed that photovoltaic technology was sufficiently complex that Chinese competitors could not seize huge advantages by leveraging economies of scale created by the Chinese market. Instead, much of the alternative energy space evolved to resemble traditional high-end manufacturing. Alternative energy development required investing big money to achieve incremental improvements in solar cell yield or expensive infrastructure deployment (e.g., to build private radio networks to connect sensors for a building's smart management). VCs quickly lost confidence and pulled their support from projects that required expensive too much work to generate mundane profit returns.[91] Until production technologies yield much larger cost breakthroughs, built on a sustainable technological edge, VCs will approach this domain with extreme caution while a few "billionaire angels" such as Bill Gates still place some larger speculative bets.

Nonetheless, the discovery process continues and a new generation of business models focuses on opportunities presented by network-based software and data that are bolstered by improved sensors (including "smart meters" that provide real-time information on individual users). These models seek specialized tasks with high payback on investment, like the management of peak load power, where a significant part of urban peak loads come from large buildings and air conditioning. New solutions use network-based software and big data analytic guidance to dramatically cut costs of peak loads. These systems also substitute the networks of public mobile operators for private radio nets to reduce capital costs and lead times. Moore's law, like improvements in the cost and performance of sensors, follows and uses big data/big analytics to manage the load management plan. With greater experience, these innovations can guide loads "circuit by circuit" at competitive prices. We also expect that during the information disruption, the more micro the observation and control points, the more valuable control analytics will be.[92]

Predictably, in the IPD, opportunities and risks will foster deeper experiments with reorganization of the business model and innovation system for electric grids. The "microgrid" has attracted increased investment in experimental systems, especially software platforms that can provide interoperable coordination of public and microgrids.[93] Instead of pushing larger and larger economies of scale in centralized generation and distribution networks, the microgrid uses IT to enable specialized "islands" of generation and distribution. These islands are intensively managed by networked IT systems to serve university campuses, manufacturing complexes, military bases, and other specialized large users of electricity. Solar and other distributed energy sources can be scaled more effectively for the target microgrid. These sources are backed by localized energy storage systems and distributed by networks that are optimized to reduce demand and lose less energy than with long-distance transmission. The systems may be less subject to large-scale grid failure, but can be backed up by the grid if local failures occur. The "closed grid" also permits greater cybersecurity with more information-intensive monitoring of the system. Like any innovation, microgrids may stumble or they could cause an economic crisis for the public grid as profitable peak load customers disappear from the rate base. In either case, they show how the IPD allows significant experiments with "strategy" and "structure" in the economy.

2.5. Six Takeaways from the IPD

To summarize, we briefly revisit six major consequences of the IPD that serve as a basis for considering the governance opportunities and challenges discussed in Parts II and III.

1. *Digital ubiquity and diversity*: Modularity and the intermingling of production and information inputs mean that many more markets will act like IT markets. More complicated divisions of labor and value will emerge, not just a few dominant digital solutions.
2. *Market disruption*: The intermingling of traditional goods with information enabled by new services and new production technologies will disrupt even traditional markets.
3. *Easier entry*: New technologies lower the cost of many forms of innovation, making entry easier. New technologies also invite novel hybrid innovations and business models that defy traditional market boundaries. Many winners and losers will organize around new business models.
4. *New regional platform clusters*: New types of regional startup clusters that cover a more diverse range of industries, expertise, and locations will thrive. Clusters could be smaller and focus on craft knowledge. The IPD will play out most dramatically in technology markets, where it can revitalize old or enable new clusters of more traditional products and services. As the IPD spreads across industries, the distinctions between high-tech and other industries will narrow.

5. *Global productive potential*: The IPD will alter interactive user experiences and big data analysis will require drawing more on global experience and feedback. Even smaller firms will rely on network clusters of specialized local talent spread worldwide.

6. *New governance solutions*: The characteristics of the IPD disruption will require rethinking many assumptions behind economic policies, including tax and tariff policies.[94] There will also be a need for more shared governance involving public and private arrangements and for an emphasis on experimentation and learning in policy to foster innovation on issues such as cybersecurity and digital privacy.

Notes

1. See Andrew McAfee and Erik Brynjolfsson, "Big Data: The Management Revolution," *Harvard Business Review*, 90, no. 10 (October 2012): 60–66, 68; and Arvind Subramanian and Martin Kessler, "The Hyperglobalization of Trade and Its Future," Peterson Institute for International Economics, Working Paper Series, WP 13–6 (July 2013), https://piie.com/publications/wp/wp13-6.pdf.

2. Our point follows directly from the classic work of Alfred Chandler on "strategy" and "structure" that showed how an earlier era of communication and transportation innovations opened the possibility of effectively serving the continental U.S. market and thus incentivized the experiments that led to the rise of the vertically integrated, multidivisional corporations that became the anchor of the first wave. Alfred D. Chandler Jr., *The Visible Hand: The Managerial Revolution in American Business* (Cambridge, MA: Belknap Press of Harvard University Press, 1977). Oliver Williamson provided a broader theoretical framework for these problems in *The Economic Institutions of Capitalism* (New York: Simon & Schuster, 1985).

3. For example, the formation of Lloyd's of London accelerated the rise of global trading and shipping.

4. In its first printing, Bill Gates, *The Road Ahead* (New York: Viking, 1997), failed to foresee the transformative significance of the Internet.

5. The market for big stars remains, although with lower profit margins and a somewhat smaller market share. Similarly, Netflix and streaming video (and pirating) decimated studio profits from DVD sales. Yet, Hollywood persisted by changing its product mix and distribution cycle to cater more to global markets such as China to replace lost DVD revenues. Lynda Obst, *Sleepless in Hollywood: Tales from the New Abnormal in the Movie Business* (New York: Simon & Schuster, 2014).

6. Boy de Nijs, "Rungis: World's largest wholesale market for fresh food," May 31, 2016, *hortidaily*, http://www.hortidaily.com/article/26574/Rungis-Worlds-largest-wholesale-market-for-fresh-food.

7. The radiofrequency identification tags made it easier to audit meat sales, even if they had kept paper payments.

8. As economic growth theory evolved, it placed more emphasis on the impact of innovation. David Warsh, *Knowledge and the Wealth of Nations: A Story of Economy Discovery* (New York: Norton, 2006).

9. Brynjolfsson and McAfee are optimists on innovation rates. Gordon and Cowen disagree. Tyler Cowen, *The Great Stagnation: How America Ate All the Low-Hanging Fruit of Modern History, Got Sick, and Will (Eventually) Feel Better* (Boston: Dutton, 2011), pamphlet; Robert J. Gordon, *The Rise and Fall of American Growth: The U.S. Standard of Living since the Civil War*, The Princeton Economic History of the Western World (Princeton, NJ: Princeton University Press, 2016).

10. McKinsey Global Institute, *Digital Globalization: The New Era of Global Flows* (2016).

11. Predictably, policy makers now devote more attention to the role of smaller firms in trade policy. Peter F. Cowhey, "Crafting Trade Strategy in the Great Recession: The Obama Administration and the Changing Political Economy of the United States," in Miles Kahler and David Lake (eds.), *Politics in New Hard Times: The Great Recession in Comparative Perspectives* (Ithaca, NY: Cornell University Press, 2013).

12. Anne Wren (ed.), *The Political Economy of the Service Transition* (New York: Oxford University Press, 2013).

13. In November 2014, Korean investors with a manufacturing background told us that rising Chinese labor prices are leading Korean manufacturers to shift plant investments to Vietnam.

14. Rainer Lanz, Sébastien Miroudot, and Hildegunn K. Nordås, "Trade in Tasks," *OECD Trade Policy Working Papers*, No. 117, 2011, http://dx.doi.org/10.1787/5kg6v2hkvmmw-en

15. See Autor, Dorn, and Hanson, *The China Syndrome*, 2013; Acemoglu, Autor, Dorn, Hanson, and Price, "Return of the Solow Paradox?," 2014.

16. See Martin Ford, *Rise of the Robots: Technology and the Threat of a Jobless Future* (New York: Basic Books, 2015); Alec Ross, *The Industries of the Future* (New York: Simon & Schuster, 2016); "The Third Great Wave," *The Economist*, Special Report, October 4, 2014.

17. One imaginative proposal is Seth D. Harris and Alan B. Krueger, "A Proposal for Modernizing Labor Laws for the Twenty First Century: The 'Independent Worker,'" The Hamilton Project, Discussion Paper 2015-10, December 2015, http://www.hamiltonproject.org/assets/files/modernizing_labor_laws_for_twenty_first_century_work_krueger_harris.pdf. The paper estimates that 0.4% of total U.S. employment currently uses such arrangements.

18. Neal Stephenson, *Snow Crash* (New York: Bantam Spectra Book, 1992). Indeed, in 2014 a resurgent Domino's leveraged its superior IT to jump ahead of its competitors. It even dropped "pizza" from its name. "Domino's Becomes a Tech Company That Happens to Make Pizza," *All Things Considered*, NPR, November 4, 2014, http://www.npr.org/blogs/alltechconsidered/2014/11/04/359829824/dominos-becomes-a-tech-company-that-happens-to-make-pizza.

19. A similar analysis is Martin Hirt and Paul Willmott, "Strategic Principles for Competing in the Digital Age," *McKinsey Quarterly*, May 2014.

20. The cost of 1 million transistors (a standard measure of computing power) was $527 in 1990, $1 in 2002, and $.05 in 2012. The cost of storage of a gigabyte of data dropped from $569 in 1992, to $1 in 2002, and to $.02 in 2012. The bandwidth cost to transmit 1000 megabits per second plunged from $1,245 in 1999, to $100 in 2009, and to $16 in 2013. Mary Meeker, *Internet Trends in 2014*, Kleiner, Perkins, Caufield, Byers at http://www.kpcb.com/internet-trends. Cowhey and Aronson (*Transforming Global Information*, 2009) stressed the importance of modularity, echoing Rich Klitgaard in dubbing this "the cheap revolution." A similar analysis is John Hagel, J. S.

Brown, T. Samaloya, and M. Lui, "From Exponential Technologies to Exponential Innovation," Deloitte Edge Center, 2013.

21. "More from Moore," *The Economist*, Technology Quarterly, September 5, 2015, p. 9, http://www.economist.com/news/technology-quarterly/21662644-chipmaking-moores-law-may-be-running-out-steam-chip-costs-will-continue.

22. Machine learning is powerful, but subject to the usual hype about new capabilities. Mathematicians point out that many predicted benefits of machine learning depend on inventing new data analytics that far exceed standard statistical tests. Artificial intelligence experts note that machine learning is not a form of autonomous artificial intelligence. Oren Etzioni, "Deep Learning Isn't a Dangerous Magic Genie. It's Just Math," *Wired*, June 15, 2016, http://www.wired.com/2016/06/deep-learning-isnt-dangerous-magic-genie-just-math/; Darryl K. Taft, "One-Third of Big Data Developers Use Machine Learning: Study," *eWeek*, July 6, 2016, http://www.eweek.com/developer/one-third-of-big-data-developers-use-machine-learning-study.html.

23. Modularity is a recurring theme of our industry interviews. "Containers" are the newest metaphor for packing complex software code into building blocks that can be slipped in and out of different service applications. Quentin Hardy, "A Small Software Company Sees a Future in Containers of Code," *New York Times*, January 13, 2015, p. B2.

24. Kal Raustiala and Christopher Sprigman, *The Knockoff Economy: How Imitation Sparks Innovation* (New York: Oxford University Press, 2012), pp. 185–191.

25. Karen A. Frenkel, "Crowdsourced in the U.S.A.," *Bloomberg Business Week*, June 29, 2012, http://www.bloomberg.com/bw/articles/2012-06-29/crowdsourced-in-the-u-dot-s-dot-a-dot.

26. For the history of modularity, see Cowhey and Aronson, *Transforming Global Information*, 2009. For details on the Google and Intel actions, see Shelanski.

27. James McQuivey, *Digital Disruption: Unleashing the Next Wave of Innovation* (Amazon Publishing, 2013).

28. Presentation and discussion with David Hardman, UK Science Park Association Chairman, at Zhongguancun Forum, Shanghai, September 12, 2013.

29. Interviews, Estonia, October 2014. "How Did Estonia Become a Leader in Technology?," *The Economist*, July 30, 2013, http://www.economist.com/blogs/economist-explains/2013/07/economist-explains-21.

30. Successful tech startups worldwide are investing in U.S. tech startups. Chinese firms like Xiaomi, JD.com, Tencent, and Alibaba invested heavily in such U.S. startups as Misfit (wearable and home tech IT), Snapchat (messaging), Riot Games (massive multiplayer gaming), and Lyft (IT enabled transport services). *Financial Times*, December 3, 2014, p. 19.

31. See, for example, "Voice from Caveman to the Next Big Thing," *Internetcentral*, https:www.ic.co.uk/news-and-events/voice-from-caveman-to-the-next-big-thing/; "Is Voice the Next Big Thing for the Internet?," NXP Software, http://www.nxpsoftware.com/blog/hypervoice-smartphones-big-thing-2/; Benedict Evans, "Voice Is the Next Big Thing in Mobile," October 1, 2014, http://ben-evans.com/benedictevans/2014/10/1/voice-is-the-next-big-thing-in-mobile.

32. Olivier L. de Weck and Darci Reed, "Trends in Advanced Manufacturing Technology Innovation," in Richard M. Locke and Rachel L. Wilhausen (eds.), *Production in the Innovation Economy* (Cambridge, MA: MIT Press, 2014), pp. 235–262.

33. Scott Kennedy, "Made in China, 2025," Center for Strategic and International Studies, June 1, 2015, http://csis.org/publication/made-china-2025.

34. Janet Fang, "NASA Just Emailed a Wrench to the International Space Station," December 19, 2014, accessed December 24, 2014, http://www.iflscience.com/space/how-nasa-emailed-wrench-space.

35. "A Bridge to the Future," *The Economist Technology Quarterly*, September 5, 2015, http://www.economist.com/news/technology-quarterly/21662647-civil-engineering-3d-printing-technologies-are-being-adapted-use.

36. Janet Fang, "3D Printed Device Detoxifies Blood Like a Liver," May 17, 2014, accessed January 26, 2015, http://www.iflscience.com/health-and-medicine/3d-printed-device-detoxifies-blood-liver.

37. This also is happening at the household level. As of August 2016, Amazon listed Cube 3D home printers for as little as $230. HP has announced its intention to undertake the challenge at all levels of production capacity. "HP Unveils Future of 3D Printing and Immersive Computing as Part of Blended Reality Vision," press release, October 29, 2014, http://additivemanufactur-ing.com/2014/10/30/hp-unveils-future-of-3d-printing-and-immersive-computing-as-part-of-blended-reality-vision/.

38. At feetz.com. Also J. D. Harrison, "SxSW Start-up Snapshot: Shoes Built by iPhones and 3D Printers," *The Washington Post,* March 16, 2015, https://www.washingtonpost.com/news/on-small-business/wp/2015/03/16/sxsw-start-up-snapshot-shoes-built-by-iphones-and-3d-printers/?utm_term=.9e60922390c9.

39. We thank David Michael for his insights. On DARPA's initiative, see http://3dprint.com/69674/darpa-3d-printing/.

40. Tesla robots, for example, use IT to multitask in ways that other manufacturers cannot match. *Seeking Alpha*, Technology Talker, "Tesla's Highly Scalable Model," posted October 28, 2014, http://seekingalpha.com/article/2604485-teslas-highly-scalable-model.

41. Ross, Chapter 1; "A Third Industrial Revolution," *The Economist*, April 21, 2012, Special Supplement, pp. 1–20; Brynjolfsson and McAfee; Jeremy Rifkin, *The Zero Marginal Cost Society* (New York: Palgrave Macmillan Trade, 2014).

42. See, for example, the minimally invasive da Vinci Surgical System being produced by Intuitive Surgical, http://www.intuitivesurgical.com/. However, the system and replacement parts are still extremely expensive.

43. De Weck and Reed, p. 254. Brad Stone, "A Bay Area Startup Spins Lab-Grown Silk," *Bloomberg Technology*, June 3, 2015, http://www.bloomberg.com/news/articles/2015-06-03/a-bay-area-startup-spins-lab-grown-silk.

44. Auto manufacturers believe that a combination of smart materials and information systems soon will allow cars to adapt dynamically to changing conditions, such as sunlight, heat, speed, and wind.

45. We thank Al Pisano for this example.

46. On the growth of nanorobotic systems to support nanomanufacturing that may change lithography, see http://www.nanowerk.com/spotlight/spotid=37884.php, posted October 28, 2014.

47. See, for example, the reporting on commercializing the research of Todd Coleman, http://www.slashgear.com/whats-inside-motorolas-digital-tattoo-31284412/.

48. *Bloomberg Business Week*, "This Lab for Hire," July 7–13, 2014, http://emeraldtherapeu-tics.org/; http://www.mysanantonio.com/technology/article/Outsourcing-scientific-tests-aids-biotech-startups-5657832.php.

49. Lee G. Branstetter, Matej Drev, and Namho Kwon, "Get with the Program: Software Driven Innovation in Traditional Manufacturing," NBER Working Paper 21752, November 2015, http://www.nber.org/papers/w21752.

50. This definition is from Shelanski's valuable review of competition policy concerning platforms. For a treatment of platform economics focused on purely digital services, see Parker, Geoffrey G., Marshall W. Van Alstyne, and Sangeet Paul Choudary, *Platform Revolution: How Networked Markets Are Transforming the Economy—And How to Make Them Work* (New York: Norton, 2016).

51. Brad Stone, *The Everything Store: Jeff Bezos and the Age of Amazon* (Boston: Little, Brown, 2013).

52. MinuteKEY promises to save consumers time. Their trademarked slogan is "make the most of every minute," accessed November 8, 2014, http://minutekey.com/. Also see "Small to Big Minute Key," *Bloomberg Business Week*, April 23, 2015, p. 48, accessed May 3, 2015, http://www.bloomberg.com/news/articles/2015-04-23/small-to-big-minute-key-unlocks-growth.

53. The survey results of Ashish Arora, Wesley M. Cohen, and John P. Walsh, "The Acquisition and Commercialization of Invention in American Manufacturing: Incidence and Impact," NBER Working Paper 20264, June 2014, echo our point that firms are becoming more reliant on open co-invention.

54. Parker et al., *Platform Revolution*; Steve Blank and Bob Dorf, *The Startup Owner's Manual: The Step-By-Step Guide for Building a Great Company* (Berks County, PA: K&S Ranch Press, 2012).

55. Eric von Hippel, *Democratizing Innovation* (Cambridge, MA: MIT Press, 2005). On a case-by-case basis, analytic gains may be small. However, when added together they can yield significant gains, as demonstrated in the totality of the supply chain management eco-system. Schumpeter, "Little Things That Mean a Lot," *The Economist*, July 19, 2014, p. 60. On digital technology and supply chains, see *Financial Times,* Special Report, "The Connected Business," October 22, 2014.

56. Breznitz and Zysman (eds.), *The Third Globalization*, deftly analyze ICT enabled services.

57. McAfee and Brynjolfsson dub this effect the "recombinant innovation" properties of digital technology. Mark Muro, "The Wrong Lesson Companies Learn from Silicon Valley," *The Wall Street Journal* blog, May 13, 2015, http://blogs.wsj.com/experts/2015/05/13/the-wrong-lesson-companies-learn-from-silicon-valley/.

58. IBM foresaw a huge upside to data analytics but struggled to establish high-margin business models comparable to those once earned by the software, services, and storage associated with mainframe computing that contributed 25% of corporate revenue and more than 40% of its profits. Robert X. Cringley, *The Decline and Fall of IBM—End of an American Icon?* (London: Mobi, Kindle edition, 2014); Steve Lohr, "Weak Results at IBM as Its Strategy Shifts," *New York Times*, October 21, 2014, p. B1.

59. See Larry Smarr, "Quantifying Your Body," *Biotechnology Journal*, 7, no. 8 (August 2012): 980–991; Eric Topol, *The Patient Will See You Now* (New York: Basic Books, 2015).

60. http://techcrunch.com/2013/01/10/dropcam-now-processing-more-uploaded-video-than-youtube-says-ceo-greg-duffy/, accessed December 24, 2014.

61. Daniela Hernandez, "Software Is Still King. Hardware Is Just Along for the Ride," *Wired*, July 8, 2013, http://www.wired.com/business/2013/07/software-is-still-king-hardware-is-just-coming-along-for-the-ride/?cid=co9596544.

62. *Nest Labs* recast thermostat control systems, traditionally an electromechanical technology, with an elegant redesign that integrated easy to use ICT control systems, accessed December 18, 2015, http://www.nest.com/about/. In early 2014, Google announced it would acquire Nest

for $3.2 billion. Rolfe Winkler and Daisuke Wakabayashi, "Google to Buy Nest Labs for $3.2 Billion," *The Wall Street Journal*, January 13, 2014.

63. "Why Did Nest Labs Buy Dropcam? *Forbes*, July 1, 2014, accessed December 11, 2014, http://www.forbes.com/sites/quora/2014/07/01/why-did-nest-labs-buy-dropcam/; Steven Levy, "Nest Gives the Lowly Smoke Detector a Brain—And a Voice." *Wired*, October 18, 2013, http://www.wired.com/2013/10/nest-smoke-detector/; Steven Levy, "Where There's Smoke," *Wired*, November 2013, pp. 164–169.

64. Breakthroughs at Nest came more slowly than Google hoped, and in mid-2016, Tony Fadell, Nest's co-founder, exited as head of Nest's "smart home division," http://www.forbes.com/sites/quora/2014/07/01/why-did-nest-labs-buy-dropcam/. Richard Waters, "Nest Chief Executive Exits as 'Smart Home' Division Loses Steam," *Financial Times*, June 3, 2016, http://www.ft.com/intl/cms/s/0/87605e7e-29ca-11e6-8ba3-cdd781d02d89.html#axzz4BVL7yLjG. Also Mark Bergen, "Dropcam founder: Selling to Nest and Google Was a 'Mistake'," *Recode*, March 29, 2016, http://www.recode.net/2016/3/29/11587344/dropcam-duffy-nest-google-mistake.

65. Liz Gannes, "Wearable Sensors Could Be an Antidote to Football's Concussion Problem," *All Things D*, November 25, 2013, http://allthingsd.com/20131125/wearable-sensors-could-be-an-antidote-to-footballs-concussion-problem/.

66. "A study by Intuit predicted that by 2020, 40% of American workers would be independent contractors," http://whatis.techtarget.com/definition/gig-economy; Eric Morath, "Gig Economy Attracts Many Workers, Few Full Time Jobs," *The Wall Street Journal,* February 18, 2016, http://blogs.wsj.com/economics/2016/02/18/gig-economy-attracts-many-workers-few-full-time-jobs/; Amy Cortese, "A New Wrinkle in the Gig Economy: Workers Get Most of the Money," *New York Times*, July 21, 2016, http://www.nytimes.com/2016/07/21/business/small-business/a-new-wrinkle-in-the-gig-economy-workers-get-most-of-the-money.html?_r=0.

67. The definition is from Investopedia, http://www.investopedia.com/terms/s/sharing-economy.asp. Rachel Botsman and Roo Rogers, *What's Mine Is Yours: The Rise of Collaborative Consumption* (New York: Harper Collins, 2010); Farhad Manjoo, "Tipping Point in Transit, BITS," *New York Times*, June 11, 2015, p. F1. See also http://www.economist.com/news/technology-quarterly/21572914-collaborative-consumption-technology-makes-it-easier-people-rent-items.

68. Viktor Mayer-Schönberger and Kenneth Cukier, *Big Data: A Revolution That Will Transform How We Live, Work, and Think* (Boston: Houghton, Mifflin Harcourt, 2013).

69. Either public policies, like privacy protection, or corporate strategies may limit reuse.

70. In early 2016 we learned of one low-profile startup in nuclear fusion that had substantial investment as a high-risk play in energy. On VC dynamics, see Lerner.

71. Lerner, p. 68; Ethan Mollick, "The Dynamics of Crowdfunding: Determinants of Success and Failure," *Journal of Business Venturing*, 29, no. 1 (2014): 1–16. Block chain technology may further lower the cost and increase the network effects of crowdsourced models.

72. http://www.crowdfundinsider.com/2014/10/53384-crowdfunded-fitness-device-moov-raises-3-million-funding-banyan-capital/.

73. When a research star departs a cluster, the star's influence on basic research in the cluster does not diminish because of the low costs of networking relationships. However, the shift reduces the number of the researcher's ideas showing up in future commercial investments in the cluster, perhaps because the commercialization decision depends on more intimate trust factors that link researchers and investors. Pierre Azoulay, Joshua Graff-Zivin, and Bhaven Sampat, "The Diffusion of Scientific Knowledge across Time and Space: Evidence from Professional

Transitions for the Superstars of Medicine," in Josh Lerner and Scott Stern (eds.), *The Rate and Direction of Inventive Activity: A New Agenda* (Cambridge, MA: National Bureau of Economic Research, April 2012).

74. We believe that "innovative industries" go beyond traditional high-tech industries characterized by high, fixed initial research and that capital costs usually are dispersed over large volumes of output at low marginal costs. Atkinson and Ezell argue that these firms often have lower marginal costs than average costs, an anomaly in the standard textbook treatment of the firm's production function. We are more concerned with how the IPD is changing the behavior of traditional, less technologically intensive industries.

75. Steven Rosenbush and Steven Norton, "Goldman Turns to Software Containers," *The Wall Street Journal*, February 25, 2016, p. C3.

76. Deutsch Bank Research, Industrie 4.0: Huge Potential for Value Creation Waiting to Be Tapped, May 24, 2014, http://www.dbresearch.com/PROD/DBR_INTERNET_EN-PROD/PROD0000000000335628.pdf; *The Economist*, "Does Deutschland Do Digital?," November 21, 2015, pp. 59–61.

77. For significant differentiators of "heavy" manufacturing processes, see Timothy Sturgeon and Richard Florida, "Globalization, Deverticalization and Employment in the Motor Vehicle Industry," Chap. 3, in Martin Kenney and Richard Florida (eds.), *Locating Global Advantage: Industry Dynamics in the International Economy* (Palo Alto, CA: Stanford University Press, 2004).

78. Discussions with one of the authors in California in April 2014 and in Paris in October 2014. More formally, see the discussion of John Hagel et al.

79. "UCSD–Tsinghua University Innovation Metrics Survey Project: Electric Vehicles" (University of California Institute on Global Conflict and Cooperation, July 2014). Executive summary, https://igcc.ucsd.edu/_files/tech-innovation-security/EV-survey-summary.pdf. This document contains only the U.S. results.

80. Nick Stockton, "How Tesla's Batteries Will Power Your Home," *Wired*, May 1, 2015, http://www.wired.com/2015/05/teslas-batteries-will-power-home/. But the proposed purchase of Solar City, its battery supplier, made investors wary. Fred Lambert, "Tesla (TSLA) Target Price Cut 26% by Adam Jonas from Morgan Stanley Following Solar City Deal," Electrek, June 23, 2016, http://electrek.co/2016/06/23/tesla-tsla-adam-jonas-morgan-stanley-rating-solarcity-scty/.

81. Tesla's promise also involved two helping hands, a large grant from the Obama energy program and the fortuitous closing of the GM–Toyota NUMMI factory that Tesla bought inexpensively and then reequipped. On software vision and good luck, see Ashlee Vance, *Elon Musk, Tesla, SpaceX, and the Quest for a Fantastic Future* (New York: HarperCollins, 2015). On predicted efficiencies, see Elon Musk, "Master Plan, Part Deux," July 20, 2016, https://www.tesla.com/blog/master-plan-part-deux.

82. Bill Vlasic and Neal Boudette, "As U.S. Investigates Fatal Tesla Crash, Company Defends Autopilot System," *New York Times*, July 12, 2016, http://www.nytimes.com/2016/07/13/business/tesla-autopilot-fatal-crash-investigation.html.

83. The estimate is from Rogue Wave, a U.S. software firm. Andy Sharman, "Automakers Spy Hazards Ahead," *Financial Times*, special report on "The Future of the Car," November 21, 2014. On Google, see the account by Brynjolfsson and McAfee, http://www.ft.com/intl/reports/future-car.

84. Automobile IT systems are still not highly "modular." Every major car manufacturer has its own version of an IT architecture. Suppliers are urging more modularity in the interfaces. So far Ford has been the most attuned to opening up its IT platform to co-invention.

85. James Vincent, "Toyota's $1 Billion AI Company Will Develop Self-Driving Cars and Robot Helpers," *The Verge*, November 15, 2016, http://www.theverge.com/2015/11/6/9680128/toyota-ai-research-one-billion-funding. Mark Bergen and Johana Bhuiyan, "GM Spent over $1 Billion on Self-Driving Startup to Keep Up with Google, Apple," March 11, 2016, http://www.recode.net/2016/3/11/11586894/gm-spent-over-1-billion-on-self-driving-startup-cruise-the-largest-y; Mike Ramsey, "Car Makers Hunger for Self-Driving Tech," *The Wall Street Journal*, March 24, 2016, http://www.wsj.com/articles/car-makers-hunger-for-self-driving-tech-1458811804.

86. Predictably, taxi companies are counterattacking in regulatory arenas as revenues and the value of their medallions plummet.

87. The sharing economy also illustrates the geographic dispersion of innovation. For example, automobile vehicle diagnostics for car owners may change because of the rise of "Fitbits for cars," inexpensive systems for monitoring car systems for maintenance and fine-tuning driver performance, to improve mileage. One Thai company began with $60,000, raised on Indiegogo, a crowdsourcing platform. That amount was more than it needed. Its system plugs into an automobile's diagnostic system and sends guidance to the owner's smartphone. Angus MacKenzie, "Drivebot Provides Real-Time Monitoring of Vehicle Health," *gizmag*, October 27, 2014, accessed October 28, 2014, http://www.gizmag.com/drivebot-vehicle-monitoring/34447/.

88. "The Rise of the Sharing Economy," *The Economist*, March 9, 2016, http://www.economist.com/news/leaders/21573104-internet-everything-hire-rise-sharing-economy.

89. See the remarks of the chief executive officer of Fiat Chrysler in Michel Sanderson, "A Car Chief's Gloomy View of the Valley," *Financial Times*, January 17, 2016, p. 7.

90. We thank Michael Kleeman and James Lambright for connecting the dots for us.

91. Dan Breznitz points out that the paucity of such plausible financial mechanisms for "grind it out" innovations is a weakness of the American innovation system in "Why Germany Dominates the U.S. in Innovation," *Harvard Business Review*, May 27, 2014, https://hbr.org/2014/05/why-germany-dominates-the-u-s-in-innovation/.

92. Opower, a disruptive software-as-a-service firm founded in 2007, sells utility companies on three continents' cloud-based software that provides a behavioral energy efficiency solution. It provides personalized information to customers about their energy use and recommends ways to save energy. On average, the more than 50 million homes that receive this information have cut their energy usage by about 2.5%, http://www.opower.com/.

93. See, for example, the blog discussion by Michael Panfils of the Environmental Defense Fund, http://blogs.edf.org/energyexchange/2014/05/22/resiliency-distributed-generation-and-microgrids-can-keep-lights-on-during-the-next-storm/.

94. For example, in an interview with a Shanghai official about this book in fall 2013, his major reaction was that Chinese tax policy is skewed to favor manufactured goods over services, a distinction that makes little sense in the future. President Trump also favors manufactured goods over services.

3   Two Cases and Policy Implications

THE SECOND WAVE of innovation put pressure on the champions of the first wave. Many behemoths disappeared or their influence ebbed significantly. Others adapted to the new ways of innovation and prospered. The same will be true with the IPD. Established market leaders will need to change; their choices can illuminate the dynamics at work. This chapter focuses on two companies in different industries, Monsanto and Qualcomm, to illustrate the disruptions and their governance implications.

The Monsanto example shows how the IPD is transforming management of the farm field. The possibilities have huge implications for the management and control of data. The market opportunities are attracting new kinds of entrants in ways that illustrate the beginnings of a new craft-based cluster. The IPD also inspires experiments in the governance of Big Data and, in terms of corporate strategy, the Monsanto story shows how a firm can embrace a conglomerate approach to organizing disruption.

The Qualcomm example shows how a second-wave winner is adapting to the next generation of innovation. Specifically, we examine how Qualcomm is engaging with the cluster dynamics in wireless health to develop new uses for its core competencies. Qualcomm's experiments illustrate the difference between an ecosystem strategy and a conglomerate strategy and lay out the evolving logic of global "platform economics."

A comparison of the Monsanto and Qualcomm cases shows how the IPD's forces are driving even the strategies of successful incumbents, which has major governance consequences. However, insights derived from these two cases do not translate into predictions of commercial success for any specific experiment.

After considering these two cases, we delve into specific governance issues that arise from the analysis in Part I and propose a policy agenda for the coming decades and a "design philosophy" to inform the strategies needed to solve the governance challenges.

3.1. Monsanto: Disruption of a Traditional Market and Governance Innovations

Digital DNA is transforming industries beyond the traditional domain of information-intensive business models. The case of Monsanto shows how technological disruption opens a new space for innovation in agriculture, the world's oldest market.

Monsanto, a leading first-wave agricultural innovator, became an embattled leader in seed and herbicide technology, including genetically modified seeds. Although its net sales declined in 2016 to $13.5 billion from its $15.86 billion peak in 2014 while its seed and genomics sales declined to $9.23 billion in 2016 from $10.35 billion in 2014, Monsanto remained well ahead of DuPont on the list of global agribusiness companies worldwide.[1] In recent years Monsanto flourished, in part by supplying inputs to booming corn crops that were planted to meet the surging demand in corn-based ethanol and other biofuels and because of the high prices generated by the commodity boom in large emerging markets. As ethanol-based biofuels lost some of their allure and the growth of global commodity markets ebbed, Monsanto and other agriculture giants began to think seriously about sustaining growth through diversification. Monsanto experimented by developing an "Integrated Farming Systems research platform."

Its first move was to buy Precision Planting in mid 2012, a firm that combined data analytics (a service called FieldScripts) and an innovative seed planter that trailed behind tractors to guide optimal planting (the spacing and depth of seeds in fields).[2] The Monsanto system promised to raise yields by 5% in two years and could ultimately raise corn productivity by 25%.[3] In late 2013, Monsanto also spent $932 million to purchase the Climate Corporation, a big data company founded in 2006 that provides weather monitoring and then forecasts crop yields. Climate Corporation builds on the cheap revolution to narrow the analytical focus to the level of the individual farm field to raise the power of big data analysis. Monsanto anticipated that its new subsidiaries would improve forward planning for new products and open a complementary market potential of $20 billion for agricultural data services.[4] Climate Corporation uses remote sensing and big data models to underwrite insurance for farmers against losses if weather outside predicted parameters causes crops planted using its suggested guidelines to fall below expected yields. More importantly, it allowed farmers to use online software services to optimize yields and reduce input (mainly fertilizer).

The Monsanto story illustrates how mobile broadband–enabled services can add new capabilities to a traditional market segment and significantly alter the business model. It also demonstrates how hardware (the Precision Planting equipment) and services (FieldScripts and Climate Corporation insurance and in-field sensor data) intersect in new integrated models. Whether the current package of value added will be compelling for farmers remains uncertain.[5] But, intensive data gathering and analysis at the micro level and the marriage of products and capabilities, such as planters and insurance packages, support our expectations about the IPD.

The previous chapter suggested that the IPD invites new types of entrants and clusters. Significantly, other specialized suppliers are emerging that rely on local knowledge. Local expertise allowed cities such as Des Moines, Iowa, to become favored locations for clusters of new applications for information-intensive agriculture.[6]

Personalized individual or business farm data are critical to the success of these models, which raises issues traditionally treated under the rubric of privacy rights. Mechanisms were needed to negotiate the terms under which data could be used by information service firms or their third-party clients. Concerns arose regarding whether Monsanto could resell farmer's private expertise (their information) to others, use the data from its services to farmers to backward integrate into farming by purchasing lower-yield farms, or even speculate on futures in commodity markets in ways that might hurt farmers.

Predictably, new types of startups emerged that claimed competitive advantages in managing risks from Big Data. Entrants like the Grower Information Services Cooperative negotiates on behalf of farmers. Big data services and new specialized service suppliers like Geosys (owned by the large Land O'Lakes farmer cooperative) emphasize the alignment of their interests with those of farmers. In addition, FarmLogs, a fast-growing startup that allows farmers to monitor the performance of their crops, served about 20% of the total row crop acres in the United States by the end of 2016.[7] These startups provide farmers with options to manage risks from new, shared production asset-information services. They are easier to create because of the disruptive changes in IT. However, these new services also raise novel governance issues.

Governance can be articulated or implemented by government agencies, private agreements, or the nonprofit sector. For example, the American Farm Bureau, the leading private U.S. farm organization, wrote a code of conduct ("Privacy and Security Principles for Farm Data"), which declares, "farmers own information generated on their farming operations."[8] Firms may not use data or supply it to third parties, except for agreed-on purposes. The principles limit what information can be revealed or shared about farmers' practices (e.g., about their use of pesticides), which corresponds closely to the traditional privacy rubric. The principles also establish a right for farmers to "retrieve their data" for use in other systems. Finally, the principles limit the use of data by technology providers for practices such as commodity speculation. Although their contracts do not yet incorporate these terms, companies like Monsanto, Deere, DuPont, and Dow have agreed in principle to this approach.

Monsanto is not alone in exploring the space opened by the IPD.[9] AGCO combine harvesters were priced at about $65,000 in 2000. By 2014, AGCO combines cost as much as $500,000 because of the added computer and informational technology.[10] John Deere, the tractor and farm equipment giant, is following a similar path in providing information and advice to farmers. Its SeedStar Mobile lets farmers monitor their activities in the field; its SageInsights provides a cloud-computing platform to consolidate the management of agronomic data and, in collaboration with Monsanto's Climate Corporation division, delivers farmers counsel on best planting choices based on weather and crop data.[11] In a related development, data analytics are being applied to manage the breeding of cattle.[12] Agricultural schools are hiring specialists in "precision agriculture." Discussions of the use of technology by such specialists stress that the formal analytics of the IPD can be more effective if harnessed to the craft knowledge of agronomic specialists. This approach often is adopted by new cooperatives or startups built around farm communities.[13]

In sum, the Monsanto case illustrates five features emerging from the IPD:

1. New, highly networked information is being applied to traditional sectors.
2. The supply of goods (tractors and specialized planters) and services (data analytics) is increasingly converging.
3. New entrants and new types of specialized clusters are emerging.
4. New risks are proliferating, especially risks associated with privacy and the use of Big Data.
5. New public and private entities are emerging to help govern those risks.

This case also shows how Monsanto is strategically approaching the IPD by creating and using a conglomerate structure. According to Robert Fraley, its chief technology officer, Monsanto now is "built on data science and services, not just chemicals, seeds, and generic traits."[14] A parallel prospect arose in March 2015 when the German chancellor, Angela Merkel, announced plans to provide all Germans, including those living in rural communities, with broadband connections with Internet speeds of 50 megabits per second by 2018. The goal was to catalyze huge improvements in digital farming. Local European champions, like Claas, a maker of agricultural machinery, or SAP, Europe's leading enterprise software specialist, hope to take advantage of world-class broadband opportunities.[15] The icing on the cake came when Bayer, the giant German conglomerate, agreed to acquire Monsanto for $66 billion in order to consolidate its strength in agricultural markets.[16]

3.2. Qualcomm: Large Technology Firms and the Growth of New Clusters

Technology giants will face many challenges in IPD. These firms seek to continue to add value within their core technological competence while marrying it to new pools of unconventional demand. Qualcomm's activities in wireless health fit this model. The Qualcomm story also shows how international innovation efforts may work in the IPD.

As background, through 2014 Qualcomm was a highly profitable technology firm that dominated a core technology (radio chips for wireless systems) for a rapidly growing global market. In 2016, its net income tumbled to $4.89 billion from $7.97 billion in 2014. However, its technological lead remains substantial and is reinforced by high levels of R&D spending, more than 18% of gross revenue.

But, significant challenges remained. First, compared to many of its rivals, Qualcomm was only mid-sized—even after years of rapid growth. In 2016 it generated annual revenues of $23.55 billion, down from 2014 revenues of almost $26.5 billion.[17] Second, although it designs and sells chips with good margins, its largest profits come from licensing its extensive patent portfolio. Third, the technology is so vital to many manufacturers that they frequently complained to their national competition authorities about the licensing terms. Irrespective of the legal merits, these complaints produced substantial political pressure in Korea, China, and other important markets for Qualcomm to modify its terms for doing business. Fourth, countries like China are heavily subsidizing entrants in the market that could challenge at least the lower end of its chip sets, thereby pressuring margins and scale economies. Adding to this challenge, as China's global economic power increases, China generates more than half of Qualcomm's revenues. China's antitrust action against Qualcomm in 2014–2015 was commonly read as a sign that the government hoped to weaken Qualcomm's strength in the Chinese market,[18] but Qualcomm nonetheless agreed to pay a fine of almost $1 billion to settle the case. In July 2015, the EU joined in and opened two antitrust investigations into Qualcomm. South Korea also raised competition complaints against the company.[19]

Qualcomm continues to dominate core wireless chip technology for mobile phones, including smartphones, but in 2015 and 2016 growth slowed as the company lost chip placements in some smartphones, especially in one generation of Samsung's highest-end offering. More critically, the smartphone market matured and slowed in its global growth cycle, a problem for all suppliers. Investors with significant stock holdings complained that Qualcomm expenses were too high, causing its returns to lag, and urged the company to spin off the less profitable chip division, a demand that management studied but ultimately rejected.

Short-term forces aside, Qualcomm must continually deal with rapidly evolving wireless information technology.[20] The future includes faster mobile data streams with greater capacity to use spectrum efficiently in 5G systems, where competitors are investing heavily in the hopes of eroding Qualcomm's dominance in key intellectual property for mobile systems. In addition, wireless capabilities will foster a stream of new applications and will produce complex architectures of mobile and fixed wireless capacities that interact seamlessly with the lowest costs and the highest reliability. Simultaneously, the major players in the mobile device market continue to demand more integration of data processing with radio capacity in a smaller set of chips. The aim is to reduce cost and complexity and simultaneously improve management of critical battery power. This led Qualcomm to integrate from the radio into microprocessor chips for mobile devices and put the company squarely in competition with Intel and other firms. (Intel, predictably, responded with its own ambitious plan to win a share in the wireless communications chip space.) Later, it became clear that Qualcomm also was investing heavily in artificial intelligence and machine learning solutions that could be executed by the local device to mitigate latency issues (delays in signal responses) and security risks created by relying exclusively on the cloud for guidance.[21]

As a major supplier of technology inputs to smartphones and other end devices, Qualcomm strives to remain relevant to emerging, potentially huge users of its core technologies. The Internet of Things, one manifestation of the IPD, implies massive wireless and mobile connectivity to everyday devices, such as household appliances, to automobiles, and to specialized new high-tech applications.[22] This is a larger universe than Qualcomm's traditional customer base of telecom carriers, network equipment suppliers, and smartphone producers. As noted in Chapter 2, the IPD creates a prospect of frequent explosions of novel demands that will change preferences about technology inputs. This happened, for example, when portable computers effectively killed the cathode ray tube display technology system. Joshua Gans's study of disruption by innovation notes that firms may recognize the need to disrupt their own business in these situations, but find the challenge of restructuring is more difficult than agreeing to sacrifice the profitability of its lead products.[23] For Qualcomm, staying aligned with new classes of wireless technology users is critical to maintaining leadership in the space.

The new wireless demand pools required Qualcomm to supplement its internal competence by aggressively acquiring firms with related radio technologies (such as advanced WiFi and Bluetooth chips). Qualcomm needed to meet evolving market demand and build its marketing expertise to fine-tune business models to new classes of customers.[24] In addition, there is a strong incentive to become expert in complementary technologies that will likely be integrated into a single chip set with a seamless hardware and software solution. As the terminal space moves to wireless health, autonomous vehicles, and robotic devices, system producers seek strong visualization and machine learning capabilities in chip sets.[25] The goal of the chipmaker is to provide a platform that allows for customization depending on function, but builds on a common core of capabilities that make it faster and cheaper to provide solutions.

Before noting two forays into new markets, we offer a note of caution. Like all large corporations, Qualcomm cannot afford to tackle many new niche markets, which can be profitable for smaller companies but are too small for a large company to organize and manage. (One analyst suggested that for a $30 billion company, the minimum potential market should exceed $1 billion.) Thus, in the IPD, many micromarkets will explode, but larger players will not dominate them.

One way to diversify in the short term is to purchase market entry into a large market that is rapidly becoming ICT intensive, such as autos. In October 2016 Qualcomm announced its plan to acquire NXP Semiconductors, a leading European supplier of chips for the auto industry, for $38 billion. Its goal is to gain a larger share of new ICT functions for vehicles by infusing Qualcomm technology.[26] This merger would more than double Qualcomm's employee numbers.

A second route for Qualcomm and other specialized firms is to directly stimulate early rounds of novel innovation entrants that complement their business strategies. Wireless health is an emerging market of potentially great scale based on a new technology ecosystem and regional cluster enabled by the IPD. It is made feasible by the IPD that combines elements of ICT and medical technology with a range of service systems, from insurance to hospital networks.

The Wireless–Life Sciences Alliance typifies the aspirations of an emerging new technology space. It aims to redefine the business models and market boundaries that traditionally define health care: "WLSA envisions a future in which healthcare is connected, consumer centric, distributed and integrated seamlessly across all providers irrespective of the venue. Digital and wireless technologies enable this vision. It will be the integration of medicine, science, technology, engineering and big data analytics that will deliver improved wellness and cost effective health care and outcomes."[27] The alliance engages with academic researchers globally, government agencies such as the National Institutes of Health and the U.S. Food and Drug Administration, and corporations spanning mass consumer markets to Big Pharma, insurance, healthcare systems, telecom carriers, and specialized information and biotech equipment companies. The organization is trying to serve as both a global and a regional technology cluster. It is based in San Diego because of the confluence of the wireless technology community anchored by Qualcomm and a leading biotech cluster.[28]

The Wireless–Life Sciences Alliance aims to circulate people and expertise across technology spaces that previously had minimal contact, such as ICT and medical technology and services. Thus, it strives to integrate primary building blocks for a new technology cluster. Shared facilities for research and experimentation are emerging. For example, the Gary and Mary West Health Institute in San Diego focuses on health solutions enabled by wireless information networks and seeks to "redesign our healthcare system around a more continuous, more responsive, 'automated, connected and coordinated' model of healthcare delivery, one specifically tailored to manage individuals both at-risk and suffering from chronic diseases."[29] Showing how financial models are changing in the IPD, this institute also houses an incubator for technology startups in which a West family investment fund has invested. Accepted companies must fit with the mission of the fund and the institute.

Interactions in the cluster also help firms invent business models relevant to novel markets. Some firms cluster around the consumer market to avoid the complexities of regulatory approval processes in the Food and Drug Administration. Fitbit, an activity tracker in which Qualcomm invested, was an early startup winner in this space. Its overlap, combining consumer electronics and athletic gear, allowed it to move horizontally into the space. Fitbit and other firms in this space keenly observe user behavior and preferences as they incrementally fine-tune product features. Hence, the device's early differentiation by design and functionality was augmented by superior marketing capabilities. Further, our interviews suggest that sustaining advantage over the long term may rest on deep analytics involving big, anonymized data gathered from users. These users typically rely on the supplier's cloud to provide data storage for workout records, individual performance profiles, and the like. The feedback performance programs offered by these applications are a valuable part of the user experience. They provide superior analytics to gently steer individuals toward better health outcomes. Thus, without employing regulated medical devices, there will be significant innovation based on data analytics driven by electronic devices for now, but eventually by breakthroughs such as networked sensors built into "smart" athletic apparel. Going forward, the "nonrivalrous" use of data may propel sustained advantage if human behavior factors such as user fatigue with daily guidance do not stunt growth.

Another strategy is to enter the regulated space by taking advantage of formal government regulations or extensive industry standards, such as ISO quality standards. This approach is safer for some firms because it shields them from the domination by mass consumer firms and because barriers to entry may make margins easier to sustain. Qualcomm Life targeted a space with these characteristics. Its website proclaimed that its mission was to provide the hundreds of millions of customers suffering from chronic diseases in OECD and developing markets with initiatives that "would immediately benefit from wireless home monitoring solutions . . . [or] . . . would benefit from handset integration of existing medical devices."[30] Its venture investments focused on monitoring and analytic systems that covered new functionalities (e.g., fertility monitoring), less expensive technologies for critical wireless health monitoring (e.g., cardiac devices), and software analytic systems tied to extensive patient monitoring systems. The company expected that better organization and integration of the patient monitoring and analysis space in hospitals would produce payoffs.[31] Many of these complex functions also require more sophisticated visualization and, especially if used outside hospitals, enough intelligence in the device to allow for autonomous action by the device under certain predefined conditions. This level of sophistication would differentiate these terminals from the mass consumer market items.

Strategies depend in part on responses to regulatory and quality control challenges. Eventually, these challenges become part of the discussion about governance. When we talked with a wide range of participants, including veterans of government, the conversations often circled back to how governance might ensure safety and security (including data protection) without seriously hampering innovation. Many challenges arise from the novelty of the capabilities. For example, wireless-controlled medical devices implanted in bodies collect data that provide feedback. As more medical devices are inserted more frequently, cybersecurity issues will loom larger.

The capabilities nurtured by the wireless health cluster could create a new IPD-induced customer pool seeking health solutions for firms like Qualcomm and its subsidiary, Qualcomm Life. Qualcomm might act as an angel investor—making smaller investments to accelerate undertakings that are too novel and too new for conventional VC funding. This approach is spreading among major tech firms. As they adapt, they evolve into something akin to a cross between angel and VC investors. In addition, firms are experimenting with the use of prizes to stimulate initial inventions. For example, Qualcomm is offering an "X Prize" for a wireless medical diagnostic device (patterned on the "medical tricorder" of Star Trek lore). Its purpose is to feed an ecosystem of new innovation groups that can generate new sources of market demand for Qualcomm chip technologies.[32]

Qualcomm also is taking this strategy global. For example, Qualcomm Ventures was established in Korea in October 2010, following a $4 million investment into Pulsus Technologies, and moved quickly to establish itself as a significant VC in Korea.[33] Ventures' QPrize was instrumental in establishing the Qualcomm brand in the small Korean VC community. Its brand was further strengthened by the establishment of Qualcomm Research Korea, which was designed to tap into research capacities in Korea by developing innovations, especially those related to wireless health. It improved the smartphone's microphone to enable human-like hearing functions and the phone's camera to enable human-like vision functionalities. Both could be licensed for more integrated medical care solutions.

Qualcomm's efforts illustrate the range of emerging technological convergence of networked information and medical devices. However, if Qualcomm or other firms defined the funding market for these fledgling efforts, an adverse selection problem would arise because its biases would shape the types of entrants and technologies rather than allowing Qualcomm to sample a diverse range of experiments. Thus, successful digital platform clusters need enough funding diversity to avoid such bias effects.

Another strategy creates an infrastructure to support an innovation environment for specialized firms with midsize product markets. The Qualcomm Life infrastructure comprises a package of a middle ware that helps convert applications built for diverse wireless operating platforms (Apple, Android, and Windows) to the ICT infrastructure needed to support them. It also includes a wireless "hub" that exchanges data gathered and requested by the mobile application and a cloud storage system for the data that complies with health privacy rules. Its "modular" design allows for plug and play by different wireless health applications that use almost any operating system or radio device.

The Qualcomm package allows wireless health application providers to avoid creating a "back end" for their device and/or software application. In addition, Qualcomm maintains a "catalog" and "roadmap" system for its users. Its catalog of solutions for wireless applications in new global markets is provided because radio spectrum and other design details vary by country. Companies can consult the roadmap for each mobile operating system in the standards-setting community to find out what it must design without participating in the standards process.[34] For Qualcomm, a core question will be whether the sophistication of these devices is sufficient to justify high-end chips instead of cheaper offerings with fewer capabilities (a $60 chip set versus a $5 chip set).

Qualcomm also invested in technologies that may alter the terms on which critical challenges for wireless health, like cybersecurity, can be addressed. In October 2014, for example, it joined GE and Andreessen Horowitz to invest in Bracket Computing. Bracket's customers include the Blackstone Group, the Department of Defense, and DirecTV. Users (e.g., a patient's health-care system) employ its encryption software to secure data in the public cloud offered by Qualcomm or others. The software simplifies the management of cloud-enabled data applications and creates a layer that allows it to operate across multiple cloud infrastructures, including those of Amazon and Google.[35]

Consider two features of these experiments. First, in contrast to the traditional conglomerate approach, Qualcomm can expand its core strengths in areas like radio technology and power-efficient computing capacity on mobile devices without diversifying into new technologies with rapidly changing business models. The company hopes that a complementary set of new functions, like intelligence, will then reinforce the value of its chip set for customer uses. Second, a major feature of markets such as wireless health that build on heavy information technology is that the true value of any single product depends on the entire solution set.[36] Economists would say that this conforms to the logic of "two-sided platforms."[37] For example, the value of a personal computer varies depending on the value of printers. So, cluster participants care about integrated approaches because they add to the cumulative value of two-sided platforms. These dynamics also introduce the possibility of "tipping" in wireless health markets.

The value and staying power of dominant solutions rest in part on the stability of the two-sided platform. The digital DNA of the cheap revolution and modularity can undercut the advantages of established innovators. For example, by 2014 a newly prevalent standard for Bluetooth low-energy radio simplified the engineering roadmap for the radio connection, thus reducing some of the Qualcomm hub's advantages for mass consumer applications. Moreover, steady growth in broadband wireless networks lowered prices for firms contracting for network services for wireless applications. One industry planner estimated that from 2011 to early 2015, the cost of one megabyte of data transport in the United States on a major wireless network dropped from $80 to $1.[38] A new set of wireless health standards issued by the Continua Health Alliance augmented by the Amazon cloud, allowed small consumer electronic startups to rapidly and inexpensively roll out new applications that complied with standards demanded by the health industry.[39] The speed and cost advantages of smaller specialists suggest that the real advantages of firms like Qualcomm were in their work on specialized solutions with insurance firms, hospitals, and other large providers requiring security, reliability, and system integration at more exacting levels.

In sum, the Qualcomm case illustrates how the IPD fostered the emergence of a new technology cluster that exemplifies the growth of novel hybrid innovations. It also highlights the interactions between governance calculations and firm strategies, such as the choice of conglomerate or two-sided platforms. The IPD also shows that both small new entrants and large technology giants have potential competitive advantages. Both cases rely on a growth model that differs from the traditional conglomerate strategy and illustrates the dynamics of digital platform economics.

3.3. Issues for Governance

It is now widely accepted that the Internet and the digital revolution change "everything." We have broken down this generalization to develop a finer-grained analysis of the implications of the digital DNA for large and smaller firms. The landscape is shifting in ways that shuffle winners and losers and redefine markets and business models. We suggested that the overall logic of regional innovation clusters changes when informed by digital cluster platforms. These changes will trigger the functional need for governance reform and the practical political economy to generate initiatives to improve governance. Because digital dynamics thrive on a global scope and scale, important issues for global economic governance are coming to the forefront.

The laundry list of governance issues is long. Next, we suggest how our analysis of the IPD could alter the way policy makers think about their choices. Our goal is to identify a set of first principles and issues that might inform efforts to craft innovations in global economic governance in a world driven by digital DNA. We highlight three issues that we will return to in the case studies in Part III. Our goal is to identify anchors for global arrangements that could allow for productive innovation by the clusters globally.

3.3.1. Promoting a Trusted Digital Environment

Several elements of the platform model depend on the use of controversial information. For example, "user co-invention" can propel continuous learning and innovation that is productive, but it may involve users' personal data, and users worry about giving strangers unlimited access to such data. Similarly, "experimentation and discovery" innovation models rely on continuous market feedback, even at the initial design stage of new products. However, modularity and the nonrivalrous character of information may make it difficult to obtain user consent to access these data. Hence, new focused methods for obtaining selective consent are needed. Similarly, cybersecurity is a growing concern for digital platform clusters because it puts the entire digital value-added component at risk.

Chapters 7 and 8 will explain why unregulated markets will yield unsatisfactory results for cybersecurity and digital privacy, two elements needed to establish a trusted digital environment. However, earnest but cumbersome regulations could inappropriately lock down data, and innovation may suffer. As Chapters 6 and 8 explain, government restrictions on data flows could tightly lock down national borders or industry regulations could restrict data circulation to ensure what is deemed to be adequate privacy protection. Both approaches would restrict innovation.

Chapter 8 argues that major elements of a flexible approach exist, but further progress will require a stronger global framework.

Marketplace innovations including marketplace governance innovation options will emerge. A major challenge for global economic governance is to find ways to advance a trusted digital environment. Governments granted the Society for Worldwide Interbank Financial Telecommunication (SWIFT) novel oversight authority to secure digitally enacted international financial flows, which was credible because the organization is accountable to collaborative review by major central banks.[40] Another market governance innovation, marketplace exchanges for personal data, could address personal data concerns raised by co-invention.[41] Chapters 6 and 8 address the privacy challenge on the cloud. Market regulations, including international trade rules, could incorporate such governance innovations, especially because evidence is emerging that trade can accelerate innovation.[42] A related public policy approach is the EU effort to keep personal user data modular. This approach already is embedded in EU "interoperability" directives. Once a user invests in an app—perhaps one to keep track of her exercise data—will she have an enforceable right to move the data easily to another application? Enhancing modularity is desirable, but the policy-making risk is that it will descend into government-dictated architectures for information applications.[43]

3.3.2. *Global Economic Governance Practices: Challenges and a Trade Agenda*

We focus on the global economic governance practices that matter for innovation. Barriers that hamper the reorganization of significant inputs must be addressed across countries and sectors. (Intellectual property is not our primary focus, but we will note how governance innovations in the marketplace may influence the organization of this input.)

Many governance changes that support digital platform clusters will be local, not global. Still, global economic governance practices should support the reorganization of major inputs to digitally enabled innovation. For example, the changing production technology system will boost demand for shared training, manufacturing, and testing facilities to enable lower costs for scaling manufactured goods in many industries. Incubators that experiment with new techniques of advanced production equipment are proliferating. To this end, in October 2014 the Obama administration offered a plan to make certain facilities at the national laboratories more accessible to small manufacturers and funded new skills-training programs for these technologies.[44]

Similarly, Chapter 6 will discuss how the cloud promotes a market-based transformation of innovation system; it is a "strategy and structure" innovation. Stunning technology-stimulated changes are resulting in new opportunities for processing and storing information as an infrastructure for innovators. Still, there are growing public policy problems related to regulating the cloud, especially because it remains shrouded in concerns over competition policy and a trusted digital environment.

Modularity is a major driver of the IPD, but global economic governance could impede modularity. For example, secret government attempts to dictate security technologies for information systems periodically come to light. Conspicuously, South Korea and China tried to mandate certain national encryption standards, which raised risks for the IPD.

An additional implication of the IPD is that market distinctions that underpin governance are blurring. So, as additive printing spreads, the line between manufactured products and services blurs. This can generate significant differences under international trade rules. Similarly, as markets experiment with the implications of growing modularity and value added to products, flexible experimental approaches to choices about governance rules are desirable. Outdated trade and regulatory rules should not arbitrarily drive how services and goods are combined or whether a solution for a customer is delivered as a digital service or as a good that embodies the digital code. We expect more markets to resemble the IT markets that now receive special liberalization treatment in the Information Technology Agreement. The scope of special agreements designed to address high-tech markets, such as the devices involved in wireless health systems, should be expanded.[45]

A related implication of the IPD is that new technologically enabled clusters based more on traditional craft knowledge will emerge. Trade secrets will matter more than patents. As SMEs in clusters that rely on trade secrets go global, more scrutiny of the appropriateness of current global regulations and rules should occur. An excellent starting point would be to address the gaps in international trade rules (that flow from the original Uruguay Round TRIPS agreement) concerning the treatment of trade secrets.[46] For example, the Trans-Pacific Partnership endorsed "adequate and effective protection of industrial designs."[47]

Finally, as globally networked clusters spread, especially those newly supercharged by platform economics, smaller firms (SMEs) should be allowed to combine and collaborate across national borders. This is already on the agenda of governments—trade policy initiatives to simplify customs and border procedures have circulated since the 1990s. But, today global action is more focused on sharing risks and intangible resources, so economic governance must help facilitate foreign direct investment involving SMEs. Practices and policies that overly burden smaller players must be revised.

TABLE 3.1

Thirteen Market Access Issues to Be Addressed in the Digital Economy Agreement

Issue	Objective
1. Expand the Trans-Pacific Partnership's domestic regulatory framework for services to include services and digital economy goods	Promote transparent rule-making, nondiscrimination among firms, and technology neutrality in policies
2. Expand "IT agreements" to cover innovation-intensive industries	Lower tariffs for all innovation-intensive industries
3. Seek liberalization for products that cross the boundaries between a good and a service	Liberalize barriers for goods that rely heavily on IT; apply most liberalizing rule
4. Liberalize intermingling of goods and services using "solutions packages"	Strike deals in areas such as agriculture and global positioning systems
5 Add nonlinear distribution and supply of audiovisual content	Address the challenge raised by the morphing of audiovisual content
6. Clarify trade-related obligations on interoperability	Make data portable among services; regulators should seek "least trade restrictive" and nondiscriminatory regulations
7. Clarify obligations of private firms to provide data for public-interest or competition purposes	Get ahead of wicked problems raised by the rise of Big Data
8. Improve protection of intellectual property for craft knowledge	Develop new intellectual property definitions, especially for trade secrets, to deal with new innovation clusters
9. Use international standards for encryption and affirm rights of qualified data controllers to use encryption	Rationalize encryption and help data controllers generate trust
10. Freedom to locate infrastructure wherever the supplier wishes	Permit the use of large global cloud hubs located in other countries
11. Freedom of customers to use extraterritorial service suppliers via public telecom networks	Do not require local presence; permit the use of public telecom networks as needed internationally
12. Customers can use extraterritorial suppliers of services via public telecommunications networks	Respect technological neutrality of services and promote interoperability as long as neutrality is respected
13. Develop investment facilitation measures as well as trade facilitation measures to benefit SMEs	Make SME investments in foreign subsidiaries or joint ventures easier in addition to exports

IT, information technology; SMEs, small and medium-size enterprises.

3.3.3. Providing Market Access while Promoting Good Conduct

A third issue, market access and conduct, has at least thirteen elements. These ele-ments are summarized in Table 3.1 and then discussed in more detail in the final chapter. Recall that the IPD impacts digitally enabled markets, disrupts traditional market boundaries, and mixes elements of technical capacity in new ways, often with surprising business models. As many traditional markets become more technology intensive and intermingle goods and services in new ways, the differences between goods and services likely will blur. Therefore, these elements are desirable for a robust trade agenda, but may not emerge from current trade negotiations.

These thirteen principles are incomplete and need clarification. Trade rules could play an important role in the overall solution set of any governance scheme that addresses marketplace innovation. And multistakeholder organizations should have a major role in solving the new governance puzzle. Part III addresses these problems in greater depth to prepare the groundwork for our proposed next generation of governance initiatives set forth in the concluding chapter.

3.4. Conclusion: A Design Philosophy of Global Economic Governance

Thus far, we have identified a series of issues that are critical to advancing the poten-tial of digital platform clusters to serve the public interest. This analysis is rooted in our conviction that the governance of the properties emerging from the IPD should be built around a set of essential design principles.

As rapid technological innovation transforms, expanding swaths of economic and social processes, we must recognize what remains unknown. Short-run fixes can thwart long-term gains of greater magnitude, but hoping that problems will cure themselves opens a road to failure. Hence, a mixture of experimentation and flexibility in governance is needed even if it is difficult to accomplish in often-volatile political environments. In Chapter 5, we will argue that the most promising approach will be to recognize the virtues of "complementarity and authority" (See the discussion of "FACE" in Chapter 9). Complementarity means that innovations for governance that arise from, and are often operated by, the marketplace and/or civil society are indis-pensable to making the IPD work effectively. Governance must be about more than government policy. Authority has a double-edge meaning. To the extent possible, it is desirable to delegate detailed design of governance arrangements to expert groups of multistakeholder organizations. Authority also requires that the basic guidelines for what these expert groups seek, as well as accountability for their performance, rests with public authorities. Global economic governance may be a mixed system of policy and civic society arrangements, but ultimate accountability rests with governments.

Notes

1. Monsanto's fiscal year runs from September to August https://www.statista.com/statistics/276270/net-sales-and-net-income-of-monsanto-since-2008/ and https://www.statista.com/statistics/276279/monsanto-seed-and-genomics-segment-net-sales/.

2. As part of a complex deal, Monsanto resold the Precision Planting unit to John Deere in November 2015. Michal Lev-Ram, "John Deere, Modern Farmer," *Fortune*, December 1, 2015, pp. 67 and 70, discusses John Deere's investment in and development of new software to manage their fields via mobile device and their partnership with Monsanto to "open data links between its machinery and Monsanto's Climate Corp. division to allow the latter to deliver farmers advice based on weather and crop data," providing Monsanto with greater access to troves of individual data.

3. Another estimate put savings at 15% to 30%. "Considerations for Adopting & Implementing Precision Ag Technologies," Precision Agriculture Series, October 2010, http://www.AlabamaPrecisionAgOnline.com.

4. Bruce Upbin, "Monsanto Buys Climate Corp for $930 Million," *Forbes*, October 2, 2013, http://www.forbes.com/sites/bruceupbin/2013/10/02/monsanto-buys-climate-corp-for-930-million/#174c18155ae1. IBM also entered the weather prediction business. Richard Waters, "IBM's Acquisition of Weather Co Is a Test for the Big Data Economy," *Financial Times*, October 30, 2015, p. 14. Including executive incentives, the total acquisition cost was $1.1 billion.

5. BluePac Partners was sharply critical of the value Precision Corp adds to farmers. It criticized the limits of its technology, including its heavy reliance on public databases. BluePac Partners, "Monsanto: Engineering EPS Growth," October 13, 2014, *Seeking Alpha*, http://seekingalpha.com/article/2556425-monsanto-engineering-eps-growth.

6. Specialist companies serving world markets, like AgDNA of Australia, are emerging in farm centers around the world, https://agdna.wordpress.com/. On Des Moines as a new service and app center, see John Eligon, "Tech Start-Ups Find a Home on the Prairie," *New York Times*, November 22, 2012, p. A1.

7. Louisa Burwood-Taylor, "FarmLogs Raises $22m Series C as CEO Vows Never to Exit to Agribusiness," Agfund News, January 11, 2017. https://agfundernews.com/farmlogs-raises-22m-series-c-with-naspers-as-ceo-vows-never-to-sell-to-agribusiness.html.

8. See American Farm Bureau, "Data Privacy," accessed March 2014 and the final principles issued November 13, 2014, http://www.fb.org/index.php?action=issues.bigdata. On Monsanto strategy, see http://seekingalpha.com/article/1729352-monsanto-now-the-big-data-buzz-hit-the-agriculture-industry, accessed October 4, 2013; Daniel Shea, "What Are They Doing at Monsanto?" *Bloomberg Business Week*, June 2014, p. 52; Schumpeter, "Digital Disruption on the Farm," *The Economist*, May 23, 2014, p. 64.

9. Work is in process that could transform another traditional industry—textiles—especially through the manufacture of smart shirts. The ATTACH (Adaptive Textiles Technology with Active Cooling and Heating) project at UCSD develops fabrics that will automatically heat or cool the wearer, potentially saving on heating and air conditioning bills, http://www.engineering.com/DesignerEdge/DesignerEdgeArticles/ArticleID/10216/Engineers-Receive-26M-to-Develop-Smart-Clothes.aspx, accessed June 7, 2015.

10. Quentin Hardy, "Working the Land and the Data," *The New York Times*, November 30, 2014.

11. Lev-Ram, "John Deere," 2015.

12. "Connected Wearables Are Changing the Dairy Industry," http://theinstitute.ieee.org/technology-topics/life-sciences/connected-cattle-wearables-are-changing-the-dairy-industry; "Stock Answers," *The Economist*, June 11, 2016, p. 15. Also, "Factory Fresh," *The Economist*, Technology Quarterly, The Future of Agriculture, June 9, 2016, on using sensors to monitor breeding schedules, health, and well-being (if the cow is getting lame/to prevent digestive "disorders"). They are also developing extremely precise genetic modification capabilities to allow specific sequences to be changed to provide livestock with resistance to specific diseases, such as providing pigs with a resistance to African swine fever resembling what is found in warthogs, etc., http://www.economist.com/technology-quarterly/2016-06-09/factory-fresh.

13. Laurie Bedford, "Dancing with Data," *Successful Farming*, March 2013; Jess Lowenberg-DeBoer, "The Precision Agriculture Revolution—Making the Modern Farmer," *Foreign Affairs* 5, no. 3 (May/June 2015): 105–112.

14. P. J. Huffstutter and Carey Gillam, "Exclusive: Pivoting after Failed Syngenta Bid, Monsanto to Build Big Data Business," *Reuters*, September 24, 2015, http://uk.reuters.com/article/2015/09/24/uk-monsanto-big-data-exclusive-idUKKCN0RO0B420150924.

15. After receiving details from farmers, SAP's prototype Digital Farming application could recommend the timing and actions farmers might embrace and could make real-time changes as weather and other conditions change. Farmers could choose to accept some or all of the recommendations. The robust broadband network would almost eliminate data clogging but also safeguard data privacy in accordance with German data protection regulations. SAP has yet to launch Digital Farming as a product, but it is moving forward. The above account is drawn from Peter Sayer, "German Industry Is Poised to Exploit Rural Broadband," *PCWorld*, March 15, 2015, http://www.pcworld.com/article/2897092/german-industry-is-poised-to-exploit-rural-broadband.html.

16. The deal will require antitrust approval to proceed. Christopher Alessi, "Bayer CEO Defends Planned Acquisition of Monsanto," *The Wall Street Journal*, October 26, 2016, http://www.wsj.com/articles/bayer-boosted-by-recently-launched-drugs-1477466756.

17. http://www.marketwatch.com/investing/stock/qcom/financials.

18. Charles Clover, "China: Monopoly Position," *Financial Times*, January 25, 2015, https://www.ft.com/content/22704a96-9ff2-11e4-9a74-00144feab7de.

19. Mark Scott, "EU Opens Antitrust Investigations into Qualcomm," *New York Times*, July 16, 2015, http://www.nytimes.com/2015/07/17/business/international/qualcomm-antitrust-investigation-eu.html?_r=0&mtrref=undefined&gwh=C0EC00D64BADC22FC0CC2C528 A7F2FE3&gwt=pay. Diana Goovaerts, "Qualcomm Facing $879M Anti-Trust Fine in S. Korea," *Wirelessweek.com*, posted July 18, 2016.

20. Ironically, the China antitrust settlement opened the way for a Qualcomm to improve its collection of licensing revenues there, and this cushioned the firm financially as it laid out its strategy in mid-2016 along the lines detailed here. Mark Hibben, "Qualcomm: Back on Track," *Seeking Alpha*, July 21, 2016.

21. "Qualcomm: Taking Artificial Intelligence to a New Level," *Seeking Alpha*, May 16, 2016, http://seekingalpha.com/article/3975394-qualcomm-taking-artificial-intelligence-new-level.

22. For example, in late May 2015 Qualcomm Technologies and Daimler AG announced a collaboration on the connected car, including in-car wireless charging. The companies plan eventually to produce intelligently connected vehicles that drive emission free. Monica Alieven,

"Qualcomm Teams Up with Daimler on Connected Car," *Fierce Wireless*, May 25, 2015, accessed May 26, 2015, http://www.fiercewireless.com/tech/story/qualcomm-teams-daimler-connected-car/2015-05-25.

23. Joshua Gans, *The Disruption Dilemma*, 2016.

24. By mid-2015, Qualcomm bought Atheros for Wi-Fi expertise, Ikanos for complementary DSL modem chips in the home, and CSR, a leader in such Internet of Things markets as evolving automotive infotainment systems.

25. Based on interviews with industry experts in 2014 and 2015.

26. Samantha Masunaga and Mike Freeman, "Qualcomm prepares for a future beyond smartphones with $38-billion purchase of NXP Semiconductors," *Los Angeles Times*, October 27, 2016, http://www.latimes.com/business/technology/la-fi-tn-qualcomm-nxp-20161027-story.html.

27. Statement at http://wirelesslifesciences.org/who-we-are/mission/, accessed October 29, 2014.

28. For example, Sentrian, a startup based in the United Kingdom and Southern California, combines biosensors with the use of a hybrid of physician insight and machine learning to generate "disease deterioration models" to inform patient management options with the goal of radically reducing hospitalization. Its London medical research base (drawing on the UK National Health System records) is combined with biomedical device expertise in California. See http://www.sentrian.com.

29. http://www.westhealth.org/institute/our-priorities/automated-connected-care, accessed October 29, 2014.

30. http://www.qualcommlife.com/company-overview.

31. Qualcomm Life and Cerner, one of the largest U.S. electronic medical record providers, announced such a partnership in April 2015, http://www.cerner.com/Cerner_and_Qualcomm_Collaborate/. Qualcomm also created a joint venture with Roche and a joint investment fund with Novartis. Andrew Ward, "Roche Agrees Digital Disease Monitoring Push with Qualcomm," *Financial Times*, January 30, 2015, p. 15.

32. Firms often also use prizes as a part of corporate social responsibility strategies to demonstrate their engagement with larger societal goals. Qualcomm named a winner of the prize in April 2017. Mike Freeman, "Dr. McCoy would be proud: Winner named in Qualcomm Tricorder Xprize," "The San Diego Union Tribune," April 13, 2017. At: http://www.sandiegouniontribune.com/business/technology/sd-fi-tricorder-winner-20170412-story.html.

33. When the first QPrize was offered in 2010, 43 companies applied. In 2013, when the second QPrize was announced, applications skyrocketed to 139. Qualcomm expanded its portfolio to 5 companies in less than two years. QC Ventures' companies are involved with consumer apps, components, network infrastructure, and gaming. Qualcomm also used the prize mechanism to incentivize innovation in Korea. In the medium term, Qualcomm Ventures wants to expand these efforts into the so-called "1000x" challenge—the prospect that data flows will increase even faster than Moore's law—and adding later-stage companies to the portfolio to mitigate risk.

34. General Electric's strategy for the "Internet of Things" is similar. GE and its partners define process solutions that improve the reliability of complex systems such as aircraft or ships. Its goal is to use ICT and sensors to reduce maintenance costs and down time on critical equipment, while fulfilling all of the required technical standards (such as ISO quality standards).

35. "Trying to Make the Cloud Safe for Corporate Data," *Bloomberg Business Week*, October 23, 2014, pp. 43–44.

36. David Evans, Andrei Hagiu, and Richard Schmalensee, *Invisible Engines: How Software Platforms Drive Innovation and Transform Industries* (Cambridge, MA: MIT Press, 2006). Also Martin Kenney and John Zysman, "The Rise of the Platform Economy."

37. Two-sided markets are economic platforms or intermediaries where two distinct user groups interact and both groups benefit from the interaction. One example of a two-sided network is a mobile phone network. People who make calls are able to connect with people who receive calls.

38. Interview, 2015.

39. Our interviewee cited MyLively.com as a low-cost, fully certified system to comply with standards health monitoring solution that combined good hardware and software with wireless service and cloud data analytics. In March 2015, the hardware for its home monitoring system (targeted for the elderly) cost $25 and service cost $35 per month. In December 2015, GreatCall, Inc., a larger firm in the elder-care market, purchased MyLively.com.

40. In Chapter 7 we discuss the three known breaches of the SWIFT system in 2015 and early 2016.

41. We suggested the desirability of commercial solutions in 2009. The Boston Consulting Group estimated the market for personal data, if turned into a property right, would be worth $140 billion by 2020. Startups such as Handshake, Enliken, and Mydex are exploring this possibility. Chapter 8 explores ways in which governments could intervene, http://techcrunch.com/2013/09/02/handshake/, accessed September 2, 2013. Kenneth Cukier, "Souls for Sale, the World in 2014," *The Economist*, p. 120.

42. Jesse Perla, Christopher Tonetti, and Michael E. Waugh, "Equilibrium Technology Diffusion, Trade, and Growth," National Bureau of Economic Research, Working Paper 20881, January 2015, http://www.nber.org/papers/w20881.

43. We are fans of data portability as an example of modularity and argued for it in our 2009 book. Assuming that, like number portability in telecoms, the regulations make certain it is done at a reasonable price and with technological flexibility, it could be beneficial. The worry is that, as with security, it could become a cumbersome industrial policy.

44. Office of the Press Secretary, the White House, Fact Sheet: President Obama Announces New Actions to Further Strengthen U.S. Manufacturing Building on the Recommendations from the Final Report of the President's Advanced Manufacturing Partnership, "Accelerating U.S. Advanced Manufacturing," October 27, 2014.

45. This insight came from the Information Technology & Information Foundation. We see it as a key corollary to our advocacy of eliminating policy distortions in the growing substitutability of goods and services and the novel intermingling of goods and services in solutions packages.

46. Stephen J. Ezell, "Ensuring the Trans-Pacific Partnership Becomes a Gold-Standard Trade Agreement," Information Technology & Innovation Foundation, August 2012, http://www2.itif.org/2012-ensuring-tpp-gold-standard-trade-agreement.pdf.

47. The agreement also requires criminal penalties for theft of trade secrets by, for example, hackers. The quote is from the Australian government summary of the agreement: http://dfat.gov.au/trade/agreements/tpp/summaries/Documents/intellectual-property.PDF.

II Global Governance in a Technologically Volatile Environment

4 Designing International Governance for the IPD
THE NEGOTIATING CHALLENGE

4.1. The Plan for Part II and III

Part I outlined how the digital DNA of the world economy is creating IPDs. The IPD is changing patterns of innovation, a key driver of long-term global prosperity. We concluded Part I by arguing that the changes in the innovation system required a careful redesign of global governance of the world economy. Part II proposes an approach to reorganizing global governance. Our strategy emphasizes partial convergence of national policies within an authoritative international framework of binding hard and soft rules of conduct. The implementation of these tasks depends on government and private-sector inputs and on substantial delegation of responsibility to multistakeholder organizations (MSOs) dominated by civil society.

The logic unfolds in three stages: We describe the *negotiating landscape*, explain the *bargaining situation*, and then imagine a *global regime* and how it might be implemented.

First, this chapter examines the changes in the global negotiating landscape for governance choices because any realistic strategy must account for the shifts transforming the global economy in the 21st century. We stress that although the landscape is in flux, a critical mass of "like-minded" nations remains in place that could coalesce into a viable "club" that begins to build a workable global regime for governing the IPD. Moreover, the IPD is rapidly, if still imperfectly, becoming a universal phenomenon. Over time, the IPD could open opportunities for all countries, thus creating a promising landscape for a global regime.

Second, Chapter 5 develops a clear picture of the strategic bargaining situation that will shape the feasible solutions open to policy makers. Hard work will be required to forge workable governance agreements. These agreements must address collective action issues, and even under the best circumstances they are fraught with risks of strategic misbehavior.[1] Effective governance will require managing the risks of cooperation and structuring governance in ways that effectively respond to the IPD. We suggest appropriate governance strategies to deal with two distinct types of challenges, "coordination" and "cooperation" challenges.

Third, the international governance regime must be developed, negotiated, and implemented. A robust regime should feature three elements. (1) It should include a mix of common international obligations that set a baseline for governance. Making progress will require creating rules that are authoritative and combine hard and soft obligations. (2) The regime should be composed of varied national policy systems that are quasi-converged around an international baseline. (3) Any sustainable regime also must contain a mechanism to increase cooperation with nongovernmental problem solvers, the MSOs. These nongovernmental players should be accountable to, and operate within rules set by, governmental authorities. They can contribute greater flexibility, experimentation, and learning to the policy mix. Moreover, MSO involvement allows actor preferences to evolve over time so that the various stakeholders become more compatible. In this way, MSOs can influence the political and economic "facts on the ground" to promote more effective governance. This analysis unfolds in Chapter 5.

Consider the global rules guiding information technology. Part I argued that information is pervasive and that economic reorganization will be central to the global economic agenda and to creating new value in the world economy. This will require further integration of global information markets. The analysis of regime design in Part II shows how trade rules could serve as an anchor point for creating a common international baseline.

Part III will show that other international instruments still are needed for a regime to function successfully. Advancing integration and convergence will require establishing a trusted digital environment, not just new trade rules. Chapters 6 through 8 will show how the mix of binding authority and flexibility might combine to achieve more effective governance given the global issues raised by the cloud and the need to create a digital environment responsive to rising concerns surrounding cybersecurity threats and the need to safeguard digital privacy. Finally, Chapter 9 summarizes our prescriptions and spotlights a path forward.

Many policy efforts by governments, such as measures to advance a trusted digital environment, will require flexible experimentation. A politically and socially free society with an open market always engages in multidimensional bargaining. For example, individuals exchange information to earn specific benefits. To find a result, someone searching for information online provides Google with small bits of personal information in exchange. Or, an actor gives up some privacy to induce fans to follow her latest movie. In this volatile, rapidly changing environment, technological surprises are frequent and the reconceptualization of markets and social relationships is ongoing. Learning is critical to policy design, which implies continuous adaptation. For example, a trusted digital environment is never perfectly secure. The best that can be hoped for is good security and a capacity to respond rapidly and effectively to significant individual and collective breaches.

Similarly, trust in privacy is not the same as universal agreement on how much and what specific kinds of privacy to protect. Privacy will be breached.[2] Tastes and political–legal traditions vary globally. What is required is that minimum common benchmarks, simpler policies, and clearer processes exist to reconcile variations. Quasi-convergence of national policies within a global framework is desirable.

There are various ways to advance binding rules to anchor global governance. We favor using trade rules because they appear to us to be the most elegant and effective starting point. Even if another starting point is ultimately chosen for reasons of political expediency, it is enormously valuable to understand why and how trade disciplines could serve the agenda as well. That said, we conclude that the implementation of trade rules is the best path forward given the need for innovations to cope with the IPD. Specifically, trade rules require adaptive learning made possible by self-consciously incorporating MSOs into global implementation processes. As MSOs evolve, they will generate standard operating procedures and capabilities that will make it easier to adapt to variations in national rules and will chip away at barriers to integrated markets.

4.2. The Negotiating Landscape

The 21st-century negotiating landscape differs sharply from that of the 1990s because of the cumulative impact of four drivers. First, as globalization progressed in recent decades, global economic power dispersed, which has implications for reforming global governance. Second, specific characteristics of the ICT market reinforced the implications drawn from our analysis of economic power. Third, the leadership roles of influential actors in agenda setting for global ICT policies changed. Fourth, the

IPD's technological characteristics, and their market implication, altered the nature of governance choices.

4.2.1. The Dispersion of Economic Power

Two major trends within the world economy set the stage for any global governance strategy. Both the interdependence of national economies and the distribution of global economic power are changing.

Many scholars have analyzed the history of globalization and the emergence of a broader set of countries whose populations joined the global middle class. Although the process of globalization was flawed, overall it made the world more prosperous and equitable.[3] A major part of this tale of transformation is the growing economic interdependence of all economies as evidenced by the role of trade in global and national gross domestic product (GDP). According to World Bank data, in 1960 (and still in 1967) trade as a percentage of global GDP was 25%. The percentage surged to 38.8% in 1980 before the recession of the early 1980s. Trade as a percentage of global GDP then grew from 39.6% in 1990, to 51.6% in 2000, and to a peak of 61% in 2006. The figure fell sharply after the collapse of the financial bubble in 2007, but regained those losses by 2011. Since then, trade as a percentage of world GDP tapered slightly and stood at 58% in 2015.[4]

These changes also increased the sensitivity of the largest economies to trade. From 1960 to 2015, U.S. trade as a percentage of GDP rose from 9.2% to 28.1%. (Excluding trade in services and foreign direct investment, America's total trade in goods in 2015 was about $4 trillion.)[5] During this period, the EU percentages rose from 39% to 83%, percentages in East Asia and the Pacific from 26% to 58%, and those in China alone from 9% to 41%.[6]

The trade statistics underplay the density of cross-national links. Part I identified the complex global production chains of goods and services that the IPD helped to enable. Another way to grasp the depth of these links is to consider the impact of foreign direct investment on traditional exporting. Today, about 60% of U.S. imports and exports flow through the internal channels of U.S. or foreign-based multinational corporations. Moreover, as foreign direct investment into the United States climbed, it reshaped U.S. manufacturing exports. In 2007, a foreign-controlled plant in the United States earned more than one in three U.S. manufacturing export dollars.[7]

Growing interdependence does not necessarily lead to global harmony. Indeed, the tensions over the displacement of markets of firms from advanced countries by emerging economies, especially China, is one of the central political economic tensions confronting global governance. This is particularly significant because OECD companies believe that as a result of China's massive industrial policies their market access to China through foreign direct investment is declining in digital industries.

The second fundamental change is the dispersion of global economic power. If we take membership in the OECD as a surrogate for wealthier economies with roughly similar philosophies about market governance, there is both an expanding geographic membership beyond its early transatlantic roots *and* a declining share of total world economic output.[8] However, despite the dramatic growth of the rest of the world economy, the OECD remains viable as a core club to advance global governance reforms for the IPD.

In 1980, the U.S share of global GDP stood at 21.9%.[9] It fell slightly to 20.8% in 2000 and 15.8% in 2015. The EU share was 30.2% in 1980, 20.4% in 2000, and 16.9% in 2015. By contrast, the share of China and India, the two most populated nations, grew from 5.3% in 1980, to 11.4% in 2000, and to 24.1% in 2015. The projected percentages for 2020 are 14.9% for the United States, 13.4% for the EU (not including the United Kingdom), and 27.9% for China and India. Table 4.1 displays these trends and also provides data for the same years for other major economies.

The bottom line is that economic power is now more dispersed than it was decades ago. Although the United States may, for example, be able to exert substantial influence in particular bilateral deals, the governance challenge in digital markets is ultimately global in nature. The United States can no longer easily push through major global initiatives alone or solely in collaboration with the EU. Hence, a core club of countries now is needed to credibly launch any new effort to propel innovations in global governance.

In 2015, advanced economies associated with the OECD and the EU and the five smaller countries associated only with the TPP together accounted for almost 45% of the global GDP.[10] (Their share would be higher still if not corrected downward to account for purchasing power parity). But although their policy preferences differ on the details, a club to launch governance reforms with about half of world output, and the lion's share of advanced technology, is a formidable platform for driving a global regime.

In contrast, the five most prominent critics of many of the traditional international economic institutions—China, Brazil, Russia, India, and Argentina—accounted for more than a quarter of the GDP for the first time in 2008, just over 31% in 2015, and they are projected to reach 33.9% of the total by 2020.[11] The fates of individual economies will vary, but the global share of the larger emerging economies will grow in future decades. For example, in the past few years, Brazil, Russia, and Argentina slipped into recession, China dipped to a significantly lower growth rate, and India nudged to a higher rate. Significantly, uncertainty will increase about how their individual market strategies will evolve and align with each other. Their

TABLE 4.1

Gross Domestic Product as a Share of the World (at Purchasing Power Parity)

Country	1950* (%)	1980 (%)	2000 (%)	2010 (%)	2015 (%)	2020 (%) (forecast)
Developing and emerging economies	N/A	36.286	43.003	53.658	57.556	60.765
Advanced economies	N/A	63.714	56.997	46.342	42.444	39.235
EU	N/A	30.174	23.689	18.971	16.918	13.403**
United States	27.3	21.927	20.76	f16.846	15.809	14.878
China	4.6	2.32	7.389	13.822	17.082	19.351
Japan	3.0	7.635	6.533	4.863	4.255	3.657
Germany	N/A	6.636	4.906	3.692	3.83	3.051
France	N/A	4.43	3.388	2.634	2.332	2.111
Brazil	N/A	4.368	3.189	3.156	2.812	2.391
United Kingdom	N/A	3.763	3.107	2.509	2.36	2.204
Italy	N/A	4.554	3.286	2.337	1.912	1.693
Russia	N/A	n/a	3.294	3.641	3.275	2.836
India	4.2	2.926	4.194	5.980	7.016	8.505
Canada	N/A	2.2	1.839	1.523	1.438	1.328
Australia	N/A	1.183	1.112	1.036	1.003	0.970
Spain	N/A	2.274	1.969	1.691	1.423	1.233
Mexico	N/A	2.991	2.444	2.010	1.962	1.890
South Korea	N/A	0.638	1.561	1.659	1.628	1.583
Indonesia	N/A	1.413	1.935	2.256	2.504	2.752
Turkey	N/A	1.145	1.323	1.333	1.4	1.401
Saudi Arabia	N/A	2.761	1.431	1.371	1.483	1.375
Argentina	N/A	1.345	0.878	0.883	0.856	0.796

Source: 1980–2021, http://www.economywatch.com/economic-statistics/economic-indicators/GDP_Share_of_World_Total_PPP/.

Source: 1950, https://infogr.am/Share-of-world-GDP-throughout-history.

** Assumes that the United Kingdom exits from the EU.

heterogeneity and volatility reinforce the opportunity for a determined club to be the catalyst for reforms enabling the IPD.

4.2.2. *Turbulence and Market Leadership in the Global ICT Sector*

As posited in Chapters 1 and 2, the IPD unleashed tremendous growth and huge changes that extended well beyond ICT markets to begin transforming traditional manufacturing and commodity sectors. However, given the ICT market's centrality to the IPD, this section more closely scrutinizes how it fits into the negotiating incentives of countries.

Next, we argue that this gigantic market has begun to deliver on its vast potential in lower-income countries. Therefore, in the long term it offers a positive-sum situation for all countries with regard to its economic returns. (This is not to say that every country will like its specific market trade-offs.) Then, we explain how the market's geographic makeup for revenues is evolving. A close examination of changes within specific segments of the ICT market suggests a long-term interdependence of market interests. (Chapter 5 shows that interdependence may not lead to cooperation, but here we argue that the potential for aggregate gains is interdependent.) The OECD share of the ICT market is larger than its share of the total world economy. In addition, the profit margins in its markets are generally higher than in the rest of the world.[12] This means that the OECD has significant market power because it remains the launching point for many, but not all, of the largest technological changes. For non-OECD firms with global ambitions in OECD markets, the terms for market access will influence their futures. At the same time, the immediate impact of the biggest emerging markets, especially China (and to a lesser extent, India), is large enough that no major global company can ignore major engagements in these markets. Thus, over the long term, there exists mutual commercial vulnerability between important emerging markets and the markets of advanced economies. The volatility of the technology adds an important element of uncertainty regarding how to frame and pursue narrow interests. A global governance strategy should try to convert uncertainty into a path for experimentation about ways of governing that evolve over time.

Table 4.2 shows that the global ICT market was worth about $3.7 trillion in 2014, far dwarfing stalwart giants like automobiles.[13] *Telecom services* accounted for almost 45% of the total and still dominate the ICT industry. Wireless and broadband continue to drive strong sector growth.[14] Meanwhile, *global spending on IT services*, an indicator of the growing value added of information, is now worth close to $1 trillion annually.

We fully endorse the consensus that efforts to increase the universal availability of ICT capabilities are good policy for both economic and ethical reasons. Thus, it is encouraging that a governance bet on private-sector investment and competition to spur availability has paid off so well in terms of communications and Internet penetration. Although supplementary government measures will be needed, the basic strategy has performed well.[15]

Mobile communications was a key enabler of progress toward universal service. An International Telecommunication Union estimate indicated that mobile cellular

TABLE 4.2

Worldwide Information Technology (IT) Spending
Forecast: 2014, 2015 (Billions of U.S. Dollars)

	2014 Spending	2015 Spending
Devices	669	685
Data center systems	142	142
Enterprise software	313	320
IT services	948	942
Telecom Services	1,614	1,572
Overall IT	3,701	3,662

Source: Gartner (April 2015), http://www.gartner.com/newsroom/id/3025217.

subscriptions exceeded 7.2 billion at the end of 2015, about 1.58 billion of them in developed countries. About 3.8 billion of these subscribers are located in the Asia-Pacific region. Similarly, the number of mobile phone users worldwide increased from about 80 million in 1995 to about 4.6 billion in 2016. In October 2014, the number of active mobile devices exceeded the number of people on the planet for the first time.[16] The number of mobile phones likely will approach 5 billion in 2017.[17] Since penetration spiked first in industrial countries, recent growth in mobile phone use has skewed toward industrializing and poorer countries. Significantly, broadband access also is diffusing. By late 2015, mobile broadband penetration reached 87.9% in industrial countries, industrializing countries were at about 40%, and the least developed countries, mostly in Africa, were at about 12% but continuing a rapid growth path.[18]

A similar story applies to metrics focused on Internet access. According to data assembled by Mary Meeker of Kleiner Perkins Caufield Byers, in 1995 the total number of global Internet users was about 35 million.[19] By 2000 the total number of global Internet users had increased 10-fold, to about 361 million, and the number increased 10-fold again to 3.732 billion by March 2017—a penetration rate of 49.6% of the global population. Since 2000, the number of Internet users has increased most rapidly in Africa (7,557%), the Middle East (4,221%), Latin America and the Caribbean (2,036%), and Asia (1,539%). The number of Internet users grew more slowly in Europe (506%), Oceania/Australia (261%), and North America (196%).[20] U.S. Internet penetration is higher than in China or India, but India now has the most Internet users and is adding more new users than China.

But where is the heart of the global ICT market? Revenues help tell the tale. The distribution of the ICT market remains more concentrated in OECD countries than is the case with the global GDP. Statista estimates that in 2014 the United

States accounted for 27% of the global ICT market, the EU for 20.7%, China for 10.8%, and Japan for 7.7%; the rest of the world held the remaining third.[21] Yet, as the Qualcomm case study in Chapter 3 illustrated, the rapid growth of the market in China and some other emerging countries led to an outsized importance of this market for global growth strategies for OECD-based companies. The transformation of the ICT market, engendered by the IPD, continues to unfold. Many waves of innovation and market growth remain in the wealthier countries. Turbulence in the global market, as it is buffeted by new waves of innovation and fresh spending, means that the traditional OECD markets will remain dynamic and relevant to all aspiring global players, including those from China and India. Indeed, our interviewees in China and the United States in 2015 and 2016 emphasized that Chinese Internet companies often have unique revenue mixes fueled by such factors as the weakness of Chinese consumer finance markets and different ways that e-commerce and social networking have intermingled in a giant market largely shielded from foreign competitors. Yet, as Chinese firms try to expand abroad, the unique characteristics of their domestic market make it more difficult for them to fit into the global IPD ecosystems.[22] This problem will become acute as issues tied to a trusted digital environment loom larger. In short, vulnerability to governance patterns for the IPD cuts both ways of OECD and emerging market firms.

Rapid changes in the organization of digital markets provide a further illustration of our point about strategic interests. For example, broadband Internet promoted convergence trends that created new distribution channels for voice, data, images, and audiovisual content and opened new growth opportunities for a wide range of market players. Network traffic patterns reflect these changes. Cisco projects that between 2014 and 2019, global mobile data traffic will increase 11-fold and exceed 200 exabytes in 2019, about three times the rate of traffic growth of wired network devices. Global mobile data traffic was 4% of total Voice over Internet Protocol (VoIP) traffic in 2014 and will be 14% of total VoIP traffic by 2019.[23] As Table 4.3 shows, Internet video streaming and downloads, propelled by instant broadband access on wireless devices, are taking an ever-increasing share of bandwidth and will likely account for more than 80% of all consumer Internet traffic by 2019. According to Cisco Systems, "globally, consumer Internet video traffic will be 80% of all consumer Internet traffic in 2019, up from 64% in 2014."[24] Broadband penetration also created a new market for "cloud" services and applications.[25] The cloud also lays the groundwork for a robust, ubiquitous Internet of Things, a critical change in the IPD. (Chapter 6 examines the cloud market in more detail.)

The mix of traffic and contours for hardware and software is in flux, underscoring the volatility of any market segment's role in the IPD. To give a sense of the magnitude of the unfolding disruptions, Table 4.4 highlights selected trends in U.S.

TABLE 4.3

Global Consumer Internet Traffic, 2014–2019

Consumer Internet traffic, 2014–2019

	2014	2015	2016	2017	2018	2019	CAGR 2014–2019
By network (petabytes per month)							
Fixed	31,548	37,916	46,527	58,125	72,938	91,043	24%
Mobile	2,050	3,430	5,599	8,906	13,587	20,544	59%
By subsegment (petabytes per month)							
Internet video	21,624	27,466	36,456	49,068	66,179	89,319	33%
Web, email, and data	5,853	7,694	9,476	11,707	14,002	16,092	22%
File sharing	6,090	6,146	6,130	6,168	6,231	6,038	0%
Online gaming	30	41	64	88	113	138	36%
By geography (petabytes per month)							
Asia-Pacific	12,193	14,571	17,871	22,470	28,374	36,391	24%
North America	8,913	11,091	14,095	17,951	22,893	28,621	26%
Western Europe	5,834	6,865	8,400	10,480	13,219	16,780	24%
Central and Eastern Europe	2,594	3,507	4,773	6,742	9,356	12,885	38%
Latin America	3,152	3,915	4,823	6,026	7,558	9,514	25%
Middle East and Africa	912	1,396	2,164	3,363	5,123	7,397	52%
Total (petabytes per month)							
Consumer Internet traffic	33,598	41,346	52,126	67,032	86,524	111,587	27%

Notes:

- Web, email, and data: includes web, email, instant messaging, and other data traffic (excludes file sharing).
- File sharing: includes peer-to-peer traffic from all recognized peer-to-peer systems such as BitTorrent and eDonkey, as well as traffic from web-based file-sharing systems.
- Gaming: includes casual online gaming, networked console gaming, and multiplayer virtual-world gaming.
- Internet video: includes short-form Internet video (for example, YouTube), long-form Internet video (for example, Hulu), live Internet video, Internet-video-to-TV (for example, Netflix through Roku), online video purchases and rentals, webcam viewing, and web-based video monitoring (excludes peer-to-peer video file downloads).

Source: Cisco Visual Networking Index: Forecast and Methodology, 2014–2019, http://www.cisco.com/c/en/us/solutions/collateral/service-provider/ip-ngn-ip-next-generation-network/white_paper_c11-481360.html.

ICT spending. Spending on cloud computing, and machine-to-machine communication, which are critical to the Internet of Things, and on cybersecurity all are growing rapidly. (Globally, the percentage of funds spent on each category varies.) The Telecommunications Industry Association calculates that total spending surpassed $100 billion in 2013 and it is expected to reach almost $175 billion in 2016.

TABLE 4.4

Major Trends in the U.S. Market (Millions of Dollars)

Year	Cloud computing	Machine-to-machine	Cybersecurity	Total
2006	N/A	180	25,500	25,680
2007	N/A	528	27,800	28,328
2008	21,700	936	28,900	51,536
2009	24,700	1,428	26,500	52,628
2010	30,600	2,160	27,400	60,160
2011	39,000	3,255	30,500	72,755
2012	47,000	5,115	34,500	86,615
2013	56,000	7,395	39,500	102,895
2014	66,000	11,760	45,000	122,760
2015	76,000	20,250	51,000	147,250
2016	86,000	31,200	57,500	174,700

TIA's 2013 ICT Market Review and Forecast, Chapter 2-3, "Major Trends," http://serving.portal.dmflex.com/8ab02188-ee2c-4018-8441-2f4fcbda6f6a/assets/2013mrf_majortrends_sample.pdf.

An analyst from a decade ago would be stunned today that cloud computing now represents the largest portion of this spending, although its share of total spending has begun to decline.

To further illustrate this point, consider how the cloud, mobility, and broadband led to a major reorganization of the global software market and the applications that it can enable. This took place because cloud-based startups, championed by business model innovation like that of Apple on its iPhone, can avoid many of the high distribution and sales costs associated with traditional packaged software. A huge and growing percentage of new software market entrants are distributing their products online.[26] The market share of mobile apps, like Pokémon GO, also is growing rapidly.[27] Precise market size is uncertain, but it is conservatively projected that the number of app downloads will reach 268 billion annually by 2017, of which about 8% of downloads are will be paid for, yielding $77 billion in revenue.[28] The largest share of downloads by volume is in Asia, but the dominant markets by revenue are the United States, the EU, and, because of gaming, Japan.[29] The Apple and Android ecosystems continue to dominate for mobile apps. As noted in Chapter 2, this app's ecosystem is part of the specialized entry patterns of digital innovation clusters. It is pervasively global, enjoys broad global market entry, and benefits consumers in wealthy and lower-income countries. Its dominant, but not exclusive, channels remain grounded in the OECD nations, however.

Advertising is a major revenue driver for the new generation of information services—ranging from search through social networking and from digital media through the stunning 2016 viral emergence of the mobile game Pokémon GO. Total global advertising spending is predicted to increase from 2013 to 2018 by almost a third, from $516 billion to $642 billion. Global digital advertising spending is growing even more rapidly. From 2013 to 2018, digital spending on advertising is expected to more than double, from $121.5 billion to $252 billion,[30] with mobile advertising expected to be about a third of that total.[31]

Online, digital advertising fuels many of the new service revenue models, and it remains predominantly OECD centric. By 2015, U.S. revenue exceeded $63 billion; China surged to second place at more than $25 billion, followed by the United Kingdom at around $10 billion, and Japan and Germany came next, at $9.2 billion and $7.9 billion, respectively.[32]

As mobile and Internet opportunities explode, entrepreneurs and established firms are devising new ways to market their products and services. The opportunities to create new offerings that are not traditional services or traditional products, but some hybrid of the two, are expanding. What remains in question is how governments and other institutions should act to promote innovation, competition, and a robust world economy. This review suggests that there is ample opportunity in terms of potential global influence for OECD countries and like-minded nations to play a vigorous leadership role. The question is whether they have the will and the strategy to do so.

4.2.3. *Shifting Leadership Roles in the World Economy*

The leadership roles and dynamics of 21st-century negotiations changed after the mid-1990s. Our 2009 book argued that during the 1980s and 1990s the United States was generally the agenda setter in negotiations about changes in global governance of ICT. This was unsurprising. The United States was by far the largest single market for ICT and it vigorously reorganized its market in light of the second-wave dynamics. Policy makers everywhere closely scrutinized America's emerging domestic policy regime so they might glean lessons from the U.S. efforts. Hence, when the United States decided that the existing global regulatory and trade rules were no longer compatible with its policy directions and that a new agenda was needed for global ICT governance, others took note.

During the 1990s, the U.S. position was bolstered by a bipartisan domestic consensus on its main global agenda. Democrats and Republicans supported competition in communication markets, policies friendly to the emergence of the IT and information networking industries, and liberalization in competition of all global services (with some caveats with regard to finance). In addition, beginning in the 1990s, a light-touch approach to the regulation of web-enabled markets such as e-commerce was favored. But bitter domestic battles raged over the precise terms under which these priorities should play out. The regulatory battles in the telecom industry fueled big payouts for the corporate lawyers and lobbyists who argued their clients' cases in government venues. Still, the divisions were navigable in terms of a common international position. Moreover, nongovernmental "civil society" groups had a low profile on the international agenda. Nongovernmental organizations (NGOs) focused mainly on domestic issues while favoring more international competition to foster innovation and lower prices. A few issues, mostly tied to intellectual property, drew their adversarial attention. They focused predominantly on intellectual property issues involving food, pharmaceuticals, or copyright issues related to media content. Privacy also began to spark international controversy, but was largely absent in discussions about ICT markets.

A few years later, the global picture looked far different. In 2012, one of us (Cowhey) spent a day discussing IT issues with a prominent advisor to the Singapore government. Singapore, he explained, watched EU policy models on new issues. The EU was busily trying to codify systematic stances on major policy issues such as privacy and had launched a sweeping reorganization of regulations of communication and information markets intended to better align policies with changing technologies.[33] In contrast, Singapore could not determine where the United States was headed. The domestic policy malaise and political polarization in the United States had stunted the policy ambitions of the Obama White House. There were several "small-bore" initiatives at regulatory agencies, but legislative efforts on privacy, security, and competition policy for IT floundered. Even as the Singapore authorities worried that the EU rules might be too rigid, they viewed U.S. initiatives as disjointed, behind the curve, and slightly incomprehensible as a strategy.

Moreover, in the wake of the serious global recession of 2008–2009, the U.S. economic policy tradition lost some of its cachet.[34] The EU's traditional caution about embracing market forces and its more preemptive regulatory stance gained global appeal. This occurred although the EU's economic track record was weaker than America's during the recovery. Subsequent revelations of vastly expanded U.S. electronic surveillance after 9/11, especially the Edward Snowden disclosures, and the implicit cooperation of U.S. ICT firms in these practices further undermined U.S. leadership. Even traditional U.S. allies grew nervous about a U.S.-led global governance regime and a market where existing policy positions and market shares allowed the U.S. government so much room for unilateral decisions on highly sensitive issues in their own jurisdictions. These developments also put U.S. ICT firms on the defensive globally on policy issues. These weaknesses are somewhat offset by the technological "facts on the ground." Leadership in shifting third-wave ICT dynamics (like the cloud) originated from a single U.S. market that could still rapidly scale innovation and was less fettered by regulatory hurdles to ICT experimentation. Thus, the United States had controlled the de facto first move in global policy discussions because of commercial leadership, but had failed to consolidate it into a leading-edge model for policy and regulation.

A somewhat brighter light was trade policy. The United States retained its roles as "demandeur" and primary agenda setter for ICT trade policies in regional and global forums. But the absence of a similarly compelling story about its domestic policy approach eroded U.S. influence at a time when the policies of the United States, the EU, and other OECD members were misaligned. Nonetheless, the OECD countries have sufficient market power to serve as a core group to initiate a broader set of international governance changes. The question, as posited in Chapter 9, is whether they can create enough domestic political consensus on the role of trade and other international economic agreements on ICT to use this leverage adroitly.

The deeper split at the global level emerged because newer economic powers such as Brazil, India, and China had grave reservations about the equity or policy mix of stalwart institutions like the International Monetary Fund, the World Bank, and the World Trade Organization (WTO). In addition, China and Brazil sought to mark out broader claims to greater global power. They increasingly sought alternative regional or bilateral frameworks for many decisions. (The election of a Brazilian, Roberto Azevedo, to lead the WTO beginning in September 2013 somewhat softened Brazil's position.) Other emerging developing countries, including Singapore, South Africa, Mexico, and Indonesia, also explored new avenues of economic diplomacy and trade alliances.[35] For example, the Pacific Alliance for trade involving Chile, Mexico, Colombia, and Peru won plaudits. Yet, support lingered for the fundamental governance structure that emerged after 1945.

The impasse at the WTO between the United States and rising economic powers over the moribund Doha Round reflected different calculations about what constituted a fair bargain. The disagreements underscored the growing philosophical divide about how to structure national regulatory and other economic policies.[36] For decades, students of globalization and interdependence assumed that efficiency incentives would nudge countries toward convergence. This assumption was thrown into question in the absence of new ways of achieving effective compromises.

Beneath the philosophizing and technocratic considerations about efficiency lurked a set of raw political calculations that influenced international negotiations. Tensions grew over global economic policies, especially policies involving trade among China, the United States, and the EU. Maneuverings took place in the context of broad tensions over their relative power to define the international rules of the coming economic and strategic order. These tensions may be reconcilable, but progress is difficult because vigorous debates rage within each power center over the appropriate policy mix. Many Chinese leaders still view the United States as determined to use the conventions of postwar cooperation as instruments to repress the ascension of Chinese economic power and influence. In addition, American leaders rightly believe that parts of the current Chinese policy resemble the mercantilist tactics found in other East Asian nations, particularly Japan during the 1970s and 1980s. Moreover, the Chinese agenda for the control of speech and news for reasons of political stability and security complicates many digital governance issues globally.[37] Still, Chinese policies are evolving, and some of their more successful firms are acquiring more global interests that require navigating access to OECD markets. In addition, the slowing of the Chinese economy since 2014 and the signs of a sustained uptick in Indian growth (a country that OECD firms believe might be more congenial to their interests over time) means that everyone's calculus of the world market is changing. This means that room for compromise still exists. But, the shift to nationalism in the United States and elsewhere could further narrow the room for productive agreement.

4.2.4. The Rise of Civil Society

The final major change took off with startling rapidity as the Internet became pervasive. More than a decade ago, one of the authors (Aronson) asked a serving EU commissioner what surprised him most about his job. He responded immediately, and with considerable irritation, that he spent a third of his time meeting with NGOs, which wanted to voice their views and lobby for their positions. Since then, NGOs have sought and gained a somewhat more prominent role in international negotiations. There are ample precedents for NGO participation in negotiations, such as in international standards–setting bodies. But in many arenas, NGO influence is new and expanding.[38] On issues such as land mines, the trafficking of women and children, and net neutrality, increased NGO awareness and activism pushed their concerns up the policy agenda. They emerged as important players in MSOs and negotiations. Inevitably, many future negotiations will include representatives and negotiators from government, the private sector, and NGOs.

Many catalysts provoked the rise of civil society. The rise of the Internet was the first catalyst. It allowed individuals and groups in different cities, regions, and countries with similar goals and ideas to coalesce more quickly and effectively, and in far more numerous variations, than in a time of slower, more costly, and less effective communications. Often the social movements empowered by the Internet led to organized protests that called for change in existing governments and their policies from outside the corridors of power. The Arab Spring, the *Indignada* movement in Spain, and the Occupy Wall Street protests are three examples.[39] More recently, peaceful efforts by labor unions and liberal politicians to derail the proposed Trans-Pacific Partnership (TPP) negotiation among Pacific nations show that those outside the circle often try to disrupt negotiations from which they feel excluded. However, government authorities increasingly recognize that a better approach is to invite those seeking change to sit at the table.

A second catalyst to civil society involvement was the greater ease of travel and larger investments by governmental and nongovernmental institutions to facilitate the creation of NGOs. This yielded more sophisticated, better-networked organizations that were better able to influence global agendas.[40]

A third catalyst, at least in more democratic societies, was that civil society NGOs are like a flock of canaries in the coal mines of politics. They are indicators and mobilizers of intense preferences and passions among people who are likely to be active in politics (voters, organizers, contributors, and shapers of mass or elite opinions). Thus, NGOs are the latest incarnation of the long-standing embrace between political leaders and civic organizations. This relationship is a source of political insight and a coalition that is evolving among sympathetic sometime allies.[41] This is especially the case in areas where governments were largely absent in coordinating and implementing certain international tasks, including financially sensitive ones like credit rating for government debt and essential technical infrastructures such as the Internet's domain name system. Hence, many observers concluded that government was waning while civil society's influence was surging.[42] Others took a more agnostic view, that both may be flourishing.[43]

Our view is that governments are still in charge, even as MSOs and their kin are growing in importance. In a field like human rights protection, which is often cited to demonstrate the growing power of NGOs and their "soft power" (e.g., in norm setting), the most effective policies evolve when governments support stronger intergovernmental agreements.[44] Moreover, governments' acceptance, or invention, of MSO governance structures is consistent with the history of delegation of authority to expert organizations by governments under certain circumstances. Standards-setting organizations were, for example, part and parcel of the "rationalization" of the world economy since the 19th century, and many important instances of MSO authority trace their roots back to that era.[45] Yet the primacy of sovereign states was unquestioned before 1945. Today, states remain the most powerful actors even while significant new divisions of labor between governments and NGOs emerge and thrive. The goal now is to explore the delegation of authority in the context of governance responses to the IPD.

Finally, although this book especially focuses on trade initiatives and MSOs as a way to deal with economic governance, other approaches are critical for use in the full digital landscape. For example, the Council of Europe's Cybercrime Convention, adopted in 2001, represented the first global attempt to address cyberthreats.

We also recognize that embracing a larger role for MSOs will raise controversies. As posited in the next chapter, MSOs perform better when firmly embedded within a larger framework of accountability to governments. But the struggle over Internet governance (discussed briefly below) shows that blueprints for governance created by scholars often run into problems because the sequence of decisions in the real world is messy. For example, the terms for reaffirming support for MSO governance of the Internet Assigned Numbers Authority (IANA) that is operated by the Internet Corporation for Assigned Names and Numbers (ICANN) provoked an extended diplomatic and civil society storm because the U.S. government needed to find a path that allowed it to relinquish its national control over core legal authorities to a MSO, even as some countries wanted to use the moment to assert intergovernmental control.

The Internet governance drama was symbolically launched at the World Summit on the Information Society, held in Geneva (2003) and Tunis (2005), which featured battles among civil society groups suspicious of the U.S. government's motives, countries wanting more governmental control, and those seeking a way to keep much of the status quo on ICANN. Matters escalated in 2011 at the Global Conference on Cyberspace, which kicked off in London. The International Telecommunication Union engaged in a bitter turf battle for control that erupted at the International Telecommunication Union Plenipotentiary in Dubai (2012), but a "truce" subsequently was arranged in Busan, Korea, in 2014. As Adam Segal documents, the NETmundial conference that convened in Brazil marked a turning point where the U.S. government's plan to relinquish its legal control over the IANA, the critical power of ICANN, assuaged countries such as Brazil that MSO governance would not be a veil for U.S. control.[46] By 2017, this change was well on its way to implementation. But other issues on Internet governance remain regarding how to achieve, as three astute analysts put it, a "shared, neutral, & global resource for human solidarity & economic progress."[47] This volume tackles one set of issues tied to economic progress.

4.2.5. The Nature of the Governance Challenge

In July 2015, there was considerable relief in the circles of veteran trade policy experts when the United States and China seemingly reached an accommodation on how to update the WTO's International Technology Agreement, a tariff reduction deal that covers a larger trade market than trade in automobiles and automotive parts.[48]

This effort removed the largest diplomatic barrier to revamping the tariff schedules that cover many new electronic goods, such as GPS devices, that emerged since the original pact was agreed on in the late 1990s. It was also one of only two noteworthy breakthroughs in a WTO-related trade negotiation in more than a decade. Yet, for all the promised economic benefits, the agreement is an old-fashioned pact about tariff reductions—the traditional staple of trade agreements. Such agreements are simple to measure, easy to monitor, and generate reasonably reliable estimates of likely benefits and costs. After all, a tariff is a tax on imports and thus does not pose novel economic issues, assuming that other market barriers do not negate the value of the tariff reductions to exporters.[49]

Many trade policy debates in the United States and other industrial countries hinged on nontariff barriers imposed in rapidly growing economies that made trade deals bad business for wealthy countries. Nontariff barriers emerged as a burning issue in negotiations with Japan by the 1980s, with China in the 2000s, and in numerous smaller disputes with Korea and other countries.[50]

Regardless of how one estimated the net benefits of trade, a consensus formed in the trade policy community that the new frontier of trade policy was tackling behind the border barriers. Examples of nontariff barriers include the following:

- Manipulation of technical standards to protect local suppliers;
- Poor protection of the intellectual property of foreign firms;
- Foreign investment limits designed to coerce technology transfers to local firms;
- Manipulation of regulatory policies to favor local firms;
- Health and safety standards that are applied unequally to favor local providers; and
- Use of state-owned enterprises as a vehicle to discriminate against foreign suppliers.

This agenda was reinforced by the belated recognition during the 1980s that the global economy had predominantly become a service economy in which goods were secondary to services as a share of GDP and jobs. Many services, such as dry-cleaning shops and hairdressers, are basically local. However, a growing share of services can be supplied across national borders by remote service suppliers (e.g., a bank in London originating a loan for a firm in Chile) or by foreign-service suppliers operating in a local market (a global accounting firm with a local office supported by staff in other offices around the world). The 1995 General Agreement on Trade in Services, negotiated during the Uruguay Round, pioneered the first application of trade disciplines to the service economy.[51]

The General Agreement on Trade in Services made issues tied to regulatory har-monization more important for the operation of trade rules because most barriers to cross-border services were regulatory restrictions. This immediately increased the WTO's focus on rules whose effects were less quantifiable, less observable, and more difficult to calculate in terms of predictable costs and benefits. These issues are challenging, and they require significantly more difficult decision-making calculus compared to tariffs.

As Part I showed, the increased intermingling of goods and services embedding ICT functions is a central feature of the IPD. The growing ICT component in services also is propelling increased trade in services. Although trade in services is more difficult to measure than trade in goods, services account for about a quarter of U.S. trade.[52]

A globalizing services industry raises strategic issues for governance strategies. The United States and twenty-three members of the WTO, including the EU, are as of 2017 continuing to negotiate a new Trade in Services Agreement, which, if success-fully concluded, would cover about 70% of world trade in services.[53] The prospects for success are unclear but the OECD plus still hold the largest share of the world market, although China and India are now the largest growth markets. As explained in Chapter 9, the terms of such a pact could strengthen some significant governing principles of the IPD.

Yet, it is critical to understand that we are only beginning to grasp the IPD's impact on the way markets function and the consequences for issues involving behind-the-border governance. To illustrate, consider just three consequences of the IPD. First, it will make the intermingling of services and goods more important in more markets. Today, tariff barriers alone are ill equipped to handle many goods in relatively integrated, global markets. Hence, the significance of behind-the-border barriers is on the rise. Second, there is growing reluctance to allow trade disciplines to be the primary arbitrators of many of the policies tied to these barriers, such as policies on privacy and digital security. Trade rules can facilitate and support, but it will take complementary governance structures to have a productive governance regime. Third, the IPD will regularly disrupt business models. Big data analysis that draws on information gathered around the globe is changing patterns of innovation. Production disruptions will reorganize global supply chains—both how we supply (imagine networks of 3D printers) and where supply originates. The question is, will national policies embrace or constrain this element of innovation? Given the IPD's further erosion of entry barriers to markets, this question will likely be especially important to SMEs dreaming of rapid global growth.[54]

In short, the IPD will continue to make governance messier. As we will discuss later in more detail, the negotiations aimed at creating the TPP and Transatlantic

Trade and Investment Partnership trade accords demonstrate how difficult negotiations can be and the desperate need for new approaches. There are no easy solutions. Sitting on the sidelines will only make problems more likely, perhaps dangerously so. Government policy makers, private firms, unions, and other NGOs will need to be determined and inventive to negotiate important and much-needed authoritative decisions. But there is reason for hope. The next chapter proposes a strategy for forging this framework.

Notes

1. Strategic misbehavior might entail defecting from commitments or failing to contribute enough to the collective goal to achieve its objective.

2. For thoughtful exchanges on the tradeoffs, see Ellen P. Goodman (Rapporteur), "The Atomic Age of Data: Policies for the Internet of Things" (Report of the 29th Annual Aspen Institute Conference on Communications Policy, Washington, D.C., 2015). Bruce Schneier provides a broad overview in *Data and Goliath: The Hidden Battles to Capture Your Data and Control Your World* (New York: Norton, 2015).

3. See especially David Held, Anthony McGrew, David Goldblatt, and Jonathan Perraton, *Global Transformations: Politics, Economics and Culture* (Palo Alto, CA: Stanford University Press, 1999), and M. Ayhan Kose and Eswar Prasad, *Emerging Markets: Resilience and Growth amid Global Turmoil* (Washington, D.C.: Brookings Institution, 2010). Economic integration through trade agreements boosted the prosperity of even large economies that are less dependent on trade. Scott C. Bradford, Paul L. E. Grieco, and Gary Clyde Hufbauer, "The Payoff to America from Global Integration," in C. Fred Bergsten, *United States in the World Economy: Foreign Economic Policy in the Next Decade* (Washington, D.C.: Peterson Institute for International Economics, 2005), pp. 65–109, calculated that gains from the WTO trade rounds enriched the U.S. GDP by about 9%. They estimated that the elimination of all remaining trade barriers would add another 4% to 5% to the U.S. GDP, a big win if it is achievable. A thoughtful critique is Dani Rodrik, *The Globalization Paradox: Democracy and the Future of the World Economy* (New York: Norton, 2012).

4. World trade is calculated as the sum of all countries' net imports (or exports). World Bank, "Trade (% of GDP) 1960–2015," World Bank national account data, and OECD National Accounts data files, http://data.worldbank.org/indicator/NE.TRD.GNFS.ZS.

5. The five largest U.S. trading partners in 2015 were the EU, Canada, China, Mexico, and Japan. In 2015, the seven largest U.S. export markets for goods were Canada, Mexico, China, Japan, the United Kingdom, Germany, and South Korea. The seven largest exporters (by value of goods) to the United States were the same seven countries, but China was in the top position. "Top U.S. Trade Partners," World Bank, "Trade (% of GDP) 1960–2015," http://data.worldbank.org/indicator/NE.TRD.GNFS.ZS; http://www.trade.gov/mas/ian/build/groups/public/@tg_ian/documents/webcontent/tg_ian_003364.pdf.

6. The World Bank, *ibid*.

7. Manufacturing Institute, *The Facts about Modern Manufacturing*, 8th ed. (2009), http://www.themanufacturinginstitute.org/~/media/D45D1F9EE65C45B7BD17A8DB15AC00EC/2009_Facts_About_Modern_Manufacturing.pdf.

8. Since the 1990s, membership expanded to cover a larger swath of Asia, Latin America, and Eastern Europe.

9. The share was 27.3% in 1950. Infogr.am, "Share of World GDP throughout History," https://infogr.am/Share-of-world-GDP-throughout-history.

10. The TPP negotiations involved the United States, Australia, Brunei Darussalam, Canada, Chile, Japan, Malaysia, Mexico, New Zealand, Peru, Singapore, and Vietnam. China, India, and Indonesia were not at the table, but might have sought TPP membership if the United States had not withdrawn.

11. *Economy Watch*, "GDP Share of World Total," June 30, 2016, http://www.economywatch.com/economic-statistics/economic-indicators/GDP_Share_of_World_Total_PPP/.

12. The twenty original members of the OECD (including Turkey) formed this "club of rich countries" in 1961. Since then, an additional fifteen countries became members. Australia, Finland, Israel, Japan, New Zealand, and seven Eastern European countries joined over the years. Three other countries, as they developed, also joined: Mexico (1994), Korea (1996), and Chile (2010). OECD, "List of OECD Member Countries," http://www.oecd.org/about/membersand-partners/list-oecd-member-countries.htm.

13. In comparison, although our calculation is imperfect, global auto output was roughly about $2.25 trillion in 2015. Based on the auto industry forum's data, http://www.oica.net/category/economic-contributions/.

14. "Gartner Says Worldwide IT Spending on Pace to Reach $3.8 Trillion in 2014," accessed February 1, 2015, http://www.gartner.com/newsroom/id/2643919.

15. Bildt Commission. Global Commission on Internet Governance, "One Internet," Final Report by the Centre for International Governance and the Royal Institute for International Affairs, 2016, http://ourinternet.org/report#chapter--preface.

16. Zachary Davies Boren, "Active Mobile Phones Outnumber Humans for the First Time," *International Business Timer*, October 7, 2014, http://www.ibtimes.co.uk/there-are-more-gadgets-there-are-people-world-1468947.

17. Meeker, "2015 Internet Report," 2015, p. 5, and Statista, cited at http://nicholasvenzke.com/modern-communication-began-with-the-telegraph/.

18. http://www.itu.int/en/ITU-D/Statistics/Pages/stat/default.aspx; http://www.itu.int/net/pressoffice/press_releases/2015/17.aspx#.VnuVqUtdFjo.

19. Meeker, "2015 Internet Report," 2015, p. 4.

20. *Internet World Stats News*, Number 110, March 26, 2017. Provided by Enrique De Argaez from http://www.internetworldstats.com/. Also, as of late July 2016, there were 1.86 billion Facebook users active monthly. Zephoria Digital Marketing, "The Top 20 Valuable Facebook Statistics—Updated March 2017," https://zephoria.com/top-15-valuable-facebook-statistics/.

21. Source: Statista 2015, http://www.statista.com/statistics/263801/global-market-share-held-by-selected-countries-in-the-ict-market/.

22. A vivid case study of this dynamic is in Paul Mozur, "Internet's Great Wall—China's Efforts to Keep Foreign Tech Firms out Handicap Its Own Start-ups," *New York Times*, pp. B1–2, August 10, 2016.

23. Cisco Visual Networking Index, 2014–2019, was updated in late May 2015. Its forecast and Methodology can be found at http://www.cisco.com/c/en/us/solutions/collateral/service-provider/ip-ngn-ip-next-generation-network/white_paper_c11-481360.html, accessed June 8, 2015.

24. *Ibid.*

25. See Martin Fransman (ed.), *Global Broadband Wars: Why the U.S. and Europe Lag while Asia Leads* (Palo Alto, CA: Stanford Business Books, 2006).

26. Joe McKendrick, "IDC: Very Soon, a Third of All Software Delivered via Cloud," August 9, 2010, ZDNet, http://www.zdnet.com/blog/service-oriented/idc-very-soon-a-third-of-all-software-delivered-via-cloud/5474.

27. Pokémon GO was released in July 2016 by its maker, Niantic Labs (spun off from Google in October 2015). Its augmented reality technology helped make it a global phenomenon. Pokémon GO, which forces gamers to move around outdoors to play, was reportedly downloaded more than 100 million times in the first month after its release. The number of users declined over time but the profitability from those who remained was high.

28. Gartner Group, "Predicts 2014: Apps, Personal Cloud and Data Analytics Will Drive New Consumer Interactions," http://www.gartner.com/doc/2628016.

29. One study suggests Japan is the largest revenue market. Tero Kuittinen, "App Market Globalization: The Big Theme of 2014," *Forbes/Tech*, posted February 5, 2014.

30. In 2016, global Internet advertising revenue exceeded television advertising revenue for the first time. Statista, the Statistics Portal. Total advertising spending, http://www.statista.com/statistics/273288/advertising-spending-worldwide/, and digital advertising, http://www.statista.com/statistics/237974/online-advertising-spending-worldwide and https://www.statista.com/statistics/273288/advertising-spending-worldwide/.

31. Pwc, "Global entertainment and media outlook 2016–2020: Internet Advertising," http://www.pwc.com/gx/en/industries/entertainment-media/outlook/segment-insights/internet-advertising.html.

32. Statista, the Statistics Portal, "Digital Advertising for Selected Countries Worldwide in 2015," accessed May 16, 2016, http://www.statista.com/statistics/459632/digital-advertising-revenue-countries-digital-market-outlook/.

33. Brown and Marsden (*Regulating Code*, 2013) provide a good overview and analysis of the EU efforts.

34. Jonathan Kirshner, *American Power after the Financial Crisis* (Ithaca, NY: Cornell University Press, 2014).

35. Kishore Mahbubani, *The Great Convergence: Asia, the West, and the Logic of One World* (New York: Public Affairs, 2013).

36. Dani Rodrik, *The Globalization Paradox*; Peter F. Cowhey, "Crafting Trade Strategy," in Kahler and Lake, *Politics in New Hard Times*.

37. Atkinson and Ezell, *Innovation Economics*, 2012 ; Tai Ming (ed.), *Forging China's Military Might: A New Economic Framework for Assessing Science, Technology, and the Role of Innovation* (Baltimore: John Hopkins University Press, 2014); Scott Kennedy and Christopher K. Johnson, "Perfecting China, Inc. The 13th Five-Year Plan," A Report of the CSIS Freeman Chair in China Studies, CSIS, May 2016, https://csis-prod.s3.amazonaws.com/s3fs-public/publication/160521_Kennedy_PerfectingChinaInc_Web.pdf.

38. Peter Gourevitch, David Lake, and Janice Gross Stein (eds.), *The Credibility of Transnational NGOs: When Virtue Is Not Enough* (Cambridge: Cambridge University Press, 2012).

39. The most thorough treatment of these social movements is Manuel Castells, *Networks of Outrage and Hope: Social Movements in the Internet Age* (New York: Polity, 2012).

40. A sophisticated analysis of the impact of organization capacity is Wendy H. Wong, *Internal Affairs: How the Structure of NGOs Transforms Human Rights* (Ithaca, NY: Cornell University Press, 2012).

41. Within limits (organizing mass protests is off limits), even Chinese political authorities show some leeway for informal civil society networks as a way to detect problems and locate trends in mass opinion. Gary King, Jennifer Pan, and Margaret E. Roberts, "How Censorship in China Allows Government Criticism but Silences Collective Expression," *American Political Science Review*, 107, no. 2 (May 2013): 1–18.

42. Timothy Sinclair, *The New Masters of Capital: American Bond Rating Agencies and the Politics of Creditworthiness* (Ithaca, NY: Cornell University Press, 2008).

43. David Lake, "Rightful Rules: Authority, Order, and the Foundations of Global Governance," *International Studies Quarterly*, 54, no. 3 (September 2010): 587–613.

44. Emilie M. Hafner-Burton, *Forced to Be Good: Why Trade Agreements Boost Human Rights* (Ithaca, NY: Cornell University Press, 2009) makes this case persuasively.

45. Craig Murphy and Joanne Yates, *The International Organization for Standardization (ISO): Global Governance through Voluntary Consensus* (New York: Routledge, 2008).

46. Adam Segal, *The Hacked World Order: How Nations Fight, Trade, Maneuver, and Manipulate in the Digital Age* (New York: Public Affairs, 2016).

47. These efforts are considered in a growing body of recent literature including: William J. Drake, Vinton G. Cerf, and Wolfgang Kleinwächter, "Internet Fragmentation: An Overview," Future of the Internet Initiative White Paper (World Economic Forum, January 2016), http://www.academia.edu/20523166/Drake_William_J._Vinton_G._Cerf_and_Wolfgang_Kleinw%C3%A4chter._2016._Internet_Fragmentation_An_Overview._Geneva_The_World_Economic_Forum_January; Laura DeNardis, *The Global War for Internet Governance* (New Haven, CT: Yale University Press, 2014); Milton L. Mueller, *Network and States: The Global Politics of Global Internet Governance* (Cambridge, MA: MIT Press, 2010); The Bildt Commission.

48. https://www.wto.org/english/news_e/news15_e/ita_23jul15_e.htm.

49. The other agreement reached in November 2014, the Trade Facilitation Agreement, was a "downpayment" on the long-stalled Doha Round designed to remove bureaucratic obstacles at borders that made trade slower and more expensive. Shawn Donovan, "Dealmaker in Charge at the WTO Faces Tough Fight," *Financial Times*, December 3, 2012, p. 2.

50. See, for example, Clyde Prestowitz, *The Betrayal of American Prosperity: Free Market Delusions, America's Decline, and How We Must Compete in the Post-Dollar Era* (New York: Simon & Schuster, 2010).

51. For an analysis of the treatment of services by trade rules before the Uruguay Round, see Ron Shelp, "Trade in Services," *Foreign Policy*, 65 (1986–1987): 64–84; Anupam Chander, *The Electronic Silk Road* (New Haven, CT: Yale University Press, 2013), Chaps. 6–8.

52. In 2014, U.S. service exports exceeded $700 billion and U.S. service imports reached almost $480 billion. America enjoyed a healthy trade surplus in services. Bureau of Economic Analysis, "International Economic Account: U.S. International Services Tables," http://www.bea.gov/scb/pdf/2015/10%20October/1015_international_services_tables.pdf.

53. European Commission, "In Focus: Trade in Services Agreement," http://ec.europa.eu/trade/policy/in-focus/tisa/.

54. The broadest study of the adverse impacts of outdated rules on SMEs is United States International Trade Commission, *Digital Trade in the U.S. and Global Economies*, Part 2 (2014).

5   Strategy and International Governance Regimes

IF THE IPD is to yield its best potential for society, it should be governed by a policy regime that is as global as possible. But classic questions remain. How should a negotiation be organized to maximize the chances of reaching agreement? When is coordination across national boundaries, and especially among governments, likely to be effective? Chapter 4 showed that global power is more dispersed and that some of the newly influential players have significant reservations about business-as-usual governance, as do countries like the United States and Britain that have had populist backlashes against some elements of globalization. Furthermore, despite the plethora of new civil society players in global negotiations, ultimate authority remains with governments. Yet, the political and technical feasibility of global governance increasingly depends on working with these players at the negotiating table and in governing complex processes that transcend national borders. The IPD adds to the stresses of managing these governance choices.

Today's challenging negotiating landscape requires nuanced, creative efforts to foster significant collaboration and progress. However, one virtue of social science theorizing is that it can reveal the deeper logic of the underlying bargaining dynamics and draw on insights gained from different arenas with comparable bargaining situations. Prisoner plea bargaining, nuclear deterrence and defense alliances, the management of sheep herds, and choices about investing in cybersecurity safeguards all are strategic choice problems. Such cases generate numerous observations that illuminate the core fundamentals that shape choices. Section I of this chapter undertakes this review. Then, after describing the nature of the bargaining challenge, Section II proposes a strategy for developing, negotiating, and implementing a sustainable, forward-looking international governance regime. The design and implementation of this governance regime will need to significantly modify the intergovernmental arrangements that anchored the world economy after 1945. We envision a scheme where the international governance regime is an "umbrella" for a variety of specialized problem-solving arrangements. As noted in the prologue, some trade policy instruments could ease the implementation of whatever mix of bilateral and plurilateral agreements involving the IPD emerge going forward. Accordingly, for intellectual clarity and expositional economy, the exploration of trade policy helps understand the possibilities for the umbrella of arrangements that could constitute a productive governance regime.

5.1. The Strategic Bargaining Problem

The worst-case scenario for IPD governance can be extracted from Daniel Drezner's excellent work on global economic governance.[1] Drezner argues that the ultimate governance choices rest with governments. He probes the interaction of two variables—the extent of agreement of the major economic powers on policies and purposes and the scale and scope of disagreement between major powers and weaker countries on policies and purposes. Four outcomes are possible. (1) Total disagreement on both variables makes meaningful coordination impossible. (2) At the other extreme, if the United States and the EU are on the same policy page and differences with emerging economies are mild, strong global policy convergence is possible. (3) When the major powers clash but major and emerging countries are in general agreement, a split policy world emerges. To simplify matters, exclude China and India. Then imagine that the EU has one preference on IPD competition policies and the United States has another view. Emerging economies line up with one view or the other. This resembled the situation in 2015 with privacy rules. (4) Finally, if U.S.–EU policy convergence is proceeding, but significant splits with emerging economies persist, then the United States and the EU might form a private club to govern their internal transactions without bridging the gap to emerging economies.

Drezner's approach opens the possibility that IPD governance is a stretch. Our case studies in Chapters 6 through 8 highlight significant existing differences. The pervasiveness of disruption by digital DNA in every phase of markets and society is vexing. Still, inventive strategy could make long-term positive outcomes more likely. Bargaining problems might be overcome if the various actors design productive compromises built on overlapping interests. In addition, policy preferences may change when persuasive arguments and convincing data are coupled with smart bargaining strategy. Countries always promote their own interests as they understand them, but policy coalitions also change in response to politics and to economic incentives. Many of these coalitions influence international governance to obtain global arrangements that complement their preferred domestic strategies.[2] A well-conceived international governance strategy can facilitate the evolution of policy coalitions that are more favorable to cooperation.

Chapters 1 through 3 emphasized that technological opportunity and nudges by competition policy authorities made modularity into a major driver of the IPD's acceleration of cheaper and easier innovation. A significant design lesson of modularity is that coordination requires sound anchor principles backed by a variety of flexible implementations, but not detailed master plans. Perfect behavior is unattainable—there are numerous rough-and-tumble interactions in modular markets. By analogy, global governance policy can aspire to be something like an application programming interface (API) in information technology. Different technical systems are embedded in a complex electronic product. A series of carefully designed interfaces can be interconnected without huge efficiency losses or crippling costs. To do so, the APIs lay down some "rules" for exchanges at the interface and everyone agrees to design according to those rules. The automatic fit with individual pieces of technology will be imperfect. But the APIs allow substantial, if not frictionless, integration into an acceptable product outcome by being transparent, predictable, and subject to ongoing technical consultations among stakeholders.[3]

We develop an outline of a strategy for governance by discussing the two predominant forms of incentive systems that influence collective action among governments. One is a coordination challenge and the other is a cooperation challenge.

5.1.1. Governance When the Strategic Problem Is Coordination

There are strong "functional" incentives for working together internationally, especially for addressing the "coordination" problem. This line of logic is promising and can help forge a system of governance, but it ignores fundamental problems that require tackling "cooperation" problems.

In coordination problems, everyone benefits from a common approach because it improves efficiency and reduces uncertainty. The forging of a globally accepted and adopted technical standard, or a system for network coordination (such as the arrangements for global air traffic control or for allocating spectrum for communication satellites), fit the concept of coordination. Scholars also focus on the vast sprawl of arrangements that coordinate global behavior that are either entirely outside the scope of formal government activity or where governments are mainly "backbenchers" that do not drive the primary decision making about and implementation of agreements. Many of these activities represent coordination problems. This work often is arduous, but success is probable on many complex issues if the work is capably done.[4]

Many important ICT issues manifest the characteristics of a coordination challenge and its cautiously sunny expectation of common gains. Many see the core issues of Internet governance, particularly the domain name and number system, as a coordination problem. In essence, this was the U.S. government position when it emphasized that there should be an MSO process to protect ICANN from government manipulation. Similarly, the cybersecurity literature contains numerous calls for this style of coordination. Recommendations that call for expanded collaboration among national cyberemergency response teams are frequent. Such teams are rapidly proliferating.[5] In addition, coordination analysis often treats policy problems as "technical" and therefore best dealt with by experts, not politicians.

The logic of coordination problems impresses many scholars because their interviews with midlevel officials involved in complex processes like standard setting extol its dynamics.[6] Thus, in technologically dynamic environments, coordination discussions often consider ways to move toward Pareto optimality. In economics, Pareto optimality occurs when no actor's situation can improve without another actor suffering a loss in welfare. If a situation is not Pareto optimal, some choices exist that allow one or more actors to improve their welfare without harming the welfare of others.[7] One way to improve efficiency is through the creation of a common technology standard.

If the economic and technological stakes are large, however, the logic of coordination may fail to capture the true risks and rewards as understood by more senior government officials and passionately committed stakeholders in the problem domain. Thus, officials at higher decision-making levels review coordination task forces when the stakes are high. For example, in the mid-1990s one of the authors (Cowhey) was asked by the leadership of the Federal Communications Commission to reassess what its engineers were reporting about the global coordination process on the crafting of a new mobile technical standard named "3G." (Third-generation wireless moved the mobile world from voice only into broadband data.) Cowhey and his boss were surprised to discover that buried in the engineering discussions was a choice about a branching point in the direction of the burgeoning mobile technology industry. Cowhey compared notes with his EU counterpart, who was undertaking a similar review of the process. They both wanted to determine why companies kept reporting that they feared that the consensus process was going awry. (For example, rumors circulated that Japanese corporate interests were hijacking the process.) Eventually, it became clear that a profound disagreement was brewing over the path for technology and that the outcome would influence the corporate fortunes of all players in the market. The engineers tried to finesse the issues, but the stakes were too high to be handled by engineers alone.[8]

More generally, coordination efforts can be undermined by at least four significant uncertainties, all of which are illustrated by the case of setting technical standards.

1. *Profound disagreements may arise about where Pareto optimality resides,* even when there is unanimous agreement that Pareto improvements are possible. Most innovation is incremental, but in technologically dynamic arenas, surprises can make large differences. Some players may define the problem as how to achieve a slight upgrade, whereas others see a different path to a much larger improvement. Fights may erupt over these matters in the wake of idealistic efforts to maximize innovation and because practical self-interest of certain players intervenes. Innovation is measured in the real world by technical improvement and by the speed to deployment, especially for networked technologies. The speed of deployment by a major actor and its like-minded allies may have profound market consequences. There are strong economic incentives that may lead players to push prematurely for a standard (to try to tip the market by being the first to provide a solution) or to drag their feet.[9]

2. *Confidence that those benefiting from a Pareto improvement will share the riches may be absent.* Importantly, a Pareto improvement may require that the winner compensate other actors so that no actor is worse off. In theory, the winner can afford to compensate others so long as the gains outweigh the payments to others. In reality, however, some standards organizations are stacked to favor a subclass of participants whose preferences predictably dominate the standard process. Those outside the inner circle know that they may never receive compensation. In some obvious cases, governments work with an industry to set a unique domestic standard that discourages entry by foreign firms. Numerous clashes occurred with China on such efforts. In more subtle cases, found even in wealthier countries, market leaders may avoid a unique standard and select standards' arrangements that play into their plans but not into those of their newer, smaller challengers. They then offer few offsetting commercial favors as side payments.[10]

3. Even if the situation appears to be optimal, some choices occur where *dissatisfaction with the status quo is not regarding its inefficiency*; the dissatisfaction regards the trade-off it embodies. As Stephen Krasner noted, at Pareto optimality the choice among various trade-offs is not determined simply by efficiency; relative power and other forces also shape preferences.[11] For

example, European public authorities' concerns with Google regarding privacy are not primarily to do with search efficiency but rather with their priorities about privacy and approaches to fostering innovation.[12] Similarly, European firms' claims that there could be alternative approaches to search and security are based on their willingness to engineer to a different value trade-off that might improve their market position. They recognize that their approach may not result in superior output.

4. An idealistic policy maker also may ask, *How do different trade-offs influence the speed of further technological advances?* Important standards' choices may influence future technology vectors as well as short-term outcomes. For example, David Sarnoff twice delayed introducing major game-changing technologies that RCA had in hand to prolong RCA's advantage. The rollout of FM radio was delayed to prolong the dominance of AM radio. Later, Sarnoff delayed the introduction of television until RCA was ready to dominate the new innovation.[13]

These four considerations explain why even technical coordination, the poster child of coordination possibilities, can explode into tense economic quarrels. Standards-setting groups working in related technology development spaces struggle against rival claims from firms about performance and possibilities. Traditional approaches to antitrust controls governed conduct in this area. Thus, considerations of rival claims to support different standards can draw governments into significant disputes.

Finally, with regard to coordination, solving a problem on paper is not the same as achieving coordinated action. After addressing questions about implementation, a variety of collective-action problems remain that create perverse incentives for actors. For example, investing in a new approach to security and privacy control may be ineffective unless a critical mass of other players deploy the same approach in a similar time frame. The result can be a stranded investment with little return—or, to quote one market participant, "What if you lead and no one follows?"

Even when problems arise, they may not scuttle coordination opportunities. Some items are so routine or vexing that it is incredibly difficult to achieve a tolerable outcome without some measure of coordination, and actors must continue regardless of impediments. The larger lesson is that during disruptive times, the success of coordination dynamics in solving problems depends significantly on whether higher-level policy constraints are in place. To achieve higher levels of political cooperation, the practices involving coordination must align with the political and policy realities. That leads to the second strategic situation—a cooperation problem.

5.1.2. *Governance When Managing a Cooperation Problem*

Cooperation problems differ from coordination problems because, as the classic prisoners' dilemma game demonstrates, the best outcome for a particular player may be the result of the worst outcome for another player. All players can lose badly when each one seeks unilateral gains at the expense of others. In contrast, the feasible strategy for cooperation results in a milder second-best outcome.

Cooperation problems are not intractable, but they require wary strategies of prudential cooperation. International trade liberalization is one such cooperation problem. Economists and trade negotiators are weaned on the specter of the great depression being worsened by "beggar-thy-neighbor" trade policies.[14] Nonetheless, the temptation to free ride when others are liberalizing is strong. If they are skillful, some countries can benefit by subtly barring access to their own market for limited periods, while other countries are opening their markets. For example, export-led industrialization strategies in East Asia regularly exhibited this tactic during their initial economic takeoff into world markets.[15] Prominent analysts such as Rob Atkinson argue that in response to the IPD, such strategies, as exemplified by policies pursued by China, will likely remain common.[16]

To mitigate conflict that may erupt during coordination exercises, numerous frameworks of higher-order rules and obligations were developed to stabilize efforts to operate within coordination motifs. Typically, these higher-order arrangements limit certain forms of strategic behavior. For example, WTO trade rules on technical barriers to trade, negotiated during the Tokyo Round (1973–1979) and updated in the Uruguay Round (1986–1994), created government obligations to use international standards.[17] To the extent that these standards are effective and appropriate, they elevate the importance of international standards organizations in the global economy.[18] Trade rules in most regional and global pacts now recognize that governments should rely on standards-setting processes that are "industry led," have participation from a wide spectrum of concerned parties, and are consensus based. These pacts also call on governments to base domestic rules and regulation on the standards that result from these processes. This limits the temptation of governments and their national companies to tilt markets by having the government mandate a particular technology that favors local interests.[19]

The WTO characterizes international standards organizations as adhering to the following principles for developing standards: transparency, openness, impartiality and consensus, effectiveness and relevance, and coherence. In addition, international standards organizations that operate globally are generally bound by rules that are strongly reinforced by competition policies in most OECD economies. These rules generally advocate that intellectual property incorporated in a standard be licensed to all parties, either royalty-free or on fair, reasonable, and nondiscriminatory terms (although there are major disputes about what that means). In the case of cybersecurity, firms are sometimes incentivized to coordinate more fully to improve best practices in an industry. If they do so, they are granted some protection against legal liability. Such incentives offset the fear that an investment in a best practice will create a cost disadvantage for the firm unless it is widely duplicated by others.

The cooperation problem is central to thinking about prisoners' dilemmas and related strategic games that plague negotiators.[20] When negotiating trade policy, for example, some countries make meager liberalization commitments at the WTO. They hope to win most-favored-nation treatment to benefit unilaterally from the liberalization commitments of other countries. Alliance defense strategies are another example, wherein NATO perennially struggled with the disproportionately large U.S. contribution, a major complaint of President Trump. Other countries held back because they were confident that the United States would "stay the course" strategically. A third example is global climate remediation plans; both the United States and China feared that the other would leave them to bear a disproportionate share of the burden for remediation. Hence, although cooperation is possible, it is not always the clear-cut, best approach for any actor. Cooperation may be superior to achieving no cooperation, but gaming for positional advantage or shirking cooperative action needed to achieve a collective good threatens the possibility of achieving significant cooperation.

The good news is that global society's ability to manage these challenges has improved substantially. Governments have invested huge amounts of financial and human capital to build capabilities that make management schemes more effective. For example, numerous studies suggest that the elaborate development of skilled international policy elites improved the ability to navigate cooperation problems.[21] In addition, work on the intersection of coordination and cooperation dynamics shows that creative leadership strategies can revitalize cooperation dynamics.[22] Moreover, recent studies of the aftermath of the post-2008 recession persuasively show that collective economic cooperation withstood the crisis reasonably well despite the fears of many that massive "defection" would occur. Although collective economic governance failed to avert the "worst downturn" since the Great Depression, the crisis could have been far worse without cross-national cooperation and coordination.[23]

The bad news, gleaned from countless laboratory experiments and studies of real-world cases, is that these cooperation challenges are persistent. International cooperative arrangements usually are less resilient than arrangements in countries with stable, prosperous domestic societies. This is because central authority is less available to enforce bargains and because the costs of bargaining, monitoring, and adjustment are higher in changing circumstances under an anarchic international system.[24] In addition, as the number of players grows and reliance on consensus rules increases, it becomes easier and more likely that laggards will embellish ineffectual half steps with large rhetorical flourishes during cooperation exercises instead of making good-faith efforts.

Achieving a threshold of cooperation is easier if there is a club of committed champions that will, for self-interested reasons, bear disproportionate costs to overcome the initial hurdles and achieve a meaningful collective effort. Ideally, policy strategies should incorporate built-in "accelerators" to improve cooperation over time beyond the minimum common denominator. We shortly will argue that network and reputational effects are two important accelerators. A third accelerator, found in trade agreements, is a format to facilitate issue linkage. Linkage makes it possible to craft trade-offs among issues where each party has strong reservations about cooperating on one issue but may do so for concessions on another issue. Carefully crafted common measures also can address perpetually corrosive issues such as high bargaining costs and tensions over good-faith adherence. These measures include formal and informal arrangements for exchanging information, monitoring behavior, and finding ways to adjust to shortfalls in meeting commitments. Adjustment mechanisms, for example, might include schemes that provide collective assistance to improve their implementation, especially when they provide aid at moments of distress or create different ways to enforce common obligations.

In addition to questions about strategy, the IPD raises two sets of perplexing challenges that make it difficult to improve cooperation. First, the IPD will rapidly subvert traditional market models, current policies, and governance institutions. The situation will change in unpredictable ways. Second, as IT becomes more pervasive, the IPD will collide with and more closely interlink with broader questions of security and liberty. Thus, some significant gaps in preferences must be addressed. We suggest a strategy for addressing these challenges next.

5.2. A Design Philosophy and the Creation of an International Governance Regime

Is there a way to forge the necessary minimum, common international rules among countries while nurturing quasi-convergence in domestic policy approaches? Here we define a design philosophy, which we call FACE, and lay out a governance framework that fits the philosophy.

The ultimate test of an international governance approach is whether the approach makes it easier to solve problems and harvest opportunities or simply exists to save diplomatic face by cooperating in some *de minimis* manner. One way to envision a path forward is to embed all particular solutions, including negotiated international agreements, around four guiding design principles that flow from the dynamics of the IPD. Together they can be summarized as FACE:

– *Flexible mechanisms*: The IPD accelerates technological change in ways that have significant implications for governance. Hence, governance frameworks must be designed to adapt and be flexible over time.

– *Accountable authority*: Governments still rule the world, and governance still requires them to make sensible compromises and decisions for which they are accountable. Ideally, governments will establish clear, authoritative expectations for solutions to serve as guidelines and assessment tools for the detailed solutions enabled by MSOs and civil society. (These guidelines will be authoritative if they provide some form of credible enforcement mechanism.) A pragmatic approach to governance also will recognize that there will be multiple international arenas for coordination horizontally. The challenge is to make navigation among these arenas easier and more efficient. This result can be achieved if relevant national and regional policy choices blend smoothly with negotiated agreements. Vertically, the nature of international agreements should emphasize subsidiarity as an organizing motif, as the EU has done in its internal work.[25]

– *Complementary governance arrangements*: Governments cannot accomplish successful governance alone. Many of the governance innovations that are needed to respond to the IPD will arise in the marketplace and in civil society. If the MSO process works properly, a successful regime will benefit from changing coalitions of political economic support. Consequently, governments should embrace more sweeping delegations of authority, retaining ultimate decision-making power. The actions of government, private firms, and civil society must complement one another.

– *Experimental problem solving*: Most scholars of the IPD agree that for many choices, there are few clear answers. In technologically dynamic environments, rules must be flexible and governance should embrace experimentation so that iteration, implementation, and learning can inform and improve the mix. Experimentation and complementarity are entwined. Experimentation is difficult in traditional governmental decision making, so leavening implementation of policy parameters with nongovernmental mechanisms is an attractive way of experimenting to improve governance. The use of MSOs in problem solving for the world economy is especially promising because MSOs can adroitly tackle problems arising from new market institutions.

5.2.1. Defining an International Governance Regime

We now turn to the governance structure. Scholars developed the concept of an international *regime* to show how countries establish a collective approach to problem solving.[26] A regime refers to the mix of arrangements needed to manage a common challenge. In an effective regime, countries do the following:

1. Share the same basic approach on *principles* (a theory of causation about how to achieve a policy goal) that can anchor their individual strategic calculations.[27]
2. Agree on shared *norms*, the main drivers of the collective challenge. Norms are locked in when government rule makers and market participants converge on expected, and acceptable, forms of behavior.
3. Create specific *rules* that translate principles and norms into specific obligations.
4. Create identifiable *decision-making and implementation arrangements*, including arrangements about how to resolve disputes.

With regard to decision making and implementation, a single institution is unnecessary because much of the action should be decentralized through MSOs. But, as Henry Kissinger famously complained about European foreign policy choices (and American diplomats complained about European privacy rules in 2010), "Who do I call if I want to call Europe?" Ultimately, some leaders or institutional processes must be mandated to make the final choices.

Our approach to governance builds on the concept of a regime. But we fine-tune the approach to address the challenges of the IPD in the 21st-century political economy by focusing on "*international governance regimes*" to highlight the role of selective clubs and nongovernmental problem solving in our framework.

The post-1945 era of regime building was mainly state centric and relied on intergovernmental institutions for the heavy lifting. We are in the mainstream in believing that governments still have ultimate authority, even more so in a time of populist skepticism about globalization. Therefore, we underscore the importance of a core *club* of governments to initiate reforms. However, political necessity and functional effectiveness require greater incorporation of civil society processes into governance.

Many IPD governance issues will involve rapidly changing technological environments and issues that go "behind the borders" of nations. They will also require coordination of numerous domestic market practices and government policies. Moreover, our discussion of cybersecurity in Chapter 7 will illustrate that many governance tasks require outcomes that are difficult to measure and complex process-oriented tasks that do not yield easily to policies focused on final results. Given these challenges, there are two classic sets of tools for responses. One focuses on delegating authority to expert agents who are ultimately accountable to governments. We will argue shortly that MSOs can be especially valuable in this situation.[28] A second set focuses on setting goals for observable efforts or on inputs to solutions, rather than on specific outcomes.[29] For example, the WTO telecommunications agreements required observable efforts to create rules that reflected specific "pro-competitive" regulatory principles, but it left signatories with substantial freedom to design the implementing rules. Similarly, to act on climate change, the United States and China agreed to observable efforts that they believe will improve the status quo, but they did not set a binding treaty target for emissions reduction.

We now discuss four positive features of successful international governance regimes.[30] First, clubs help initiate problem solving. Clubs are especially important in arenas with novel governance problems for two reasons.

One reason is that club members must make a special effort to join and participate. For example, membership in many informal negotiating groups is by invitation only. Only countries that show themselves to be serious about finding a solution, even if they are somewhat skeptical about its feasibility, are included. Social science researchers have repeatedly demonstrated that if it is difficult to join a club, then those who gain admission are more likely to trust that the other club members are serious about making progress. The willingness of applicants to overcome membership barriers is indicative of their attitude and approach to others and thus their reliability in helping to create the core club.[31]

Another reason is that many investments in new capabilities for companies or individuals raise the question of whether enough actors will adopt the approach for it to pay off. Unless everyone moves together, there may be no movement at all. In clubs, by contrast, everyone may not move together, but enough will move to make it worthwhile. For this reason, trade deals often include a final review of compliance plans of member states before the countries formally accept the new obligations. Accordingly, analysts also should distinguish between the viable and the ideal. Many countries do not live up to the ideals of a trade deal or to other forms of seemingly authoritative international codes. Hence, policy makers and stakeholders ask whether there is enough compliance on the core parts of the code to achieve roughly what was envisioned.

As a practical matter, the threshold effect in these fields will require careful coordination with the related challenge of the timing of costs and benefits. Upfront costs and delayed benefits are a more difficult proposition on which to mobilize action than one in which there are prominent early benefits. This is doubly so because of fears of defection. The incipient club could disintegrate, perhaps leaving significant stranded political and financial capital and foregone opportunities in other policy directions. For example, it is valuable to bind trade agreements with enforcement to ease fears of abandonment. However, to achieve acceptance of the trade deal, negotiators must show early, valuable deliverables.

The second feature of international governance regimes is that they emphasize cooperation "accelerators" of reputational and networking effects to complement the established practices used by regimes to lower bargaining and information costs. To qualify as an international governance regime, there must be meaningful agreements on both its principles (causal problem-solving theories) and its norms (acceptable patterns of behavior) that are translated into core rules for the regime. Perfect agreement or compliance, however, is neither feasible nor, in a dynamic world, healthy in the long run.

Governments enjoy concrete advantages, such as better lending rates, as they build reputations for good conduct. Compliance with a strong club's codes can generate positive "reputational effects" because many players judge reputation in global negotiations and markets using both historical conduct and updated information. Moreover, in the IPD age, "network effects" matter. As a governance practice gains greater adherence from more players, the practice delivers more value to each adopter.[32] As explained later, expert problem solving and delegation to MSOs can enhance these benefits.

Third, although every regime needs some level of authority (an expectation that important players agree to abide by specific rules) to complement regime principles and norms, international governance regimes give more emphasis to soft rules combined with delegation to MSOs.

Richard Cooper and many subsequent analysts of economic interdependence argued that different types of rules and international cooperation schemes depend on the level of interdependence.[33] We agree. One issue is the geographic scope of the rules. Chapter 7 will show that some problems, such as cybersecurity, require authoritative international baselines and careful monitoring of MSO activity by a global club of major regulators. Other problems are mainly regional in their impact. If regional policy remedies do not interfere with global commercial transactions, strong international agreements are unnecessary. Partial convergence of national policies usually suffices without international codes being created beyond the non-discrimination obligations set by trade rules.

What types of rules are possible? At the heart of our response is the distinction between soft and hard rules. Soft rules create the expectation that participants will undertake certain tasks. In WTO rules, for example, soft rules are central to the framework for telecommunications. Hard rules can impose an absolute ban on certain forms of conduct. For example, national treatment obligations ban differential treatment of foreign and domestic firms. Similarly, tariff negotiations produce a series of hard rules designed to set specific tariff schedules.

The problems of uncertainty and different national strategic contexts intersect when dealing with policy choices related to the IPD, such as cybersecurity. Many solutions seek commitments to build capabilities that conform to quality assessment rules. An example of a soft rule would be an effort to strengthen cross-border regional cybersecurity that uses commitments to create cyberemergency response teams with best practice standards. Similarly, cybersecurity will evolve depending on how insurance markets interact with liability rules set by government and best practice standards determined by MSOs. How insurers deal with losses from cyberbreaches of security and privacy will be important.

Whatever the mix of soft and hard rules, the regime must create a minimum international baseline that facilitates partial convergence of national policies and civil society practices, which can gain credibility over time, as actors come to rely on norms of interdependent behavior.[34]

Fourth, some form of dispute resolution and sanctioning mechanism is needed whose scope, features, and degree of authority depend on the nature of the problem. Going forward, hybrid mechanisms likely will dominate. At one extreme are voluntary codes developed in conjunction with governments, such as the elaborate mediation and arbitration system that governs disputes over the implementation of the International Cyanide Management Code for certifying good corporate practices in safely managing cyanide used in gold mining.[35] At the other extreme are the WTO treaty obligations and its dispute settlement mechanism (with enforcement sanctions). However, the WTO has evolved to feature reliance on many MSO arrangements. Similarly, Trade Records Analysis of Flora and Fauna in Commerce, an MSO run by conservation NGOs, is the formal monitor for compliance to the Convention on the International Trade in Endangered Species, a treaty that obligates police action against violators.[36] Similarly, central banks enforce rules for the international payments system. They agreed on regulatory best practices that build on self-interest to incentivize major market powers to at least partially enforce best practices through unilateral action. (The cybersecurity actions of the central banks reviewed in Chapter 7 reflect this logic.)

5.2.2. Testing the Idea in a More Traditional Regime: The WTO

Many efforts to create international governance regimes for the IPD will be "lighter weight." They will include fewer elaborate international treaty agreements and less powerful intergovernmental arrangements for sanctioning. But the realities of global commerce still will dictate a strong imprint on regime choices by the foundational rules governing global trade. WTO practices illustrate many of the design features that we envision and showcase an intergovernmental arrangement that, out of necessity, deals with features of the MSO system introduced as the world economy evolved.

A short review of the WTO agreement on basic telecommunication services (referred to as the Basic Telecommunications Agreement [BTA]) is illustrative. The agreement depended on, and then reinforced, the emerging quasi-convergence on a new regime. In the new regime, the causal principle was that market competition was the best way to organize communication infrastructure and services. This principle applied both to the entry into the national market by global firms and to global networks. This principle led to hard rules that set forth specific rights to market entry through investment, which, for example, permitted telecommunications network facilities to deliver cross-border communications services. The BTA also crafted rules, dubbed "pro-competitive regulatory principles," that reflected the emerging consensus among national regulators about forms of government competition guidelines that were needed for the market to succeed. These soft rules were designed to achieve certain tasks and create appropriate capabilities. For example, one important principle required the creation of a government authority (a regulatory body) that was independent of the major telecom operator to govern the market using a system of transparent rule-making. When this principle was adopted in the late 1990s, it constituted a major change for many countries that previously allowed their state-controlled telecom firms to set their own rules. Governments can no longer allow their telecom operators to self-regulate, but otherwise governments retained considerable flexibility in organizing decision making.[37]

The BTA emerged from an organization with nearly universal membership,[38] but the agreement depended on a club of important countries, driven notably by the United States, Japan, the EU, and a few of the then–newly emerging economies. The leaders recognized that if they could agree on the intersection of a new global trade deal and the new regulatory regime, ICT would have a stronger policy framework.[39] The other OECD countries cooperated, and together these countries wielded enough market influence to propel a global negotiation forward. Working together as a negotiating group within the larger negotiation, the club members agreed that if a group controlling a large majority share of the world market signed on, they would be willing to tolerate "free riders," which were granted market access without opening their own markets.[40] To reach this outcome, the negotiators of the core participants made a list of "must have" countries and a list of "nice to have" countries. If a trade deal was reached, they were content to work to expand adherence by other countries to the pact afterward, which is what happened. Even as the negotiators closed in on a final agreement, they discussed ways in which their national regulatory authorities and international development institutions could cooperate more intensively. The ongoing task was to sort out the regulatory issues that would convert the telecom agreement into a supportive framework for global market integration. Crucially, their final choices hinged on local market characteristics.[41] Although the focus in the 1990s was to successfully network governmental regulatory authorities, the same logic remains relevant in our efforts to negotiate flexible implementation featuring MSOs.

Getting to the right trade rules is a chicken-and-egg problem. The political feasibility of a trade agreement depends on a forward-looking assessment of the chances of gaining meaningful market access on a continuing basis. This requires a converging approach to problem solving by a club of countries, ideally linked to an agreed-on international trade regime or some other form of authoritative international agreement with enough teeth to improve confidence. Stakeholders are more likely to reach this conclusion if they believe that a trade pact will help advance regulatory convergence that enhances the chance of improved market access to a significant share of the world market covered by the pact.[42]

What would a trade framework with a partially converged national regulatory regime for a trusted digital environment look like? In contrast to the 1990s, when the BTA emerged, important trade frameworks attuned to the IPD are unlikely to grow from a universal trade agreement. One alternative may be "plurilaterals" that resemble the International Technology Agreement or the proposed WTO Trade in Services Agreement. But for many important behind-the-border issues, deals likely will emerge from a network of regional and bilateral arrangements anchored by a core club of OECD countries.[43] This club would de facto become the nucleus of an international trade regime that could eventually emerge at the WTO. There also could be parallel agreements that address the critical IPD issues of privacy and information security where trade agreements alone cannot establish a common minimum framework. In their original language or in their implementation strategies, the trade deals should be "friendly" to such parallel efforts.

Given the nature of the IPD governance challenges and the changing negotiating landscape, successful negotiations in the future will require that MSOs play a larger role. Tariffs and quotas differ from regulatory and policy barriers addressed in trade codes tied to nontariff barriers and services. This is partly because success at reducing measurable barriers and reducing harder-to-measure barriers of indeterminate character and magnitude are different challenges. The implication of the IPD for trade is that the intermingling of information and services, even in traditional goods, is growing. As a result, measurable wins and losses are more difficult to judge in trade negotiations and their incomes. This ambiguity increases when privacy, cybersecurity, and other non–trade policy issues posed by the IPD are added to the mix. Volatile, fast-changing technical environments where the tasks are as much about changing processes, incentives, and efforts as they are about assured specific outcomes are the new normal. Going forward, expert MSOs will be ever more essential, even for a traditional arrangement like the WTO.

5.2.3. The Role of MSOs in International Governance Regimes

Stepping back from the special case of trade, the "glue" permitting an international governance regime for the IPD would combine appropriate authoritative rules and a set of expert MSOs with flexible expertise. In the context of Internet governance, the Bildt Commission defines an MSO as a "model in which affected stakeholders who want to participate in decision making can, yet where no single interest can unilaterally capture control."[44] Part III will demonstrate that the scope of eligible membership of MSOs will necessarily differ depending on their task. One argument posits the presumptive guideline for recognition should be that the MSO membership is expert and self-organizing, as was the case with the bottom-up process that created the Internet Engineering Task Force (IETF). In general, such a guideline would help safeguard against governments organizing MSOs in a top-down manner. Regardless of the specific membership guideline, this chapter previously discussed helpful precedents in WTO agreements on structural and process guidelines for one important set of MSOs, technical standards organizations.

To understand the full significance of MSOs and the lessons that can be learned from their successes in many organizational contexts, it helps to recognize that putting an emphasis on MSOs is consistent with the pioneering work on principal-agent delegation of authority. These relationships play out in different contexts, including business and government,[45] theories of optimal contracting,[46] relational authority structures in global governance (based on a limited hierarchy that demonstrates mutual benefit),[47] and investigations of influential NGO roles in global governance.[48]

As previously noted, when it is difficult to measure outcomes and evaluate complex process-oriented tasks, a classic approach is to rely *on accountable problem solving by semiautonomous agents.* MSOs can prove especially valuable here.[49] Those who study MSOs stress that their success depends on presenting a sufficient value proposition to stakeholders to persuade them to accept limits on their choices.

Two critical insights help organize our insights. First, MSOs trade their expertise and energy (special effort beyond some hypothetical "norm") and, in return, receive tacit or explicit consent from stakeholders to lead the effort to solve a problem. Their expertise should be plausibly tied to the causal theory underpinning the regime. Hence, the MSO must establish its expertise and its commitment to some agreed-on goal and not just represent and bargain about individual interests. The MSO's expertise can enhance its reputational and networking advantages. These improve reputations of both the public and the private governance regime members by, for example, lending the weight of their expert opinion to the solutions that they help devise for members and perhaps undertaking verification tasks about compliance.

They bolster networking effects by moving quickly, by global metrics, and by opening the possibility of first mover advantages. MSOs also help to create a network of government officials within a high-value global network of experts, which is a source of benefit for the officials. The MSO arrangements also can reduce the transaction costs of gathering reliable information, bargaining, and applying necessary expertise to decisions.[50]

A second critical insight is that delegation of authority must be accountable to others in a meaningful way. This means that its work is transparent and that if it missteps, it is subject to external critiques and sanctions.[51] For example, the working groups of the IETF that develop Internet standards are composed of individuals acting in their personal expert capacity who work within the guidelines and general purposes laid out by senior experts on the Internet Architecture Board.[52] The working group is the primary driver of a new standard, but its work is subject to final approval by the board to ensure that the group is in sync with the views of board Internet experts. The group's work is transparent, so final decisions are not presented as "take it or leave it" recommendations. The decision-making process is partially but not fully autonomous from the immediate interests of the largest stakeholders.[53]

Even if MSOs gain the trust of other players, how will they fit into overall governance?[54] The history of the IETF and ICANN illustrates a situation that almost certainly will arise in IPD governance. Initially, some MSOs will start working in a fairly obscure, technical niche broadly supported under the logic of coordination by interested stakeholders in governments and civil society.[55] They may later become central to more politically and economically sensitive tasks. This happened to IETF and ICANN as the Internet became the dominant approach to organizing global networking. Today, governments face established institutions. Displacing them comes with costs and may not be fully attuned to the cooperation dynamics now at work. Cowhey and Mueller dubbed this a situation of "implicit delegation" because governments must decide whether they will accept the existing arrangement and monitor it more closely, as they did in the case of the IETF's operations and the participation of countries like China. Alternatively, they could try to exert their authority to force modifications of the agent while retaining its main features. This is how the U.S. government proceeded as its approach to ICANN evolved. Finally, as often occurs in domestic and international governance, governments could replace or supplement the agent with a different one, as some countries proposed for ICANN.[56] Although strong MSOs exercise some autonomy and authority, they ultimately reside in a framework of government tolerance. On digging deeper, it will become clear that MSOs often rely on supportive "backstopping" by governments.[57]

Unlike many advocates of the MSO approach, we argue that because of the dynamics of the Internet, in the digital arena successful MSOs will operate in a framework of coordinated regulatory action by major governments. Credibility increases when the MSO role and government authority are interdependent. The independent role of MSOs in implementation adds credibility to government efforts, perhaps even in determining sanctions when a legal instrument other than a trade agreement is involved. But to be trusted with their authority and be sustainable politically, MSOs must be accountable to government authorities.[58]

But what happens if there is not effective government accountability?[59] Prakash and Potoski examined the cost-benefit ratio for companies working under standards of the International Organization for Standardization (a nongovernmental MSO composed of private-sector delegations from member countries) for best practices for managing air and water pollution.[60] Two issues about how these codes drive capacity investments are important. First, confirming David Vogel's findings, there is little evidence of a race to the bottom.[61] Many firms standardize globally around corporate practices to meet their obligations in countries with high protection standards. They also seek credit for deploying their standard corporate practices in low-protection countries. Thus, they do not race to the bottom in countries with weak legal protections, and they are not particularly motivated to do business in a country because it has low standards. However, firms also may not race to the top level of protections. In developing countries with stronger mandated protections, few companies went beyond the local legal mandates because the added effort was more costly than the perceived benefits. Second, where local regulation was weak, firms opted to concentrate on correcting problems based on the level of public attention (in this case, prioritizing air pollution measures).

The behavior of firms, as Prakash and Potoski note, resembles the way political leaders focus their effort on projects that win the most goodwill, even if technocratic considerations might argue for a more balanced portfolio. The cautionary tale is that MSOs, left to their own devices, choose policies that improve the status quo. Their policy choices also may be more efficient and more adaptable over time than cumbersome governmental rule-making. But, their policy choices may not be socially optimal and, like political processes, they include complex variables that influence whether one system of certification dominates or many systems are complementary or rivalrous.[62] Hence, public accountability is still needed as a safeguard. The most important check on MSOs is the careful assertion of public authority to designate the expected deliverables from a policy. This can be accomplished with a formal decision or through the clear intent to make a decision in the absence of further action by the MSOs.

Many NGOs see any substantial role for the private sector in MSOs as suspect. They worry about being sold out by corporate and government leaders. Their distrust was evident in the debates over the merits of the TPP trade agreement proposed by the Obama administration. But the preferences of NGOs and union critics may be at odds with the democratic consensus in their country. Yet, it is difficult to imagine timely, flexible problem solving on IPD issues in the absence of private-sector expertise and cooperation because marketplace actors across the globe usually organize productive resources. Many MSOs can only operate appropriately if they incorporate members of the larger civil society, however. In addition, leaving policy exclusively to MSOs to decide is a recipe for abdication of democratic accountability and an invitation to deadlock. MSOs must be accountable to appropriate government oversight.[63]

The MSO process will occasionally be contentious, but it offers an avenue for creative problem solving and flexibility. Further, as the parties hammer out implementation practices, MSOs likely will build political economic coalitions that begin to influence policy preferences that can accelerate coordination dynamics over time.

In short, the ideal is to hold governments accountable while trying to change the implementation and learning cycles associated with government policies. Delegating more of the implementation to stakeholders can reduce the number of formal rules and the amount of rule-making needed. Regulators, both past and present, recognize that rule-making is cumbersome, no matter how often and how sensibly it is reformed. Opening the delegation to qualified experts from global civil society encourages stakeholders to evolve as advocates for more convergence and promotes greater interoperability among national policies. As the API experience noted earlier shows, perfect convergence is an impossible dream, but a combination of common international rules and a sound mechanism for implementation and learning could allow for enough "quasi-convergence" for governance to be effective.

5.2.4. A Concluding Synthesis

Given the design philosophy of FACE, we argued that the right mix of authoritative rules will allow for diversity in national policies but still create enough of a common minimum baseline to make the global dynamics work more smoothly. An implementation system that delegates a greater role to MSOs can allow for the flexible experimentation that improves governance of the IPD and reduces the demands for detailed hard rules in international agreements. As practical experience accumulates, this approach can promote greater alignment of actors' preferences. Simultaneously, the political economic coalitions that influence policy can recalculate their interests as the facts on the ground change.[64] This approach— "partial convergence"—may begin in a club of influential committed actors, but can evolve into a dominant global policy mix. Taken together, this provides an alternative path forward.

The strongest approach would build on these six characteristics at a minimum:

1. *A threshold effect achieved through a club*: A broad core "membership" provides the regime with significant market and political heft. Even within the club, there must be an inner core that drives it forward. Ultimately, nonmembers might be convinced that club membership is needed to become a global player.[65]

2. *An "umbrella" of authoritative rules, based on common principles and norms, whose scope varies according to the nature of market integration*: Shared principles and norms allow self-guidance and monitoring of good-faith behavior. To the extent possible, these principles and norms should be pervasive globally to establish a framework in which to nest a variety of problem-solving arrangements.[66] For example, a single set of authoritative global rules is unnecessary for many problems. Partial convergence of national policies will frequently suffice without any specific international codes being created. Similarly, specialized, often overlapping, working groups may be the most effective route to solving some problems. To the extent possible, however, they must operate within common principles and norms with some teeth.

3. *Quasi-convergence that emphasizes flexible mixes of hard and soft rules and policies within a common policy regime*: The IPD produces disruption and surprise in how markets and social processes operate and in how actors understand their interests and equities. This is especially true for cybersecurity and privacy, where achieving the best is impossible and the way to achieve the "good" may rapidly change. In addition, the "correct" answer for one sector, such as finance, may be the wrong choice for social networking, global manufacturing networks, or other industries.

4. *Expert, fragmented implementation that fosters issue linkage for creating rules*: The WTO allows for issue linkage during bargaining to establish rules. Linkage makes productive, complex bargains easier to negotiate and allows for more fragmented contributions to implementation. For example, the WTO welcomes inputs from expert and MSO groups. These inputs made trade obligations such as the Codex Alimentarius for food safety and technical standards set by international standards organizations more practical.[67] The best approaches and processes will vary across markets. To establish the regime, different forms of expert working groups that operate at the national, transnational club, and global levels must be co-opted. For example, as noted in Chapter 2, the IPD will introduce the equivalent of "hacking" into many biomedical devices for "off-label" applications. This will increase pressure for more timely medical safety certification in many countries.

Fragmentation also may reward narrow definitions of the MSO mandate. The specialization of tasks and mandates strengthens the prospects of global standards setting. This logic is illustrated in the reform of ICANN, which was especially difficult because it conjoined two separate governance problems into one structure.[68] The technical task of managing the reliability of the core operation of the root was vested in IANA. IANA also undertook the policy-setting task of determining which types of names and numbers rules (e.g., which top-level domains) to embrace. IANA also tackled related issues such as property rights and assignment criteria. Such tasks would be easier to mandate in the future if they were separated, because each poses a distinct management and subject-matter challenge. Separation also would make each task easier to reform because those worried about the politics of policy setting would not worry about degradation of the technical efficiency of the root management.

5. *Transparency*: Transparency in significant doses builds legitimacy and trust in contemporary global society.[69] Analysts of strategic behavior argue that solutions are more credible if information about both decision making and compliance is available. Under these conditions, it is possible that obligations are "self-enforcing" and that actors will comply with the regime, partly to show that they can be trusted to abide by their commitments. Learning, essential in a dynamic landscape, is improved with transparency. For example, the failure to disclose breaches of cybersecurity and privacy seriously hinders collective action because it reduces the costs of inadequate protection and slows learning about emerging risks. However, transparency does not equal full disclosure. It means that there are regular ways to monitor decision making, for instance, by making timely inputs and requiring reporting about compliance.

6. *Public accountability of governments and MSOs*: Expert decision-making groups and multistakeholder entities cannot report just to themselves. As the number of international flows increases, a denser networked environment arises for commerce, communications, and the interaction among experts, advocates, and governments.[70] Some networked arrangements are highly asymmetric, with one or more nodes dominating flows. Many of the remaining interactions display little formal structure. Recall that the rising density of action in national societies led to more elaborate organizing rules and structures. Similarly, when flows are more symmetrical, there should be a growing array of accountability mechanisms among MSOs to serve as checks and balances.[71] Properly used, these mechanisms reinforce the transparency and accountability that builds confidence in MSOs. But

when political controversy arises, both the ends (which values have priority) and the means (what strategy is credible to create trust) require some form of ultimate public accountability. Accountability is politically necessary and provides assurance that the expert group is a reliable agent working in society's best interest. Like it or not, and many cyberlibertarians do not, the world is still organized around states that have ultimate accountability and authority for public order, civil liberties, and markets. (There also is an endemic problem created by the possibility of defection by those who are unwilling to make sufficient effort to adhere fully to MSO solutions that require common levels of implementation. However, national regulatory authorities can bolster the effectiveness of MSOs when this problem becomes pervasive.)

In sum, our approach recognizes a political economic landscape that is more fragmented than the milieu in which the classic post–World War II international institutions emerged. More fundamentally, we begin with the premise that the processes of the world technological and economic systems change more quickly and are stretching many of our conventional governing frameworks. As a result, we advocate an approach that emphasizes a structure of government authority that embraces decentralized and flexible problem solving while maintaining principles and norms of collective public accountability. Although we relied on multilateral trade pacts as the starting point for our analysis, other approaches could also work, including building a web of bilateral regulatory and trade agreements with parallel commitments. Our approach does not solve all the problems of the IPD, but it fosters improved problem solving in this era of innovation. Chapter 9 lays out specific recommendations built on this approach to governance design.

Notes

1. Daniel Drezner, "The Global Governance of the Internet: Bringing the State Back In," *Political Science Quarterly*, 119, no. 3 (Fall 2004): 477–498.

2. Karen Alter, *The New Terrain of International Law: Courts, Politics, Rights* (Princeton, NJ: Princeton University Press, 2014). Miles Kahler, "Economic Crisis and Global Governance: The Stability of a Globalized World," in Kahler and Lake, *Politics in the New Hard Times*, pp. 27–51.

3. For years, APIs were the subject of antitrust fights. One player could hold a dominant market position, making it possible to manipulate the APIs connecting its technology to restrict incipient competitive challenges. Intellectual property fights also can surface over the control of important APIs. See Richard Walters, "Android Legal Fight Is a Landmark Moment for Software Economy," *Financial Times*, May 20, 2016, p. 14. As with modularity, policy can, and in important

ways has, limited this risk. By analogy, we take as a given that a legitimate "policy API" partly constrains the behavior of dominant powers. David A. Lake, "Rightful Rules," noted that this is true of most successful hierarchical relationships in international politics. Peter F. Cowhey, "Domestic Institutions and the Credibility of International Commitments: The Cases of Japan and the United States," *International Organization*, 47, no. 2 (Spring 1993): 299–326, argued that U.S. dominance after 1945 was more acceptable to its allies because domestic political checks on its foreign policy were reasonably transparent and predictable.

4. Scholars who characterize the coordination problem assume varying degrees of harmony. Daniel W. Drezner, "Globalization, Harmonization, and Competition: The Different Pathways to Policy Convergence," *Journal of European Public Policy*, 12, no. 5 (October 2004): 841–859, is more cautious.

5. Chris Vallance, "Cyber Emergency Response Team Launched by UK," *BBC News Technology*, March 31, 2014, http://www.bbc.com/news/technology-26818747.

6. Most scholars have limited access to senior officials involved in the ultimate political deal making. Andrew L. Russell, *Open Standards and the Digital Age—History, Ideology and Networks* (Cambridge: Cambridge University Press, 2014).

7. This basic concept was introduced by the Italian economist/sociologist Vilfredo Pareto in his 1906 *Manual of Political Economy*.

8. For the details of what became a serious transatlantic dispute, see Cowhey and Aronson, *Transforming Global Information*, 2009, Chap. 8.

9. Timothy F. Bresnahan and Pai-Ling Yin, "Standard Setting in Markets: The Browser War," in Shane Greenstein and Victor Stango (eds.), *Standards and Public Policy* (Cambridge: Cambridge University Press, 2012), pp. 18–59.

10. For a past case involving Europe, see Neil Gandal, David Salant, and Leonard Waverman, "Standards in Wireless Telephone Networks," *Telecommunications Policy*, 27, nos. 5–6 (June–July 2003): 325–332.

11. Rewards may follow from getting one's way on where to sit on the frontier. For example, a national regulatory system may more closely align to the selected alternative than those of other countries. Stephen D. Krasner, "Global Communication and National Power: Life on the Pareto Frontier," *World Politics*, 43, no. 3 (April 1991): 336–366.

12. See "Should Digital Monopolies Be Broken Up?," *The Economist*, November 29, 2014, p. 11, http://www.economist.com/news/leaders/21635000-european-moves-against-google-are-about-protecting-companies-not-consumers-should-digital.

13. Tim Wu, *The Master Switch: The Rise and Fall of Information Empires* (New York: Knopf, 2010), pp. 125–128, 138–139, and 151–153.

14. Charles P. Kindleberger, *The World in Depression, 1929–1939* (Berkeley: University of California Press, 1973, 2013).

15. Paul Krugman (ed.), *Strategic Trade Policy and the New International Economics* (Cambridge, MA: MIT Press, 1986).

16. Robert D. Atkinson and Paul Hofheinz, "China's Dangerous Digital Agenda," Project Syndicate, February 23, 2015, https://www.project-syndicate.org/commentary/china-digital-agenda-by-robert-d--atkinson-and-paul-hofheinz-2015-02?barrier=true.

17. Knut Blind and Axel Mangelsdorf, "The Trade Impact of ISO 9000 Certifications and International Cooperation in Accreditation," 2012, http://www.law.northwestern.edu/research-faculty/searlecenter/events/innovation/documents/Blind_Mangelsdorf_SEARLE_Final.pdf.

18. Tim Büthe and Walter Mattli, *The New Global Rules: The Privatization of Regulation in the World Economy* (Princeton, NJ: Princeton University Press, 2011), emphasize this point.

19. The logic of trying to optimize policy based solely on issues of coordination of private actors can ignore the strategic dilemmas created by internation rivalries. For a time, Japan dictated that telecom equipment follow uniquely Japanese standards. This favored Japanese equipment makers at home, but hampered their export possibilities. Similarly, China tried to impose WAPI, its homegrown 802.11 wireless networking standard, which was available only to Chinese companies. A U.S.–China trade dispute flared. The ISO rejected the WAPI standard and China ultimately withdrew it.

20. See Duncan Snidal, "Coordination versus Prisoners' Dilemma: Implications for International Cooperation and Regimes," *American Political Science Review*, 79, no. 4 (December 1985): 923–942.

21. See, for example, Emilie M. Hafner-Burton, Brad L. LeVeck, David G. Victor, and James H. Fowler, "Decision Maker Preferences for International Legal Cooperation," *International Organization*, 68, no. 4 (Fall 2014): 845–876.

22. Randall Calvert, "Leadership and Its Basis in Problems of Social Coordination," *International Political Science Review*, 13, no. 1 (January 1992): 7–24.

23. Stephan Haggard, "Politics in Hard Times Revisited: The 2008–9 Financial Crisis in Emerging Markets," in Kahler and Lake, *Politics in New Hard Times*.

24. Randall W. Stone, "Institutions, Power, and Interdependence," in Milner and Moravcsik (eds.), *Power, Interdependence, and Nonstate Actors in World Politics*, pp. 31–49.

25. "In areas outside the Union's exclusive competence, the principle of *subsidiarity*, laid down in the Treaty on European Union, defines the circumstances when it is preferable for action to be taken by the Union, rather than the Member States," http://www.europarl.europa.eu/atyourservice/en/displayFtu.html?ftuId=FTU_1.2.2.html.

26. Stephen Krasner, "Regimes and the Limits of Realism: Regimes as Autonomous Variables," *International Organization*, 36, no. 2 (Spring 1982): 497–510.

27. Ideally, causal theory helps in practical analysis and problem solving. At a minimum, it serves as what Thomas Schelling called a "focal point" that can serve as a strong anchor for converging expectations in the absence of direct communication. Thomas C. Schelling, *The Strategy of Conflict* (Cambridge, MA: Harvard University Press, 1960), pp. 111–113.

28. Dan Honig, "Navigation by Judgment: Organizational Autonomy and Country Context in the Delivery of Foreign Aid," Kennedy School Working Paper (October 2014), http://sites. bu.edu/neudc/files/2014/10/paper_59.pdf; Philippe Aghion and Jean Tirole, "Formal and Real Authority in Organizations," *Journal of Political Economy*, 105, no. 1 (February 1997): 1–29. Charles F. Sabel, "Beyond Principal-Agent Governance: Experimentalist Organizations, Learning and Accountability," in Ewald Engelen and Monika Sie Dhian Ho (eds.), *De Staat van de Democratie. Democratie voorbij de Staat*, WRR Verkenning 3 (Amsterdam: Amsterdam University Press, 2004), pp. 173–195.

29. Martin Weitzman, "Prices vs. Quantities," *Review of Economic Studies*, 41, no. 4 (October 1974): 477–491; David Victor, "Fragmented Carbon Markets and Reluctant Nations: Implications for the Design of Effective Architectures," in Joseph E. Aldy and Robert N. Stavins (eds.), *Architectures for Agreement: Addressing Global Climate Change in the Post-Kyoto World* (Cambridge: Cambridge University Press, 2007).

30. These features evolved out of necessity. There is no long-term trend to granting more authority to international regimes, but all else being equal, a track record of reasonably successful problem solving in a regime builds coalitions of support because actors value predictability and invest in strategies based on the regime's strong points. This may not translate into support for more centralized regime authority because modularity undercuts centralization even as it enables coordination. Moreover, conditions may change and lead to a demand for regime transformation.

31. Not all membership "hurdles" are legitimate functional criteria; racial or religious barriers to joining private clubs are illegitimate hurdles. George W. Downs, David M. Rocke, and Peter N. Barsoom, "Is the Good News about Compliance Good News about Cooperation?" *International Organization*, 50, no. 3 (Summer 1996): 379–406; Joe Waz and Phil Weiser, "Internet Governance: The Role of Multistakeholder Organizations," *Journal of Telecommunications and High Technology Law*, 10, no. 2 (2013): 333–350; Emilie Hafner-Burton, Edwin Mansfield, and Jon Pevehouse, "Human Rights Institutions, Sovereignty Costs, and Democratization," *British Journal of Political Science*, 45, no. 1 (2013): 1–27; David Victor, "Fragmented Carbon Markets."

32. Part I discussed network effects. On reputation, see Michael Tomz, *Reputation and International Cooperation: Sovereign Debt across Three Centuries* (Princeton, NJ: Princeton University Press, 2007).

33. Richard Cooper, *The Economics of Interdependence* (New York: Columbia University Press, 1968); Robert O. Keohane and Joseph S. Nye, *Power and Interdependence* (Boston: Little, Brown, 1973).

34. Hard and soft lie on a continuum; they are not black-and-white distinctions. We draw on Kenneth Abbott and Duncan Snidal for the concepts of obligation, precision, and delegation in international agreements. "Hard and Soft Law in International Governance," *International Organization*, 54, no. 3 (Summer 2000): 421–456. We collapsed some of their distinctions, but our approach is compatible. To illustrate how our argument applies in policy realms outside trade, see Hafner-Burton, Mansfield, and Pevehouse on human rights and Chris Brummer, *Minilateralism: How Trade Alliances, Soft Law and Financial Engineering Are Redefining Economic Statecraft* (Cambridge: Cambridge University Press, 2014), Chaps. 3 and 4.

35. The code emerged in a multistakeholder process reporting to the United Nations Environmental Program. It emphasizes site-specific solutions achieving certain levels of agreed standards of practice. Governments retain the right to impose alternative regulations, http://www.cyanidecode.org/about-cyanide-code/dispute-resolution#sthash.CjNMmuh6.dpuf.

36. Jessica F. Green, *Rethinking Private Authority, Agents and Entrepreneurs in Global Environmental Governance* (Princeton, NJ: Princeton University Press, 2014).

37. Amazingly, during the Clinton administration Cowhey and the chairman of the Federal Communications Commission had to place a call to the new German minister with authority for telecommunications to inform him that Germany had agreed to WTO rules that made it unacceptable to keep certain technical rule-making solely in Deutsche Telekom's hands. The minister was surprised, but German policy changed within months.

38. After prolonged negotiations, China joined the WTO in late 2001, Saudi Arabia joined in December 2005, and Russia joined in August 2012.

39. Although each country determined that some formula to expand market competition was critical to better telecom policy, each major country faced regulatory dilemmas that were better handled with a combination of trade rules and regulatory convergence. See Cowhey

and Aronson, 2009, and Peter Cowhey and John Richards, "Dialing for Dollars: Institutional Designs for the Globalization of the Market for Basic Telecommunication Services," in Aseem Prakash and Jeffrey Hart (eds.), *Coping with Globalization* (New York: Routledge, 1999), pp. 148–169.

40. The principle of most-favored nation treatment under the WTO agreements, a core rule for the WTO, normally obligates countries not to discriminate between their trading partners. If one country grants another country a special favor (such as a lower customs duty rate for one of their products), then it must extend the same favor to all other WTO members. Most-favored nation status also applies to the General Agreement on Trade in Services (Article 2). See http://www.wto.org/english/thewto_e/whatis_e/tif_e/fact2_e.htm.

41. Rudolf Adlung and Aaditya Mattoo, "The GATS," in Aaditya Mattoo, Robert M. Stern, and Gianni Zanini, *A Handbook of International Trade in Services* (New York: Oxford University Press, 2007), pp. 48–83.

42. Classic free trade advocates like Jagdish Bhagwati argue that unilateral liberalization is a first best policy. But in the real world of trade policy, some degree of negotiated reciprocity is critical to political sustainability.

43. Until the TPP was abandoned in 2017, the Transatlantic Trade and Investment Partnership negotiation with Europe and TPP negotiations showed that the OECD club could arrive at overlap through separate, sequential negotiations.

44. Bildt Commission, Global Commission on Internet Governance, "One Internet," Final Report by the Centre for International Governance and the Royal Institute for International Affairs, 2016, p. 22, http://ourinternet.org/report#chapter.

45. David A. Lake and Mathew McCubbins, "The Logic of Delegation to International Organizations," in Darren Hawkins, David A. Lake, Daniel Nielson, and Michael J. Tierney (eds.), *Delegation and Agency in International Organizations* (New York: Cambridge University Press, 2006).

46. Sanford J. Grossman and Oliver D. Hart, "The Costs and Benefits of Ownership: A Theory of Vertical and Lateral Integration," *The Journal of Political Economy*, 94, no. 4 (1986): 691–719.

47. Lake, "Rightful Rules," 2010.

48. Gourevitch, Lake, and Stein, *The Credibility of Transnational NGOs*, 2012.

49. See citation in Note 28 and Matt Andrews, *The Limits of Institutional Reform in Development: Changing Rules for Realistic Solutions* (Cambridge: Cambridge University Press, 2013).

50. See the discussion in Jessica Green, *Rethinking Private Authority*, 2014.

51. Gourevitch, Lake, and Stein, *The Credibility of Transnational NGOs*, 2012.

52. See the IETF website, https://www.ietf.org/. More generally, see William J. Drake and Monroe Price (eds.), "Beyond Netmundial: The Roadmap for Institutional Improvements to the Global Internet Governance Ecosystem," August 2014, http://www.global.asc.upenn.edu/app/uploads/2014/08/BeyondNETmundial_FINAL.pdf.

53. The Bildt Commission, Global Commission on Internet Governance, "One Internet," Final Report by the Centre for International Governance and the Royal Institute for International Affairs, 2016, p. 106, also stresses the importance of transparency for the legitimacy of MSOs. http://ourinternet.org/report#chapter.

54. Some analyses stress the characteristics of individual leaders. Others stress the intensity of engagement of certain countries (e.g., Switzerland in setting standards for watches) or the ways

that countries organize their national standards bodies to influence global standards. However, these questions of influence are secondary when determining how a successful MSO helps an international governance regime work more effectively. On leadership and national influence factors, see Gourevitch, Lake, and Stein; Büthe and Mattli; and Murphy and Yates.

55. Green analyzes these as cases of "entrepreneurial" private authority, an apt categorization.

56. The WTO's entry into basic telecommunications was met with howls of protest from International Telecommunication Union officials because the WTO was trespassing on their "turf." The WTO ultimately shared some aspects of the International Telecommunication Union's traditional domain and dominated other aspects. Peter Cowhey and Milton Mueller, "Delegation, Networks and Internet Governance," in Miles Kahler (ed.), *Networked Politics: Agency, Power and Governance* (Ithaca, NY: Cornell University Press, 2009).

57. David Lake treats strong MSOs providing critical governance services, such as credit-rating agencies, as "relational authorities" and argues that their power is independent of government. We agree that they have some autonomy, as a theory of delegation predicts, but suggest that they must keep important government stakeholders satisfied. Lawrence White, "The Credit Rating Industry—An Industrial Organization Analysis," NYU Center on Law and Business Working Paper 01–001, April 2001, shows how credit-rating organizations rest on government tolerance, https://www.bis.org/bcbs/ca/lwhit.pdf.

58. Lesley K. McAllister, "Regulation by Third Party Verification," *Boston College Law Review*, 53, no. 1 (1-1-2012): 1–64. Also see Hafner-Burton, Mansfield, and Pevehouse.

59. Two broad reviews that touch on these issues are Deborah D. Avant, Margaret Finnemore, and Susan K. Sell (eds.), *Who Governs the Globe?* (Cambridge: Cambridge University Press, 2010). Also see A. Claire Cutler, Virginia Haufler, and Tony Porter (eds.), *Private Authority and International Affairs* (Albany: State University of New York Press, 1999).

60. The ISO 14001 guidelines are for management practices. They posit that best practices in firm processes for pollution management will significantly mitigate pollution, but they do not attempt to set social objectives for acceptable levels of pollution. Aseem Prakash and Matthew Potoski, "Global Private Regimes, Domestic Public Law: ISO14001 and Pollution Reduction," *Comparative Political Studies*, 47, no. 3 (March 2014): 369–394.

61. David Vogel, "The Private Regulation of Global Corporate Conduct," in Walter Mattli and Ngaire Woods (eds.), *The Politics of Global Regulation* (Princeton, NJ: Princeton University Press, 2009), pp. 151–188.

62. Graeme Auldt, *Constructing Private Governance: The Rise and Evolution of Forest, Coffee, and Fisheries Certification* (New Haven, CT: Yale University Press, 2013).

63. Business interests, in a surfeit of excess caution about regulatory risks, can derail MSO discussions. If MSOs are not accountable to a government authority, there can be deadlocks on solutions that are inequitable and undermine the public interest. For example, the NGO–business sector discussion on privacy and facial recognition technology requested by the Federal Trade Commission broke down. Absent a clear signal from the commission that a rule would be promulgated if the MSO failed to reach consensus, the discussion deadlocked. Similarly, deadlocks on credit card security among business groups persisted until the Federal Trade Commission intervened to force progress. Andrea Peterson, "The Government's Plan to Regulate Facial Recognition Tech Is Falling Apart," The Switch, *Washington Post*, June 16, 2015, http://www.washingtonpost.com/blogs/the-switch/wp/2015/06/16/the-governments-plan-to-regulate-facial-recognition-tech-is-falling-apart/?wpisrc=nl_tech&wpmm=1.

64. An example of changing facts on the ground was the conversion of U.S. health insurance providers to support Obamacare. As they studied the policy, they realized that it would open a substantial new pool of clients for coverage. We envision a path for a "race to the top" at the global level, not a "race to the bottom." See David Vogel.

65. We borrow significantly from Thomas Schelling's concept of a "k-group." Schelling defines the k-group as "the minimum set of members that can benefit from the production of a public good, even if no other members contribute to its provision." The definition is from Ellis Krauss and Benjamin Nyblade (eds.), *Japan and North America* (New York: RoutledgeCurzon, 2004), p. 383. They follow Thomas C. Schelling, *Micromotives and Macrobehavior* (New York: Norton, 1978), Chap. 7.

66. We thank David Victor for suggesting the notion of an umbrella. The value of nesting was first established in Vinod Aggarwal, *Institutional Designs for a Complex World: Bargaining, Linkages, and Nesting* (Ithaca, NY: Cornell University Press, 1998).

67. Kal Raustiala and David G. Victor, "The Regime Complex for Plant Genetic Resources," *International Organization*, 58, no. 2 (Spring 2004): 277–309.

68. On the IANA process, see the Bildt Commission, pp. 110–114; Milton L. Mueller and Brenden Kuerbis, "Roadmap for Globalizing IANA: Four Principles and a Proposal for Reform, Internet Governance Project Working Paper," March 2014, http://www.internetgovernance.org/wordpress/wp-content/uploads/ICANNreformglobalizingIANAfinal.pdf.

69. This same logic applies to small, local societies. The Nobel laureate Elinor Ostrom stressed the importance of monitoring in local efforts to sustainably manage natural resources. See her Nobel Prize lecture, "Beyond Markets and States: Polycentric Governance of Complex Economic Systems," December 8, 2009, video at http://www.youtube.com/watch?v=T6OgRki5SgM; http://www.nobelprize.org/nobel_prizes/economic-sciences/laureates/2009/ostrom_lecture.pdf.

70. Miles Kahler, *Networked Politics*, 2009.

71. Nelson W. Polsby, "The Institutionalization of the U.S. House of Representatives," *American Political Science Review*, 62, no. 1 (March 1968): 144–168. Gary Cox, *The Efficient Secret: The Cabinet and the Development of Political Parties in Victorian England* (Cambridge: Cambridge University Press, 1987), examined institutional changes in British Parliamentary government during the 19th century.

III Creating a Trusted Digital Environment in an Era of Quasi-Convergence

6 Global Policy for the Cloud

"AS TIME GOES By," *Casablanca*'s classic song, begins with poignant lines: "You must remember this. A kiss is still a kiss." Would that the cloud was still just a cloud. The technological marvel that is the cloud is transforming information processing, the nature of information applications, and data storage. Its digital DNA is altering the economic stakes and technological dynamics of all digitally enabled markets. In short, the cloud is central to everything in the IPD.

Why is it so difficult to reach global agreement on how to govern the dynamics of the cloud and how governance might be improved? Our short answer is that the cloud has triggered a geopolitical tug of war over the control of today's information economic drivers. Complicated clashes among industries over the use of the cloud to create fresh value and capture the lucrative value added that the cloud helps generate also are underway. Many industries wish to use cloud dynamics to improve their economic performance, which provides an incentive to cooperate to remove obstacles to cloud deployments. This is the coordination logic that was described in the previous chapter, which also demonstrated that mixed motives created by the logic of cooperation could bedevil coordination because industries and governments are contesting how these gains will be distributed. Moreover, given the cloud's security and privacy implications for digitally enabled markets, political tensions are spreading over how to secure a "trusted digital environment." Any governance solution for the cloud must develop ways to govern market competition and innovation dynamics that are compatible with stronger security and privacy protections.

The argument unfolds in five sections. Section 6.1 explains what is distinctive about the cloud and clarifies the cloud's impact on the workings of digitally enabled markets. Section 6.2 explores why the economic stakes are high for global ICT markets and discusses the impact of the cloud on the broader economy. Section 6.3 summarizes the responses of governments to the cloud's emergence. Special attention is paid to government measures to speed the cloud's deployment as well as to regulatory worries that raise caution flags for global cloud markets. Section 6.4 considers the political economy of the policy dialogue. The final section focuses on possible governance solutions by considering how trade policy approaches could facilitate the creation of an international "baseline" for the quasi-convergence of national policies and easier navigation among varying national schemes.

6.1. The Technology of the Cloud and Its Intersection with Digital Markets

6.1.1. Understanding the Cloud

The cloud[1] differs from the computing architectures that dominated from the 1980s until recently. Simply stated, the cloud enables users to access remotely located computing resources on demand and pay for what they use. The cloud's architecture separates suppliers and users, dynamically allocates ICT resources, and provides metering for reporting and billing.[2] Users no longer need to make major investments in their own IT infrastructure to have access to world-class capabilities. This harkens back to the early reliance on computer "timesharing" networks that remotely accessed mainframe computers. What is new is that the cloud is dynamically scalable on demand and allows users far more "modularity" at far lower prices. Its users can flexibly mix and match their own value added because the cloud encompasses multiple technical configurations and service mixes.

The United States pioneered the dominant models for e-commerce, software, and integrated hardware–service models (such as the iPod and, later, the integration of music streaming services with smartphones). Hence, predictably, U.S. firms were the first to master cloud technology and build the necessary infrastructure for their own global operations. Amazon was the pioneer in creating global cloud networks that took advantage of economies of scale and scope and improved reliability for their services. Microsoft and Google followed rapidly in the sale of cloud services and other new entrants soon flooded the cloud market.[3] Apple, IBM, and other IT firms built private clouds to support their service offerings (ranging from iTunes to Watson), as did global banks and other firms with vast scale and special regulatory concerns about security.[4]

Many discussions about the cloud, such as estimates of market size and share, stumble over critical distinctions about its service model. *Infrastructure as a service* is the fundamental building block for cloud infrastructure, but provides the lowest value-added service. Users dynamically and remotely access raw machine and network resources and use them as needed; they control what is loaded onto the infrastructure (e.g., operating systems and deployed applications) but do not control the underlying infrastructure. The *platform as a service* model, which allows users to create end applications to leverage the cloud provider's offerings, is a step up in value-added engagement. These users rely on cloud service to provide elaborate support capabilities such as software tools to help their users exploit the underlying cloud infrastructure, including programming languages, program libraries, services, and development and collaboration tools.[5] Many new entrants, such as Cask, have created a host of specialized software tools independent of the infrastructure-as-a-service provider. The highest value-added model for cloud services, as well as its largest revenue stream, is *software as a service*, as exemplified by Google Applications or Microsoft 360 email. Users do not manage or control the underlying infrastructure or create the basic application. Applications interface through client devices such as a web browser or through dedicated programs such as Outlook. Many Indian companies, which provided outsourced, back-office data entry services, use the cloud for what they call "*business processing as a service.*"[6]

In addition, the cloud deploys a *hub-and-spoke network*. Most large-scale data operations are transnational and are handled through a network of regional hubs whenever legally possible. (The limitations are discussed later.) Operationally, the cloud hubs work together to manage peak demand. To illustrate, Amazon Web Services (AWS) reduces the total capacity necessary to handle peak demand by time shifting between its data centers in different global time zones.[7] Hubs also are critical for managing massive amounts of global data for large multinational companies, for NGOs, or for public institutions that must coordinate their international operations or public-sector data related to issues such as infectious diseases patterns.

Engineering economics favor state-of-the-art hub facilities that work at major economies of scale and scope. The cloud requires significant resources, space, power, cooling, and machines, so locations are chosen based on complex operational requirements.[8] To enable iCloud, Apple opened its first major cloud data center in North Carolina in late 2010. The 500,000 square foot data center was powered partly by 200 acres of solar panels. This facility is now comparatively small. More massive data centers exist in Ireland, India, and China, and smaller nations, such as Haiti, are studying the potential of cloud-hosting centers. In 2016 the largest center operating in the United States was the 2.2 million square foot Switch SuperNap in Las Vegas. By comparison, the Range International Information Hub in Langfang,

China covers 6.3 million square feet, almost the size of the Pentagon, was scheduled to be completed in late 2016.[9]

Cloud hosting is rapidly diffusing globally as prices continue to fall.[10] The private cloud infrastructures of governments, companies such as Ford, and the major banks already are globally distributed to improve their speed in interactions and reliability. Further, even in firms like Amazon, much of the smaller-scale work in cloud services already takes place in the spokes of local cloud facilities.[11] The dynamic sharing among cloud facilities, especially to manage peak demand, is increasing. Moreover, many of the applications running on the cloud, such as tracking trucks and managing traffic across border crossings, are inherently international. To be optimal, cloud facilities must be flexible and free to promote the unrestricted movement and management of data across borders.

The configuration of this hub-and-spoke network inevitably is subject to significant policy influences, so understanding the implications of the engineering and economic logic of the architecture is critical. The early cloud leaders remain on top of the market, especially in basic infrastructure. Their position is reinforced because the largest market for cloud services remains in North America.[12] But a hub-and-spoke system characterized by rapid demand growth offers abundant opportunities for competitive entry for companies in all countries as owners of giant data centers and as suppliers of specialized cloud services. Some of the largest public data centers in the United States in 2015 were Switch Communications, DuPont Fabros, and Terremark (a subsidiary of Verizon since 2011).[13] New operators are springing up in the wealthier countries, such as Numergy in France and Next Generation Data in Britain. In addition, in March 2015 the Chinese e-commerce giant Alibaba opened a cloud computing facility in the Silicon Valley to support Chinese companies doing business in America and to compete with Amazon, Google, and Microsoft, which dominate the U.S. market.[14] A similar pattern is emerging in poorer nations on all continents where local cloud providers will have some "home court" advantages.[15]

Three other features of cloud systems are important for policy debates, especially those involving security and privacy. First, different levels of security measures are needed for different data. Minimum standards apply to all data, but certain types of data require greater security because of the risks associated with its loss or theft. Cloud systems routinely classify and organize data and price their services based on the minimum level of required security. If a client wishes, major cloud providers offer higher levels of security. Second, cloud data are not anonymous. They are contractually managed for a client and always carry an identity tag to the client, except in private clouds, which do not always use tags. This is critical for privacy and security issues. A client—say, Siemens—is obligated under German law to protect privacy and security in certain ways. The contract with the cloud provider can stipulate that its data be handled in a manner required by German law. If the client does not insist on the required German protection level, it can be taken to court in Germany. If the cloud provider does not provide the protections in the contract, the client can sue the cloud provider. In short, cloud users can stipulate how data should be organized. Legal systems, in theory, enforce the arrangement.[16] Third, in tension with the second point, the cloud involves some practical issues on legal jurisdiction. They are symbolized by conflict over the power to subpoena records in a criminal case. For example, suppose the German government seeks access to data of a German citizen for an alleged crime in Germany. If the information is on an Amazon server in Germany, Germany still must go to an American court for the authorization to search. In the age of the cloud, this type of situation is generating tension because it is no longer the occasional oddity.[17]

To summarize, five characteristics are at the heart of engineering and economics of the cloud market. First, cloud computing can be supplied in a variety of manners, ranging from the private clouds of a single organization to a public commercial resource owned and managed by a private entity. Second, three different business models for cloud services exist: infrastructure as a service, platform as a service, and software as a service. Third, a global hub-and-spoke network emerged because it provides economies of scale and scope, responds well to data management needs (including cross-border applications), offers redundancy to ensure reliability, and has advantages for peak load management. There is growing diversification of facility locations and an increasing array of competitive entrants in large data centers and cloud-enabled services, including by firms from emerging economies. The rise of these new players responds to data sovereignty demands and provides greater geographic distribution for response times, redundancy, and peak load management. Fourth, cloud data can be stored according to different levels of desired security and applicable privacy rules. Fifth, distributed global storage and processing of data make a traditional legal issue, defining the extraterritorial jurisdiction of countries over their companies, a factor of growing prominence in cloud governance.

6.1.2. The Cloud and Digitally Enabled Markets

The complexity of cloud configurations makes it difficult to understand its economic significance for digitally enabled markets. Following Zysman and Breznitz, we distinguish three dynamically evolving layers of digital intersection. Players are competing to capture the value within each layer and among the three layers: terminals (as conceived in the Internet of Things), networks, and information (technology–services–applications–software).[18]

As noted previously, the IPD transforms how value is created and marketed, how profits are taken, and how business models change. Firms are creating hybrid innovations that mix and match traditionally distinct markets, including markets for traditional goods and commodities. The cloud and IT modularity, which embody the "cheap revolution," are two major factors shaping the way new digitally enabled markets are emerging. It is radically reshaping the economics and trade patterns of ICT service and hardware markets, including in developing economies.[19] For example, the $67 billion merger of Dell and EMC in 2015 was an effort to reposition these hardware giants for a cloud-centric age.[20]

To understand the implications of the cloud, consider how information services are being fundamentally reorganized. Software as a service disrupted the economics of software provision (by making distribution cheap and reducing piracy) and opened new challenges to business software packages from Microsoft and Adobe and to SAP and Oracle databases. SalesForce.com also is a child of the cloud. If cloud-enabled social networking could not scale robustly, social networking firms like Facebook could not exist. Uber, Airbnb, and other newly emerging giants of the "sharing economy" rely on cloud infrastructure and mobile broadband.

In the prior era of computing, high IT infrastructure costs reinforced the dominance of the early leaders. Today, the cloud allows lower costs and specialized entry into information services and fosters specialized IT services and applications. It allowed BlaBlaCar, a French ride-sharing venture, to take a different road than Uber. Similarly, Maverick, a globally ambitious YouTube channel that emphasizes Korean pop culture, depends on the cloud.

Further disruption will occur because computers and smartphones soon will be a minority subset of terminal devices in a cloud environment. The information capabilities of new "terminals" such as smart vehicles and buildings, supported by network-connected sensors, will create new competitive advantages. Thus, Google dominates search but also is moving into manufactured devices, smart terminals for household functions, parts of automotive systems, ride-sharing services in China, and other new areas. Rivals worry that if the search leader/dominant big data firm is reinforced by expertise in verticals such as household security and climate control, it could "eat everything." More prosaically, Google could become an all-purpose data analytic leader that dominates new digitally enabled applications. As iTunes showed, smart terminals could seize value from content providers or create value that leaders of other markets otherwise could not glean. For example, Apple and Samsung are racing to create medical monitoring devices for consumers in competition with conventional medical equipment makers.[21]

The automobile giants also want to leverage their control of vehicles into the information and network layers to create "verticals" by leveraging their control of their cars' firmware to offer all-purpose solutions that preempt efforts by rivals such as Google, Microsoft, and Alibaba. Similarly, as posited in Chapter 3, firms such as Monsanto and Qualcomm are using the cloud to enter new product markets outside their traditional core businesses. In addition, huge telecom carriers (and their equipment suppliers, like Ericsson) are anxious to enter cloud computing and provide value-added services for data security in cooperation with telecom equipment suppliers or provide "content distribution networks" for video to compete with firms like Akamai.

In short, the cloud alters the dynamics of the ecosystem of all digitally enabled markets. This is why the stakes are so high.

6.2. Measuring the Economic Stakes

Our next challenge is to measure the economic stakes for global markets with respect to the information and communications market and the impact of the cloud on general economic activity. First, we ask, as the cloud becomes pervasive, how can its impact be measured? The size of cloud-related activities in the ICT industry must be estimated to capture the direct value of cloud services for verticals, such as automobiles. Then, we consider the impact of cloud services on economic growth. As the cloud expands, so will its impact. Market forecasts are notoriously unreliable and the macroeconomic analyses make assumptions from limited data. Still, policy makers rely heavily on selective data when considering cloud governance. As the newspaper editor in a classic Western movie noted, "When the facts become legend, print the legend."[22] Legends and speculation fuel political dynamics in explosive markets.

For example, estimating the size of cloud markets depends on how the analyst distinguishes infrastructure and software services. Nonetheless, all estimates of the size and impact of the market growth of the cloud are remarkable. In November 2014, a senior executive of a major IT firm told us that the company was stunned at the speed of the transformation—"the global market for computing changed dramatically in just the past twelve months." Although this firm had proclaimed the critical importance of the cloud for several years, it was still astonished.[23] Table 6.1 shows that in early 2016 Gartner Research forecast the public cloud services market would reach almost $110 billion (excluding advertising) in 2016.[24] Remarkably, Gartner forecasts that global cloud-computing business will almost triple, from $23 billion in 2016 to $67 billion in 2020.[25] To illustrate further, AWS, by far the largest public cloud service (about an order of magnitude larger than the runner up, Microsoft), increased its revenues from $3.1 billion in 2013 to $4.6 billion in 2014 and almost $7.9 billion in 2015.[26] Revenues were projected to pass $10 billion for 2016.[27] Despite

TABLE 6.1

Worldwide Public Cloud Services Forecast (Millions of Dollars)

	2016	2017	2018	2019	2020
Cloud Business Process Services (BPaaS)	40,812	43,772	47,556	51,652	56,176
Cloud Application Infrastructure Services (PaaS)	7,169	8,851	10,616	12,580	14,798
Cloud Application Services (SaaS)	38,567	46,331	55,143	64,870	75,734
Cloud Management and Security Services	7,150	8,768	10,427	12,159	14,004
Cloud System Infrastructure Services (IaaS)	25,290	34,603	45,559	57,897	71,552
Cloud advertising	90,257	104,516	118,520	133,566	151,091
Total market	209,244	246,841	287,820	332,723	383,355

Source: Gartner (February 2017)

this impressive record, the biggest money rests with digital ad revenues (propelled by cloud-enabled analytics) and value-added information services that are slowly displacing part of the profit centers of producers in traditional industries.

Even as the market exploded, prices dropped. Even larger economic implications arise from radically cheaper computing and Big Data that will drive changes in innovation and general economic patterns. For example, consider their impact on SME enterprises. AWS is a platform for numerous startup firms that require cloud services—from simple web services to media streaming. In the past, these startups needed to buy servers, lease high-speed network lines to their offices, employ technology specialists to manage the servers and disk drives, and constantly risk being under capacity if a product was quickly adopted that suddenly required a massive new investment. With cloud services, SMEs' capital commitments vanish and their cloud-provided resources grow dynamically at declining prices. Detailed estimates for SMEs in India, for example, suggest the cost for IT capabilities had declined by at least a third by 2010.[28] Greater reductions followed. This reduction in upfront capital and operational execution risks means that startup firms and those experiencing significant growth have a better chance of survival and success. This translates to more startups, more jobs, and more local innovation.

EU case studies argued that the cloud could boost cumulative EU GDP growth and job creation,[29] primarily through faster expansion of SME activity resulting from lower initial entry costs for new products and businesses and faster business expansion.[30] Today, the cloud is helping maintain the quality of services, making it cheaper to handle "peak demand" periods for ICT, and beginning to increase productivity growth. These trends should translate into wage improvement. The distribution of benefits among nations depends on factors such as the percentage of their economies involved in the most ICT-intensive sectors. In descending order, these include banking, finance, and business services, followed by manufacturing and then transport, communication, government, health, and education services.[31] Today, perhaps 20% of the economy is extremely information/Internet intensive, but the Internet of Things is rapidly opening up the other 80%.[32] Predictably, the EU set ambitious objectives for the use of Big Data to advance health care, smart grids to manage electricity consumption, and improved fuel and time savings to enhance transportation. The OECD cites one estimate that the global value for transportation efficiencies could be worth $500 billion annually by 2020.[33]

Another significant benefit for SMEs and for emerging markets is innovation in distribution and payments for IT services. The cloud enables mobile phone applications that require less software code and are cheaper to develop. This trend is opening the market to new developers, including those from developing countries with context-specific knowledge that enables successful tailored solutions. The economics of PC ecosystems normally resisted this kind of inexpensive systems solution for specialized market niches. The growth of various cloud-enabled "stores" (not just Apple's or Alibaba's mass consumer stores) also is creating digital payment systems that lower the cost of supporting local and global markets. This enables the expansion of SMEs from countries with less flexible financial systems than those in the United States.[34]

In short, in addition to lowering distribution costs, the cloud is creating a global market for service, content, and program providers. It is an evolutionary step in computing as a general platform technology, much like electricity. This market is supported by a powerful payments system, just as app stores enable independent application developers to reach millions of customers. This combination of the information disruption and the creation of new business models permits cloud-enabled service architectures to blossom. In addition, many highly specialized engineering and skilled support services needed for local innovation clusters can be supplied transnationally. This allows entrepreneurs with local expertise, even those in poorer economies, to innovate on a local, regional, and global scale. These cloud applications include mobile health services and other "social service applications." As a result, countries are taking a fresh look at the cloud with a new calculus. For example, Kenya is developing a network of data centers to try to become a regional cloud hub.[35]

The broader lesson is that the cloud benefits developed and developing countries that use cloud infrastructure/services. Even in Africa, investors in fiber-optic cables plan to ring the continent and are engaged with applications' developers and users of cloud services to expand the demand pool that will support the economics of those fiber rings.

The IPD has two further implications. First, the logic of macroeconomic analyses is that, other things being equal, as economies use more data, they become healthier. This is why analysts worry about weaknesses in the communication infrastructures of poorer countries and about digital divides in data use by income or region in wealthier countries. Another worry is that significant data usage gaps exist among wealthy countries. The United States and Korea both used roughly 65 gigabytes of data per month per capita in 2014. In contrast, the EU average (as well as that of France and Germany) was about 25 gigabytes of data per month per capita.[36] Among major European countries, gigabit usage ranged from a high of 58 gigabits per month per capita use in Sweden to a low of about 18 gigabits per month per capita in Spain and Italy.[37] Much of the difference lies in the prominence of digital consumer video consumption in Korea and the United States compared to Europe. But even after eliminating consumer video and trying to focus only on data for business use, Germany trails the United States in its digital use by about 45%.[38]

The EU has repeatedly expressed the need for Europe to rapidly become digitally enabled. Our interviews with EU officials in 2016 (before the Brexit vote) suggest that they may be resigned to American dominance of the infrastructure market. But they hope to construct a single EU digital market that will encourage more local entry into niche infrastructure ventures and the emergence of a vibrant EU ecosystem for platform- and software-as-a-service markets. Such a market, they predict, will be larger and more profitable than infrastructure services as digital data in the cloud climbs from 20% of EU data in 2013 to 40% in 2020, with efficiencies generating a 1.9% boost in EU GDP by 2020 worth 206 billion Euros.[39]

Second, the information disruption means that more of the overall value in every type of good and service is in its information content. As broadband continues to intersect with the cheap revolution and modular ICT capabilities and the Internet of Things emerges, big data analytics mean more than better search engines or superior targeted marketing that is driven by data on the web. It creates the dynamics of nonrivalrous use and co-invention by users and other suppliers. Big data analytics also drives mix-and-match architectural innovations that span traditional market segments and rely on novel combinational forms of research and discovery. Further innovation is prompted by user experiences with formal feedback mechanisms and observations of product use. Incremental innovation leads to more tweaking, but more than tweaking is involved. Today, users also can observe and experiment on a global scale. Globalization makes the pursuit of markets easier, but globalization also drives discovery and innovation.[40] Thus, the cloud and its information dynamics are part of a fundamentally new disruptive innovation system.

6.3. The Policy Importance of the Cloud

New technological capacities inevitably provoke second thoughts about their implications. Next, we review prominent aspirations and worries expressed in policy debates and provide an overview of government responses to the cloud's emergence.

Ricardo Tavares has usefully divided policy-related debates into two groups.[41] First, some policy discussions focus on which incentives are most appropriate to promote the cloud, propel its deployment, and facilitate its use for economic and social objectives. Second, regulatory and competition policy discussions consider ways to deal with possible flaws in the workings of the cloud market and those in related big data analytics markets.[42] Table 6.2 provides a breakdown of these policy approaches.

Most *enabling policies* are intended to strengthen the use of the cloud by providing complementary economic and social assets. Most of these policies are uncontroversial. Debate continues about which policies are effective, but there is little fear that they significantly distort global markets. Enabling policies that include elements of regulatory policy are more complicated. The overwhelming majority favor digital connectivity and agree that governments should adopt policies to promote connectivity by fostering competition and, if needed, by adopting additional measures to promote it.[43] However, the debate regarding the terms of access to communications networks for information application providers is deeply contentious; the global debate about "net neutrality" mainly regards these issues.[44] Here, it suffices to note that the outcomes influence who provides what value added in a cloud-centric world.

Beyond net neutrality, a variety of policies are designed to bolster local information infrastructures. One approach is to use government procurement to favor local suppliers over foreign competitors in the provision of cloud computing. Similarly, almost all recommendations related to cloud computing endorse moving faster to embrace cloud-enabled e-government. But procurement policies and use policies for e-government frequently become entangled regarding the terms under which access to the network should be provided and on related regulatory restraints on network practices and pricing. As recognized by government officials, issues surrounding public data access to private corporate data will raise complicated issues over intellectual property rights and compensation.

TABLE 6.2

Enabling and Regulatory Policies for the Cloud

A. Enabling policies

Providing complementary assets for cloud-based innovations:

1. Ensure access to government data and resources for new cloud applications.
2. Provide investments in and coordination of "vertical" applications such as health care, energy conservation, and transportation efficiencies.
3. Provide technical assistance to small and medium-size enterprises to identify and use cloud-enabled capabilities.
4. Address human capital issues such as training labor forces to be responsive to opportunities opened by the cloud ecosystem.

Policies that include elements of regulatory policy:

5. Ensure the availability of ubiquitous connectivity for the cloud ecosystem at competitive prices and on nondiscriminatory terms.
6. Promote e-government-enabled public investment in cloud systems and ensure data gathered by e-government are available for universal use.
7. Ensure government access to private data if necessary for public-interest reasons, such as public health monitoring.

B. Regulatory policies

Jurisdictional policies:

1. Resolve conflicting or uncertain legal jurisdictions that arise from cross-border data flows and multicountry facilities of cloud computing systems.
2. Resolve data sovereignty claims.

Creating a trusted digital environment:

3. Enact transparent policies for effective privacy protection of business, institutional, and personal data, including secondary uses of data by other commercial parties.
4. Enact transparent policies to ensure appropriate security of data stored or transmitted in the cloud and of cloud operations (to safeguard against outages).
5. Provide safeguards on third-party access to data stored in the cloud (e.g., U.S. government subpoenas of personal data for antiterrorism programs).

Competition policies:

6. Achieve interoperable technical standards and policies designed to avoid consumer and small and medium-size enterprise lock-in (so customers can switch cloud service providers more easily, often called data portability).
7. Ensure that dominant suppliers of cloud computing or of search and other data analytic services do not act anticompetitively. This could include looking at property rights (and thus rights to payments) from data.

The jurisdictional and trusted digital environment regulatory policies, sometimes bolstered by instincts to protect local competitors, are at the heart of demands for "data localization."[45] Countries use regulatory mechanisms to clarify and adjudicate jurisdictional authority over national data and enforce privacy and security safeguards. If proper user "consent" is provided, most regulatory frameworks allow data to cross borders or to be shared. This means that a great deal of business-to-business information flows operate within contractual relations where many privacy issues are resolved.[46] For example, in the United States, nongovernmental governance structures were created to regularize many data-handling issues involving farmers' data.

In addition, governments are taking steps intended to create a trusted digital environment that bolsters privacy, data security, and cyberinfrastructure operations.[47] These issues pose major questions about cloud operations and the movement of data across borders.

Chapters 7 and 8 explain how disagreements among countries over the specific rules governing privacy and security partly play out. These clashes were intensified by the revelations in June 2013 that the National Security Agency was secretly tapping into the communication traffic flowing into and out of the United States and that the agency routinely subpoenaed personal data on U.S. information company servers, including the data of foreign nationals. They also accelerated demands for data localization rules. EU and Chinese policies garnered the most attention, but Australia, Canada, Brazil, India, Indonesia, Malaysia, Korea, and others instituted similar policies. Chander and Le summarized these restrictions: (1) prior consent of a user before data are sent abroad,[48] (2) copies of all data sent abroad are retained on an in-country server, (3) bans on exports of certain classes of data, such as personal medical records, and (4) taxes on the export of data. In practice, major differences exist regarding information flows to individuals and to or among businesses. The most important movement toward creating international governance regimes for these measures has emerged in bilateral negotiations (such as those between the United States and the EU discussed in subsequent chapters) and in both regional and WTO trade negotiations. We return to these discussions later in this chapter.

Along with privacy and security and related jurisdictional issues, probably the thorniest issue associated with the cloud is *competition policy*. The increasing information intensity of all products and services, as well as the associated dynamics of Big Data, suggest that the dynamics of information markets will continue to spread globally. This process is fueled by the dynamics of network tipping (a result of Metcalfe's law)[49] and by increasing returns to scale phenomena.[50]

Competition involves specific markets and market structures. For governance purposes, it rarely begins in the abstract, but the IPD and digital platform dynamics call many of the conventional market definitions and measures used to judge market performance (such as prices) into question.[51] In a new technology environment, this is a challenge for even the most adroit regulators with responsibility for competition policy. In our experience, governance decisions begin in the context of an implicit or explicit "first premise" about the market because choices rarely play out with perfect information or free of political economic passions. Hence, if digital platform clusters grow in significance for most industries, thus upsetting conventional wisdom, policy makers must decide how much to worry about intellectually interesting efforts to paint the worst-case scenarios for competition.

In the United States, competition agencies begin with a premise that consumers gain advantages over time from innovation that is accelerated by healthy competition.[52] Even oligopoly does not automatically translate into consumer losses if, as Schumpeter pointed out, oligopolists compete vigorously to dislodge existing solutions by innovating.[53] As a result, when weighing market situations, competition authorities are careful not to favor short-term consumer benefits over long-term innovation considerations. The trick is to distinguish between problems that cause short-term maladies, which are almost inevitable in markets undergoing rapid reshuffling of their markets, from those that will seriously distort market performance in the longer term, as judged by consumer benefits and innovation. Although they are willing to require major remedies when they determine that a long-term problem exists, in practice, U.S. authorities have adopted more of a "wait and see" attitude with regard to market complaints.[54] Significantly, when making these judgments, the political economic pressures on the U.S. regulators are more manageable because the leading companies are largely American. This means that the regulators are sorting through complaints of "hometown" rivals.

The situation in jurisdictions like the EU is substantially different where there is some element of "them versus us" when confronting the American firms dominating their markets. Although U.S. competition authorities believe that their EU counterparts are not acting on protectionist logic, other parts of the European governance establishment reflect strands of hometown protection.

A second factor in the EU and many other countries is a competition policy tradition of preemptive action to correct possible market problems created by prior industrial policies. EU competition authorities cut their teeth on combating the pervasive influence of government-owned or -organized EU competitors. Furthermore, many of the East Asian market economies had long stretches of experiments in "industrial policy" to encourage local entrants' success in world markets. Even in an era more supportive of open markets, the policy legacy is one of broader sympathy for proactive market interventions.

Differences in leanings from first premises must be worked out in the context of the specific market situations fueled by the cloud. Many advocates worry about the dangers associated with the power of tipping resulting from network effects and the economies of scale associated with information-gathering and -processing infrastructures. Their fears are amplified because these same firms are the leaders in artificial intelligence and machine learning. This leads to warnings that a few oligopolists rooted in "pure" digital industries will control the core value of digital markets and then might spread into and take control of some traditionally non-IT markets.[55]

Popular discussions about competition often stall because of the failure to distinguish among the three different business models embodied under the "cloud" rubric or because they focus on the size of the competitors instead of on the "harm" they might perpetrate. Consider the case of infrastructure as a service. As noted, scale economies matter for the cloud. Being big has advantages, but harm is difficult to detect. Scholars of platform economics (see Chapter 3) would expect competition among strategic business models to promote the emergence of the cloud ecosystem. Moreover, high profit margins alone are not a test of competition. They reflect rewards in riskier businesses that involve high fixed costs.[56]

The largest cloud suppliers of infrastructure as a service are engaged in vigorous price competition, partly because of competition within their own ranks and partly because new entrants vigorously join the rapidly growing market. The largest public cloud venders (AWS, Microsoft second, and then Google, followed by IBM) continue to engage in intense price wars. In March 2014, Google sparked a major drop in cloud pricing, perhaps to foreclose any chance that Amazon would develop a cloud-based cash cow. The wars continued. In January 2016, after yet another cut, AWS boasted that it had cut prices fifty-one times. Google claimed that they still were much less expensive, in part because artificial intelligence advances allowed them to reduce power use in their data centers by 15%.[57] The providers were able to maintain solid profit margins because ICT infrastructure costs also continued to decline, however. This suggests both price and service differentiation competition. Further, the largest players' expectations about how markets should operate continually evolve. However, as prices fell and cybersecurity breaches proliferated, users grew more concerned with security than with price or agility.[58] This proliferation of specific user demands abetted by rapid market growth, plus deep financial pockets of firms like telecom carriers, has induced continued large-scale entry in the market to provide market discipline to the Big Three (Amazon, Microsoft, and Google).

Competition fears run deeper than the usual checklist of issues about dominance of infrastructure as a service. One fear is that the Big Three of the cloud will leverage their vertically integrated businesses to create structural advantages in software as a service. This concern emerges most dramatically in debates regarding EU competition policy safeguards for Google. We focus on this dispute because it illuminates many possible complaints involving all of the market leaders.

Google has about 90% of the search market in major European markets, which exceeds its U.S. share by more than twenty-five points (63.4% in January 2017) . EU competition policy complaints contend that Google uses its search engine to favor its related suite of IT services and its most lucrative advertisers on its search results. EU officials worry that this could skew competition in ways that harm consumers. Microsoft and many other American companies also criticize Google. When the U.S. Federal Trade Commission addressed these issues, it found no harm comparable to allegations made by the U.S. government when it brought its antitrust case against Microsoft's practices in the 1990s, while Microsoft still dominated computing software platforms.[59] The largest difference between the U.S. government cases against Microsoft and Google was that search engines are less able to lock in their customers than a computer system.[60]

If search were the only issue, then, as the EU competition commissioner originally proposed, some changes in the rules governing Google's search results would suffice. But concern about Google goes deeper. Many fear that the Google model of organizing information and providing services is intended to lure customers at zero cost into Google's domain (including its Android mobile operating system) and to gather users' data to generate profits. The harshest critics, often in the EU Parliament, charge that Google offers "free" service in return for building an ecosystem whose logic fundamentally undercuts privacy.[61] Critics complain that cloud-fueled tipping and scaling fueled by the cloud gives Google an unfair advantage.[62] Therefore, they call for the breakup of Google and for tougher protection of privacy and security. The EU antitrust regulator filed a "statement of objections" accusing Google of breaching EU antitrust rules in July 2016, the fourth complaint within one year.[63] (Non-EU complaints about digital diversity also exist.)

These broad anxieties have ascended to the highest political levels. At one time, the French government sought "digital sovereignty" with "made in France" labels for cloud computing and related digital services and devices. It also considered taxing the functional equivalent of Internet searches.[64] The German chancellor, Merkel, expressed interest in creating a EU Internet to enable European companies to keep EU data in Europe.[65] Similarly, the EU commissioner in charge of its digital agenda called for a secure European cloud capacity.[66]

The specific charges on competition relate to how Google can marry search with the cloud to organize and retrieve every sort of content. In short, critics worry that powerful infrastructure in the cloud reinforces Google's dominance in a major platform for software as a service, another facet of cloud services.

In a world of digital DNA, two cautions immediately arise regarding this logic. First, technology continues to shift rapidly. Google established its dominance in a world of personal computing. The shift to mobile devices is a threat because Google is far less dominant in mobile where specific apps for services bypass general search engines and reliance on social networking as a portal to the Internet erodes Google's market position.[67] Instant messaging apps also are becoming platforms that support their own ecosystem of apps. Down the technological road are uncertainties about how the rise of voice (fueled by machine learning and artificial intelligence) and virtual-reality interfaces may change the market. Second, the IPD causes constant change in business models. Network dynamics have made social networking, an area where Google has floundered, into an enormous factor. Here, Facebook has dominated the global landscape, abetted by its Instagram and WhatsApp subsidiaries, and made itself into the principal rival of Google for digital advertising.[68] Cultural differences also generate openings for rivals. In China, Tencent's WeChat messaging app is dominant. And LINE is a successful Korean-owned (by Naver) Japanese rival to WhatsApp.

Still, it is worth considering a scenario where Google remains resilient in its leadership in search. European authorities have identified three knotty problems created by dominance. One is the terms on which Google uses others' content. For example, the ire of German and French publishing groups ignited a push for stricter terms of competition action against Google.[69] European newspaper publishers complained that Google ignored their property rights to content and that they should be paid for any access to their materials.[70] This represented major money for publishers because, by one estimate, a major newspaper market like the United Kingdom has seen ad revenue for print drop by 50% since 2000 (to about 700 million pounds), whereas total British Internet ad revenue soared to levels roughly five times as large.[71] This content dispute was more about how to divide economic rents than about competition or innovation.[72] Moreover, the dispute is not unique to Google. Online content providers, including newspapers and magazines, worry that they could be intermediated by a "news feed" service like the one promoted by Facebook. Although a partner like Facebook might help provide a faster, more powerful platform, the publishers would cede the information feedback to Facebook, which maintains the platform. This would provide Facebook, which has an edge in gathering information on consumer behavior, with a huge advantage for targeting digital advertising.[73]

The EU plan for a single digital market announced in 2016 raised a possibility that will require payments by Google if it posted excerpts of content from, for example, newspapers with its links. Critics have dubbed this plan the "snippet tax."[74] The commission pointedly noted that it will not tax hyperlinks only, but will decide whether to tax snippets later. U.S. officials noted to us that the German commissioner for the digital economy, Gunther Oettinger, has a strong interest in such an adjustment in copyright payments.

Second, the EU competition authority has argued that Google illegally favors its own advertiser-supported content and services over other suppliers.[75] Whatever the merits of the specific complaint, the revenue involved for Google on these applications, where it badly trails Amazon, is negligible. The real issue is whether the general learning cycle from providing search will give Google unmatched advantages in countless other vertical applications.[76] As of mid-2016, many predicted that Google would face a multibillion-Euro fine for abusing its web search monopoly.[77]

Both of these controversies turn on how one views the power of digital platforms and their staying power. Some platforms are "stickier" than others. Other platforms, like major digital stores, can be difficult for entrants to replicate, although the costs to duplicate them or to significantly differentiate from them are manageable. Still, firms with market power require oversight, especially if the IPD allows a few digital firms to take commanding positions in multiple nondigital markets.

Many platforms are less sticky than often assumed, probably because first mover and tipping advantages rest on a market's specific consumer surplus characteristics.[78] Google tipped the market for search because its main business was in the general consumer search market, where network effects and scale economies lowered the costs of delivering new service features. Google's command of Big Data also helped it improve its ability to respond to innovation, reinforced its quasi-monopoly in search, and boosted its revenues as it learned to better match search results to advertiser needs. Some predict that Google could secure generalized oligopoly, but this is an overgeneralization.

Many digital and digitally infused markets have segmented supply chain and consumer demand preferences, which allow different types of platforms to emerge. Dating sites keyed to religion and other factors show the variety of consumer demand.[79] Similarly, regional cultural factors may favor local suppliers of social networking applications, such as Snow from South Korea.[80] The variety in the hardware and software of gaming systems also show how supply chains can differ. The proliferation of specialized applications and products enabled by the IPD may blunt some competition worries about platform monopolies. In addition, platforms can create interdependencies such as those between computers and printers, which limit market participants' pricing and supply decisions in ways that defy normal expectations about market power.[81]

The same phenomenon appeared in digital services. Providers of credit cards and online payment systems, such as PayPal and Stripe, learn from the pattern of user transactions and either provide new services independently or sell their analyses to third parties. This allows large retailers to use mobile technology to invent new payment systems that bypass traditional payment systems.[82] If they owned their own system, they would not need to pay fees to Visa and other card issuers. They also would own the information generated by their credit transactions. This is one reason why ambitious Japanese firms, such as SoftBank and Rakuten, are investing in innovative financial services that could be profitable niches in e-commerce and points of vulnerability for Google. Similarly, in China, firms like Alibaba and China PnR are carving out major financial alternatives.[83]

The production disruption reinforces diversification. As new production techniques make products cheaper and smarter, more software and information are embedded in end products. The growth of updatable "firmware" produces specialized information-gathering and analytic systems that share many characteristics with gaming systems. More generally, the Internet of Things opens the way to specialized platforms and cloud applications. Google faces increased competition threats as mobile devices replace computers as the access point for information because people often bypass search in favor of specialized "apps." Google implicitly recognized this diversity in its race to enter traditional manufactured product markets, such as autos, while also promoting its Android operating system for mobiles. Growing diversity also implies that a more complicated division of labor will evolve in the digital platform space. Google and a few other firms could dominate the cloud and some verticals even as the value added created by digital technology grows more diverse across a wider array of goods and services. Still, the EU competition authorities in 2016 began a probe of whether Google's licensing practices for Android discriminated against competitors.[84]

The third competition issue noted by the EU, the development of interoperable standards, arises because cloud vendors and cloud service offerings may have different system standards for data storage formats and other items. As happened when Microsoft and Apple competed over software platforms, there is concern that customers, especially individuals and SMEs, will be "locked in" once they commit to a cloud vendor because it is costly to move their data to another vendor. This also applies to cloud-enabled applications like Fitbit—it is difficult to transfer personal workout data from a PC to an Apple device.

Compatible standards can temper the risk that new entrants will be frozen out by lock in. The flip side of using policy to induce standardization is the risk that innovation will slow down or freeze altogether. Although technology develops rapidly, competing platforms (standards systems) promote experimentation and induce greater competitive efforts among rival systems. It is risky to prematurely pick the "best" technology; the process could be hijacked for industrial policy purposes. Over time, however, translators and other cloud-based solutions diminish platform island issues. Well-funded startups now offer their own platforms to enable interoperability among cloud applications of diverse companies.[85] Moreover, large users are pressuring vendors for easier inter-operability options.

In short, experimentation and contestation exist regarding the terms of sharing the underlying digital platform. These activities push contending parties to make rival claims for new policy interventions. However, it is difficult to pinpoint the "right" technological disruption from the viewpoint of the public interest. "Easy" clear cases arise, but the big issues frequently require trial-and-error testing to determine appropriate parameters. Private market responses may be more efficient over time than a new policy intervention. Sometimes governments can accelerate innovation using strategic policy interventions, but they must empower learning and experimentation and also consider a wide range of responses to problems, including private and civil society solutions.[86]

In addition to appropriately weighting the value of innovation, a prudent governance approach to competition policy should recognize the following:

1. *Modular flexibility remains important in all phases of the IPD.* Lowering the transactional costs of mixing and matching all assets, including intellectual property, personal information, and pieces of equipment, is central to successful innovation and robust competition. (Modularity can be consistent with strong intellectual property. A modular world will mix traditional intellectual property and techniques such as technology commons or open-source projects.)

2. *Competition among technologies and business models should be encouraged.* Central command and control guidance, such as mandatory national technical standards, can restrict innovation. But governance can use other measures, such as performance standards and investments in shared assets, to achieve the balance between moving public-interest goals forward and allowing technological and business experimentation.

6.4. The Political Economy Informing the Cloud Debate

The cloud is not just a philosopher's stone that elicits passionate, but also disciplined thinking about the optimal governance of the digital world. It also touches on conflicting political goals and market ambitions. We had conversations on four continents with government officials, corporate executives, and NGO leaders. They saw themselves as engaged in a long battle to curb U.S. commercial dominance during the past two decades and worried that the cloud could open the door to two more decades of U.S. dominance of the IT space. U.S. dominance during the 1980s and 1990s was symbolized by "Wintel" (the intersection of Windows and Intel processors as architectures) and was reinforced by complementary software (e.g., Oracle) and hardware (e.g., Cisco and Qualcomm). Now, they fear that Google, Microsoft, and Amazon, the leaders of cloud computing, will dominate information markets and new markets created by the Internet of Things. The cloud is a new architecture with large economies of scale. U.S. firms are ahead on the learning curve for creating cloud infrastructure and operations. They already are deeply entrenched in the digitally enabled markets that the cloud is transforming. Furthermore, cloud capabilities may allow other U.S. giants (such as Apple, IBM, and Facebook) to dominate many of the most lucrative IT applications.[87] Hence, the leaders we spoke with were nearly unanimous in hoping to avoid another era of overwhelming U.S. technological dominance. Given their additional misgivings about American security and privacy policies, the global stage was arranged for trouble.

Thus far, we have analyzed the debate surrounding competition policies to anchor governance of the cloud and the general concerns about American dominance of the ICT in some detail. It also is useful to add nuance on the market positions and policy approaches, in short, to provide perspective on specific policy stances. Despite the policy conflicts, a common assumption exists that any strategy for ICT and the IPD must embrace a central role for the capabilities of a cloud-enabled world. Therefore, everyone has interests, albeit mixed ones, in identifying governance anchors that make the world market more predictable. This is the classic challenge of a coordination benefit that is entangled in a cooperation challenge, explained in the previous chapter.

The United States is a status quo power with regard to the cloud because it extends the evolution of the U.S. approach to IT. The U.S. share of the world market for "lower-end" cloud functions outside its borders was perhaps 85% circa 2013, but the Information Technology and Innovation Foundation estimated that restrictive measures for the cloud could reduce that share to 55% in a few years.[88] The U.S. response to others' concerns was tardy and timid, however. In 2009, U.S. IT business leaders initially bet that the growing rumbles about the cloud would pass quickly, requiring only minor policy adjustments, perhaps including a few new rules for international trade. As many in the corporate community became more worried by the Obama administration's economic agenda, their skepticism about Obama initiatives on data privacy and security regulation also grew. Yet, without a proactive domestic strategy, crafting a forceful U.S. international strategy for these issues became more difficult.

To fill in the global tableau, we briefly extend our discussion beyond the familiar American landscape. Suspicions about the cloud elicited different international responses. We consider four market centers to illustrate the different political economic incentives—Japan, Korea, China, and the EU—and then discuss interests of large, influential global users.

Japan remains the dominant center for Asian corporate R&D. Despite decades of slow growth, Japan has many strong companies, especially specialized suppliers to other businesses.[89] Its strength in IT and telecoms ebbed after the early 1990s, however, when Japan missed the shifts to Internet-enabled computing and the new mobile communications architectures. Predictably, Japan is not a prominent cloud player internationally because its firms mainly focused on the relatively insulated Japanese domestic market and the overseas subsidiaries of Japanese firms.[90]

A new generation of competitors is again expanding the Japanese global position. The main innovators in services are two unconventional, entrepreneurial companies. SoftBank is Japan's largest firm through its control of Yahoo! Japan. (Yahoo! Japan and Yahoo!'s Alibaba stake were not part of the deal in which Verizon purchased Yahoo! in July 2016.)[91] Rakuten is the dominant Japanese e-commerce firm.[92] SoftBank and Rakuten are both partly services conglomerates and partly investment bankers for service firms worldwide. SoftBank leads the most successful set of Japanese IT expansions outside Japan (such as its $100 million investment in Tokopedia, an Indonesian e-commerce firm, and its even larger stake in Snapdeal, a similar firm in India). Yahoo! Japan also invests in thousands of e-commerce and information application firms and is the majority owner of Sprint, the third largest U.S. telecom carrier. Its minority share in Alibaba, the Chinese giant, is its crown jewel. Rakuten describes itself as building ecosystem mixing finance, e-commerce, and other services (through such purchases as that of Vibe, the large messaging app based in Cyprus). Both firms are focused on innovative financial payments and credit systems enabled by the cloud.[93] Japan's other leading services firms depend on cloud dynamics for much of their large service properties.[94] The Japanese leadership position in the massive online gaming industry is mainly a result of its gaming companies that specialize in mobile apps, not traditional hardware and software units like those of Nintendo.

With regard to hardware, foreign penetration of the Japanese market for equipment and services has improved markedly but remains less prominent than in other countries. The strengths of Japanese firms in telecoms, terminals, and IT equipment have become specialized product offerings for industrial groups' IT systems and components (such as chips for equipment enabled by the Internet of Things, robotics, and video displays for every kind of terminal).[95] For example, on the terminal layer, in July 2016, shortly after the Brexit vote, Japan's SoftBank launched a $31 billion bid to acquire ARM Holdings, a British designer of semiconductors used in mobile devices.[96] The acquisition was completed in September 2016.[97]

Japanese information services benefited from a home base that remains, because of language barriers and customer habits, attuned to domestic suppliers. As a result, even as Japan has adopted cybersecurity policies similar to the mix of other industrial democracies, ferment over the cloud did not markedly fan Japanese public concerns regarding privacy. Although Japan's privacy regime borrows from the EU model, its application is more relaxed. The rules do not restrict the location of cloud infrastructures or the movement of data.

Korea, in contrast to Japan, enthusiastically embraced global ICT standards and built on the revival of U.S. ICT fortunes in the 1990s. A group of Korean chaebols (including Samsung, LG, and SK hynix) emerged as global leaders in computer chips and many kinds of terminal equipment, including computing, telecoms, and audio-visual.[98] Korean telecom carriers traditionally cooperated with government industrial policy goals to upgrade Korean technology leadership. Early on, they deployed 3G wireless technologies and championed the use of code-division multiple-access wireless platforms that came to dominate the core of 3G networks. This fed the demand base of Korean telecom terminal makers. Telecom terminals, especially Samsung's, are its strongest entry point into expanded value shares. Korea's strategic weakness was software, even for Samsung, in mobile operating systems.[99] Thus, Korea strived to be a leader in creating 5G, the next generation of broadband wireless technology.[100] At the same time, as explained in Chapter 1, Korea tried with mixed success to build a larger ecosystem for startups resembling the Silicon Valley model.

Korea's successful domestic IT service companies were built on two main strengths. First, they were early leaders in leveraging Korea's high-penetration, high-bandwidth networks. From the start, Korean broadband Internet speeds were among the fastest anywhere and its broadband penetration exceeded 100%. This allowed Korean firms to experiment with rich visual interactive environments. Second, they optimized for local language and culture (especially Korea's devotion to mobile online gaming). The Korean search leaders at the end of 2015 were Naver, with a 77% share, and Daum, with a 20% share.[101] Naver's LINE Corp. is the dominant messaging app for Japanese users under the age of forty, and it has expanded briskly in Taiwan, Thailand, and Indonesia. This led to a successful billion-dollar initial public offering in June 2016.[102] This second strength was augmented by the growing popularity of Korean culture, such as pop music, globally. These new entrants, as noted in Chapter 1 benefited from the Park government's effort to decrease its reliance on traditional chaebols.

Local firms were reinforced by Korean security rules (privacy rules) that were implemented in response to North Korea. One such rule forbids South Korean mapping data to reside on servers outside the country, which effectively blocked Google from using its vast geospatial data and mapping expertise to build market share in search.[103] The Korean government also planned to use cloud computing to upgrade its technology to capture 10% of the global market by 2018. It incentivized government agencies and firms to convert to cloud operations, but its focus on security tilted markets toward "private cloud" deployments instead of the public cloud. Amazon, Microsoft, and the cloud subsidiaries of KT and SK, the two dominant Korean carriers, dominate the Korean market.[104] Korea's leverage on digitally enabled markets is built on terminal equipment and digital service (such as gaming) partnerships with networks that are embracing cloud computing. There are signs of progress in Northeast Asia. Still, the efforts to expand to the United States and Southeast Asia have had only limited success.[105]

China is engaged in a tug of war between liberalization and mercantilism.[106] After entering the WTO in 2001, it opened its market to global competition and is now the largest or among the largest markets for many OECD technology firms. As China moves from low-value, export-led manufacturing growth to higher-value-added exports, many influential policy makers want China to become the largest supplier to major technology markets. They believe that to move up in value, China must boost its R&D and infrastructure investment to supplement conventional policy tools. Hence, the government is providing generous financial support for its firms and instituting measures to rapidly advance priority technologies. For example, the Ministry of Science and Technology in the 12th Five Year Special Plan in 2012 singled out cloud technology.[107] Beijing now provides financial support and presses its agencies and state-owned enterprises to contract for cloud services. Regional governments also promote public–private partnerships to create cloud facilities in their areas.

China's policies go beyond normal industrial promotion; they also exercise policy muscle to erode the position of foreign firms. China's continuing refusal to liberalize markets for many priority technology areas stalled the Information Technology Agreement negotiations until July 2015.[108] Foreign firms and their home governments are anxious about pressure for technology transfer to Chinese firms and about subsidies in the tens of billions of dollars by state-guided banks and state-owned enterprises to some technology exporters. They worry about technology standards that favor Chinese firms and about government administrative guidance to opt for Chinese suppliers. China also used competition policy tools to charge that foreign firms acted in anticompetitive fashion against Chinese firms. This industrial policy mix is reinforced by Chinese concerns that an unbridled Internet is politically risky. Their definition of privacy and security diverge significantly from that used by the EU and others. Most recently, they justify policies designed to create Chinese control over core ICT technologies.[109]

However, reformers exist. A cluster of academic experts, government officials, and business leaders favor less intervention and more market opening. Rhetorically, President Xi endorsed greater reliance on market competition as the primary economic driver, but progress to implement such measures is underwhelming. In our

2016 discussions with Chinese leaders, there is great enthusiasm for small-scale entrepreneurship, such as the "makers movement," but they remain guarded on crucial details of state-owned enterprise reforms. In addition, foreign firms are skeptical about state-funded "private" investment funds that target strategic technology priorities such as semiconductors.[110] They may, as Chinese officials suggest, be more market oriented but their control structures apparently allow for substantial government guidance, thus allowing for a disguised form of state subsidy.

Significantly, a cadre of Chinese IT companies expanded globally as China developed its robust, largely Chinese-owned Internet ecosystem.[111] The three initial successes among hardware companies were Lenovo in computers, Huawei in telecom equipment, and ZTE in mobile handsets. A fourth entrant, Xiaomi, uses a blended service and mobile handset model. In parallel, the Chinese government shielded Alibaba, Tencent, Baidu, and 360 Search, the entrepreneurial domestic juggernauts of the Chinese Internet service world, from outside competition. (In 2015, Baidu had a 54.3% share of the Chinese search market, but was losing ground to Qihoo 360, with a 29.2% share, and Sogou, with a 14.7% share.)[112] These companies spawned a host of wealthy technology leaders, which are taking their companies and investment funds into world markets, including Silicon Valley. They are actively pursuing global market integration while taking value from the Chinese telecom firms. These incumbents retain enormous protected markets that generate dependable profits, as the telcos are losing value added to IT service and equipment firms.[113] More boldly, Alibaba has built two cloud centers in Silicon Valley to meet regional customer demands and perhaps in part to respond to AWS plans to provide services in China.[114] In addition, hybrid plays of cloud computing and robotics (an industry in which China is one of the top four globally) are emerging from Chinese entrepreneurs, such as CloudMinds, which has research and operations centers in both China and California.[115] But these ventures also run into problems in their overseas operations because the software architectures and services developed in the protected Chinese market must be revamped considerably for global operations.

The EU embraced a muscular response to the cloud. Except for SAP, Europe lacks large world leaders in general IT and services markets. (Europe did spawn Skype, several specialized services companies, and ARM Holdings, which designs low-power-consumption chips for mobile devices.)[116] The dearth of major players in the pure IT space provokes continuing consternation in Europe. European economic strategists favored accelerating movement toward a single European digital market to help its startups grow in a market larger than America's.[117] This included the free movement of data within the EU, including ending restrictions on the movement of sensitive data such as patient health information. It would also include measures to make cloud-computing suppliers subject to certification procedures and measures to make it easier for users to switch cloud suppliers. These would, in theory, support the needs of specialized user groups. They also favored strategies designed to create "shared assets" and identified specific strengths and weaknesses that might help bolster Europe's efforts to build "industry verticals" on its strengths in telecom equipment and services. Setting technical standards and guidance on improving interoperability of applications, especially for public-interest purposes (such as energy, transportation, and health), featured prominently in EU planning.

Europe's major telecom equipment players are Ericsson and Nokia (which took over Alcatel–Lucent, the third major player in January 2016). These suppliers are expanding into cloud security technologies and other value-added functions through software additions to their network equipment offerings.[118] They seek a comparative advantage against challengers like Huawei in higher-end networking technology. For example, Alcatel–Lucent is tightly focused on ultrabroadband, Internet Protocol networking, and cloud infrastructure through software defined networks for cloud centers. These firms all seek a larger value share at the intersection of IT and communications networking.

European telecom carriers comprise one of the largest EU business associations. Spain's Telefónica, Norway's Telenor, and other major carriers that operate in several countries outside of Europe believe that EU telecom regulations stifled network investment for advanced broadband.[119] They also complain bitterly that EU competition policy prevented the creation of a consolidated network of large EU-wide carriers. Like telecom carriers everywhere, they wanted to expand their possibilities beyond the traditional telecom network services. (Mobile expansion boosted their growth for a decade, but mobile profit margins are sagging.) They complain that they need a "level playing field" against IT companies that are taking over communications markets for long-distance calling and messaging by offering Internet services that bypass traditional telecommunications regulations. Further, these IT crossovers into the telecom domain operate under different security rules than large telecom operators because they do not control the core physical infrastructure.

National regulators prize achievements related to competition policy, so, predictably, operators' policy complaints created major political headaches in Europe. Europeans enjoy relatively inexpensive broadband because competitors can resell the network capacity of large carriers while selectively investing in supplemental infrastructure.[120] But by early 2014, major political leaders, including Merkel and François Hollande, came to favor reviving the core of the EU ICT sector and sought to advance the single digital EU communications market and to permit significant cross-border mergers to create integrated European players.[121] Implicitly, European authorities want to help their telecom carriers expand in the IT world. But complications sometimes arose, as when German privacy policies caused Deutsche Telekom to launch an email service that routes German emails only through the German network.[122] We anticipate that entry into cloud services, in ways that mirror Verizon's approach, will follow.

In addition, the explosion of mobile video available on the Internet and mobile devices persuaded the EU to focus on audiovisual media services. In March 2010, the EU Parliament approved the Audiovisual Media Services Directive (2010/13/EU) to improve coordination of certain laws, regulations, and administrative action of member states. The rise of the cloud and the country of origin challenges it raises for policy makers led in mid-2015 to new consultations that updated the directive, yielding in May 2016 a new legislative proposal by the EU Commission to amend the directive.[123] Major new elements of the amended proposal focused on simplifying and clarifying cooperation procedures about country-of-origin principles and reducing burdens on television broadcasters to deal with issues raised by Netflix and other providers of content using the cloud.[124]

Europe's other strength is in verticals. As discussed previously, some worry that big data companies might use their IT capacity to seize market value from traditional goods and services impacted by the IPD. Some successful EU sectors, such as transportation equipment, where products are becoming dependent on IT, are at risk.[125] As the Internet of Things evolves, products like cars have become information terminals, and industry associations and the EU Commission favor cooperative programs that blend an industry's specialized IT capabilities with, for instance, public infrastructure development.

The EU introduced digital technology programs for roads, railways, and electric utilities. This public policy made sense, but it is easier to implement EU privacy rules in business-to-business or business-to-government agreements. Privacy rules make big data companies' tasks more complicated, so the implicit bonus is for European verticals. A subtle dynamic is at play here. By definition, regional transportation and energy patterns are optimized regionally. Those projects that succeed can serve as demonstration projects for bidding on projects in other regions. It is less important for these infrastructure projects to observe and experiment globally than to engage with data for commercial purposes at a regional level.

The EU rules do not preclude U.S. cloud-based operations. (For example, Microsoft won EU approval of its cloud storage privacy rules because it used its policies on privacy as a differentiator for its cloud operations.)[126] The political economic incentives for the EU, given its market strengths, are to expand from the network into the IT space and to organize verticals that work from terminals (e.g., a vehicle) upward into the IT space in cooperation with network firms. Cloud policies and privacy and security considerations can be attuned to this foundational principle.

When global ICT rules were set during the 1980s and 1990s, a group of powerful international ICT users helped drive the project forward. This group included many financial institutions, large multinational manufacturing firms, and other companies. Given their early embrace of globalized ICT, financial institutions and other service firms were particularly invested in updating the rules. Some major chief executive officers personally spent time on the effort to signal its importance. The U.S. Coalition of Service Industries and its counterparts elsewhere continue to support developing common rules for the cloud infrastructure. However, given the increasing dependence on ICT, the absence of a similar level of political attention among chief executive officers of huge corporate users today is striking. This may reflect tensions over the possible entry of ICT firms into the downstream markets of their users.

In sum, the future political economy of cloud governance will depend largely on whether important users decide that the status quo suffices. Perhaps the heavily IT-focused financial industry, given its specialized regulatory structure, has adequately hived off its interests from broader ICT policy. For large global manufacturers that embraced the IPD logic, cloud restrictions have yet to slow them down. Cloud capacity rises and prices fall. Restrictions on data movement are worrisome, but so far business-to-business data sharing of corporate data has not received top-level attention by data authorities. The next chapter considers cybersecurity for financial industries. Cybersecurity is a huge priority for these firms, but they do not see it as a cloud issue. In short, although they support the cloud, it is low on their shopping list for government policy.

6.5. Government Policies: Attempts at Trade Deals to Set an International Baseline

The commercial implications of the cloud finally led to serious consideration of the way in which international trade rules may provide a partial response to major IPD governance challenges. But can trade rules contribute a fuller governance solution if MSOs are substantially involved in implementing policy? If so, would this also create conditions that encourage partial convergence of national regulatory systems, but recognize that full harmonization is neither possible nor desirable?

If the political will to compromise on a core principle exists, negotiators excel at determining details. On major tasks such as the cloud ecosystem, negotiators will fail unless they reach an understanding about common principles. The principles of cause and effect and normative expectations were discussed earlier. Here, we focus on the basic principles and what they might mean for the market. We identify the promise and the problems.

Negotiations rarely begin in a policy vacuum. Prior agreements usually set precedents and boundaries. The same is true when tackling the cloud ecosystem. Although several Free Trade Agreements have gone further, the foundational texts are the WTO deals that grew out of the Uruguay Round and the policy principles embedded therein. However, it is essential to incorporate MSOs and NGOs in the mix to successfully implement and monitor new trade agreements in an era of rapid technological disruption and new arrays of political economic power. That is the task of trade negotiators in the future.

The cloud ecosystem is partially covered by trade obligations. General obligations on all services are set out in the Uruguay Round General Agreement on Trade in Services. Annexes for specific service industries drill down into specific commitments for market access and into specific hard and soft obligations for conduct and institutions. These agreements cover information and telecommunication services. Arguably, cloud computing, since it is a remote computer-processing and storage system delivered by telecom facilities, already is covered by the Uruguay Round texts.[127] This includes cross-border data flows.[128] The prior agreements simplify the task for trade negotiators because some elements can be repeated in a more specific context for the cloud ecosystem. In addition, the negotiation can clarify the meaning of past commitments. That said, there is a substantial difference between inferring obligations from past commitments and reaching practical agreement on their meaning for new market situations.

In 2011, the United States and the EU collaborated at the WTO's Council for Trade in Services to develop a set of starting principles for dealing with ICT in a Trade in Services Agreement (this agreement is a plurilateral negotiation in which China does not participate). The idea was to build on the legacy of past WTO agreements.[129] Several of the principles draw from frameworks that inform all service trade rules. They include obligations of transparency in rule-making and decisions, cooperation to improve international development (digital divide concerns), and the creation of a strong regulatory authority independent of the suppliers and with authority to perform its duties. One principle built on the 1997 Basic Telecommunications Agreement obligation to create appropriate institutional arrangements and decision processes for making choices about radio spectrum. Other principles reaffirmed the Basic Telecommunications Agreement's principle that it should be straightforward to get a license to provide competitive telecom services and that entrants had the right to interconnect on cost-effective terms with the major public telecom networks. (A cloud-enabled service might want its own telecom delivery network to major customers.) Yet another principle encouraged negotiators to grant full foreign participation in the sector, including through the right of foreign ownership. All of these were tweaks on the original Basic Telecommunications Agreement obligations.

At their core, the three crucial principles discussed next speak to how the General Agreement on Trade in Services framework should be clarified for the cloud ecosystem. Both sides agree on the need to at least partially exempt financial services. The EU insisted that measures to protect privacy and security be exempted from these principles as well, at least until the conclusion of a satisfactory U.S.–EU agreement on data privacy protection.

First, the *Cross-Border Principle* affirms the free flow of data internationally for commercial services. It affirms the right of a foreign company to access its own business data across national borders to provide a service. A bank that needs to check on customer accounts from its servers located abroad may do so. If a search engine needs to access mapping data from a regional center abroad to answer a query, it may do so, as may the search engine's customers. Foreign suppliers also may access publicly available data in other countries (e.g., official national income accounting data).[130]

Second, the *Local Infrastructure Principle* affirms that suppliers are free to locate infrastructure wherever they wish. Using large cloud hubs located in other countries would be permitted.[131] A company would not need to create a local subsidiary. Thus, a Facebook user in Thailand could use Facebook services and facilities in the United States if she wished, and Facebook would not need to set up a Thai subsidiary. This principle also grants Facebook equal treatment to a local social media company when it seeks access to network resources. Imagine that Google Auto needed spectrum for a private network to serve Thai vehicles that use Google Auto for a car's navigation system. Google should be treated the same as Thai firms when competing to obtain needed spectrum.

Third, the *Open Network and Network Access Principle* reinforces the right of customers to use extraterritorial suppliers of services via public telecommunications networks. It also states that government policy should respect technological neutrality in how a service is technically organized and delivered.[132] (As an example, companies could deliver new software or video content either by broadband networks or by traditional compact discs.) To paraphrase, there are different technical architectures for different folks. But this principle also recognizes the desirability of promoting interoperability as long as the neutrality premise is respected.

Taken together, free flow of data, freedom to choose where to locate facilities, and nondiscriminatory access to network resources needed to deliver cloud services would provide a robust bottom line for the market. This is a good start, but two types of problems arise related to market access and the conduct and obligations involving a trusted digital environment.

The now abandoned TPP negotiation somewhat fleshed out these issues (see Chapter 9), but at a global level it is the Trade in Services Agreement talks that best symbolized slow progress. Until signs of significant progress became evident in early

2016, the U.S.–EU trade initiative on cloud markets was stalled.[133] Australia offered two principles at the General Agreement on Trade in Services discussions that took an important step toward addressing these issues. They suggested the following:[134]

1. "Online consumer protection: Members should recognise the importance of maintaining and adopting measures to protect consumers using electronic commerce in order to enhance consumer welfare and confidence in electronic commerce. Members should also encourage cooperation between their respective national agencies responsible for consumer protection on activities related to cross-border electronic commerce."

2. "Online Personal Data Protection: Members should adopt or maintain a domestic legal framework, which ensures the protection of the personal data of the users of electronic commerce. Governments should share information on their experiences in protecting the personal data of the users of electronic commerce."

To briefly summarize, the cloud is reshaping the economics and technological characteristics of the world's digital DNA. The cloud's dynamics favor international technical architectures and therefore impinge on domestic markets. Governments have responded with some ambivalence. They try to stimulate use of the cloud because of its performance advantages, but they worry that the cloud may reinforce American dominance of IT markets in coming years. They also fear that giant U.S. corporate leaders enabled by the cloud are implicitly channeling U.S. governance values about trade-offs concerning the balance of competition and innovation, including safeguards for privacy and security. We explored the ways that these concerns become entangled with the protection of local industries because cloud dynamics are upsetting business models far beyond the markets for purely digital products. We further illustrated the complexities of the political economy of the cloud by examining the different arrays of interests of Japan, South Korea, China, and the EU. We concluded by showing how issues propelled by the cloud began to shape negotiations in trade policy as governments began to look for an acceptable common ground on these governance issues. The rest of Part III and then Chapter 9 lead to our conclusions about a way forward on governance.

Notes

1. We draw heavily on Peter Cowhey and Michael Kleeman, "Unlocking the Benefits of Cloud Computing for Emerging Economies—A Policy Overview," October 2012, https://www.wto.org/english/tratop_e/serv_e/wkshop_june13_e/unlocking_benefits_e.pdf.

2. Peter Mell and Tim Grance, "The NIST Definition of Cloud Computing," U.S. National Institute of Science and Technology, Special Publication 800-145, September 2011, http://dx.doi.org/10.6028/NIST.SP.800-145.

3. Amazon, Microsoft, and especially Google are vertically integrated and involved in all aspects of the cloud, including processors, data centers, domestic and international network assets (dark fiber), and major ownership in undersea fiber-optic cable systems. Their investments impact the quality of service, interconnection, costs with last-mile providers, and the quality of their delivered products to customers. Apple also is a major cloud player; its iTunes, iCloud, and other Apple services are cloud based, albeit in private Apple clouds.

4. The cloud can be deployed in three different configurations. First, it can be the private capability of a single organization. Some manufacturers (like GE) took this path. Second, it can be a shared private resource of a consortium of users. Third, it can be a public commercial resource that is owned and managed by a private entity and is available to any user on commercial terms, as are Amazon's cloud offerings. Peter Mell and Tim Grance, "The Cloud Dividend-Part One: The Economic Benefits of Cloud Computing to Business and the Wider EMEA Economy," The Center for Economics and Business Research, December 2010. Note that hybrid models also are possible.

5. Naadhi, an Indian IT service firm, moved its project monitoring-and-reporting application to the cloud to enable prospective customers to try it before they fully committed to the service.

6. James Crabtree, "Bangalore Steps Out of the World's Back-Office," Financial Times, July 21, 2015, p. 12.

7. "Microsoft—The Economics of the Cloud, 2010," http://news.microsoft.com/download/archived/presskits/cloud/docs/The-Economics-of-the-Cloud.pdf.

8. Michael Armbrust et al., "A View of Cloud Computing," Communications of the ACM, 53, no. 4 (April 2010): 50–58.

9. "The 5 Largest Data Centers in the World," Forbes, accessed May 19, 2016, http://www.forbes.com/pictures/gikh45hdm/range-international-info/#7512c4951e99. "Switch Starts 2016 as the World's Largest Colocation Data Center to be 100% Green," accessed July 15, 2016, https://www.supernap.com/news/switch-largest-data-center-100-percent-green.html.

10. "Silver Lining: Tech Giants Are Waging a Price War to Win Other Firms' Computing Business," The Economist, August 30, 2014, pp. 59–60, and "The Cheap Convenient Cloud: As Cloud-Computing Prices Keep Falling, the Whole IT Business Will Change," The Economist, April 18, 2015, pp. 60–61.

11. Amazon announced new data centers for China, India, Canada, and the United Kingdom to be built in 2016. All would be hubs of local networks. Leslie Hook, "Amazon's Cloud Puts Retail Unit in the Shade," Financial Times, January 27, 2016, p. 14.

12. See the July 2015 estimates of Synergy Research, https://www.srgresearch.com/articles/big-four-cloud-providers-are-leaving-rest-market-behind.

13. Data Center Knowledge, Special Report, "The World's Largest Data Centers," accessed December 13, 2014, http://www.datacenterknowledge.com/special-report-the-worlds-largest-data-centers/.

14. John Ruwitch and Paul Carsten, "Alibaba Opens First U.S. Cloud Center, Enters Hotly Contested Market," Reuters, March 3, 2015, http://www.reuters.com/article/2015/03/04/us-alibaba-group-usa-cloud-idUSKBN0M002Y20150304.

15. ABB estimated that 5.75 million servers are added annually. In India, HCL, E2E, and others operate cloud-supporting data centers. In Mexico, Amazon and Google operate cloud-serving centers, as does Telmex, the dominant Mexican telecommunications carrier. In South Africa, Vodacom and Teraco operate several centers and a new firm, Pamoja, is deploying a Pan-African cloud service based in South Africa, Kenya, and other African nations. ABB, Powering the Cloud—ABB Infographic, 2014, accessed December 14, 2014, http://www.abb.com/product/ap/db0003db004052/e950c90f13518ffbc125788f0030bda0.aspx.

16. In 2010, a divisional chief technology officer of a major IT company explained this to us, but these requirements were largely overlooked in public debates on privacy and the cloud. A work using similar logic is Daniel Castro, "The False Promise of Data Nationalism," The Information Technology & Innovation Foundation," December 2013, http://www2.itif.org/2013-false-promise-data-nationalism.pdf.

17. Jennifer Daskal and Andrew Woods, "Cross-Border Data Requests: A Proposed Framework," *Lawfare*, November 24, 2015, https://www.justsecurity.org/27857/cross-border-data-requests-proposed-framework/.

18. John Zysman and Dan Breznitz (eds.), *The Third Globalization*, 2013.

19. "Measuring international trade related to cloud computing is challenging. Official data give a partial impression of related developments." "UNCTAD Information Economy Report 2013: The Cloud Economy and Developing Countries," p. 20. Additional useful data are at UNCTAD, "Information Economy Report 2015: Unlocking the Potential of E-commerce for Developing Countries."

20. "Partly Cloudy," *The Economist*, October 17, 2015, pp. 67–68.

21. Examples include Android Auto, Apple's HomeKit, and Samsung's Smartthings, Jessica Twentyman, "The Connected Business: Wearables and Cars stimulate Demand," *Financial Times* December 10, 2014, p. 2, http://www.ft.com/intl/cms/s/0/945c903c-7564-11e4-a1a9-00144feabdco.html#axzz3wokP2z5y.

22. From the 1962 classic "The Man Who Shot Liberty Valance," directed by John Ford and starring James Stewart and John Wayne. Maxwell Scott, playing the newspaper editor, when asked by his reporter why he was not going to print the true story that was told in the movie, responded, "When the facts become legend, print the legend." http://www.imdb.com/title/tt0056217/quotes.

23. This market flip surprised many IT firms and cloud leaders. Richard Waters, "The Connected Business: IT Incumbents Learn to Love the Cloud," *Financial Times*, December 10, 2014, p. 1.

24. Michael Kleeman states that this is just the revenue for the direct services provided by cloud providers, not the total revenue generated by all parties that use cloud services.

25. Quentin Hardy, "Google Races to Catch Up in Cloud Computing," *New York Times*, July 24, 2016, http://www.nytimes.com/2016/07/25/technology/google-races-to-catch-up-in-cloud-computing.html?_r=0.

26. Statista, http://www.statista.com/statistics/233725/development-of-amazon-web-services-revenue/.

27. Jack Clark and Ashlee Vance, "Amazon's Cloud Is Worth How Much?," *Bloomberg Business Week*, April 27–May 3, 2015, pp. 30–31. Dan Frommer, "Amazon Web Services Is Approaching a $10 Billion-a-Year Business," *recode*, April 28, 2016, http://www.recode.net/2016/4/28/11586526/aws-cloud-revenue-growth.

28. Monica Sharma, Ashwani Mehra, Haresh Jola, Anand Kumar, Madhvendra Misr, and Tiwari Vijayshri, "Scope of Cloud Computing for SMEs in India," *Journal of Computing*, 2, no. 5 (May 2010): 144–149.

29. Federico Etro, "The Economic Impact of Cloud Computing on Business Creation, Employment and Output in Europe," *Review of Business and Economic Literature*, 54, no. 2 (2009): 179–209.

30. Using a finer-grained analysis, the Copenhagen-based Centre for Economic and Business Research estimated annual economic benefits in France, Germany, Italy, Spain, and the United Kingdom would exceed 177 billion Euros annually by 2015, creating about 445,000 net new jobs annually by that date. Ann Metter and Anthony D. Williams, *Wired for Growth Innovation: How Digital Technologies Are Reshaping Small and Medium-Sized Businesses* (Brussels: Lisbon Council, 2012).

31. The most ICT-intensive sectors spend up to 5.4% of total revenues on ICT. Centre for Economic and Business Research, "The Cloud Dividend-Part One: The Economic Benefits of Cloud Computing to Business and the Wider EMEA Economy," December 2010, p. 22, http://uk.emc.com/collateral/microsites/2010/cloud-dividend/cloud-dividend-report.pdf.

32. Hofheinz and Mandel, "Bridging the Data Gap," 2014.

33. OECD, "The Impact of Internet in OECD Countries," OECD Digital Economy Papers, No. 200, OECD Publishing (2012), http://dx.doi.org/10.1787/5k962hhgpb5d-en.

34. U.S. trade negotiators learned of efforts to restrict cloud-enabled payments systems in countries such as Thailand and Korea that traditionally provided extra shelter for local financial institutions. The usual rationale is the protection of privacy. In May 2015, an APEC meeting on the Internet economy took up this issue for future policy consideration. (Based on a private email summary provided to the authors by a participant.)

35. The cloud also enables changes by reducing the cost of terminals on high-bandwidth networks and providing networked intelligence capabilities critical to reliability and cost management of remote monitoring, management and billing systems, and marketing and sales support.

36. Hofheinz and Mandel, "Bridging the Data Gap," 2014, p. 3.

37. Patrick Brogan, "U.S. Internet Usage and Global Leadership are Expanding," *USTelecom Research Brief*, August 12, 2015, Charts 4 and 5, p. 6. This report uses Cisco data, http://www.ustelecom.org/sites/default/files/documents/081215%20Internet%20Usage%20%26%20Global%20Leadership.pdf. For an alternative calculation with a similar bottom line, see Jacques Bughin, Eric Hazan, James Manyika, Peter Dahlstrom, Sree Ramaswamy, and Caroline Cochin de Billy, "Digital Europe: Pushing the Frontier, Capturing the Benefits," McKinsey Global Institute, June 2016.

38. Hofheinz and Mandel, "Bridging the Data Gap," 2014. Cisco estimates that "Global Internet traffic in 2019 will be equivalent to 66 times the volume of the entire global Internet in 2005. Globally, Internet traffic will reach 37 gigabytes (GB) per capita by 2019, up from 15.5 GB per capita in 2014." "The Zetabyte Era—Trends and Analysis," http://www.cisco.com/c/en/us/solutions/collateral/service-provider/visual-networking-index-vni/VNI_Hyperconnectivity_WP.html.

39. European Commission, "Why We Need a Digital Single Market," https://ec.europa.eu/priorities/sites/beta-political/files/dsm-factsheet_en.pdf.

40. James Manyika et al., "Big Data: The Next Frontier for Innovation, Competition and Productivity," McKinsey Global Institute, May 2011.

41. Ricardo Tavares, "Rise of the Machines," *InterMEDIA*, 42, no. 3 (Autumn 2014): 26–30. The further subdivisions are ours.

42. Drawn from OECD, "Exploring Data-Driven Innovation as a New Source of Growth: Mapping the Policy Issues Raised by 'Big Data,'" January 30, 2012, http://www.oecd-ilibrary.org/science-and-technology/exploring-data-driven-innovation-as-a-new-source-of-growth_5k47zw3fcp43-en; OECD, "Cloud Computing: The Concept, Impacts and the Role of Government Policy," OECD (2014) Digital Economy Papers, No. 240, OECD Publishing, http://www.oecd-ilibrary.org/docserver/download/5jxzf4lcc7f5.pdf?expires=1468651718&id=id&accname=guest&checksum=AD29829B95723CD6E4045E67C6D1B05A.

43. See the Bildt Commission recommendations, Global Commission on Internet Governance (The Bildt Commission), "One Internet," Final Report by the Centre for International Governance and the Royal Institute for International Affairs, 2016, pp. 31–45, http://ourinternet.org/report#chapter which, like most economists, endorses competitive markets mixed with supplementary measures when necessary. See *The World Bank News*, "World Bank Supports New Actions to Improve Connectivity," November 6, 2014, http://www.worldbank.org/en/news/feature/2014/11/06/world-bank-supports-new-actions-to-improve-connectivity-of-land-locked-countries.

44. The world closely monitored the U.S. fight over net neutrality. On February 26, 2015, the Federal Communications Commission, by a 3–2 party-line vote, reclassified broadband to fall under Title II, making it possible to use its authority over "common carrier" activities to implement net neutrality principles. The commission declared that it would intervene in response to provable complaints of significant violations of the principles but not impose detailed regulations. An adroit summary is available at http://arstechnica.com/business/2015/02/fcc-votes-for-net-neutrality-a-ban-on-paid-fast-lanes-and-title-ii/. The commission's authority to impose "net neutrality rules" was upheld by the U.S. Court of Appeals of the District of Columbia Circuit in June 2016. Cecelia Kang, "Court Backs Rules Treating Internet as Utility, Not Luxury," *New York Times*, June 13, 2016, http://www.nytimes.com/2016/06/15/technology/net-neutrality-fcc-appeals-court-ruling.html.

45. We draw on the excellent overview of the limits on cloud computing imposed by government policies: Anupam Chander and Ulyen P. Le, "Breaking the Web: Data Localization vs. The Global Internet," April 2014, http://papers.ssrn.com/sol3/papers.cfm?abstract_id=2407858. Also see Anupam Chander, *The Electronic Silk Road*; Amir Nasr, "Data Localization Would Harm U.S. Economy, Tech Experts Warn," *Morning Consult*, July 13, 2016, https://morningconsult.com/2016/07/13/data-localization-would-harm-u-s-economy-tech-experts-warn/.

46. For example, see the auto industry principles announced on December 9, 2014, http://www.autoalliance.org/index.cfm?objectid=865F3AC0-68FD-11E4-866D000C296BA163.

47. See Irene S. Wu, *Forging Trust Communities: How Technology Changes Politics* (Baltimore: Johns Hopkins University Press, 2015).

48. In theory, this would include written consent prior to sending an email abroad.

49. Metcalfe's law states, "The value of a telecommunications network is proportional to the square of the number of connected users of a system (n^2)." It is attributed to Robert Metcalfe, the co-inventor of the Ethernet.

50. W. Brian Arthur, *The Nature of Technology: What It Is and How It Evolves* (New York: Free Press, 2011).

51. Shelanski, "Information, Innovation," 2012.

52. Richard Gilbert and Willard K. Tom, "Is Innovation King at the Antitrust Agencies? The Intellectual Property Guidelines Five Years Later," *Antitrust Law Journal*, 69, no. 1 (2001): 43, 44.

53. In these models, the dominance of oligopolists could decline unless they grasp new technology opportunities. This pushes leaders to continue to innovate or face "creative destruction."

54. A thoughtful comparison of the U.S. and EU approaches is Inge Graef, Sih Yuliana Wahyuningtyas, and Peggy Valcke, "Assessing Data Access Issues in Online Platforms," *Telecommunication Policy*, 39, no. 5 (February 2015): 375–387.

55. Astra Taylor, *The People's Platform: Taking Back Power and Culture in the Digital Age* (New York: Metropolitan Books, 2014).

56. Atkinson and Ezell (*Innovation Economics*, 2012) rightly point out that high-innovation industries can have some special characteristics that can lead to higher profit margins without harming consumers or competition.

57. "Cloud Chronicles," *The Economist*, August 27, 2016, pp. 46–47, http://www.economist.com/news/business/21705849-how-open-source-software-and-cloud-computing-have-set-up-it-industry; Quentin Hardy, "Google Races to Catch Up in Cloud Computing," *New York Times*, July 24, 2016, http://www.nytimes.com/2016/07/25/technology/google-races-to-catch-up-in-cloud-computing.html?_r=0.

58. See Michelle Jones, "Google, Apple, Netflix: A Trifecta To Kill Amazon?" *Valuewalk*, August 4, 2014, accessed December 9, 2014, http://www.valuewalk.com/2014/08/google-apple-netflix-trifecta-kill-amazon/. Also, Tamlin Magee, "Cloud 'Pricing Wars': Why Google, AWS and Azure Price Cuts Should Not Be Top Priority for Cloud Customers," *ComputerworldUK*, March 1, 2016, accessed May 21, 2016, http://www.computerworlduk.com/cloud-computing/what-does-cloud-pricing-war-mean-for-business-in-2016-3633765/.

59. The Federal Trade Commission confirmed charges that Google searches favored those advertising through Google or others' links to Google services. But it found consumer benefits that justified the practice. Preventing incidental harm to competitors was not the purpose of the antitrust protection. http://www.huffingtonpost.com/2013/01/03/google-antitrust-settlement-ftc_n_2404721.html.

60. Robert Litan, *Brookings Brief*, December 10, 2014. Alex Barker and Jeevan Vasagar, "Incoming EU Digital Chief Lashes out at Google," *Financial Times*, October 29, 2014.

61. As a compromise, the Bildt Commission, Global Commission on Internet Governance (The Bildt Commission), "One Internet," Final Report by the Centre for International Governance and the Royal Institute for International Affairs, 2016, p. 62, http://ourinternet.org/report#chapter. urged a consumer option of paying for services such as search if a consumer wished to deny any collection of the user's search data.

62. Chrome, Google's web browser, captured a 48.65% global share in June 2016 (up from a 29.49% global share in August 2015), surpassing Internet Explorer for the first time in March 2016. During the same time frame, usage of the Internet Explorer browser plummeted from 50.15% to 31.65% in June 2016. The Google search engine had almost a 95% global share for mobile and just over 70% for desktop. Data from http://www.netmarketshare.com/, accessed July 20, 2016. Also see Robinson Meyer, "Europeans Use Google Way, Way More Than Americans Do," *The Atlantic*, April 15, 2015, http://www.theatlantic.com/technology/archive/2015/04/europeans-use-google-way-way-more-than-americans-do/390612/; and Matt Southern, "Bing's Share of the Search Market Is Growing Faster Than Google's," *Search Engine Journal*, May 20, 2016, accessed

May 21, 2016, https://www.searchenginejournal.com/bings-share-search-market-growing-faster-googles/164425/.

63. Natalie Drozdiak and Sam Schechner, "EU Files Additional Charges against Google," *The Wall Street Journal*, July 14, 2016, http://www.wsj.com/articles/google-set-to-face-more-eu-antitrust-charges-1468479516?mod=djemalertTECH. In addition, as of April 2016, Google required cell phone manufacturers to include Google add-ons, which are not open source and have restrictive licensing rules. The European commission complains especially about three issues: "handset-makers that wish to pre-install Google Play must, among other apps, also add Google Search and make it the device's default search service; if they want to share in Google's ad revenues they have to exclusively pre-install Google Search; and if they pre-install Google's apps on any of their models, they must commit to install only Google's standard version of Android on each and every one of their models." The EU feels these policies stifle competition, harm competitors, and hamper innovation. "Android Attack," *The Economist*, April 23, 2016, http://www.economist.com/news/business/21697193-european-commission-going-after-google-againthis-time-better-chance; Nicholas Hirst, "Google's Winning Card against Europe: Time," *Politico*, April 25, 2016, http://www.politico.eu/article/why-the-ec-may-ultimately-lose-the-android-case/.

64. Chander and Le, "Breaking the Web," 2014, p. 12.

65. Chander and Le, "Breaking the Web," 2014, pp. 15–16. At one point Chancellor Merkel stated, "we'll talk about European providers that offer security for our citizens, so that one shouldn't have to send e-mails and other information across the Atlantic. Rather one could build up a communication network inside Europe." See "Protection: Angela Merkel Proposes Europe Network," *BBC*, February 15, 2014, http://www.bbc.com/news/world-europe-26210053.

66. Patrick Lane, "Data Protectionism, The World in 2014," *The Economist*, November 18, 2013, p. 118, http://www.economist.com/news/21589110-global-computing-cloud-geography-will-matter-more-data-protectionism.

67. These points were made repeatedly to us in conversations with senior IT executives in 2015–2016, although they split on their predictions on how well Google would handle the risk.

68. Boris Marjanovic, "Facebook Is an Economic Castle Guarded by an Unbreachable Moat," *Seeking Alpha*, December 22, 2014, http://seekingalpha.com/author/boris-marjanovic/articles. Richard Walter, "Facebook Flexes Muscles over Digital Advertising," *Financial Times*, January 29, 2016, p. 13.

69. Brad Stone and Vernon Silver, "Google's European Nightmare," *Bloomberg Business Week*, August 10, 2015, pp. 50–57.

70. The worries of U.S. publishers about how to interface with social media companies, such as Facebook, were noted in Chapter 2. U.S. publishers made strategic decisions about whether their user base is strong enough for them to impose a "pay wall," a fee for access to their detailed content. Or will they need to settle for a share of ad revenue generated by visits to their site?

71. Estimate cited in Henry Mance, "Rewriting the Story," *Financial Times*, February 10, 2016, p. 7.

72. FT View, "Europe's Best Days on the Internet Could Lie Ahead," *Financial Times*, January 2, 2015, p. 6, http://www.ft.com/intl/cms/s/0/3da2fe12-844f-11e4-bae9-00144feabdco.html#axzz3wokP2z5y.

73. Facebook could provide the platform to host the mobile version of the *Washington Post*'s "front page." David Carr, "Facebook Offers Life Raft, but Publishers Are Wary," *New York Times*, October 27, 2014, p. B1. Mike Isaac, "2 Drug Chains Disable Apple Pay, as a Rival Makes Plans," *New York Times*, October 27, 2014, p. B1.

74. Mike Masnick. "Europe Is about to Create a Link Tax: Time to Speak out against It," *Techdirt*, June 14, 2016. European Commission, Digital Single Market—Commission Updates EU Audiovisual Rules and Presents Target Approach to Online Platforms," May 25, 2016, http://europa.eu/rapid/press-release_MEMO-16-1895_en.htm.

75. An astute, pithy overview of the biggest IT competition issues in the EU in mid-2015 is Nicholas Hirst, "Internet Offers Rich Pickings for Antitrust Regulators," *Politico.EU*, June 4, 2015, p. 1.

76. A. B. Bernstein, Weekend Media Blast: "That Is What It Is Really All About," April 24, 2015.

77. Christopher Williams, "Google Faces Record-Breaking Fine for Web Search Monopoly Abuse," *The Telegraph*, May 14, 2016, accessed May 21, 2016, http://www.telegraph.co.uk/business/2016/05/14/google-faces-record-breaking-fine-for-web-search-monopoly-abuse/.

78. Our thinking owes much to Tanjim Hossain and John Morgan, "Quality Beats First-Mover Advantage: The Quest for Qwerty," *American Economic Review: Papers and Proceedings*, 99, no. 2 (March 2009): 435–440; Tanjim Hossain and John Morgan, "When Do Markets Tip? A Cognitive Hierarchy Approach," *Marketing Science*, 32, no. 3 (May-June 2013): 431–453.

79. One well-funded startup told us that declining costs allow for specialized architectures. Moreover, Google monetizes its free services in ways that require compromises that limit its flexibility. Quixie, for example, takes advantage of Google's growing use of paid links on search results to open a wedge for its specialized search engine for apps. In this sense, Quixie is more like a matching service for consumers seeking apps. Parker, Van Alstyne, and Choudary argue that these challenges for platform leaders can arise because it is difficult to curate complex platforms to maintain a quality experience for users.

80. Paul Mozur, "A South Korean Copy of Snapchat Takes Off in Asia," *New York Times*, July 5, 2016, http://www.nytimes.com/2016/07/06/technology/snapchat-snow-korea.html.

81. Platforms and many of these hybrid products exemplify "two-sided markets." Evans, Hagiu, and Schmalensee, *Invisible Engines*, 2006.

82. Many U.S. firms still use checks to pay for most items, but new payment platforms and processors such as AribaPay are beginning to change that. In its first year of operation, AribaPay processed $5 billion, reducing the number of employees needed to deal with payment systems. Olga Kharif, "How Cloud Companies Are Killing Checks," *Bloomberg News*," March 12, 2015, http://www.bloomberg.com/news/articles/2015-03-12/cloud-companies-push-digital-payments-to-u-s-businesses.

83. One major Asian investor suggested to us in August 2015 that Alibaba could be a huge competitive threat to China's banks. China PnR laid out its strategy, including payments systems for SMEs and peer-to-peer lending to Cowhey in a May 2016 meeting in Shanghai.

84. This probe seems to be a classic antitrust issue of "tying" by a dominant producer, a requirement that to use a key product (like Android), customers must also accept a bundle of other products in ways that discriminate against competition. European Union Press Release, "Antitrust: Commission Sends Statement of Objections to Google on Android Operating System and Applications," April 20, 2016, accessed May 10, 2016, http://europa.eu/rapid/press-release_IP-16-1492_en.htm.

85. See Janakiram MSV, "6 IoT Startups That Make Connecting Things to the Cloud a Breeze," *Forbes*, April 13, 2015, http://www.forbes.com/sites/janakirammsv/2015/04/13/6-iot-startups-that-make-connecting-things-to-the-cloud-a-breeze/#4110deb3308a.

86. Cowhey and Aronson, *Transforming Global Information*, 2009, argued that the pattern of interventions by the U.S. government in ICT markets over many years shaped the modular architecture of the industry in a way that produced vast benefits. But the U.S. government tried to avoid dictating particular technology choices by the market and left large parts of emerging conduct open to minimal regulation.

87. Farhad Manjoo, "Tech's 'Frightful 5' Will Dominate Digital Life for the Foreseeable Future," *New York Times*, State of the Art, January 20, 2016, and Farhad Manjoo, "Global Battle Lines Form as U.S. Technology Companies Expand," *New York Times*, June 2, 2016, pp. A1, B7.

88. *Ibid.*

89. "How to Keep Roaring: Special Report on Business in Asia," *The Economist*, May 31, 2014.

90. NTT and KDDI, the traditional dominant telecom carriers, began providing cloud services, especially to Japanese firms around Asia. Concerns arose. See Kenji Kushida, Jonathan Murray, and John Zysman, "The Gathering Storm: Analyzing the Cloud Computing Ecosystem and Implications for Public Policy," *Communications & Strategies*, 85, no. 1 (March 2012): 63–85. Steve Vogel, "Japan's Information Technology Challenge," in Breznitz and Zysman.

91. Softbank, which held a 4% stake in Yahoo! until 2011, drove Yahoo! into search leadership in Japan, but by the end of 2015 Google had a 57% share of search in Japan compared to 40% for Yahoo! Japan. *Return on Now*, "2015 Search Engine Market Share by Country," http://returnonnow.com/internet-marketing-resources/2015-search-engine-market-share-by-country/; Brian Solomon, "Yahoo Sells to Verizon in Saddest $5 Billion Deal in Tech History," *Forbes*, July 25, 2016, http://www.forbes.com/sites/briansolomon/2016/07/25/yahoo-sells-to-verizon-for-5-billion-marissa-mayer/#6e0e93a071b4.

92. Rakuten also invests in diverse information service firms globally. *Bloomberg Business Week*, "Japan's Billionaire Brawl," October 21–27, 2013. Our discussions with SoftBank and Rakuten executives and numerous leaders in Japanese cyberpolicy in 2015–2016 inform this discussion.

93. Rakuten's chief executive officer, Hiroshi Mikitani, is so determined to make it a global company that he pursued a policy of "Englishnization." "All meetings, presentations, documents, training sessions and emails inside the company are conducted entirely in English." *The Japan Times*, Opinion, "Rakuten Forges Ahead in English," May 23, 2015, http://www.japantimes.co.jp/opinion/2015/05/23/editorials/rakuten-forges-ahead-english/#.V5_cKTkrKrc.

94. Niconico, another Japanese social networking leader, mainly builds on Japan's success at generating "cute" characters. Keiichi Murayama, "Japan Technology and Innovation: Animated Bears and Bunnies Score a Hit with Bug Business," *Financial Times*, December 8, 2014, p. 3.

95. Ulrike Schaede, *Choose and Focus: Japanese Business Strategies for the 21st Century* (Ithaca, NY: Cornell University Press, 2008). Kana Inagaki, "Japan Technology & Innovation, Sharp Displays May Be the Shape of Things to Come," *Financial Times*, December 8, 2014, p. 1.

96. Leslie Picker, Mark Scott, and Jonathan Sable, "SoftBank Makes Bet on Internet of Things," *New York Times*, July 19, 2016, pp. B1, B3.

97. Tom Warren, "SoftBank completes $31 billion acquisition of ARM," The Verge, September 5, 2016, http://www.theverge.com/2016/9/5/12798302/softbank-arm-acquisition-complete.

98. Some elements of old industrial policies die slowly. When Hyinx faced bankruptcy in the low-margin, capital-intensive market for DRAM memory chips, the government engineered a bailout.

99. Song Jung-A, "Samsung Heir Faces Investor Test over Shake-up," *Financial Times*, December 1, 2014, p. 15.

100. Monica Alleven, "South Korea Pushes Forward on 5G, Promises Global Cooperation," *Fierce Wireless Technology*, October 23, 2014, http://www.fiercewireless.com/tech/story/south-korea-pushes-forward-5g-promises-global-cooperation/2014-10-23.

101. *Return on Now*, "2015 Search Engine Market Share by Country," http://returnonnow.com/internet-marketing-resources/2015-search-engine-market-share-by-country/.

102. Alexander Martin, "5 Things about Messaging App Line and Its IPO," *The Wall Street Journal*, June 10, 2016, http://blogs.wsj.com/briefly/2016/06/10/5-things-about-messaging-app-line-and-its-ipo/.

103. Chander and Le, "Breaking the Web," 2014, pp. 22–23. On broader controversies over cloud policy, see Information Technology Industry Council letter of July 3, 2013, to director Jung-tae Kim of the Ministry of Science, ICT, and Future Planning.

104. Research and Markets, "Cloud Computing Market in Korea, 2014–18," summarized at http://finance.yahoo.com/news/cloud-computing-market-korea-2014-190000124.html, posted April 13, 2014.

105. "Getting the Message," *The Economist*, May 31, 2014.

106. Atkinson and Ezell, *Innovation Economics*, 2012.

107. Cloud computing development goals include the following: "(1) establishing cloud computing technology and standard system and making breakthrough on key technologies; (2) improving the service capability of servers and building cloud servers capable of dealing with 100 million concurrent accesses . . . and (5) demonstrating the application of cloud computing services in key areas and industries and promoting cloud computing application and service models in various industries." Elizabeth Cole et al., "12th Five Year Plan for the Development of Cloud Computing in China," *Lexology*, http://www.lexology.com/library/detail.aspx?g=a86168b8-3cb5-4fdc-93bb-17fa34d0f37e.

108. More than technology hardware is protected. Chinese web video companies, like Sohu, benefit from the prohibition of Western competitors like Google's YouTube. On the Information Technology Agreement, see the *New York Times* account, December 13, 2014. *The Economist*, "Online Video in China, the Chinese stream," November 9, 2013, pp. 67–68.

109. Atkinson and Ezell, *Innovation Economics*, 2012.

110. Scott Kennedy, "Made in China 2025," Center for Strategic and International Studies, June 1, 2015, http://csis.org/publication/made-china-2025o. Also Kennedy and Johnson, "Perfecting China, Inc.," 2016.

111. Dieter Ernst, "The Information Technology Agreement, Industrial Development and Innovation—India's and China's Diverse Experiences," UCSD Institute on Global Conflict and Cooperation, February 2014.

112. Evonne Guan, "Chinese Search Engine Landscape—Baidu Losing to 360 and Sogou," *Daoinsights*, January 28, 2015, http://daoinsights.com/chinese-search-engine-landscape-baidu-losing-to-360-and-sogou/. Rebecca Li, "Top 3 Chinese Search Engines: What B2B Marketers Need to Know," Komarketing, July 27, 2016, https://komarketing.com/blog/top-3-chinese-search-engines/.

113. The largest Chinese carrier, China Mobile, shows signs of becoming more international and moving toward the cloud ecosystem.

114. Catherine Shu, "Alibaba's Cloud Unit Opens Its Second U.S. Data Center," *Techcrunch*, October 9, 2015, https://techcrunch.com/2015/10/09/alibabas-cloud-unit-opens-its-second-u-s-data-center/.

115. We thank Yiru Zhou for this example. http://en.cloudminds.com/.

116. "Start Me Up," *The Economist*, August 6, 2011, pp. 45–47. Japan's SoftBank announced its intention to acquire ARM Holdings in July 2016.

117. Interviews in Paris and Brussels in the summer of 2016 supplemented official documents in this account. Commission Staff Working Document, A Digital Single Market Strategy for Europe—Evidence and Analysis, European Commission, SWD (2015) 100 final, June 5, 2015. Copenhagen Economics, "The Economic Impact of a European Digital Single Market, Final Report," March 2010, http://www.epc.eu/dsm/2/Study_by_Copenhagen.pdf.

118. Interviews, fall 2014.

119. EU regulations embrace net neutrality and impose strict interconnect obligations at low prices on all competitors to major telecom carriers.

120. Major U.S. carriers are obligated to offer network capacity to smaller competitors, but the regulatory approach uses a considerably lighter hand. Cable television is a second network infrastructure at the local level, which is less pervasive throughout the EU.

121. Alan Livsey and Robert Armstrong, "Lex In-depth: European Telecoms," *Financial Times*, November 19, 2014, p. 7; Daniel Thomas and Alex Barker, "Analysis: Scrambled Signal," *Financial Times*, July 7, 2014, p. 6.

122. Chander and Le, "Breaking the Web," 2014, pp. 15–16.

123. European Commission, "Digital Single Market: Audiovisual Media Services Directive," https://ec.europa.eu/digital-single-market/en/audiovisual-media-services-directive-avmsd.

124. Other issues receiving attention include the promotion of European works, the prohibition of hate speech, and the protection of minors, including on video-sharing platforms. It also enshrines the independence of audiovisual regulators and the role of the European Regulators Group for Audiovisual Media Services. European Commission, "Digital Single Market: Revision of the Audiovisual Media Services Directive," https://ec.europa.eu/digital-single-market/en/revision-audiovisual-media-services-directive-avmsd.

125. Some verticals should benefit because the IPD freshens and strengthens their traditional industrial control systems. For example, Siemens' strength in industrial equipment rests on its mastery of traditional SCADA control systems (a type of specialized software and computing system to control an industrial process, like power turbines).

126. James Fontanella-Khan, "EU Approves Microsoft's Cloud," *Financial Times*, April 11, 2014.

127. The relevant General Agreement on Trade in Services service category is "computer and related services."

128. This is the position of EU trade negotiators based on our interviews. Joshua Meltzer, *Supporting the Internet as a Platform for International Trade Opportunities for Small and Medium Sized Enterprises and Developing Countries* (Washington, D.C.: Brookings Institution, February 2014).

129. Trade policy aficionados will want to know that the context is WTO work on trade in e-commerce services. That is a secondary detail for our purposes. Communication from the EU and the United States, Contribution to the Work Programme on Electronic Commerce, S/C/W/338, 13 July 2011 (US-EU ICT Principles).

130. The verbatim text is *"Cross-Border Information Flows:* Governments should not prevent service suppliers of other countries, or customers of those suppliers, from electronically transferring information internally or across borders, accessing publicly available information, or accessing their own information stored in other countries."

131. The verbatim text is *"Local Infrastructure:* Governments should not require ICT service suppliers to use local infrastructure, or establish a local presence, as a condition of supplying services. In addition, governments should not give priority or preferential treatment to national suppliers of ICT services in the use of local infrastructure, national spectrum, or orbital resources."

132. The verbatim text is *"Open Networks, Network Access and Use*: Governments, preferably through their regulators, should promote the ability of consumers legitimately to access and distribute information and run applications and services of their choice. Governments should not restrict the ability of suppliers to supply services over the Internet on a cross-border and technologically neutral basis, and should promote the interoperability of services and technologies, where appropriate."

133. European negotiators contend that a final Trade in Services Agreement could be reached in late 2016. Interviews in Brussels, June 2016.

134. Communication from Australia, Suggestions on ICT Principles, Contribution to the Work Programme on Electronic Commerce, WTO, S/C/W/349, September 26, 2012.

7   Cybersecurity as a Governance Challenge

CLOUD GOVERNANCE AND considerations about creating a trusted digital environment intersect. As a result, greater consensus is needed on how to strengthen privacy rights and increase the security of digital transactions. This chapter discusses the fundamentals of the cybersecurity challenge for commerce. It explains that simple solutions are impossible because collective action problems rule out a technical fix and the incentives for substantial voluntary improvements are insufficient to force action. Moreover, much of the practical problem solving is likely to be sector specific. Hence, we turn to one sector, financial transactions, to examine governance options through an analysis of two efforts to build a trusted digital environment.[1]

The first case study analyzes the Society for Worldwide Interbank Financial Telecommunication. SWIFT is an unusual MSO, a society of international financial institutions that secures financial transfers across borders. The case of SWIFT helps us refine our argument about what is required for an international governance regime to succeed in a complex, technologically dynamic space. Any regime is more likely to succeed if it addresses threshold challenges for creating a core club, authoritative minimum international baselines, and partial convergence of national policies. Robust regimes also tend to rely on MSOs that are credibly expert, transparent to important stakeholders, and accountable to governments.

SWIFT highlights several refinements to the arguments. It shows how MSOs' management of cooperation challenges can make coordination easier. It illuminates factors that influence the choice and form of the international baseline for quasi-convergence. In this instance, the baseline is built on interlocking national regulations of cross-border services that are reviewed by the Bank for International Settlements (BIS). In short, the SWIFT case clarifies how our guidelines illuminate these situations.

The second case examines a less unified international response to a financial security problem—cybercrimes tied to credit card transactions. In this case, the EU and the United States tackled the issue and interacted with MSOs differently. Achieving coordination to reduce cybercrime through security safeguards required both MSO leadership and backstopping by public authority at the domestic level. The main market risk was less global and more regional in its impact. There were overlapping sets of global actors in the marketplace and in the regional MSOs and similar security problems in Europe and the United States. The result was a quasi-convergence of rules. However, given the nature of the risks, the dangers were more about improving efficiency and fine-tuning risk than about repelling major threats to the international financial markets. Thus, the need for an international baseline was more circumscribed because large market centers moved roughly in parallel. The critical role of an "international baseline," established by the General Agreement on Trade in Services, was to ensure that tougher security measures did not explicitly, or de facto, discriminate on the basis of the national origin of the financial service supplier or block international financial transactions.

7.1. The Common Challenges

Cybersecurity is a large and growing problem. In late 2014, Sony was the victim of the most extensive commercial hack in U.S. history. Terabytes of date and emails were stolen and released. Sony's data files were wiped clean and the computers themselves were destroyed. Apparently, the hack was committed in retaliation for a comedy, *The Interview*, about assassinating North Korea's Supreme Leader. This hack highlights four classes of challenges that permeate all forms of likely threats: crime, privacy, cyberwarfare, and espionage.[2] Many of the issues regarding data cybersecurity privacy are corollaries of these security issues. Although we recognize the interdependence of all four threats, this chapter focuses on cybersecurity governance and commercial transactions.[3]

As with any newly recognized threat to public safety, the level of risk tends to be overblown. Careful studies of cyberattacks suggest that estimates of the magnitude of their financial harm are systematically exaggerated, partly by those seeking defensive solutions against attacks.[4] Still, even when properly sized, there is ample justification for improved defenses. Singer and Friedman persuasively argued that cybersecurity policy should have four goals: (1) *confidentiality*—is vital to personal privacy,

(2) *integrity*—a hacked signal should never be sent to an individual's pacemaker, for example, (3) *availability*—the system should always work, and (4) *resilience*—the system should recover rapidly after an attack.

Why is improving cybersecurity such a difficult governance challenge? It is useful to think of three classes of problems for defense.

1. *The technology curve of the IPD creates important advantages for attackers* for three main reasons. First, as IT becomes more pervasive, new opportunities arise for direct and back-channel attacks. For example, today it is possible to attack a computer system from a networked printer or to use an Internet WiFi link to hack a heart pacemaker. Moreover, the growing reliance on Internet protocols and modularity in software creates a more universal "language" for designing attacks. This, in turn, provides larger target markets that lower the costs of designing specialized attack vehicles.[5] Second, there is no "technically perfect" security solution because new software code is inherently subject to bugs and risks. Further, IT applications change rapidly, creating new capabilities with unpredictable side effects and vulnerabilities. Third, there is no "human-proof" system that is not vulnerable to a discontented Edward Snowden, so long as users put their passwords next to their computers or continue to use "1234" or "password" as their password.

2. *Offense is easier and cheaper than defense.* It is difficult to locate and attribute blame to the perpetrators of attacks for four reasons.[6] First, offense is profitable and well organized. There are underground, sophisticated markets to support every form of capability for cybercrime, many with military significance.[7] Second, attribution ("Who did it?") is difficult, although not always impossible. Cyberspace is global, creating an expansive field of initial suspects. Even if the computer that launched an attack can be identified, the computer's control may have been hacked by another party. Third, defense is difficult because the detection of an attack can be delayed and imperfect. It may take considerable time to recognize and identify a breach. Even when a network monitor detects "something happening," there are swarms of transactions that originate for many purposes and for many reasons. Initially, it may be a major challenge to determine whether an attack is underway.[8] Fourth, mechanisms for sharing information about cyberattacks and pursuing investigations of cybercrime internationally are weak, although they are needed to improve response times and deter security attacks. At present, only the Council of Europe's 2004 Convention on Cybercrime provides for processes to share information and to cooperate on cybercrime

enforcement (through mutual legal assistance agreements to authorize electronic surveillance).[9]

3. *Institutional incentives make it difficult to figure out the right mix of strategies to reduce cybersecurity risks.*[10] Market incentives do not align properly with how actors would need to change investments and behavior to ease the cybersecurity problem. Four classic incentive problems are illustrative.[11]

First, initiatives for consumers and producers can invoke *misaligned incentives*. For example, card and account holders usually are shielded from catastrophic financial losses from hacked credit and financial accounts, so consumers may value security less than speed and ease of use. Similarly, cyberdefenses require constant updating because of the "offensive edge" for cyberattacks, but many companies underinvest in cyberdefenses to avoid high upfront costs. They gamble that losses will come later and will be manageable. Moreover, even a routine software update for security purposes can be costly because it may require shutting down key systems for hours. Worse, the updates may create unintentional problems separate from cyberattacks. Similarly, particular protections (such as the special protection for information like Social Security numbers in the United States) may require a broader set of security measures than initially imagined to achieve the narrow purpose or skew cyber strategies to narrowly protect a few risks at the expense of more systematic defenses.

Second, *asymmetric information* is endemic. In 1970, George Akerlof famously analyzed the "market for lemons" problem in used cars that arose because it was impossible for consumers to verify which cars were better.[12] Therefore, the market for used cars undervalued "high-quality" cars and overvalued, in sales numbers and prices, "lemons." Similarly, in IT security, consumers are challenged to determine which solutions for protection are superior and therefore they undervalue the best ones. In addition, underreporting of damage from cyberattacks is chronic because companies fear the upfront cost of bad publicity or lawsuits. These worries limit the incentives to fix problems and deny valuable information about risks to other market participants.[13]

Third, *externalities* abound. A collective action problem exists in regard to reducing many cybersecurity risks. Internet-based risks and other systemic problems face the "weakest link" problem—weakly protected actors may introduce risks that undercut the value of protective investments. From the viewpoint of society, socially optimum incentives for investment in protection by consumers are reduced because strongly protected actors can produce positive externalities that benefit the protection of the entire system. Yet the "good" actor is not fully rewarded for its behavior; others glean part of the benefit without paying for it. Finally, a classic externality factor, network effects, increases the value of a product as more users embrace it. This discourages investment in security engineering. Hence, a software maker faces a trade-off between fast, high-impact deployment that quickly adds users and time-consuming engineering for security. IT companies often opt for faster commercial deployment to gain leadership.

Fourth, *mixed motives* arise when, for sensible reasons, national and global laws and regulations allow governments' substantial latitude to deal with security risks. This latitude may foster new security policies that impinge on liberty and privacy. When the commercial realm uses security rationales to impose measures that stack markets in favor of preferred incumbents (e.g., national firms against foreign competitors), how can the public interest be protected? This last issue reached its highest profile in regard to various draft Chinese regulations that would mandate special technical standards, restrictions on movement of data, and disclosure of software source code, all in the name of cybersecurity protection.[14] But China is not alone in mixing market protection with security. For example, U.S. firms worry that EU security standards may be set up under rules that restrict access by U.S. firms, despite EU assurances to the contrary.

A complex challenge such as cybersecurity requires a multipronged strategy. It is important to invest in public capabilities to prevent or respond to cyberemergencies and also to align the incentives for markets to meet confidentiality, integrity, reliability, and resilience goals. Two major questions are, How can we achieve alignment without making markets less productive and innovative? and How can we ensure that security is not used as an excuse to impinge on other important values in unreasonable ways?[15]

There are no magic bullets for policy. R&D, of course, is always an option. Increased government investment in R&D technologies to respond to particular cyberthreats can mitigate specific risk factors. Information sharing is a second tool. All major governments have created sector-specific working groups for public–private collaboration to share information and best practices on threat management. Some of these groups provide classified information to firms to help them identify attackers. Privacy advocates worry that such exchanges could feed private-sector information on citizens to intelligence and surveillance agencies. Meanwhile, leading IT firms developed new private threat exchanges. About 250 major U.S. IT firms share information derived from their real-time, threat-monitoring logs. Homeland Security representatives and in-house counsels to minimize antitrust concerns monitor these corporate activities. A third response is to enhance resilience by creating new capabilities. New cyberemergency response teams and international networking collaborations are emerging from these teams.[16] A fourth tactic is to modify criminal codes and procedures for law enforcement collaboration, including international treaties to increase the deterrent value of criminal justice and the improvement of the often slow and frustrating mutual legal assistance treaty processes.[17]

The case of the Internet of Thing (IoT) outlined in Part I is illustrative. The IoT will be ubiquitous. Large and small firms will compete for market share. In the consumer product realm, cybersecurity provisions, especially those that impact smaller new entrants, could fail to find the right balance between safety and innovation. Inevitably, the cybersecurity toolkit will include a mix of efforts to improve technical standards to bolster safety, certification of products for cybersafety, and new liability rules for breaches or cybersafety practices, including rules mandating disclosure of cybersecurity breaches.

These measures are all reasonable. But how will they really work? For example, it seems attractive to require stringent testing and certifications of new IoT offerings. A precedent exists. Traditional household appliances organizations such as the Underwriters' Laboratory (renamed UL), funded by insurance companies, successfully offered simple, quick, and inexpensive testing of new products. However, smaller firms might be deterred because IoT products involving complex software and hardware mixes could make certification testing slower and more expensive. In addition, maintaining strong IoT security depends on regularly updating software and many new products will incorporate elements of open-source software to lower the cost and speed of developing new offerings.[18] This encourages innovation, but security updating of open software often is uneven. Striving for maximum risk reduction in IoT consumer offerings could drive control of the market to large incumbent firms that are better equipped to handle the complexities and costs of certification and to assume possible liability risks.[19]

The IoT example shows why it is important to assess the risk:reward ratio when evaluating how to strengthen cybersecurity. Good cybersecurity rules evolve when their commercial consequences and the degree of public risk that they entail are carefully assessed. Many actions will necessarily be sector specific because risks vary by sector. We turn now to the high-risk part of the global economy, the flow of financial payment, because of our focus on global governance.

First, we examine global and national efforts to respond by creating a shared global capacity that was enforced effectively by a club of central banks as a de facto safety regulation. Second, we examine ex post liability rules that required certain safe practices to shield companies from liability for cybercrimes and show how mandatory reporting rules can help propagate cybersecurity.[20] But these capabilities did not spring fully envisioned from a blueprint. They required trial and error and political economic strategizing.

7.2. The Story of SWIFT

Financial flows among financial institutions nationally and globally are huge. For decades, they have far exceeded trade flows or annual global GDP. These payments systems undergird the entire world economy. If they falter, they can crash the reliability of financial markets. In the domestic markets of all reasonably well-governed countries, there is a highly regulated, centralized payments system organized by a national central bank.

By contrast, the international financial flow system traditionally was more fragmented and less well organized. For example, the international telex system was built on bilateral relations among a small number of banks in major financial centers. It was slow, the volume of transactions was low, and it was costly to use. Moreover, the transactions were labor intensive and time-consuming and lacked flexible common "formats" to address the growing complexity of financial transactions. When financial flows across national borders accelerated during the 1960s and 1970s, the financial institutions, mainly money center banks, sought a more robust and efficient mechanism.[21] They began exploring the then-emerging field of computer networking as a means to provide a system that was more effective than the publicly available telecommunications network.

Ultimately, in 1973, after the demise of fixed exchange rates, the banks created SWIFT, a global nonprofit institution to oversee and manage the cross-border payments infrastructure. The member institutions own SWIFT and SWIFT is "responsible for providing the network, standards, products and services that allow member institutions . . . to exchange financial information."[22] By 2016, its membership grew to more than 200 countries and territories and more than 11,000 financial institutions. In 2015, SWIFT processed more than 6.1 billion secure messages.[23]

SWIFT became the backbone of the global payments system. Its hallmark benchmarks are reliability, confidentiality, and integrity. These values mirror those of a sound domestic payments infrastructure. However, SWIFT never participates in the actual financial transactions—it is a payments network, not a financial institution.

SWIFT operates its own specialized network and does more than just promise efficiency. Liability obligations imposed by its owners reinforce its stated security goals. If it makes errors in its messaging tasks, SWIFT accepts limited liability for losses. It also has a mandate to maintain the confidentiality of transactions it handles. To accomplish these tasks, SWIFT destroys the transaction data as soon as the transaction is completely validated. By all accounts, it has succeeded in delivering on its mandates. On its peak day in the first half of 2016, it processed almost 28.3 million messages conveying cross-border financial flows. As a technical infrastructure, SWIFT is fast, it scales as volume grows, and costs per transaction keep falling. This "industrialization of finance" lowered and continues to lower the cost of a transaction by almost 85% from 2001 to 2012, from $.26 to $.04 US. Between 2010 and the end of 2015, SWIFT reduced its prices by 57%.[24] As prices declined, traffic grew in

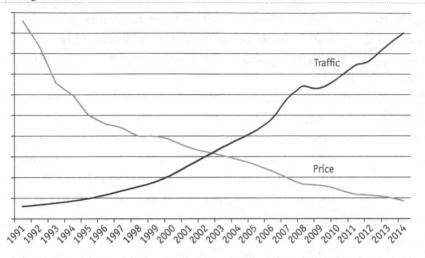

FIGURE 7.1: Sustained cost reductions for all members of the Society for Worldwide Interbank Financial Telecommunication over twenty years.

parallel. Figure 7.1 shows the price charged by SWIFT versus the growth of traffic from 1991 to 2014.

SWIFT also is designed, and periodically modified, to remain a competitively neutral asset in the global financial market. Although SWIFT might appear to be a fruitful example of coordination, it is the product of a more complex political economic story. We first discuss the creation of the core club of this MSO and the growth of the larger stakeholder community.

At the dawn of computer networking for payments, bankers cared deeply about reliability and confidentiality, but were not focused on cybersecurity.[25] The banks wanted to enable much higher transaction volumes in a more flexible and efficient way. Yet, the potential technical advantage created by coordinated investment in an improved long-term capability was insufficient to create SWIFT. Its proponents faced the usual challenge that short-term costs often trump long-term gains, especially when dealing with a function long considered a pure "cost" overhead by financial institutions. In addition, there was uncertainty about whether enough major players would voluntarily work together, which raised worries that investments in cybersecurity might be stranded in an incomplete network. This threshold challenge was surmounted in 1973 when SWIFT was created. Because it is a service facility, not a profit-maximizing entity, surpluses are returned to the co-op owners. (The rebate on messaging fees was 32 million Euros in 2015, or about 10%.)[26]

How did SWIFT conquer the threshold problem? Its initial takeoff occurred because it solved two short-term problems that framed the choices about financial transactions. The first was a *competitive* problem for major money center banks.

How could they head off First National City Bank (renamed Citibank in 1976)? First National City Bank was then the leader in correspondent banking for international transfers and a pioneer in the computerization of banking, including the installation of ATMs. It intended to create its own international payments network to serve the industry, which would have provided it with a new source of competitive advantage in an era of rapidly increasing international flows. The founders of SWIFT wanted to deliver these capabilities to develop a competitive market alternative to First National City Bank, not to solve a security or privacy problem.[27] At its founding, SWIFT had 239 member banks from fifteen countries.

SWIFT also benefited from a second boost to takeoff by solving a pressing *political* problem that was slowing the development of a single European market—the unification of financial payments systems that were fragmented along national lines in the European Common Market. The European Commission became a major proponent for SWIFT as part of the solution for achieving internal market unification.[28]

To be viable, SWIFT had to maintain trust over time among the stakeholders, especially through transparency and accountability. The location of the headquarters was a first step in that direction. Brussels was chosen because it had a favorable legal system for a co-op and was deemed neutral as a location in the London and New York bank rivalry and the Anglo-American rivalry with continental European banks. In Brussels, there would be no hidden regulatory vetoes by the Federal Reserve, the Bank of England, or their most powerful European counterparts.[29] This was important because at the time there was no extensive international code for cross-border financial flow transactions to provide an anchor for national regulators faced with difficult choices.

The design of the ownership system further contributed to transparency and accountability. SWIFT cleverly balanced the fact that full members are regulated nationally with a global organization's management. Seats on the board are distributed according to the share of transactions by country. The largest six countries by transaction volume each are allocated two seats, the next ten have one seat each, and all other countries vote on which countries will fill the three remaining seats. Board shares are adjusted as market shares change. Thus, influence is redefined over time, and a strong activist board ensures that there is significant transparency in decision making. To supplement the board as a source of information and voice, SWIFT created an annual forum, the SWIFT International Banking Operations Seminar. Every year since 1978 (except in 2001 when the meeting was canceled in the wake of 9/11), thousands have gathered to talk shop and markets and to exchange opinions on trends in global finance that may influence SWIFT planning. The forum also serves as an avenue for marketing new SWIFT offerings.

Initially, the expertise challenge was surmounted by relying on a multinational leadership team drawn from major banks and an open-procurement tender for the computer network technology that permitted a credible path for growth. The tender also alleviated another hidden worry, that selecting IBM would play into the technology plans of the leading American banks. The ultimate winner, Burroughs, was deemed competent, slightly behind the leading edge of IBM, but good enough and small enough to be dictated to by the fledging client.

SWIFT also became the International Organization for Standradization (ISO) forum for setting standards for many international financial payments transactions, which cemented its centrality to the industry's technical consultation networking process. As network analyses show, this provided SWIFT with significant influence over the network.[30] The ISO role enhanced SWIFT's credibility by introducing a separate set of rules that made it transparent and accountable to a broader range of companies in its role as a standards forum. The growing range of institutional checks and review processes among MSOs supplemented oversight by governments of individual NGOs with specialized interests because the MSOs themselves represented a broader range of stakeholders and expertise.[31]

A new stakeholder challenge arose when the growing complexity of financial markets introduced major new players, which were not traditional banks, but had significant payments flows and needed a payments system. This created two new challenges. First, what rights would nonbank financial institutions be granted to use the SWIFT system? Second, could a network system be designed to handle the complexities of their transactions? (Added complexity, compared to traditional interbank transfers, made quality control and regulatory reporting more difficult.) These two challenges tested policy adaptability and the continuing credibility of expertise.

A twofold solution gradually emerged. First, SWIFT expanded the range of full members and authorized network users to include all institutions that fell under detailed regulatory oversight, such as securities brokers and dealers. It granted lesser rights to less regulated financial institutions, which could connect to full members for payments, but could not otherwise transact SWIFT business. It also permitted clearly identified groups of specialized users—entities such as corporate treasurers of major global firms—to use the network for transactions among themselves. Second, SWIFT redesigned the standards and architecture of its new Internet-enabled network to separate the transport functions from the pure business details of transactions. Recall that this kind of "mix-and-match" standardized interface ("modularity") is a core feature of the growing information intensity of products.

One byproduct of adjusting membership and policy, while embracing modular design, was that SWIFT avoided a split in standard setting in the financial industry and remained the anchor for global flows. In 2015, MSO stakeholders still seemed satisfied.

Apparently, until 2015, nobody "cracked" SWIFT's network, but even before then, SWIFT offerings that combine the "messaging module" with agreed-on information for completing the transfer had problems. The head of security of one global bank told us that a skilled team examines multiple transactions daily where the information on the transaction falls "below guaranteed accuracy" or the transaction exceeds a certain size. After the review, the examining team determines whether the transaction should be accepted or refused.[32] Cybercrime is a major worry because all major financial institutions now contend with numerous daily probes of their security systems.[33] Even if there are no transmission errors in functions performed by SWIFT, the transaction may be flawed because of other errors.

In February 2016, the Bangladesh central bank suffered an $81 million theft from its New York Federal Reserve Bank account. Shortly thereafter, it was reported that in December 2015 a similar, much smaller, but perhaps related attack struck a Vietnamese commercial bank. In both cases, sophisticated malware was used to mimic SWIFT messages and persuade the receiving banks to transfer funds.[34] Then, in May 2016, litigation was filed that revealed a third successful fraudulent penetration. In 2015, cybercriminals tricked Wells Fargo Bank into making a $12 million transfer that it believed came from instructions from the Banco del Austro in Ecuador. In its suit, the Banco del Austro claimed that Wells Fargo should have recognized that the SWIFT messages were bogus; Wells Fargo countered that the Banco del Austro allowed thieves to breach their security, obtain legitimate credentials, and transmit fully authenticated SWIFT messages.[35] Critically, in all three cases hackers managed to impersonate legitimate SWIFT users and to even subvert the message confirmation safeguard, but the transmission system itself was not compromised. The challenge facing SWIFT led to refreshing the classic tools of cybersecurity by tightening best practices for credentialing messaging systems, certification of security practices, and information sharing.[36]

As this history shows, the fate of cybersecurity safeguards for a sector is closely related to commercial realities. Looking forward, the SWIFT system faces long-term technological challenges as business models for finance evolve. The core of the SWIFT security system is a "public key" encryption system that opens an encrypted channel between banks on demand. Beyond the impersonation issues just noted, the challenge for this approach is that although it is cost-effective for large payments, it may not be able to adapt to a world of billions of "micro financial transactions" from mobile devices each day. In addition, it may not be able to handle a multitude of interactions among Internet devices that involve no human being. The management of huge numbers of transactions and the explosion of microtransactions could make the public key technology too cumbersome and expensive in the future. Moreover, as financial chief information officers seek total systems security approaches, and not just short-term fixes, dissatisfaction may rise because the public key encryption technology does not resolve the human risk factor in payments. Even if the key is never violated, that does not prove that the rest of the transaction was not compromised. Markets are exploring numerous technologies, including blockchain technology projects sponsored by major banks, which would meet security, logistical, and cost-management goals.[37]

So, how can the SWIFT system be flexible and maintain its broader accountability to governments? Central banks never cede total freedom of action to commercial actors because of the hazards they could create for financial markets. Moreover, SWIFT must work with many central banks, not just one. How does it achieve accountability?[38]

Because shareholder representation is calculated on the basis of relative national transaction shares, SWIFT faces a commercial and a political reality. Unless the major commercial players trust SWIFT and believe their views are taken into account, they will pull out. In addition, governments of the largest market centers must be confident that their financial institutions will have a voice in governance.

Oversight by proxy (e.g., major private banks of major nations participating in board governance) is insufficient to satisfy wary central bankers worried about SWIFT's "systemic character."[39] Thus, central banks organized to provide more direct accountability. Since 1998, the G10 central bankers have reviewed SWIFT's security and reliability by accepting the Belgian central bank as the lead in examining its operations. In addition, as membership expanded to deal with financial complexity, overseers acknowledged that more countries played significant roles in the global financial system. In 2012, the most influential central banks created a SWIFT Oversight Forum to examine items such as systemic risk, the integrity of the infrastructure, and data confidentiality. SWIFT's board also mandated an annual external audit of its security system.[40] These measures sufficed even though some central banks wanted more control.

One potential threat to the integrity and universal trustworthiness of SWIFT is the worry that political leaders might instruct their central banks to expel banks from one or more country from the club, thus making it difficult or impossible to transact large-scale business in the world economy. This has happened once before. In February 2012, the U.S. Senate Banking Committee threatened sanctions against SWIFT to pressure it to cut its ties with blacklisted Iranian banks. After first resisting efforts to force it to sanction Iranian banks, in March 2012 SWIFT disconnected thirty Iranian banks deemed to be in breach of existing EU sanctions from its international network.[41] Following the lifting of sanctions, Iranian banks reconnected to the network in February 2016.[42]

Similarly, beginning in late 2014, the United States and the EU ratcheted up sanctions against Russia in response to its aggressive support of rebels fighting the Ukrainian government. There was increased speculation that, as a last resort, Russia and its banks could be expelled from SWIFT. If invoked, this so-called "nuclear option" would have isolated Russia, but would also have further undermined SWIFT's standing as an independent, trustworthy institution.[43] Russia threatened to retaliate.[44] This time, citing the concern that such an action could risk the integrity of its network and operations, SWIFT firmly resisted pressure to cut off Russian banks from its network.[45]

The SWIFT review process also operates within a system of de facto authoritative rules. The principal central banks address matters on payments systems by building on principles issued by the BIS and other clubs of financial authorities. This helped to anchor significant quasi-convergence of national rules, making oversight of SWIFT by a lead central bank possible.[46]

Established in 1930, originally as a vehicle for facilitating German reparations after World War I, the BIS is an unusual institution. It is not a traditional private bank that primarily conducts financial operations for its own account; instead, today it acts as an agent of its central bank members, including for certain financial transactions. The BIS also is a facilitating forum and provides the analytic support system for discussions on international financial regulation among the leading central banks. Thus, the BIS is a kind of hybrid MSO.

The BIS is not a universal membership organization, but it represents the world's largest financial markets.[47] Its recommendations and principles, developed by its staff in intensive consultation with the central banks, do not have the force of international treaty, but they are supported by the major financial nations. Further, cross-border financial transactions fall under individual national regulatory jurisdiction, so reaching agreement on global regulations is challenging. The ability of central banks to regulate is embodied in the 1975 BIS "Basel Concordat," which stipulated that the home country of a bank was responsible for regulating it to achieve financial soundness and that a country hosting a foreign bank had regulatory power over its operations in that country.[48] The Concordat gave countries the right to refuse entry to a bank from a country deemed to have inadequate regulation for soundness in its home country. This meant that the central banks of the major financial markets might, by mutual consent, unilaterally enforce guidelines for payments systems. These guidelines are "authoritative," as defined earlier.

Oversight and monitoring tend to be specialized in any arena. Large institutions are subjected to examination by multiple regulators, which often do not regularly speak to each other. Such specialization took place at SWIFT, leading to an imbroglio that sheds light on how privacy issues are deeply intertwined with cross-border data flows and security considerations in the world after 9/11 (see Chapter 8).

Until 2016, SWIFT appeared to be secure and adept at addressing controversies over privacy ("confidentiality" in banking parlance). It carefully aligned market stakeholder incentives with expertise and worked flexibly, while enhancing transparency and accountability. Its shareholders reinforced its mission by making it accept liability for the security of its transactions. There were controversies, but it adapted continuously. The operation of SWIFT illustrates the logic of coordination, but coordination is only possible because SWIFT solved the cooperation problems. Coordination is embedded using careful strategic positioning. Moreover, SWIFT operates within governmental and intergovernmental supervision.

Going forward, SWIFT still could provide a critical piece of cybersecurity global management because its national commercial membership is subject to strict national regulations and because of collective, if somewhat less institutionalized, action by central banks. SWIFT also has mastered an important technical problem—ensuring security and reliability in a tightly controlled function. This is practical because a small number of sophisticated institutions are focused on addressing a well-understood global problem, standards. Thus, although significant questions about the implementation of global financial policies always remain, SWIFT has a narrow focus and the largest players are aligned.

In summary, SWIFT reflects the dynamics outlined in Chapter 5 but introduces five refinements.

1. Ad hoc compromises caused a sufficient political economic coalition to emerge to surmount the threshold challenge for a club.
2. Hard work was required to maintain and keep incentives aligned and mission and trust within the MSO's core group, while growing the stakeholder community beyond the core group. Over time, government authorities also actively and tacitly delegated more authority to SWIFT and then monitored it.
3. SWIFT's experience showed that the complexity of an organization must be considered because it may hinder an MSO from rapidly adapting to a changing technological environment.
4. The international baseline for convergence can evolve from management of a coordination problem by important national central banks and de facto partial convergence by parallel regional regulatory authorities. The baseline was never inscribed in formal international rules. (The BIS guidelines are

not legally binding, but they bind most of the world's major financial institutions by their incorporation into binding national policies.)

5. The security challenge for IPD governance may complicate the oversight of MSOs that cannot take full advantage of civil society capabilities. Measures may need to clarify legal jurisdictions and then create transgovernmental measures to enhance confidence through transparency and monitoring of one country's agencies by those of another country.

Providing security for cross-border flows is a collective vulnerability of the financial system. The MSO is trusted to derive the detailed solution, but it is closely scrutinized under collectively agreed-on standards. SWIFT's responsibility to safeguard the technical infrastructure for the payments system meant that trade rules were minimally important for central bankers. What mattered was that national practices were anchored to the ongoing work of clubs of central bankers (and related regulators' clubs) that had the ability to coordinate on the overall principles for payments systems. Within that connective tissue of policy and government oversight, SWIFT managed the technical task with great operational autonomy and political economic dexterity, which mitigated controversies that could have undermined the logic of coordination.

7.3. Consumer Protection and Credit Card Fraud in a Digital Era

We turn now to the messy set of financial cybersecurity risks associated with consumer credit cards and cybercrime. The possibility of an "international governance regime" covering cybersecurity for consumer financial services depends on the quasi-convergence of domestic policy regimes. The risks are significant, but do not imperil the overall credit card service system globally. Moreover, there is de facto convergence because of the core group of commercial global players. So, how are matters progressing at a domestic level? This mini-case compares U.S. and EU decision making.

Market regulation in the United States is partly a product of the American constitutional system of divided powers and federalism, fragmented authority, and oversight structures. To safeguard the security of critical cyberinfrastructures, for example, each sector has its own arrangement. In recent years, however, a uniform template and legal authorities emerged at the federal level for each sector.[49] A sector coordinating council of significant government agencies with a sector "lead agency" takes the point on cybersecurity action. There is also an Industry Sector Advisory Committee that serves as a mixed U.S. government–private stakeholder forum in each sector to share critical cybersecurity information and advocate for best practices.

As the Web and e-commerce grew, consumer financial services emerged as an early focal point for cybersecurity. E-commerce raised cybersecurity problems for two reasons. First, a growing share of all commerce is on the Web, making hacking of electronic financial transactions a major risk. Second, sophisticated retailers and insurers retained customer financial data for a variety of purposes. It appears that retailers and insurance firms were slower to recognize the need to invest heavily to protect their data than were financial or ICT enterprises. Their data remained more vulnerable to outside attacks of hackers for criminal purposes than the data of entities that invested earlier.

By contrast, the finance sector traditionally required confidentiality and reliability in its services. Financial institutions held other peoples' money, not just their data. Cyberattacks, at the extreme, were a new form of bank robbery. Hence, cybersecurity presented a new challenge for a long-standing policy and business requisite. It is not surprising that the first Industry Service Advisory Committee, created in 1999, was for financial services.

Building on its long-time role in consumer protection, the Federal Trade Commission (FTC) emerged as the lead U.S. agency for consumer cyberfinancial crime. When the cyber problem became salient to the middle- and upper-income citizens flocking to e-commerce, Congress responded with legislative protections for consumers. The new rules held consumers virtually harmless for credit card fraud, which reduced the incentives of consumers to devote resources to prevent fraud.[50] Instead, the main motivation of consumers was to avoid the bother of replacing credit cards and updating their records. The laws also protected merchants from major liability so long as they exercised some minimal due diligence— checking credit card credentials for in-store transactions and demanding security code validations for online purchases. The main liability rested with credit card payments processors and banks/financial institutions that issued the credit cards. Visa and MasterCard, which together accounted for 84% of the world market share by dollar volume in 1984 (and 83% in 2015), represent and supply vast networks of financial institutions that issue their credit cards.[51] American Express, a freestanding firm, issues charge cards that are independent of the banks.[52] Since the card issuers had the most exposure, they also had the greatest incentive to invest in fighting cybercrime.[53]

The major credit card companies and their principal financial institutional members/partners provided the core group for an MSO. Because merchants use similar equipment or procedures for different types of payment cards, the credit card industry required sufficient unity to act together to force necessary changes on merchants.

Individual action by a specific credit card issuer was either not technically feasible or likely to cost them market share to other card issuers.

In short, the number of payments card systems was relatively small and incentives to act collectively were huge, which in September 2006 made it easier to meet the threshold challenge and successfully launch a new entity, the Payment Card Industry Security Standards Council.[54] This new MSO created and administered a set of "Data Security Standards." The credit card financial institutions rewrote their contracts with merchants to require adherence to the standards, which set forth twelve general security rules. The group then issued specific implementing instructions (e.g., merchants should not store customers' security code information), monitored compliance by the merchants, and allowed for contract enforcement actions if the standards were not implemented.

Problems remained. Merchants were slow to accept the new contracts because the rules required new merchant investments in equipment, software, and training, as well as business system reforms.[55] Moreover, the scheme recognized that for merchants, the incentives for compliance still rested significantly on monitoring and enforcement mechanisms.[56] These mechanisms were difficult to execute because the monitoring costs were high. When cyberbreaches occurred, there were disputes over whether the merchant was in compliance with the standards or whether the standards were deficient.

Recall that the standards emerged from a trade group that did not represent merchants and consumers. In addition, the standards covered various types of commerce that involved many fragmented businesses. Predictably, there were significant continuing problems.

In addition, public accountability and the relationship between MSOs and government authorities are important. In 2005, the FTC was looking for a way to address cybercrime related to charge and credit cards. It reviewed the Payment Card Industry rules and accepted them as the basis for federally enforced protection against cybercrime.[57] In effect, the FTC decided to judge the liability of merchants for a cybercrime based on their compliance with the Payment Card Industry standards. Analysts report that this signal sharply increased the rate of adherence to the new standards because it made the contractual issue irrelevant and raised the stakes for enforcement. As losses continued to climb and the public perception of risk escalated (as customer identities were hijacked and their financial data were hacked), retailers realized that they needed to recalculate their interests. Thus, U.S. regulators created new rules that imposed liabilities on merchants that failed to adopt chip and pin technology by October 2015. Swiping credit cards will phase out; microchips will replace magnetic stripes on the back of almost all cards in the United States.[58] Predictably, the transition will be bumpy because retailers are saddled with new costs for transitioning to the new chip cards and complain that the banks are getting most of the benefits.[59]

The FTC action was consistent with contemporary regulatory practice. For example, the Federal Energy Regulatory Commission delegates the task of proposing new operational standards for systems reliability (including cybersecurity) to the North American Electricity Reliability Corporation (which includes Canada). The Federal Energy Regulatory Commission has the right to approve or remand the standard for further work and can initiate a demand that the North American Electricity Reliability Corporation develop a standard to address a particular problem. If adoption lags, the Federal Energy Regulatory Commission also has the power to enforce compliance with the standards.[60]

Simultaneously, financial institutions confronted by proliferating numbers of breaches of credit card security began to launch lawsuits against merchants to recover their losses from breaches. This strategy, which is likely to be costly and extended, introduced animosity into a long-standing commercial relationship. As a result, the payments card industry created a dispute settlement mechanism to address arguments about liabilities and compensation among the credit and charge card companies, merchants, and banks. This form of dispute settlement system usually results in smaller, rapidly negotiated compromises that lower the long-term stress on the relationship.

The complex emerging mix of private and public authority provokes complaints that the negotiation process raises protections too slowly. Further, the incentives remain skewed, promoting significant action by the credit and charge card industry, less by merchants, and even less by consumers. This influences the choice of options for strengthening protection. For example, the industry reached an agreement to require multiple forms of identity authentication for card transactions to enhance security. Disputes arose, however, about what constituted the most cost-effective and technology-smart solution. The decision was unbalanced because merchants shouldered less liability and therefore were reluctant to make capital expenditures for new card terminals that would use a chip and pin system of added validation.

The EU had a more urgent problem and took a different decision-making route. Credit card fraud was significantly higher in the EU than in the United States. (Before changes in security were introduced, the UK loss rate in 2004 was about $.14 cents on every $100, compared to the U.S. rate of about $.05 cents that same year.)[61] The EU recognized that the liability regime was skewed toward responsibility by the card industry and that greater legitimacy and political urgency might emerge from engaging merchants and consumer groups. To move the process along, the EU initiated a public consultation process to identify alternatives that might provide more security. By then, considerable support existed in the United States for the chip and pin system as the best way to improve authentication of transactions. The strongest support came from the major American credit and charge card companies. Hence, the expert community and a business core group lined up around a previously negotiated solution. The commission then built on this momentum to push its independent drive to facilitate a single European payments system to promote European financial unification. This action was followed in 2015 by EU requirements on enhanced encryption and authentication that addressed a long-standing EU concern over low European public trust of electronic payments systems.[62]

The EU never mandated a change to chip and pin technology, but it informally signaled that it would be pleased if the credit card system required that merchants use the technology so long as they were still held harmless. The switch took time, but more than 70% of terminals came into compliance within a few years. This example of cybercrime and consumer financial services highlights six important points.

First, de facto convergence was facilitated by a common diagnosis of the problem on both sides of the Atlantic. U.S. and EU liability rules for credit and charge card fraud drove the response to cybercrime by the card suppliers, the merchant intermediaries, and customers. In both jurisdictions, the rules initially slanted to provide maximum protection from loss to consumers, then to merchants, and only then to credit card suppliers. Thus, the similarity of the approach to liability, and some of the perverse consequences it induced, set the foundation for the evolving security regime.

Second, the regional MSOs had core overlapping members. U.S. and EU private associations of stakeholders built around the payments card industry organized the efforts to introduce enhanced security, in essence defining the options for upgrading security. The card suppliers bore the brunt of the financial risk, but they recognized that a solution required a larger, more autonomous set of organizers to enhance transparency and legitimacy while supplying sufficient public accountability. Payment credit industry rules emerged in the United States. A more formal process of public–private consultation emerged in the EU.

Third, the MSOs relied on U.S. or EU regulators to backstop their efforts. The relevant public agencies in both regions partnered with MSOs to institute changes. Their approaches differed slightly. The FTC held hearings and decided to embrace the Payment Card Industry standards as a basis for evaluating liability claims under consumer protection laws that were more general than cybercrime protection. The EU consultation process led the commission to signal that the card industry's proposals were acceptable policy that enhanced movement toward a single European payments market. Both processes provided for public accountability and mitigated the risk that purely voluntary negotiations would lag in providing a socially optimal level of protection. Both regions took considerable time and engaged in experimentation to determine the most effective option. The rules emerged from learning by doing.[63]

Fourth, history shaped the easiest path for government action. The U.S. government treated this primarily as a consumer protection and privacy issue. Even among the frayed U.S. agencies overseeing financial questions, this was not central to the operation of the already unified national financial market. The relevant legal authority was consumer protection, an FTC stronghold. In contrast, the EU approached this as part of the continuing effort to achieve a common financial market. Consumer protection and privacy were of secondary importance. This gave the issue a higher place in the overall EU policy agenda than it had in the United States.

Fifth, the market problem was viewed mainly as a domestic problem in the United States and as a EU problem in Europe. This was because customers of payments card issuers were protected by the national rules of the customer's home market, although there were major common players, including some international credit and charge card companies and banks. Moreover, for the small, affluent market of "multination" consumers, some of whom held cards from several nations, there was enough convergence of U.S. and EU rules that the dissimilarities were manageable. Reforms also converged. Efforts to strengthen security differed in execution—chip and pin systems were prevalent in the EU well before 2014, but the United States mandated adoption by late 2015. Both regions enhanced consumer protection of data by adding requirements for card "authentication" while shielding against financial risk. In short, convergence and a limited form of extraterritorial reach of national rules reduced the need for a common international code.

Sixth, international trade rules served as a background frame to reduce the risks of increased regulation for foreign firms. In the professionally paranoid world of regulatory and trade policy, where everyone looks for subtle intended or unintended risks, trade rules eased some of those risks. For example, the General Agreement on Trade in Services financial services agreement requires "least trade restrictive" rules in addition to national treatment.[64] The agreement's obligations also require transparency in the development of financial services and the U.S. and EU national commitments for financial services ensured market access for payment card organizations and their right to move payments across borders in most circumstances. The risk of bad behavior remains despite a WTO obligation. Thus, at least in sophisticated bureaucracies, national policy makers tend to design to the "test" unless they want to defy the spirit of the WTO. These obligations establish parameters around the potential solution sets that simplified the bargaining issues. Ultimately, the global card industry might prefer a uniform approach, but it received substantial realignment of liability incentives in parallel major markets. Meanwhile, the United States and the EU each dealt with its own economy with slight variations in approach. In addition, the credit and charge card industry, as well as its users, continued to operate on a global scale because the solutions were similar and did not limit the mobility of credit card transaction availability by national boundary.

What have we learned? Although few international instruments for comprehensive cooperation on cybersecurity exist, this review of efforts to manage cybersecurity problems suggests several lessons. Leaving aside defense issues, even in the commercial marketplace most of the action is at the level of sector-specific arrangements. A more general approach might yield improvements, such as those noted about cooperation among cyberresponse teams, information sharing, and improving legal assistance treaties to deal with cyberthreat. But the specific challenges of individual markets likely will lead to parallel special arrangements. There also is broad agreement on many of the causal dynamics behind cyberrisks. This agreement on the causal issues leads to some parallelism in the sector and market-specific governance responses.

The governance arrangements in both cases were sensitive to the legacy of prior regulatory arrangements for the market and the level of global interdependence involved in the security challenge. Cross-border payment flows required a common international solution. SWIFT evolved in a market with strict Central Bank oversight of national payments systems and had to conform to the expectations and regulatory power of central banks. Similarly, cyberfraud in payments by credit and debit cards was seen mainly as a domestic problem. The United States defined cyberfraud as a matter of consumer protection because of the FTC's legal authorities. The EU saw it as a matter of consumer protection and of integrating the EU's internal financial market. Therefore, cyberfraud was higher on the policy agenda in the EU.

MSOs drove the practical problem solving and membership dynamics mattered. Their membership dynamics (overlapping memberships for credit cards and a carefully managed global membership and board of directors system in SWIFT) reduced incentives for market manipulation in the name of security and provided a credible club of committed actors for governance. The MSOs also depended on government backstopping to make their proposals effective and the MSOs were accountable to government oversight. SWIFT in particular exemplifies the challenge of finding the right intergovernmental accountability arrangements for MSOs playing a significant role in major issues.

Notes

1. Our thinking about global financial standards and their implementation is informed by Layna Mosley, "Regulating Globally, Implementing Locally: The Financial Codes and Standards

Effort," *Review of International Political Economy*, 17, no. 4 (October 2010): 724–761; Büthe and Mattli, *The New Global Rulers*, Chaps. 4 and 5.

2. Our analysis does not cover four special considerations about cyberwar: (1) The *complexity of risk* is more difficult to gauge when dealing with cyberwar (what is protected, from whom, and with what consequence?). (2) *Cross-domain issues*—cyberwar does not take place in a military vacuum—the potential link to "kinetic" warfare adds complexity. (3) *An ill-defined strategic environment*—there is nothing comparable to present "focal points" for strategic calculation (i.e., certain national borders or "no first use" norms for nuclear weapons), including an agreed-on concept of what cyberwar is, that emerged in the later stages of the Cold War. (4) *A blurred boundary* between cyberwar and cyberespionage. Ronald J. Deibert, *Black Code: Inside the Battle for Cyberspace* (Toronto: Random House, Canada: 2014). P. W. Singer and Allan Friedman, *Cybersecurity and Cyberwar—What Everyone Needs to Know* (New York: Oxford University Press, 2014), pp. 34–36. William J. Lynn III, "Defending a New Domain: The Pentagon's Cyberstrategy," *Foreign Affairs*, 89, no. 5 (September/October 2010): 97–108; Joseph Nye, "Nuclear Lessons for Cyber Security," *Strategic Studies Quarterly* (Winter 2011): 18–38, https://citizenlab.org/cyber-norms2012/nuclearlessons.pdf.

3. As an example of how to deal with the crossover with espionage, consider the escalating U.S.–Chinese recriminations on cyberespionage for commercial purposes. This led to a joint declaration on cybercrime by the presidents of the two governments in September 2015. Some China security experts believe this declaration resulted in some reduction in the Chinese activity. Nigel Inkster, *China's Cyber Power* (London: Institute for International Strategic Studies, 2016).

4. Ross Anderson et al., "Measuring the Cost of Cybercrime," http://www.econinfosec.org/archive/weis2012/papers/Anderson_WEIS2012.pdf.

5. David D. Clark and Susan Landau, "Untangling Attribution," *Harvard National Security Journal*, 2, no. 2 (2011): 25–40, http://harvardnsj.org/wp-content/uploads/2011/03/Vol.-2_Clark-Landau_Final-Version.pdf. For a comprehensive statement of all risks see: Marc Goodman, *Future Crimes* (New York: Knopf Doubleday, 2015).

6. Issues of cyberwar cover many of the same points as criminal and corporate cyberattacks. See Richard A. Clarke with Robert K. Knake, *Cyber War: The Next Threat to National Security and What to Do about It* (New York: Ecco, 2010).

7. This includes a "zero-day" exploit market for espionage/military/terrorist purposes. Zero-day attacks originate from undiscovered bugs that open a system to attack. They may be sold secretly to interested parties, including in secret auctions. Charlie Miller, "The Legitimate Vulnerability Market: Inside the Secretive World of 0-Day Exploit Sales," Workshop on the Economics of Information Security, 2007, http://weis2007.econinfosec.org/papers/29.pdf.

8. Singer and Friedman, *Cybersecurity and Cyberwar*, 2014, p. 75.

9. In addition to the EU, non-EU signatories include the United States, Japan, Australia, and a handful of small countries. Michael Vatis, *The Council of Europe Convention on Cybercrime, Proceedings of a Workshop on Deterring Cyber-attacks: Informing Strategies and Developing Options for US Policy* (Washington, D.C.: National Academies Press, 2010).

10. Kenneth Cukier, Viktor Mayer-Schönberger, and Lewis Branscomb, Ensuring (and Insuring) Critical Information Infrastructure Protection, Kennedy School of Government, RWP05-055, October 2005, http://papers.ssrn.com/sol3/papers.cfm?abstract_id=832628

11. Our discussion of incentives follows the logic of Tyler Moore, "The Economics of Cybersecurity: Principles and Policy Options," *International Journal of Critical Infrastructure*

Protection, 3–4 (December 2010): 103–117. Also see Tyler Moore and Ross Anderson, "Economics and Internet Security: A Survey of Recent Analytical, Empirical and Behavioral Research," in Martin Peitz and Joel Waldfogel (eds.), *The Oxford Handbook of the Digital Economy* (New York: Oxford University Press, 2012).

12. George A. Akerlof, "The Market for "Lemons: Quality Uncertainty and the Market Mechanism," *The Quarterly Journal of Economics*, 84, no. 3 (1970): 488–500. Carfax reduced the information gap.

13. Singer and Friedman *Cybersecurity and Cyberwar*, 2014.

14. Paul Mozur and Jane Perlez, "China Quietly Targets U.S. Tech Companies in Security Reviews," *New York Times*, May 16, 2016; "China Pushes Change in IT Infrastructure by Strengthening Regulation of Cyber Security," *Linklaters*, April 8, 2015, http://www.linklaters.com/Insights/AsiaNews/LinkstoChina/Pages/China-pushes-change-IT-infrastructure-strengthening-regulation-cyber-security.aspx.

15. European Union, "The Directive on Security of Network and Information Systems (NIS Directive), July 6, 2016, https://ec.europa.eu/digital-single-market/en/network-and-information-security-nis-directive.

16. The EU's NIS Directive similarly mandates response teams and sector-specific organizational cooperation.

17. Nicole van der Meulin, Eun Jo, and Stefan Soesanto, "Cybersecurity in the European Union and Beyond: Exploring the Threats and Policy Response" (New York: RAND Corporation, 2015), http://www.rand.org/pubs/research_reports/RR1354.html. Jonah Force Hill, "Problematic Alternatives: MLAT Reform for the Digital Age," *Harvard National Security Journal*, January 28, 2015, http://harvardnsj.org/2015/01/problematic-alternatives-mlat-reform-for-the-digital-age/.

18. UL launched a Cybersecurity Assurance Program to check whether products have reasonable security practices and software safeguards. It cannot ensure that products are "safe."

19. We developed this example in discussion with several cybersecurity experts. We particularly thank Stefan Savage. Also see Singer and Friedman, pp. 176 and 205; Shane and Hunker. Federal Trade Commission, "FTC Report on Internet of Things Urges Companies to Adopt Best Practices to Address Consumer Privacy and Security Risks," 2015. Karen Rose, Scott Eldridge, and Lyman Chapin, "The Internet of Things: An Overview," The Internet Society, October 2015.

20. As early as 2000 Hal Varian urged, "Liability should be assigned to the parties best able to manage the risk." "Managing Online Security Risks," *New York Times*, June 1, 2000, cited in Susan Landau, *Surveillance or Security? The Risks Posed by New Wiretapping Technologies* (Cambridge, MA: MIT Press, 2013), p. 242.

21. In 1961, only eight U.S. banks maintained branches outside of U.S. borders. Only four of them had more than four branches: First National City Bank (Citibank) seventy-seven, Chase twenty-four, Bank of America fourteen, and First National Bank of Boston ten. The realm of foreign exchange was a sleepy backwater because fixed exchange rates instituted by the Bretton Woods system were usually stable. Jonathan David Aronson, *Money and Power: Banks and the World Monetary System* (Thousand Oaks, CA: Sage, 1978).

22. Although the analytic frame is ours, the empirics on SWIFT's history and operation draw heavily on the illuminating definitive history of SWIFT: Susan V. Scott and Markos Zachariadis, *The Society for Worldwide Interbank Financial Telecommunication (SWIFT)—Cooperative Governance for Network Innovation, Standards, and Community* (New York: Routledge, 2014).

23. https://www.swift.com/about-us, accessed June 4, 2016.

24. https://www.swift.com/insights/press-releases/swift-announces-major-price-reductions-for-2014. https://www.swift.com/insights/press-releases/swift-to-deliver-a-57_price-reduction-by-the-end-of-2015. The phrase and cost analysis is from Scott and Zachariadis.

25. Fears about reliability were justified. Indeed, a year after SWIFT's founding, on the afternoon of June 26, 1974, the shaky Bankhaus Herstatt was forced into liquidation by its German regulators. Earlier that day, Bankhaus Herstatt received a sizeable Deutsche Mark payment in Frankfurt from New York. Herstatt had promised to deliver dollars to the New York sending banks in return. Time zone differences meant that Herstatt received the funds before it was shut down, but could not deliver the dollars to the counterparty banks after it was ceased. A significant financial crisis ensued, which led to the implementation of a new global settlements system to make certain that payments between banks were finalized and executed in real time.

26. https://www.swift.com/insights/press-releases/swift-announces-10_rebate-on-2015-messaging.

27. Scott and Zachariadis, *The Society for Worldwide Interbank Financial Telecommunication*, 2014, p. 16.

28. Interview, Paris, October 2014. SWIFT is careful to tout the ways in which it facilitates the Single European Payments Area. Dominic Broom, "Forging a Path to the Future of Payments," *Swift Connectivity for Corporate Treasurers*, 2014, pp. 5–8.

29. This issue has plagued institutions like ICANN because its incorporation in the United States made other countries believe that the U.S. government had the advantages of a legal and judicial system built around its policy penchants, thus reinforcing U.S. government dominance.

30. A cogent review of the network literature is Miles Kahler's "Networked Politics: Agency, Power and Governance," the opening essay in his edited volume of the same title.

31. Brown and Marsden, *Regulating Code*, 2013.

32. Discussed with the head of security for an international bank, Paris, October 2014.

33. It was revealed in February 2015 that a sophisticated international group of hackers bilked banks in Russia, Eastern Europe, and elsewhere out of hundreds of millions of dollars, often causing ATMs to spit out wads of bank notes to waiting accomplices. This was not a breach of SWIFT, but a direct defrauding of the banks. David Sanger and Nicole Perlroth, "Bank Hackers Steal Millions via Malware," *New York Times*, February 15, 2015, p. A1, 11, http://www.nytimes.com/2015/02/15/world/bank-hackers-steal-millions-via-malware.html?_r=0

34. "Heist Finance," *The Economist*, May 28, 2016, p. 67; Michael Corkery, "Hackers' $81 Million Sneak Attack on World Banking," *New York Times*, April 30, 2016, http://www.nytimes.com/2016/05/01/business/dealbook/hackers-81-million-sneak-attack-on-world-banking.html; and "Once Again, Thieves Enter Swift Financial Network and Steal," *New York Times*, May 12, 2016, http://www.nytimes.com/2016/05/13/business/dealbook/swift-global-bank-network-attack.html.

35. Devlin Barrett and Katy Burne, "Now It's Three: Ecuador Bank Hacked via Swift," *The Wall Street Journal*, May 19, 2016, http://www.wsj.com/articles/lawsuit-claims-another-global-banking-hack-1463695820.

36. SWIFT, Customer Security Programme, May 27, 2016, https://www.swift.com/ordering-support/customer-security-programme-csp.

37. Interviews with entrepreneurs in the cybersecurity industry revealed that many firms claim performance advantages from new technologies.

38. Our analysis was informed by parallels to J. Lawrence Broz and Michael Brewster Hawes, "U.S. Domestic Politics and International Monetary Fund Policy," in Hawkins, Lake, Nielson, and Tierney.

39. Scott and Zachariadis, *The Society for Worldwide Interbank Financial Telecommunication*, 2014, p. 43.

40. SWIFT requires top-of-the-line redundant cybersecurity protections. By contrast, SITA, which provides high-speed network communications to and between members from the air transport, deals with less sensitive material and does not require the same level of cybersecurity protection. See http://www.sita.aero/solutions-and-services/solutions#sthash.NcyIWcUS.dpuf.

41. Jonathan Fahey, "European Sanctions Have Begun to Block the Iranian Banking System off from the Rest of the World," *Business Insider*, March 15, 2012, http://www.businessinsider.com/iran-banking-swift-2012-3.

42. Andrew Torchia, "Iranian Banks Reconnected to SWIFT Network after Four-Year Hiatus," *Reuters*, February 17, 2016, http://www.reuters.com/article/us-iran-banks-swift-id USKCN0VQ1FD.

43. Valentin Schmid, "Financial Sanctions against Russia: The Nuclear Option," *Epoch Times*, March 29, 2014, http://www.theepochtimes.com/n3/column/588433-financial-sanctions-against-russia-the-nuclear-option/.

44. "Russia Threatens SWIFT," *The American Interest*, January 26, 2015, http://www.the-american-interest.com/2015/01/26/russia-threatens-swift/.

45. In this same statement, SWIFT rejected calls to cut off Israeli banks from its network. "SWIFT Sanctions Statement," October 6, 2014, https://www.swift.com/insights/press-releases/swift-sanctions-statement.

46. This linkage of common principles, national payments systems, and collective oversight of SWIFT is illustrated in a report by the Australian central bank: "In April 2012, the Bank for International Settlements Committee on Payment and Settlement Systems (CPSS) and the Technical Committee of the International Organization of Securities Commissions (IOSCO) released *Principles for Financial Market Infrastructures* (the Principles). These update, harmonize and strengthen the pre-existing standards for payments, clearing and settlement systems, including the CPSS's *Core Principles for Systemically Important Payment Systems* . . . against which self-assessments of [the Australian payments system] have to date been carried out. . . . This new tier—the SWIFT Oversight Forum—comprises representatives from 25 central banks and monetary authorities, plus the chair of the CPSS secretariat." Reserve Bank of Australia, Payments System Board Annual Report, 2012, accessed November 24, 2014, http://www.rba.gov.au/publications/annual-reports/psb/2012/html/oversight-high-value.html.

47. As of 2016, there were sixty central banks that were members of the BIS. Together, they represented about 95% of the global GDP. "The Board of Directors may have up to 21 members, including six ex officio directors, comprising the central bank Governors of Belgium, France, Germany, Italy, the United Kingdom and the United States. Each ex officio member may appoint another member of the same nationality. Nine Governors of other member central banks may be elected to the Board." https://www.bis.org/, accessed June 4, 2016.

48. Carl Felsenfeld and Genci Bilali, "The Role of the Bank for International Settlements in Shaping the World Financial System," *University of Pennsylvania Journal of International*, 25 *Economic Law* 945. Michele Fratianni and John Pattison, "An Assessment of the Bank of International Settlements," Paper for the International Financial Advisory Commission, December 26, 1999.

49. Jeffrey Hunker, "Global Leadership in Cybersecurity: Can the U.S. Provide It?" in Shane and Hunker.

50. Middle- and upper-income citizens are more likely to vote, so Congress is sensitive to their interests. See Moore and Anderson, "Economics and Internet Security, 2012.

51. In 2015, Visa held about 55.52% share of the global card market, followed by MasterCard with 26.27%, China's rapidly growing UnionPay with 12.79%, American Express with 3.21%, and Japan's JCB with 1.23%, whereas Diners/Discover fell to 0.98%. *Yahoo! Finance*, "The Nilson Report Releases Global Card Report 2015," May 9, 2016, http://finance.yahoo.com/news/nilson-report-releases-global-cards-153000667.html.

52. Payments cards come in two distinct types—charge cards and credit cards—that are often lumped together. A charge card, like the American Express card, allows cardholders to make a purchase, which is paid for by the issuer of the card. This creates a debt of the cardholder to the issuer, which is supposed to be repaid in full, usually each month. Credit cards, such as Visa and MasterCard, are usually linked to banks and other financial institutions. They provide revolving credit to the cardholder. If the designated minimum payment is made each month, there are no late fees, but an interest charge is levied on the unpaid balance, often backdated to the date of purchase.

53. According to Visa, about 6 cents per $100 of sales was lost to fraud and crime. Mark MacCarthy, "Government and Private Sector Roles in Providing Information Security in the U.S. Financial Services Industry," in Shane and Hunker, p. 92.

54. The founding members of the Payment Card Industry Security Standards Council were American Express, Discover Financial Services (founded by Dean Witter, but independent since 2007), JCB (Japan Credit Bureau), MasterCard, and Visa. The Council, which claims to act independent of its members, was designed to manage the evolution of the Payment Card Industry.

55. Cultural differences and different levels of security and privacy concerns by customers arise. For example, the norm in most of Europe is that merchants present terminals to customers that they bring to the table. Customers never surrender their cards. Most Americans blithely surrender their cards to a waiter, who takes it away and then brings it back with the charge slip. Americans trust that restaurant workers will not purloin the card number and pin for later use. In Korea, the norm is for the customer to take the card to the cashier, so that they are never separated from the card.

56. Card fraud keeps rising. In the wake of the massive hacking of the credit card data at the national retailers Target and Home Depot, the adverse publicity factor for big merchants may incentivize them to strengthen their security because it may cause them to lose market share. The hack of up to 80 million customer records from Anthem, the health insurance giant, revealed in early February 2015, was even more devastating to public confidence. Health identification records are more valuable on the black market than information stolen from retailers and commercial sites because these records can be used to file false medical claims.

57. This account draws on MacCarthy, "Government and Private Sector Roles," 2012, pp. 69–100.

58. The U.S. industry will migrate to the new Europay, MasterCard, and Visa (EMV) standard for interoperation of circuit cards card system by October 2015. EMV will use microchip-enabled credit cards. Banks can issue cards that require a PIN number instead of a signature, but the switch to PINs will not be required in October 2015. "October 2015: The End of Swipe-and-Sign Credit Card," *The Wall Street Journal*, February 6, 2014, http://blogs.wsj.com/corporate-intelligence/2014/02/06/october-2015-the-end-of-the-swipe-and-sign-credit-card/.

59. Rachel Abrams, "Chip Cards Give Stores New Gripe vs. Banks," *New York Times*, November 17, 2015, pp. B1, B6, http://www.nytimes.com/2015/11/17/business/chip-credit-cards-give-retailers-another-grievance-against-banks.html.

60. Hunker, pp. 48–49, in Shane and Hunker, *Cybersecurity*, 2012.

61. Mark Scott, "A More Secure Credit Card, European Style," *New York Times*, December 2, 2014, p. F5, http://bits.blogs.nytimes.com/2014/12/02/preparing-for-chip-and-pin-cards-in-the-united-states/.

62. Noëlle Lenoir argues that this was a case where privacy protection has created a commercial advantage for European payments system: "Data Protection in Europe vs. the United States," *Politique Internationale*," No. 151 (Spring 2016): 77–83.

63. MacCarthy, "Government and Private Sector Roles," 2012.

64. Wendy Dobson, "Financial Services and International Trade Agreements," pp. 289–337, in Mattoo, Stern, and Zanini; World Trade Organization, Council for Trade in Services, Committee on Trade in Financial Services, Financial Services, Background Note by the Secretariat, S/C/W/312, S/FIN/W/73, February 3, 2010.

8 Data Privacy

CAN WE CREATE a consensus about how global governance can advance a trusted digital environment? The previous chapter examined the dynamics of cybersecurity. Here we analyze privacy debates that involve perennially sensitive issues about the rights of citizens, a domain that does not fit tidily into the cubbyholes of economic policy. Thus, privacy represents a major challenge for global economic governance.

We argue that, despite intense political heat, many of the necessary elements required for a club to launch an international governance regime for privacy already exist. We identify these elements and then suggest which pieces are missing. Chapter 9 then proposes a way to link elements of a privacy regime to trade rules for the digital economy, including the cloud ecosystem.

Our analysis has five parts. Section 8.1 reviews the logic of the privacy challenge. Flaws in market incentives undermine efforts to use voluntary agreements to achieve a socially optimal outcome on privacy protection. Some level of governance intervention is needed. Fortunately, international governance measures can address the common causes of lapses in privacy protections. The remaining policy gaps arise from the mix of constitutional authorities and political economic conditions that any international agreement would need to accommodate.

Section 8.2 examines ongoing efforts to forge international agreements on privacy protection through the OECD and, later, through APEC (Asia-Pacific Economic Cooperation). We introduce principles that could advance a consensus on a "causal theory" for regime action. Although these principles are not authoritative, they establish the possibility of a common international baseline.

Section 8.3 analyzes the U.S.–EU privacy disputes and the possibility of mutual recognition of their privacy protection regimes and of surveillance practices. We review the events leading to the EU's rejection of the Safe Harbor Agreement by the European Court of Justice in October 2015 and the new agreement announced in early February 2016 to replace it. The analysis shows how legal traditions and political economic factors caused the application of the OECD Principles to become a source of continuing tension. We also examine the feasibility of using interlocking, national regulatory measures to create an international baseline.

Section 8.4 considers how innovation in global "civil society" might shape the governance of privacy. We revisit the history of SWIFT to draw additional lessons from the resolution of a transatlantic privacy dispute that involves government surveillance. We then show how marketplace accommodations and governance innovations that spring from civil society blur the differences in official policy frameworks. As the facts on the ground change, the space for creative governance adaptations expands.

Finally, in Section 8.5, we highlight necessary elements of a desirable regime that are absent from existing principles.

8.1. The Logic of Privacy Policy

Privacy is a complex field for legal analysis. We do not pretend to analyze the subtlest legal details. Instead, we probe the logic and political economy of privacy first principles as a basis for international governance. We simplify to clarify the fundamentals. To begin, privacy depends partly on the state of cybersecurity. A cyberattack or a lapse in routine data security practices can lead to the disclosure of confidential data. In this context, the question is, How much security protection must be assured to meet privacy requirements? There are difficult operational questions associated with this challenge. A second challenge has proven even more difficult politically: What privacy guarantees for personal data are required?[1]

Privacy concerns are growing in parallel with expanding commercial and governmental use of big data analysis. Privacy worries are further fueled by proliferating numbers of data breaches.[2] To clarify the core logic of privacy issues, for now assume perfect cybersecurity is possible. If only those with proper authorization could access the data, what would holders of personal data promise to protect and what would they be legally required to protect?

This raises three questions. The first question involves "citizen-to-government" privacy protection. How and when may governments subpoena or use covert means to access personal data without consent? In short, what personal data are legal authorities barred from accessing without prior consent? As the U.S.–EU comparison in Section 8.3 shows, this is more of a security/legal enforcement issue than a privacy issue. It is closely intertwined with legal and constitutional traditions that address privacy values.

Second, does the legal and administrative framework give meaning to any privacy policy? Who decides on the penalties and should they include redress for grievances about data accuracy or reputational harm if the data are made public? The third question involves the equivalent of "civilian-to-civilian" privacy protections involving commerce. What types of protection of private information are guaranteed in everyday commercial transactions? Should only medical information be highly protected or all personal details? What are the specific forms of the protection? When can the original collector of data share it?

To further clarify the universal challenges of citizen-to-citizen privacy in the marketplace, imagine a common global constitutional framework. In this unified legal system, privacy issues remain difficult to resolve because of five conditions that economists acknowledge can distort market performance.

1. *Personal information has collective goods properties* because it is nonrivalrous (not exhausted by one-time use) and many can continue to use it. As discussed in Chapter 2, this creates an externality that yields value to the original collector of the information for the original purpose, as well as additional value that derives from as-yet undetermined uses. But users have imperfect knowledge about the changing uses and risks for information. They are unclear about the value of their personal information and they have inconsistent preferences about how to value information that changes over time.[3] These difficulties tend to undermine the efficiency of market exchanges. If they depend purely on market devices, users are unlikely to achieve their optimal level of personal data privacy.

2. *The absence of clear property rights for private information* can raise challenges. When clear property rights exist, complex societal dynamics are easier to resolve. When property rights reside with the state or community (as in tribal rights to fisheries), it is simpler to assign costs and benefits and to negotiate about their consequences.[4] Property rights also make the transfer of rights more efficient. Unfortunately, privacy property rights remain murky.

3. The *governance remedy may excessively lock down personal information and fail to enhance consumer welfare.* Economic and legal analysis shows that individuals may benefit if information is disclosed. A classic example is that consumers want to be "known" to be good credit risks. Demonstrated high credit scores reduce risks to lenders and allow them

to make loans on more favorable terms, thus providing advantages for some consumers. Hence, individuals can benefit most when personal information is set in an ongoing give-and-take relationship. The rise of "free search" and other Web applications adds a new factor. Search in particular has radically changed the way information shapes our lives and commerce. Yet it is funded mainly using data generated by search users to sell ads displayed on search engines. Similar dynamics apply to other web apps. This is a market bargain—free service in exchange for information sharing. Or, as is often said in Silicon Valley, "If you're not paying, you're the product."

4. *As technology changes, the value relationships shift.* Three examples illustrate the impact of technology. First, as data analytics increase in power, data from different transactions for different purposes can be reaggregated to build profiles of individuals that may reveal more about a person than they intended to disclose.[5] Second, powerful data analytics permit growing price and service discrimination, as with rewards or discounts offered in "loyalty" programs.[6] By ceding information, an individual may get a better deal. Third, information uses evolve. The growth of the steam-driven printing press propelled the proliferation of newspapers at the beginning of the 20th century. These newspapers unleashed worlds of information for users and thereby "nationalized" information about high-profile people and firms to their fame and infamy.[7] Today, web search engines perform the same function more efficiently. In addition, citizen-to-citizen disclosure of private information impacts the distribution of social returns. Broader circulation of information about "newsworthy" individuals and firms may help or harm them. Either way, there is a demand for information that, judging by the proliferation of gossip-oriented media, is highly valued by the public.[8]

5. *Regulation imposes costs on society* as a whole. Compliance and monitoring can be expensive. Efficiency losses follow because rules rarely are totally efficient for all market transactions. As posited in Chapter 6, in the IPD it can be costly to restrict flexible exploration of data and data-enabled services and products. This is risky for the EU, the region with the toughest privacy restrictions, because its economy is considerably less data intensive than is the U.S. economy. Studies suggest that the EU's privacy and data localism rules could result in further economic losses of 2.3 to more than 5% of the GDP depending on the final mix of rules.[9] Whether these estimates are correct and whatever the offsetting social benefits, regulations impact society beyond individual costs and benefits.[10]

In sum, governance can help optimize social returns from privacy information markets, but achieving the right balance of costs and benefits is difficult and ever changing. And, as noted in Chapter 6, cloud computing means that the incidence of extraterritorial disputes regarding privacy will increase markedly. What are the implications for an international governance regime for privacy? We explore efforts to create a baseline of consensus on international governance next.

8.2. The Search for International Baselines

Recall that an international governance regime requires principles (a theory about how collective effort can intervene to solve a problem) and norms (expected acceptable behavior). It also requires a clear notion of the institutions that are accountable to government authorities for decision making.

The effort to define an international baseline for privacy protection began in earnest in 1980 when the OECD laid out eight guides for problem solving in response to the operations of the early computer networks. They were far-sighted, addressing many of the key dilemmas of privacy governance.[11] Calls to revise the OECD guidelines came as attention to the privacy implications of Big Data increased, especially when it flowed across global boundaries. In 2011, APEC added further governance practices in its Cross Border Privacy Rules.[12] Two years later, four additional guidelines emerged in the 2013 OECD revisions. (These guidelines, principles, and rules are listed in the appendix to this chapter.) These rules could evolve into a common floor for expected behavior among most of the leading Asian economies and several Latin American countries that are APEC members. India is not an APEC member, but might follow since these rules evolve from traditional democracies. But, their compatibility with Chinese culture, goals, and processes is an open question.

We integrate and reorganize these guidelines to clarify their unifying logic because they have become the de facto baseline for most privacy guidelines, including those worked out in MSOs. Together, the OECD and APEC created a causal theory that embraces the advancement of privacy by requiring five basic building blocks. (The first three emerged in the 1980 OECD statement.)

The core premise is the "consent principle," which holds that personal data collection requires the consent of the user. This applies the problem-solving logic of standard contractual thinking—I agree to exchange my data for something offered by a supplier that I want—and consumer protection laws to the terms for privacy protection. Data can only be used for terms specified in the original consent or for uses that are necessary to fulfill the purpose of the consent or "are not incompatible with those purposes." Although the interpretation of this term might provide wiggle room, the "use limitation" provision further clarifies that to use the data for purposes other than those covered by the original agreement, consent must be obtained again from the individual or a government agency. We routinely enter into such contracts on e-commerce sites.

Consent also entails an added condition that acts, in a way, akin to how consumer protection laws limit the terms of a sales contract for buying a car. They address the information asymmetry between the individual user and the company seeking the data by ensuring that the consumer automatically receives certain protections. Specifically, consent only will include data collection that is legally permissible, is proportional to the purpose for which the user consents, and is accurate. These limitations address the problem that a user cannot fully know ex ante what information is required for a task and cannot easily detect all the ways that information might be collected. The conditions put the burden on the data collector to conform to all legal requirements and to act in a way that would fit the reasonable expectations of the user, if the user had adequate knowledge.

The second building block creates a continuing practical right; there must be an identifiable "accountable agent" (a data controller). The data controller must ensure that the data are always safeguarded by reasonable security practices, even if shared with another party. Data might be withheld from other parties that do not provide comparable security practices. The controller also must be transparent about its evolving data collection and policies. It also can deal with user questions and provide effective redress for complaints about the data. This proactive measure goes beyond individual complaints and allows users to understand how the use of their information can morph over time.

The third building block is appropriate data security protection. The 2013 OECD Principles specified new security obligations and endorsed privacy protection based on risk assessment practices. A privacy management program "provides for appropriate safeguards based on privacy risk assessment; is integrated into its corporate governance structure and establishes internal oversight mechanisms."[13] This approach should also be embraced by all other organizations with which data may be shared. This principle is consistent with the idea that protection priorities should be tailored to continually evolving assessment of risks. No absolute protection requirements are provided that apply equally to all risks for all data. In 2013, the OECD also embraced provisions for "review" and "notification" that call for cooperation with appropriate privacy enforcement or monitoring authorities to assess the risk management program. The review might be undertaken by MSOs acceptable to public authorities. In addition, it introduces an obligation to notify privacy enforcement authorities of security breaches, which addresses a problem noted earlier.[14] The incentives for security management are weaker if an individual firm does not need to fully disclose breaches to an appropriate authority.

The fourth building block, also in the 2013 extensions, created soft rule expectations about required national capabilities and who will be accountable in governments. As noted in Chapters 4 and 5, in international governance regimes it is crucial to identify who is in charge and ensure that participating governments have the capabilities to fulfill the expectations generated by the regime's principles and norms. Like the WTO's BTA, the principles leave room for the precise form of the government authority; in this case a data-protection authority or a regulatory commission (like the FTC) both fit the expectation. But the authority must be independent and have sufficient expertise and authority. (As discussed shortly, the EU had serious reservations about whether the FTC had sufficient authority to meet EU privacy rules.) The provisions also call for the creation of capabilities to cooperate on international privacy law enforcement, especially those that strengthen information sharing and set common metrics on privacy protection.

The APEC rules break additional ground. They outline government obligations to create governance capabilities and endorse government delegation of some privacy work to MSOs. They create a set of explicit "recognition criteria" for MSOs that seek the power to certify compliance with the APEC rules. Certification requires endorsement by the privacy authority of an APEC member economy. (This is in line with the prescription in Chapter 5 that MSOs must be accountable to governments.) The APEC rules also edge from being purely voluntary to being "authoritative" because they provide a cooperation mechanism among member economies that helps them enforce and implement privacy rules by creating a Joint Oversight Panel for the rules.[15] Still, much remains to be done because real differences remain over the EU application of OECD Principles and because, even within APEC, only the United States, Japan, and Mexico have firmly committed to implementing the APEC rules by mid-2015. Still, there are reasons for hope. For example, Singapore, South Korea, and other countries have adopted privacy rules that resemble those of the EU.[16]

The fifth building block principle sets conditions that justify transborder data flows. The conditions embrace a balancing act. They affirm that the same obligations for privacy management apply if data move across national borders. They also endorse the right to move data across borders *only* if the other country honors equivalent privacy guidelines *or* the data controller introduces a strong risk-management practice system. Thus, either a country or a company's practices may qualify as a sufficient guarantee for data moved across borders. This introduction of conditionality on the right to transfer data across borders creates favorable incentives for forming a club because everyone is not licensed to transfer data. It resembles the "mutual recognition agreements" sanctioned under trade rules where countries can acknowledge equivalency of national technical certifications and thus allow "one-stop certification" among equivalent countries.

The five elements must be in place to create a regime. But obstacles remain. Two issues stand out. First, disagreement exists over how to balance preventive precautions against incremental remedies. Second, a significant difference remains over how to treat government-to-citizen privacy safeguards.

To understand the split on precaution versus post hoc remedies, consider the difference between the APEC Privacy Framework and the EU approach to the OECD Principles. A strong common foundation exists because both endorse transparency, review, and notification as keys to effective risk management. However, the APEC Framework "concentrates on actual or potential harm as a result of disclosing information, rather than individuals' rights pertaining to their information. The OECD Privacy Principles enjoy support amongst EU and other governments' legal regimes. By contrast, there is no legal precedent for the APEC Privacy Framework. To date, its major supporters are certain global corporations."[17] The similarities between the OECD and APEC frameworks were predictable, given their overlapping memberships. But the EU is not an APEC member, and it is the major advocate of strong precautionary protections. Thus, the balance in how the APEC rules are interpreted reflect an approach much more common to the United States and Asia than to the EU.

As noted in Chapter 6, as of mid-2016, the EU was reluctant to import the provisions of the OECD Principles wholesale into trade agreements. The EU, for example, took data privacy off the table from the Transatlantic Trade and Investment Partnership negotiations. What were the sticking points? The OECD Principles lay out minimum standards that can be supplemented with additional measures to protect privacy and individual liberties, even if they impact transborder data flows.[18] But the EU worried that if the minimum standards were translated into trade agreements, the United States might not stiffen its federal privacy enforcement powers. The EU was even more concerned that there would be insufficient checks on surveillance of EU citizens by U.S. intelligence agencies. The EU was therefore unwilling to consider coverage in the Transatlantic Trade and Investment Partnership until these issues were resolved. Then, the populist politics of 2016 on both sides of the Atlantic scuttled the TTIP for the forseeable future.[19]

The more general problem about government-to-citizen privacy guarantees is that governments hate to be pinned down on national security matters and many countries use digital surveillance.[20] For example, the EU avidly cooperated in the implementation of digital surveillance rules laid out by the U.S. Communications Assistance for Law Enforcement Act in 1994 and it was the first to embrace the use of mobile communications to reveal geographic locations.[21] U.S. officials also argued strongly to the EU that the large U.S. institutional bureaucracy, spread across all three branches of government, is more scrupulous in monitoring privacy rights in the United States than what exists in the EU.[22] Thus, the domain of surveillance is hard to tackle comprehensively. However, its crossover to commercial privacy issues is a significant thorn to using the OECD and APEC blueprints as a basis for an international regime. Moreover, a hot political issue is the question of extraterritorial jurisdiction as it relates to criminal and national security searches, for example, when the U.S. government issues a search warrant for a European citizen's cloud data held by a U.S. firm in a European facility.

To drill deeper into these obstacles, the next section examines the U.S.–EU conflicts regarding privacy protection. Both politics and constitutional traditions are at play, but we cite some established methods of third-party monitoring that suggest a way forward.

8.3. The U.S.–EU Debate Regarding Privacy

The U.S.–EU debate regarding privacy is important because it is difficult to imagine any club growing into an international governance regime without the participation of both of these actors. As market-based democracies, the U.S. and EU approaches to privacy protection have much in common, but the pervasiveness of digital information touches sensitivities that turn nuances in policy stances into jagged edges for international coordination.

The EU began developing a comprehensive framework on privacy protection for commercial transactions much earlier than the United States. The General Data Protection Directive of 1995 anchors the EU data privacy regime.[23] The 1995 directive and subsequent measures taken through 2012 had three apparent purposes.[24] The first was to enhance the 1980 OECD Guidelines with added protections, such as the right to know to whom personal data is disclosed and the right to appeal to courts and to be notified of data breaches by their national authorities. The 1995 directive also included a soft law requirement that mandated independent data-protection authorities. The second measure was to ensure that privacy protections do not hamper internal EU data flows, but the directive may limit some flows outside the EU. The third measure was to encourage the EU's member states to collectively embrace e-commerce by enhancing consumer confidence in the privacy of user information.[25] Significantly, security and criminal matters were exempted from the reach of the directive.

The earlier EU engagement grows from three significant differences between the EU and U.S. legal and political systems. The differences in the constitutional and legal systems lead to different implications for framing privacy choices, and further political and economic differences arise from their political processes.

The first legal difference is constitutional. The EU has a constitutional guarantee of privacy, but the U.S. Constitution only contains a specific guarantee against certain types of intrusive government surveillance. Both reflect historical experiences with government authority. The Fourth Amendment of the U.S. Constitution provides guarantees against unreasonable search by government, a legacy of the resentments against the agents of the British crown during the Revolutionary War. This amendment produced a long record of jurisprudence and legislation about what constitutes an unreasonable search in specific historical and technological contexts. A further constitutional consideration relates to the protection of freedom of expression. Courts have interpreted this to mean that the First Amendment protects certain types of privacy disclosures, considering them protected "speech." Some other national constitutions, including those of Japan, South Korea, South Africa, and Ireland, have equivalent protections, but there is no EU equivalent to the American First Amendment's protections of freedom of speech. Predictably, Europe found "the right to be forgotten" of greater value than free speech protections. Moreover, in response to the ways that the Nazi government used government registries and other information for political persecution and genocide, the EU constitution broadly protects privacy.[26] This, in turn, is reinforced by stronger German and Austrian national constitutional protections of privacy.

Second, the two legal systems differ in important ways. EU law descends from the Napoleonic code system that sets forth sweeping laws and rules and from which judges "deduce" the correct answers. This tilts the EU toward reliance on preemptive codification. The EU directives follow in this spirit as they try to update classifications of technologies on a regular basis and create frameworks for regulating them. It also led the EU to something of a "precautionary principle" to protect privacy.

The United States operates under a common-law tradition that emphasizes case-by-case adjudication that yields legal precedents that periodically crystallize into broader principles that interact with formal laws and regulations.[27] In the absence of broad constitutional protection for "citizen-to-citizen" privacy issues, the United States relies on sector-specific protections that address specific problems as they emerge. The protection of information about children, patient's medical records, and individuals' credit cards all have specific legislative protections that are quite strong.[28] In short, in the United States privacy is treated as a consumer protection issue focused on fraud. By contrast, the EU tends to equate privacy with fundamental rights such as freedom of expression.[29]

Agencies like the FTC, which has become, de facto, the lead federal agency on privacy, have teeth. Still, all agencies are required by law to analyze the economic costs and benefits likely to result from their interventions. This framework induces the FTC to value voluntary protections by industry and then supplement as needed, as we explained in regard to the FTC's work on financial security.

Third, structural differences in the political systems also have reinforced legal differences. The U.S. system of divided powers and federalism poses more checks on national legislative action and authority on privacy than typically are found in parliamentary democracies.[30] Together, they tilt the U.S. system on civilian-to-civilian protections to narrower remedies that respond to accumulated experience.[31] This allows experience to build and experiments with solutions to evolve. Recall that users benefit in various ways from Big Data enabled by the IPD. Thus, it is unclear that rapid action is the best action when learning about the scale of a possible problem and the cost and feasibility of various remedies. Still, this lag also allows time for vested interests to develop and strengthen around practices that are profitable for the firms, but may harm privacy. These active interests make passage of privacy protection initiatives more difficult.

In a system of selective protection, public opinion influences corporate practices. Much of U.S. privacy policy is contractual. For example, a contract is set when the box is checked on the terms-of-service agreement to use Facebook or Google. In the social media world, specific terms of services can generate controversies that go viral. These viral protests influenced firms to make privacy terms for service more meaningful and intelligible, even when government has yet to act. As a result, revisions of user terms of service emerged to bolster privacy protections.[32] In sum, the U.S. system tilts toward strong a priori rules for protection of certain classes of highly sensitive data and toward a more experimental and reactive system of decision making related to other privacy concerns.

The EU political structure also influences its policy bent. The primordial authority of the European Commission is the promotion of an integrated European market. This issue of legal "competence" influences how issues are framed. The 1995 Data Protection directive had its roots in building a stronger, unified European market for e-commerce. More ambitiously, EU leaders persistently seek greater centralization of authority to promote a united Europe, a goal that faced nationalist backlash by 2016.

Questions of European market integration often become entangled with privacy debates. Frustrations over progress on creating a vigorous European IT market led to a major EU Digital Single Market strategy in 2015 to enhance market integration.[33] Meanwhile, the Council and Parliament agreed on April 26, 2016, to Regulation 2016/679, which would replace the General Data Protection Regulation with stronger provisions by 2018. Commission officials admit that the intersection of the two will unify privacy safeguards and serve as the basis for the commission to insist on the removal of many of the restrictions on cross-border data flow (e.g., by cloud computing) within the EU.[34]

The evolving role of the EU Parliament in European decision making also influences privacy policy. Most European democracies, but not the United Kingdom, have political structures that favor rule by multiparty coalitions. Smaller parties often push specialized agendas that appeal to a distinct, but committed, minority of voters.[35] This opens the way to coalitions of strong privacy advocates and smaller political parties coalescing as a minority veto on policies with major privacy implications. Such coalitions may be particularly strong in lower turnout, as often happens in EU parliamentary elections. This encourages strong positions on the left or right that can mobilize small cadres of voters on high-profile, sensitive issues such as privacy.

Moreover, given the EU Parliament's limited powers, its leaders are not strongly vested in the fate of any ruling national party. Further, parliamentary parties divide policy leadership on issues to build their individual reputations. This invites "position-taking" politics that emphasizes certain policy stands rather than compromise for governance. Privacy has emerged as a special claim of the EU Parliament in advancing the single European market agenda while strengthening its role in decision making.

For example, it is striking how much the Green Party's privacy preferences influenced the powerful German delegation. Both of Merkel's potential governance partners, the Greens and the Free Democratic Party, usually took stronger civil liberties positions than her own party. This was understandable in a leftist party like the Greens, given the history of the Third Reich and East Germany, and in a party like the Free Democratic Party with a strong libertarian suspicion of surveillance. The Greens and their parliamentary allies adamantly sought the strongest possible privacy protection. According to our interviews, Merkel never pushed back hard against these pressures because their support on other issues was higher on the chancellor's priority list. In addition, she ceded leadership inside her government to the Free Democratic Party on privacy.[36] Whatever Merkel's personal views, she has found it expedient to support their privacy demands in the EU Parliament.[37]

The EU Parliament does not dictate ultimate decisions. In the past, the council and the commission overrode parliamentary worries on security. But, Parliament can generate political pressure and delay decisions by the council and the commission. Two factors make the council and the commission responsive to privacy concerns. First, as argued in Chapter 6, privacy and security considerations influence political economic cloud interests to favor a more Eurocentric cloud. The absence of world-leading, EU-wide IT companies means that EU leaders rarely hear "one of their own" advocate for balancing operational realities and opportunities in the

IPD. Second, the commission's path to creating a single digital market in Europe is politically tricky. This is so partly because of the overlapping authorities of EU national data-protection bodies that oversee transborder data flows within the EU.

Institutional innovations depend on political forces that produce permanent advocates that translate political sentiments into a stream of policy initiatives. To varying degrees, advocates turn ideas into administrative decisions. This happened with data-protection authorities fostered by the 1995 directive. These authorities came to favor stronger EU privacy actions but, fortified by coalitional politics, they were reluctant to cede their individual national authority.[38] Collectively, they had bargaining power over the terms for unifying increased authority in Brussels.[39]

These forces coalesced in January 2012, when the EU began a process to strengthen its 1995 data-protection directive (Directive 95/46/EC) by creating a EU regulation, its strongest form of legal action. The General Data Protection Regulation (Regulation (EU) 2016/670) was adopted on April 27, 2016, and is enforceable beginning May 25, 2018. The commission agreed to mandatory practices and privacy safeguards even on an extraterritorial basis (it applies to all non-EU companies that process the data of EU residents even if they are not established in the EU). It also contains an "opt-in" standard to signify explicit "consent" for specific data uses (for example, reversible user agreement to use "cookies" on websites visited). The regulation covers all companies that handle personal data and mandates "privacy-by-design" protection. It also requires firms above a certain size to create a data protection officer and providers to accommodate users who wish to move data from one supplier or country to another. The regulation obligates the data protection officer to notify the supervisory authority of breaches without undue delay. Thus, it specifies the circumstances under which data may leave the EU—if a company was certified as secure or the country where the data would reside was deemed secure. Penalties for noncompliance can reach 4% of worldwide turnover.[40]

The debate over the proposal was intensified by the Snowden revelations, which first leaked in June 2013. In March 2014, the EU Parliament endorsed the legislation, but final passage proved elusive.[41] Then, in November 2014, a European Court of Justice ruling proclaimed the "right to be forgotten." This ruling gave priority to privacy rights over freedom of expression or commercial considerations and provided extraterritorial reach to firms with any digital EU presence.[42]

The United States and the EU struggled to find a way for firms to handle differences in transatlantic privacy rules even before the new directive was proposed. In 2000, they negotiated the U.S.–EU Safe Harbor Agreement on privacy. It stipulated that, subject to certain conditions, U.S. companies, such as airlines,[43] that fall under FTC and Department of Transportation jurisdiction, could register with the U.S. Department of Commerce for "safe harbor" status and operate under U.S. privacy rules because, theoretically, they offered "equivalent" protection.[44] In effect, except in the fields of finance and telecommunications, most companies could "self-certify" by registering and agreeing to the framework principles. (A less noticed set of arrangements allowed business-to-business data flows using standard contractual templates approved by the EU that actually controlled the majority of transatlantic data. We discuss them in Section 8.4.3 of this chapter.)

From the viewpoint of global regime building, this was a bilateral agreement to promote quasi-convergence of national regulatory systems. But the Safe Harbor Agreement also had an intra-EU implication. The truly EU-wide information companies—operating ubiquitously and serving a wide range of customers—were mostly American. Thus, the Safe Harbor was a workaround for U.S. firms to overcome the lack of EU institutional capacity. Predictably, from the start, the Safe Harbor Agreement attracted criticisms from European national data authorities that were suspicious of U.S. rules and their enforcement. The agreement was amended in 2004 to exclude the Foreign Intelligence Surveillance Act. Despite the Snowden revelations, it was renewed in December 2013 with new provisions that made corporate policies on privacy more transparent, added additional auditing of the practices, and gave better access on cost-effective terms for dispute settlement to users.

These considerations fit with the revised 2013 OECD Principles. Although U.S. enforcement of the Safe Harbor Agreement stiffened, most notably when the FTC charged that Google violated the agreement when it failed "to give consumers notice and choice before using their information for a purpose different from that for which it was collected,"[45] worries that Google, in particular, was weakening privacy protections increased. In addition, the government-to-citizen surveillance issue continued to escalate as a result of the Snowden revelations about the extent of U.S. surveillance of foreign nationals.[46] In short, U.S. national security officials had wrongly discounted warnings by economic policy officials and U.S. firms about the risks of a blowback on U.S. firms from expanded electronic surveillance.[47]

In addition, questions in Europe and elsewhere intensified about the 1986 Electronic Communications Policy Act, which held that for security purposes or to fight crime the United States "could allow law enforcement access to email or other data that is more than 180 days old *without a warrant*."[48] Corporate and government critics on both sides of the Atlantic complained that the safeguards in the system to limit dangers to privacy were insufficient[49] and non-Americans were indignant that foreign nationals did not have the U.S. constitutional protections afforded to American citizens in regard to surveillance. Moreover, the EU worried that U.S. firms could be forced to turn data over to the U.S. government no matter where the data were stored, a matter that exploded in a dispute among the U.S. government, Microsoft, and Ireland over a U.S. warrant under the Electronic

Communications Policy Act that required Microsoft to turn over data on Microsoft servers in Ireland of a person who "claimed to be an Irish resident." Microsoft, with the support of the Irish government, contested the U.S. warrant in court and argued that the United States should have used the mutual legal assistance treaty process to request the data.[50] In a win for privacy advocates, on July 14, 2016, the U.S. Court of Appeals for the Second Circuit overturned a lower court ruling and ruled that Microsoft was not required to hand over to the U.S. government a customer's email that was stored in Ireland.[51]

To try to turn down the heated criticism, a blue-ribbon panel appointed by the Obama administration endorsed curbing some practices, including the observation of U.S. citizens communicating with foreign nationals. It also urged more safeguards on gathering data on foreign nationals, more transparent reporting on U.S. practices, and the development of a common approach for surveillance with several U.S. allies.[52]

Progress was too slow for the critics. On October 6, 2015, the European Court of Justice held the Safe Harbor principles to be invalid because they did not require *all* organizations entitled to work with EU privacy-related data to comply with them, thus providing insufficient guarantees.[53] The court observed that "national security, public interest and law enforcement requirements of the United States prevail over the safe harbor scheme, so that United States undertakings are bound to disregard, without limitation, the protective rules laid down by that scheme where they conflict with such requirements. The United States safe harbor scheme thus enables interference, by United States public authorities."[54]

The European court's decision did not provide a grace period, which put pressure on both sides to rapidly renegotiate an acceptable solution. On February 2, 2016, the "Privacy Shield" pact was agreed on.[55] Final approval on both sides came on July 12, 2016.[56] The United States assured the EU that American law enforcement and national security agencies would only access Europe's data subject to "clear limitations, safeguards and oversight mechanisms."[57] Further, U.S. firms will need to agree to a set of standards on how personal data are processed, while guaranteeing individual rights. The Department of Commerce will ensure the companies post those promises publicly, which makes them enforceable under U.S. law by the FTC.[58] U.S. companies also will require enforceable contracts, consistent with the pact, to move EU data to third countries. The new pact provides Europeans with new ways to ensure that companies handle their data in an appropriate manner. If a complaint is lodged, the companies will have a deadline to respond. EU citizens also may go through their local data-protection authorities to complain to the FTC. The pact also sets up a no-cost "Alternative Dispute resolution" process for consumers, including arbitration if needed. The pact requires an annual report that monitors

Department of Commerce compliance with the Shield and consultations with the commission on the report. In parallel, the United States will set up a new ombudsperson at the State Department to respond to complaints about potential access to data by the national intelligence community.

The EU Commission saw the Privacy Shield as a delicate balancing act as it tried, successfully, to win the support of the national data-protection authorities and to forestall a successful challenge at the European Court of Justice by the numerous privacy groups that announced that they intended to sue.[59] (Immediately, in July 2016, one suit challenged the business-to-business data flow contracts that channel much transatlantic traffic).[60] To satisfy national authorities, an additional safeguard on data retention needing to be deleted or anonymized by companies that left the Shield was inserted after February 2016. Although some policy advocates were dissatisfied, the commission did not link extrajurisdictional disputes, such as the Microsoft–Ireland case, to the Privacy Shield. U.S. officials adamantly rejected the linkage and many EU members' legal authorities worried that fiddling with precedents would undermine their extraterritorial powers in areas such as tax evasion. The two sides also agreed that corporate disclosure of government warrants would remain a voluntary corporate choice.

After signing the Shield, the commission remains especially concerned with how it will be implemented. The FTC is viewed in Europe as less proactive in pressing privacy complaints. Thus, the compliance behavior by companies monitored by commerce will be critical to success. In addition, the ombudsperson provision is novel and, predictably, likely to be subject to pushback by U.S. intelligence agencies.

The Privacy Shield agreement won plaudits from major U.S. information tech firms. But, some U.S. analysts argue that the laws already are outdated.[61] In addition, "[one] example is the issue of unambiguous consent, which policymakers fail to define clearly, and might be incredibly difficult to obtain in a few years' time, when IoT applications will have become more widespread and will originate an almost uncontrolled flow of personal data. . . . [Moreover,] the age limit to require parental consent for the use of 'information society' services (i.e. social media and similar) will be set by each member state between 13 and 16 years old. This is likely to be disruptive for both online companies and young users."[62]

Complicating matters further, on June 23, 2016, Britain voted 52% to 48% to leave the EU. Residents of London and Scotland, the most educated, and the young favored remaining in the EU. The older voters, lower-middle-class voters, and more rural voters voted to exit. The next morning, the Conservative prime minister Cameron announced that he would step down, and by the end of the trading day on Friday, the pound closed at its lowest level against the dollar in three decades.

Britain's divorce from the EU is scheduled for late March 2019, but it immediately raised questions about transatlantic privacy and trade negotiations. But in the end, if the United States and the United Kingdom have made the Privacy Shield workable, it would seem unlikely that the United Kingdom would follow a significantly different path than its major economic partners.

Two final observations about the Privacy Shield are important. The first is that, like the case of financial issues and cybersecurity, much of the heavy lifting on creating an enforceable framework is being done by bilateral regulatory agreement. Ultimately, the Privacy Shield is a unilateral action by the EU, and it can be revoked at any time. The United States has the power to decide on how it precisely implements the pact, but the EU has the final decision on continuing or withdrawing. The second observation, equally significant, is that once the Privacy Shield is in place, EU officials strongly suggested to us that they would like to see international trade agreements that could be a more general umbrella within which the Privacy Shield could reside and become an anchor for a broader international agreement on data flow and privacy.

What are the options going forward? Before discussing a grand design for an international baseline, we probe more deeply into the other side of international regimes: governance innovations from civil society.

8.4. MSOs and Privacy

Any international governance regime should embrace policies and rules set by governments and governance innovations that arise from civil society. Regimes depend on expectations about typical behavior, especially of influential actors, and on shared understandings of problem-solving premises. In a rapidly evolving domain such as privacy, many of these expectations are shaped by the strategies and experiments of civil society.

This section explores these civil society innovations for privacy. To begin, we revisit the case of a successful MSO, SWIFT, that in executing its mission confronted a clash between security and privacy goals. This leads to a deeper examination of what is needed to manage a characteristic international conflict. Then, we turn to two sets of additional innovations: "market accommodation" and "market governance" by civil society actors.

8.4.1. Managing Privacy and Security Issues That Intersect in a Global MSO

Oversight and monitoring frequently are specialized. Financial institutions, for example, are not part of the U.S.–EU Safe Harbor program; the EU directives on

privacy exempt data involving security matters, and large institutions often are subject to multiple regulators, which communicate with each other only sporadically.
This specialization and fragmentation in regard to SWIFT led to an imbroglio that
shed light on how privacy issues became more deeply intertwined with cross-border
data flows and security considerations after 9/11. The resolution of the controversy
suggests some guidelines for the future.

Recall that SWIFT is subject to coordinated oversight by national central banks.
The G10 central banks (circa 2002–2006) knew that SWIFT was complying with
U.S. government subpoenas for SWIFT data as part of its Terrorist Finance Tracking
Program to detect and disrupt terrorist networks. This information was shared with
the European Central Bank as a G10 participant. Honoring traditional pledges of
regulatory secrecy that involve bank reviews, the central banks did not inform the
European Parliament or the European Commission and apparently shared the infor-
mation (if at all) only with security ministries in their home governments.

In 2006, the *New York Times* reported on the arrangement, creating a European
public uproar. The European Data Protection Supervisors and the majority of the
EU Parliament demanded curtailment or abandonment of SWIFT's compliance
with the U.S. subpoenas. The controversy continued actively through 2010. This suggests several lessons for the politics of security and privacy issues in the transatlantic
region.[63]

Lesson one is that deep institutional divisions within the EU influence these
issues. One divide was between the governments represented on the European
Council, the European Commission, and the European Parliament. This was partly
a function of different institutional interests and dynamics. Several prominent governments on the council, including France and the United Kingdom, pushed hard
to settle the matter quickly and ensure continued U.S. access.[64] These governments
maintain deep intelligence links to the United States that are not available to many
smaller EU members or to the commission.[65] In July 2009, the council instructed
the commission to reach closure and find a way to allow continued U.S. access to
European data. For its part, the commission staff was frustrated and angry (especially with the European Central Bank) that it was kept out of the loop on these
matters.[66] This reflected the commission's mixed progress on gaining competence
on hard-core security issues. A byproduct of this weak competence is that the intelligence agencies of EU member states are more reluctant to play a publicly identifiable role in EU parliamentary discussions than their U.S. counterparts do with
Congress.[67] Because of its populist dynamic, the European Parliament also takes a
strong position for maximum data protection. In 2010, the EU Parliament rejected a
draft 2006 agreement between the commission and the United States on the terms
by which the United States could demand confidential data from SWIFT. (National

governments, preoccupied with winning approval of the Treaty of Lisbon, were caught by surprise by the Parliament initiative.)[68]

Lesson two is that the politics of security and privacy are passionate and complicated. Splits inside the national governments partly reflected typical turf battles among ministries with competing mandates. The German interior minister, for example, forcefully rejected the strict privacy demands of other cabinet ministers.[69] But for reasons discussed earlier, the Merkel government was the strongest advocate for firmer privacy controls among the major European economic powers.

The method for resolving the dispute reflected classic techniques for dispute resolution, agreements to narrow the scope of the issue and then the use of third-party inspectors. The first breakthrough came in June 2007, when the Belgian data protection supervisor ruled that SWIFT's cooperation with the United States did not violate European rules. This finding accompanied a unilateral commitment by the U.S. government to cooperate with implementation changes announced by SWIFT.

SWIFT always had bargained with the U.S. Treasury to limit the demands to specific searches to prevent terrorist attacks. SWIFT hired auditors to confirm the scope and appointed internal "scrutineers" to independently review and block data transfers, if necessary. The U.S. Treasury (the responsible U.S. agency) reaffirmed the narrow purpose (counterterrorism) for which the data would be used, the safeguards in place to guarantee this, and a shorter period for retaining the subpoenaed data (five years). To further reassure the EU Parliament, the United States allowed a senior French judge with experience in security matters to review the system, including its protections for civil liberties.[70] The judge ruled that the program was valid in its purpose and procedures.

The SWIFT response to European concerns also included the kind of market accommodation in technical infrastructure predicted in Chapter 6. SWIFT altered its technical infrastructure, separating European and transatlantic zones for data. (Data on intra-EU transactions now are held exclusively in Dutch and Swiss centers, instead of being held in the United States and the Netherlands.) This meant that intra-EU data remained primarily within Europe's legal jurisdiction. Data involving transactions with the United States or most of the rest of the world also reside in the United States.

As noted, the EU Council intervened in 2009 with instructions that even the data stored in the EU should be accessible to the United States, as long as it was subject to appropriate safeguards. Although EU privacy advocates still argued that the strategy of preempting terrorism networks using this form of scrutiny was unlikely to work and not worth the risks to civil liberties, the governments relied on U.S. intelligence sharing to bolster their own security programs.[71] They did not want access to the U.S. analytic capacities restricted.

Chapters 4 and 5 showed that to be credible, arrangements for transparency and accountability for MSOs are needed. That was the compromise. A Europol (the EU association of police authorities) official was installed on a permanent basis in the U.S. Treasury office that monitors privacy safeguards with the power to reject unwarranted subpoenas. (Europol was more disposed to the program than data protection supervisors, but still accountable to European authorities.) The compromise was easier because the United States and the EU remain broadly aligned in their political and security ambitions. The precedent of third-party monitoring involving disparate political military interests, such as the nuclear nonproliferation work of the International Atomic Energy Agency, is well established.

Even with the accommodation with the United States, SWIFT faced a second major governance challenge—the rising interest in using blocks on financial flows to sanction countries such as Iran and Russia.[72] Again, the United States was the main mover, but several other countries added their support. This raised the question of whether SWIFT can be a neutral, trusted infrastructure for all countries if some countries can order it to block specific financial transactions. SWIFT defenders note that as a private institution it has no immunity from the national laws of its home country, Belgium, or from valid extraterritorial orders from the United States and other countries.[73] Some countries already are exploring the idea of creating a rival to SWIFT, although it is unclear whether a limited network outside the major financial centers would have sufficient scale and scope to function efficiently.

Meanwhile, as most major countries increased scrutiny of criminal and security-related financial transactions by requiring that financial institutions "know your customers"(KYC) and maintain documentation of the relationships, SWIFT launched a KYC Registry with a dozen of its major correspondent banks to be a centralized repository for key parts of the compliance process.[74] SWIFT and its programs are collectively scrutinized by a forum of national central banks, which will provide a degree of international review and scrutiny of how KYC compliance is being handled by the U.S. government.

8.4.2. Marketplace Accommodation

Chapter 6 suggested that formal regime rules for the cloud should leave ample space for civil society innovations in cloud governance. Governance changes often flow from marketplace governance institutions or from the rise of implicit (and sometimes explicit) patterns of behavior by leading marketplace players that create "normative" expectations for the market among influential players.

Firms operating cloud infrastructure are adapting to an environment influenced by governmental pressure for greater localization. There is ample precedent for this.

Immediately after World War II, the U.S. government and the auto industry adapted to political pressures for localization.[75] It became a de facto norm of the international automotive industry that countries were obligated to open their markets to foreign suppliers, but they could do so by allowing auto imports or by granting market access to those wishing to establish local production facilities, mostly local assembly. These facilities provided political and economic side payments in exchange for market access in a politically sensitive industry. Over time, industry structure changed and its global political economy evolved enough to allow the Uruguay Round negotiators to agree on trade reforms that removed some of the worst market inefficiencies.

The hub-and-spoke system for cloud services allows some room for multinational cloud providers to set a normative expectation of "best efforts" at national or regional localization. There are signs that this is occurring. For example, in 2014, Amazon's AWS announced plans to create a cloud center in Frankfurt to meet German "cultural preferences" and local data-protection rules.[76] Amazon also cited benefits of reducing latency on its services and reducing failure rates through more redundancy in the expanding EU market for cloud services. Previously, AWS relied on an Irish center and on nine locations outside the EU, including in Singapore, California, and Oregon. IBM announced a similar wave of major new regional cloud facility investments to accommodate policy sensibilities.[77] Non-American firms also are following this route. Xiaomi, a Chinese mobile handset firm whose business model depends on cloud-enabled services, is building facilities outside China. The firm claims that this will improve performance, but most observers believe that Xiaomi also wants to assuage India, Indonesia, and others whose policies favor data localization.[78]

Another type of market adjustment would create a code among cloud centers and operators to certify firms that embrace techniques designed to reduce surreptitious surveillance. Two certification options are "sharding" and encryption technology for data flows involving the cloud centers. Sharding distributes data in a way that makes it difficult to identify the person or entity associated with a piece of data.[79] Encryption of data flows is a response to government surveillance of the traffic on fiber-optic cables flowing into U.S., British, and perhaps other cloud centers.[80] The demand for centers located outside those countries increased on the theory that this would make it more difficult to carry out such intercepts. The introduction by cloud operators of high-level encryption on cloud traffic would reduce the risk of surveillance.

U.S. national security officials worry that encryption may become the new norm for the cloud, which would make it impossible for cloud providers to comply with court orders to supply customer data. This is Apple's preference. Indeed, in March 2016, the FBI sought Apple's help to reset the password of the iPhone 5C issued by San Bernardino County, California, to the shooters who killed fourteen and injured twenty-two of their co-workers in December 2015. The FBI wanted to access data from the phone's iCloud backup. Apple refused. The FBI filed suit, but dropped the suit when it found other parties who were able to gain access to the phone.[81] The issue will linger because even Apple will not be able to decrypt more advanced operating systems on their phones.

8.4.3. Innovations in Marketplace Governance

Marketplaces also can create market codes of conduct or new collective facilities. MSOs can play a powerful role to help fill in the gaps around the baseline international rules and to implement national rules in ways that foster quasi-convergence of national policies over time.[82] They build on the basic logic of conditionality and on accountable agents. The confidentiality and security of personal data depend on the contractual relations among the data suppliers, data users, and intermediaries. There are at least four signs that such codes are emerging to ease the problems around the cloud.

1. One way to reduce the political and practical difficulty of a problem is to break it down into more manageable pieces. The "low-hanging data" for such an effort is business-to-business data storage, processing, and transmission. For many industries, it should be possible to craft voluntary industry-specific data codes. Such codes may come in three types: industry specific, process-oriented, and hybrid public–private guidelines. For example, industry-specific guidelines are burgeoning in industries like agriculture and autos. Most such guidelines build on the basic framework of the OECD Principles and then work out what this means for specific business groups and their customers. Most business-to-business data flows raise coordination problems where there are strong incentives to find a workable solution. Even strict rules for cloud data, if they are not obviously incompatible with the thrust of the government's data policies, usually can accommodate detailed voluntary guidelines among companies. However, the task also requires active ongoing management of the issues.

2. Another approach is to create a general MSO framework for corporate privacy management and accountability practices that responds to new government privacy guidelines. The ISO created its ISO 27018 guidelines for public clouds for this purpose. Although the ISO documentation recognizes that this is not a full substitute for corporate compliance programs, its tries to simplify privacy management when dealing with the EU and similar frameworks. It sets out four explicit goals: (1) help public cloud providers

comply with legal privacy obligations, (2) enhance transparency (and thus credibility) of management practices to secure private data, (3) create a framework to help simplify contracts with customers and other companies for management of data stored in the cloud, and (4) strengthen the ability to deliver necessary audit and compliance functions.[83]

Even within such frameworks, there are trade-offs between flexible general guidelines and detailed practices, which provide more guidance, but less flexibility. Predictably, MSOs are emerging to help address these challenges by reaching consensus on which problems are most important and then suggesting specific steps to improve performance. One MSO, the Centre for Information Policy Leadership (a think tank hosted by a law firm and supported by corporate membership), formed working groups to identify risk-management frameworks. They invite public officials to their meetings to help vet the work, without any obligation to embrace it.[84] Such MSO efforts may provide practical definitions for the OECD Principle that endorses risk management.

3. A third development is the rise of hybrid public–private frameworks for privacy management. Binding corporate rules authorized under the EU privacy guidelines through its Working Party on Article 19 provide one example. Binding corporate rules provide a standardized contract format for companies to allow them to meet their privacy obligations when they share personal data with, for example, outsourcing firms outside the EU that handle company business processes.[85] Similarly, the APEC rules create a process for MSOs to be recognized as qualified agents by member economies to certify compliance with APEC privacy rules. This also indicates a way to collectively review such certifications.

4. Another promising contribution to governance is the increased disclosures by firms that address government-to-citizen privacy issues. In response to governments' demands for access to their records, several leading U.S. cloud-based firms now publish annual transparency reports. These reports do not identify the subjects of the searches or the reasons they were authorized. They anonymize information by lumping the cases together. These reports begin to establish some transparency and a sense of proportion about who is doing what.[86] Companies now also are publishing comparative national statistics on such demands showing that although the number of U.S. requests far exceeds those of other countries, India, the United Kingdom, and France all make substantial numbers of demands.[87] It is striking that these

innovations parallel transparency recommendations made in 2013 by the U.S. presidential blue-ribbon panel on intelligence gathering.

In summary, intergovernmental policy disputes persist, but civil society is innovating to reduce the gaps among policy pronouncements. Innovations and accommodation in market governance are redefining operations that emphasize flexible risk management and continual review of practices. They are beginning to create new normative expectations about privacy behavior. In addition, the EU and APEC frameworks are starting to redefine ways in which MSOs can be officially recognized and held accountable as implementation authorities for international governance frameworks. The next question is, What might an international governance regime look like?

8.5. Summary Analysis

If some governance is needed to better optimize social returns from privacy information markets and benefits and costs are associated with the disclosure of private information that evolve with technology, what are the implications for an international governance regime for privacy? We draw five initial conclusions.

First, there already is substantial agreement on the causal theory and norms expected in such a regime. The OECD and APEC Principles and the implementing framework of the U.S.–EU Privacy Shield Agreement contain most of the elements of a strong consensus on the underlying principles and norms for a regime. The Privacy Shield Agreement also suggests an authoritative international baseline, but its framework is too easy to revise unilaterally. Further, despite the agreement on principles, greater clarification of the principle of "location neutrality" for privacy protection is needed. The location where personal data resides should not influence the level or standard of privacy protection. It should not matter whether information is on a personal computer or in the cloud. It should not matter whether the cloud facility is in the United States or the EU (the EU standards of protection are the privacy standards for German citizens.)

Second, there are huge differences in handling government-to-citizen privacy. The goal should be to minimize the gap and, to the extent possible, isolate it from the rest of the privacy framework. Although it is politically unpleasant to acknowledge, all countries want the power to monitor citizens and to address security or criminal problems. For example, India, despite its robust democracy, has virtually no legal framework for privacy protection, especially on government-to-citizen privacy.[88] Moreover, they benefit from sharing the results of intelligence investigations on common security threats. That is why the member governments of the EU Council insisted on a resolution of the Safe Harbor dispute with the United States that preserved America's ability to conduct intelligence activities. A serious constitutional, politically sensitive concern remains to ensure that police and security needs do not overwhelm constitutional privacy protections. Although countries may disagree on how to balance the two concerns, they can work to reduce the gaps and provide some monitoring mechanisms to address international grievances. Then they should separate governance arrangements geared to protect privacy from discussions about the scope of national security policies. Away from the political limelight, there are opportunities to improve data privacy and data security in the everyday conduct of the global marketplace. Allowing a data-intensive global economy to soar may generate an economic growth spurt. Security issues that are difficult to resolve should not blunt this possibility.

If taken in the context of a governance regime for a trusted digital environment, four actions might narrow the gap on security issues and improve the tractability of privacy regimes.

1. In return for other policy concessions for criminal matters, countries might agree to rely on mutual legal assistance treaties or working parties of like-minded countries when requesting privacy data of foreign citizens. Authorities might voluntarily refrain from using their unilateral subpoena power over the stored data of U.S. and other cloud companies.
2. Countries might support the right of "data controllers" to increase the transparency of government requests for data by issuing annual aggregated and anonymized reports to alleviate security concerns over disclosure.
3. Soft-law rules could encourage the emergence of policy standards for communications surveillance that emphasize proportionality of the surveillance risk, review by a competent independent authority, and the transparency of safeguard procedures when requested by another member country.[89]
4. Countries could support a principle, similar to SWIFT's dispute resolution process, that allows U.S.- and E.U.-approved experts to verify compliance with Privacy Shield agreements when disputes arise regarding government subpoenas for personal data of foreign nationals of like-minded countries.

Third, some variations in national and regional rules and practices are inevitable because constitutional traditions and public preferences about a trusted digital environment differ. For example, the EU's insistence on a right to be forgotten grows from popular sentiment and its constitutional commitments on privacy. The only viable approach is to seek an authoritative international baseline that creates a framework for relatively compatible interfaces among national rules. Three interlinked pieces are needed: (1) acknowledge that countries have a right to add additional protections beyond the international baseline to safeguard privacy and security considerations; (2) negotiate trade commitments to limit cooperation problems, such as disguised industrial policies, through market access rules for the cloud, and (3) in cooperation with like-minded countries, create a framework of agreed-on soft rules in a trade pact that define positive obligations of governments to protect privacy. These soft rules should include provisions to explicitly recognize the role of MSOs in implementing privacy regimes. Achieving agreement on common capabilities and approaches in a binding set of commitments would help Privacy Shield frameworks flourish.

Fourth, all frameworks for privacy governance already permit MSOs to play a prominent role in their implementation because government privacy frameworks provide insufficient certainty and clarity for major market participants. They demand more detailed expertise to establish greater granularity.[90] The goal should be to expand the role of MSOs by formally acknowledging their part in implementing an international governance regime, while simultaneously underscoring their accountability to governments. This approach should help counter the internal collective action challenges that can cause MSOs to fall apart.[91] MSOs also can simplify the problem of implementation if they require Safe Harbor agreements or their equivalents to deal with regulatory fragmentation and transaction costs. In the EU and other integrated regional markets, the Safe Harbor promotes regulatory simplification. It is unlikely that the United States will agree to new binding international commitments that increase privacy without a practical guarantee of a measure such as Safe Harbors.

Fifth, the governance structure should welcome learning and experiments because as IT evolves, new ways to better meld public and nongovernmental governance will be needed. For example, big data analysis makes it possible to offer customized contract terms for the use of data for different classes of users.[92] Various new schemes should help individuals manage privacy choices more effectively without impinging on their right to make choices using technology-assisted "nudges" to call attention to trade-offs involved in their choices.[93]

The final chapter applies these five conclusions to the creation of an international governance regime for the digital economy and a trusted digital environment. We show how they can be melded with options in trade policy to achieve our policy goals.

Notes

1. EU directives provide a standard definition of personal data: "EU Data Protection Directive 1995/46/EC is applicable to the automated processing of personal data and other processing of

personal data that form a part of a filing system." The directive defines personal data as any information that relates to an "identified or identifiable natural person." Many business-to-business data exchanges are not between "natural persons," but they include such data in their corporate data. Cited in Daniel Dimov, "Differences between the Privacy Laws in the EU and the US," January 10, 2013, INFOSEC Institute, http://resources.infosecinstitute.com/differences-privacy-laws-in-eu-and-us/.

2. For example, between 2005 and 2014, 229 European data breaches involving more than 640 million breached records were reported. British records were compromised most often. Commercial records accounted for almost 90% of the breached records and hackers accounted for almost 88%. Philip N. Howard and Orsolya Guylas, "Data Breaches in Europe: Reported Breaches of Compromised Personal Records in Europe, 2005–2014," Center for Media Data and Society, CMDS Working Paper 2014.1, pp. 7–10.

3. Allesandro Acquisti, Leslie John, and George Loewenstein, "What Is Privacy Worth?," *Journal of Legal Studies*, 42, no. 2 (2013): 249–274. Yang Wang, Pedro Giovanni Leon, Xiaoxuan Chen, Saranga Komanduri, Gregory Norcie, Kevin Scott, Alessandro Acquisti, Lorrie Faith Cranor, and Norman Sadeh, "The Second Wave of Global Privacy Protection: From Facebook Regrets to Facebook Privacy Nudges," *Ohio State Law Journal*, 74, no. 6 (2013): 1307–1335.

4. Harold Demsetz, "Toward a Theory of Property Rights," *American Economic Review*, 57, no. 2 (May 1967): 347–359; Jamie Lund, "Property Rights to Information," *Northwestern Journal of Technology and Intellectual Property*, 10, no. 1 (Fall 2011), http://scholarlycommons.law.northwestern.edu/njtip/vol10/iss1/1.

5. Although there are debates regarding the effectiveness of the technique, anonymization of data can ease the risk. One proponent is Castro, "The False Promise of Data Nationalism," 2013.

6. Users may not appreciate the full value of the information that the retailer gathers from them. Information can be bundled and resold to others for marketing analysis. Moreover, economic theory shows that perfect price discrimination is optimal for producers, not consumers. But consumers benefit in a variety of ways in areas such as service quality, which may improve with discrimination. Andrew Odlyzko, "Privacy, Economics, and Price Discrimination on the Internet," in L. Jean Camp and S. Lewis (eds.), *Economics of Information Security* (Dordrecht, The Netherlands: Kluwer, 2004), pp. 187–211.

7. Lior Jacob Strahilevitz, "Towards a Positive Theory of Privacy Law," 125 *Harvard Law Review 2010* (2013). Whitfield Diffie and Susan Landau, *Privacy on the Line: The Politics of Wiretapping and Encryption* (Cambridge, MA: MIT Press, 1999).

8. Strahilevitz, "Towards a Positive Theory of Privacy Law," 2010 (2013).

9. Mathias Bauer, Hosuk Lee-Makiyama, Erik van der Marel, and Bert Verschelde, *The Costs of Data Localization: Friendly Fire on Economic Recovery* (Brussels: European Centre for International Political Economy, Occasional Paper No 3/2014), http://www.ecipe.org/app/uploads/2014/12/OCC32014__1.pdf. Also see Matthias Bauer, Fredrik Erixon, Michal Krol, Hosuk Lee-Makiyama, and Bert Verschelde, *The Economic Importance of Getting Data Protection Right: Protecting Privacy, Transmitting Data, Moving Commerce* (Brussels: European Centre for International Political Economy, 2013); Daniel Castro and Joshua New, "10 Policy Principles for Unlocking the Potential of the Internet of Things," Center for Data Innovation, December 4, 2014. Daniel Castro and Alan McQuinn, "The Economic Costs of the European Union's Cookie Notification Policy," The Information Technology and Innovation Foundation, November 2014.

10. Jules Polonetsky and Omer Tene, "Privacy and Big Data: Making Ends Meet," 66 *Stanford Law Review On-Line*, September 3, 2013, pp. 25–33, summarizes a symposium exploring many of these challenges.

11. Privacy critics such as Bruce Schneier in *Data and Goliath* praised the guidelines.

12. The OECD work can be found at http://www.oecd.org/internet/ieconomy/oecdguidelinesontheprotectionofprivacyandtransborderflowsofpersonaldata.htm. Many issues of interpretation of the 2013 work are left to examples found in a "Supplementary Explanatory Memorandum" accompanying the principles. See Monika Kuschewsky, "OECD Privacy Guidelines—What Has Really Changed?" *Privacy Laws & Business International Report*, December 2013, pp. 15–17. On APEC rules, see http://www.apec.org/Groups/Committee-on-Trade-and-Investment.aspx.

13. "OECD Privacy Framework," 2013, quoted from 15/a/iii and iv.

14. *Ibid.* 15/b and c.

15. http://www.cbprs.org/GeneralPages/About.aspx, accessed December 30, 2014.

16. See the Public Consultation Issues by the Personal Data Protection Commissions, Proposed Regulations on Personal Data Protection in Singapore, February 6, 2013, https://www.pdpc.gov.sg/legislation-and-guidelines/public-consultations/proposed-regulations.

17. From http://www.apec.org/Groups/Committee-on-Trade-and-Investment.aspx.

18. OECD Privacy Framework, paragraphs 4 and 6.

19. Anne-Sylvaine Chassany, Shawn Donnan, and Guy Chazan, "France Urges Brussels to Halt TTIP Talks," *Financial Times*, August 30, 2016, http://www.ft.com/cms/s/0/154ecba2-6e82-11e6-a0c9-1365ce54b926.html#axzz4IyXosTTR.

20. The United Kingdom strongly supports extensive surveillance if it is subject to judicial review. Germany and France are more discrete in public, but those familiar with signals intelligence know that they have strong surveillance capacities. Other countries, like India and China, use extensive surveillance without much judicial supervision. Mark Scott, "British Court Rules in Favor of Electronic Surveillance," *New York Times*, December 6, 2014, p. A6; Ben Hubbard, "Twitter Backer of ISIS Is a Clean-Cut Executive in India, British Channel Says," *New York Times*, December 13, 2014, p. A7.

21. Diffie and Landau, *Privacy on the Line*, 1999, pp. 196–201.

22. Interviews with U.S. officials in 2015 and 2016. Passage of the USA Freedom Act in 2015 also strengthened the U.S. case by both narrowing the terms for collecting data by surveillance efforts and making reforms in the Foreign Intelligence Surveillance Act court that reinforced the hand of privacy advocates. Expanded surveillance authorities in France after terrorist acts (in the form of La loi relative au renseignement, law number 2015-92) and elsewhere also underscored the universality of surveillance practices. Segal, *The Hacked World Order*, 2016.

23. EU Data Protection Directive 1995/46/EC applies to any natural person. Infosec report.

24. Brown and Marsden, *Regulating Code*, 2013, pp. 52–57.

25. The e-Privacy Directive 2002/58/EC "states that [cookies] can be installed on devices of subscribers only after an explicit consent of the subscriber or the user is provided. It should be noted that such a consent could be obtained only after the subscriber have been provided with the information required by the e-Privacy Directive and after having been offered the right to refuse such access." Quote from *Infosec report*.

26. The protections are in the European Convention on Human Rights and in the EU Charter of Fundamental Rights.

27. On the evolution of Supreme Court reasoning on privacy, see Diffie and Landau, *Privacy on the Line*, 1999.

28. The three acts are the Children's Online Privacy Protection Act, the Health Insurance Portability and Accountability Act, and the Fair and Accurate Credit Transaction Act. The Privacy Act of 1974 is the cornerstone of legislation that defines limits and procedures for U.S. government collection, storage, and sharing of U.S. citizen data.

29. Mark Scott, "Penny Pritzker on the Privacy Shield Pact with Europe," *New York Times*, March 8, 2016, http://www.nytimes.com/2016/03/09/technology/penny-pritzker-on-the-privacy-shield-pact-with-europe.html?_r=0.

30. Peter F. Cowhey and Mathew D. McCubbins (eds.), *Structure and Policy in Japan and the United States: The Political Economy of Institutions and Decisions* (Cambridge: Cambridge University Press, 1995).

31. Strahilevitz ("Towards a Positive Theory of Privacy Law," 2010 [2013]) speculates that the distinctive U.S. approach to privacy may also result from the fact that its electoral rules tilt elections toward lower rates of voter turnout than in most democracies, thus changing the mix of citizens who influence political choices.

32. The Pew Research Center reports that more than 90% of Americans believe that they have lost control over their privacy. Mark Scott, "Where Tech Giants Protect Privacy," *New York Times*, December 14, 2014, p. SR 5.

33. Stuart N. Brotman, "The European Union's Digital Single Market Strategy: A Conflict between Government's Desire for a Certainty and Rapid Marketplace Innovation," Center for Technology Innovation, Brookings Institution, May 2016, http://www.brookings.edu/~/media/research/files/papers/2016/05/24-digital-single-market/digital-single-market.pdf.

34. Interviews with EU officials, June and July 2016. Salli Anne Swartz, "Privacy v Security," Presentation to 2016 ABA SIL Europe Forum, May 30–31, 2016, Rome, Italy.

35. Strahilevitz, "Towards a Positive Theory of Privacy Law," 2010 (2013).

36. Merkel leads a coalition government with the Free Democratic Party, a small party. Courting the Greens is at minimum a good political insurance policy. Our account relies on interviews with European and American leaders with intimate knowledge of this issue.

37. Adam Segal reports that the NSA bugged Chancellor Merkel's mobile phone. German authorities later denied this claim. However, Amicelle details how U.S. government officials, including Hillary Clinton, personally wooed German officials on the privacy decisions in the Safe Harbor. Anthony Amicelle, "The Great (Data) Bank Robbery: Terrorist Finance Tracking Program and the 'Swift Affair,'" May 2011, Sciences Po—Center for International Studies and Research, http://papers.ssrn.com/sol3/papers.cfm?abstract_id=2282627.

38. Abraham Newman, *Protectors of Privacy: Regulating Personal Data in the Global Economy* (Ithaca, NY: Cornell University Press, 2008).

39. James Panichi, "Ministers to Discuss Data-Protection Compromise," *European Voice*, November 27, 2014, p. 3.

40. Text of the regulation is at http://ec.europa.eu/justice/data-protection/reform/files/regulation_oj_en.pdf. W. Scott Blackmer, "GDPR: Getting Ready for the New EU General Data Protection Regulation," *InfoLawGroup LLP*, May 5, 2016, http://www.infolawgroup.com/2016/05/articles/gdpr/gdpr-getting-ready-for-the-new-eu-general-data-protection-regulation/.

41. The EU Parliament approved the proposed directive in a vote in March 2014, http://europa.eu/rapid/press-release_MEMO-14-186_en.htm.

42. People in public life might not have this right and the duty to forget arguably rested more heavily on search engines. Nick Graham, "New EU Guidelines on "Google Spain: Right to Be Forgotten," December 2, 2014, *Dentons*, http://www.privacyanddatasecuritylaw.com/new-eu-guidelines-on-google-spain-right-to-be-forgotten. But also see "On Being Forgotten," *The Economist*, May 17, 2014, p. 15. For examples of why some feel the need for a right to be forgotten,

see Jeffrey Toobin, "The Solace of Oblivion," *The New Yorker*, September 29, 2014, http://www.newyorker.com/magazine/2014/09/29/solace-oblivion.

43. Personal Name Records collected by airlines and the travel industry provide detailed information on travelers. Even after trips are completed or canceled, this information may be retained. Security organizations argue that this information can help deter terrorist operations, but the EU Parliament and other privacy organizations raised concerns on privacy grounds. The EU's national security agencies and European airlines finally rallied to save the program. The EU negotiated similar agreements with Canada and Australia. Abraham L. Newman, "Transatlantic Flight Fights: Multi-level Governance, Actor Entrepreneurship and International Anti-terrorism Cooperation," *Review of International Political Economy*, 18, no. 4 (2011): 481–505. The text of the December 14, 2011 U.S.–EU Passenger Name Record agreement is at https://www.dhs.gov/sites/default/files/publications/privacy/Reports/dhsprivacy_PNR%20Agreement_12_14_2011.pdf.

44. The Export Administration of the U.S. Department of Commerce listed the agreed-on principles of Safe Harbor that would guide self-certification. They were similar to the OECD Principles. http://2016.export.gov/safeharbor/eu/, accessed December 18, 2016.

45. "FTC Charges Deceptive Privacy Practices in Google's Rollout of Its Buzz Social Network: Google Agrees to Implement Comprehensive Privacy Program to Protect Consumer Data," March 30, 2011. From the FTC website, https://www.FTC.gov.

46. The chief laws of concern were America's 1978 Foreign Intelligence Surveillance Act and the Patriot Act of 2001. For a collection of key documents on the NSA and Snowden revelations, see http://apps.washingtonpost.com/g/page/world/nsa-revelations-in-documents/734/.

47. In a June 25, 2015, letter to Congress, major tech companies and industry groups called for legislation to extend data privacy protections to citizens of countries that are U.S. allies. Seventeen different tech groups and firms including Google, Microsoft, the Internet Association, and BSA signed. The Software Alliance noted "a significant erosion of global public trust in both the U.S. government and the U.S. technology sector" since Edward Snowden leaked information on sweeping U.S. surveillance programs in 2015. The full letter is at http://bit.ly/1J6Cozz.

48. "It's also used by law enforcement to justify forcing U.S. companies to hand over data stored in overseas centers, again without a warrant." Mark Sullivan, "White House Call for Upgrade to Law Protecting Consumer Cloud Data from Law Enforcement," July 29, 2015, http://venturebeat.com/2015/07/29/white-house-calls-for-upgrade-to-law-protecting-consumer-cloud-data-from-law-enforcement/.

49. Legislation created a special court (drawn from the ranks of U.S. judges) to review requests for surveillance for national security purposes. A vigorous debate continues over whether its mandate and practices suffice to ensure constitutional protections. David D. Cole, "Confronting the Wizard of Oz: National Security, Expertise, and Secrecy," *Connecticut Law Review*, 44 Rev. (2012): 1627–1635. For a succinct criticism of issues about due process, see Center for Democracy and Technology, "Electronic Communications Privacy Act Primer," May 13, 2015, https://cdt.org/insight/electronic-communications-privacy-act-primer/.

50. Alex Ely, "Second Circuit Oral Argument in the Microsoft–Ireland Case: An Overview," *Lawfare*, posted September 10, 2015, https://www.lawfareblog.com/second-circuit-oral-argument-microsoft-ireland-case-overview. Also see Frederick T. Davis, "A U.S. Prosecutor's Access to Data Stored Abroad—Are There Limits?," *The International Lawyer*, 49, no. 1 (Summer 2015): 1–20.

51. The Second Circuit's ruling on *Microsoft v. United States* (14-2985) is at http://law.justia.com/cases/federal/appellate-courts/ca2/14-2985/14-2985-2016-07-14.html. Also see Richard Waters, "Microsoft Wins Battle with US over Data Privacy," *Financial Times*, July 14, 2016, https://www.ft.com/content/6a3d84ca-49f5-11e6-8d68-72e9211e86ab. The complexity of the problem is illustrated in Orin Kerr, "The surprising implications of the Microsoft/Ireland warrant case, *The Washington Post*, Novermber 29, 2016, https://www.washingtonpost.com/news/volokh-conspiracy/wp/2016/11/29/the-surprising-implications-of-the-microsoftireland-warrant-case/?utm_term=.e2f254738ac9.

52. "Liberty and Security in a Changing World," Report and Recommendations of the President's Review Group on Intelligence and Communications Technologies, December 12, 2013. Also Adam Segal.

53. A detailed overview to mid-2015 is Richard J. Peltz-Steele, "The Pond Betwixt: Differences in the US–EU Data Protection/Safe Harbor Negotiation," *Journal of Internet Law*, 19, no. 1 (July 2015), http://papers.ssrn.com/sol3/papers.cfm?abstract_id=2637010. Also see Farrell and Newman, "The Transatlantic Data War."

54. "Judgment in Case C-362/14 Maximillian Schrems v Data Protection Commissioner: The Court of Justice Declares That the Commission's US Safe Harbour Decision Is Invalid," Court of Justice of the European Union, October 6, 2015, p. 3; Mark Scott, "U.S.–Europe Data Transfer Agreement Is Ruled Invalid," *New York Times*, October 7, 2015, pp. B1, B10.

55. U.S. commerce secretary Penny Pritzker's perspective is explained in Mark Scott, "Penny Pritzker on the Privacy Shield Pact with Europe," *New York Times*, March 8, 2016, http://www.nytimes.com/2016/03/09/technology/penny-pritzker-on-the-privacy-shield-pact-with-europe.html?_r=0. Department of Commerce, EU–U.S. Privacy Shield, https://www.commerce.gov/privacyshield.

56. Remarks by U.S. secretary of commerce Penny Pritzker at EU–U.S. Privacy Shield Framework Press Conference, https://www.commerce.gov/news/secretary-speeches/2016/07/remarks-us-secretary-commerce-penny-pritzker-eu-us-privacy-shield.

57. European Commission—Press Release, "Restoring Trust in Transatlantic Data Flows through Strong Safeguards: European Commission Presents EU–U.S. Privacy Shield," February 29, 2016, http://europa.eu/rapid/press-release_IP-16-433_en.htm.

58. In parallel to the Privacy Shield, to strengthen the new approach and to fight terrorism and crime, on June 2, 2016, the EU agreed to enhance protection of personal data transferred across the Atlantic. This umbrella agreement sets limits on data use and requires agencies to receive consent prior to transferring data. But ongoing disruptions make it certain that disputes will still arise. "EU, US sign data protection deal," *Yahoo! Tech*, June 2, 2016, https://www.yahoo.com/tech/eu-us-sign-data-protection-deal-161934121.html.

59. Based on interviews in Brussels in June and July 2016. Also: https://www.statista.com/statistics/267161/market-share-of-search-engines-in-the-united-states/.

60. There are many U.S. privacy critics. Electronic Privacy Information Center, "Max Schrems v Irish Data Protection Commissioner (Safe Harbor)," https://epic.org/privacy/intl/schrems/. Eric David, "Facebook's EU Woes Continue as Regulators Clamp Down," *Silicon Angle*, May 26, 2015.

61. Nick Wood, "EU Strikes Data Protection Deal," *Total Telecom*, December 16, 2015, http://www.totaltele.com/view.aspx?ID=492175.

62. Luca Schiavoni, "EU Data Protection Regulation Is a Necessary Step, but Practical Implementation Will Still Be Problematic," Ovum press release, December 16, 2015, http://www.ovum.com/press_releases/analyst-view-eu-data-protection-regulation-is-a-necessary-step-but-practical-implementation-will-still-be-problematic/.

63. We draw heavily on Amicelle's excellent account of the SWIFT dispute but the interpretation is ours. Our view of institutional disputes is consistent with Abraham Newman, "Transatlantic Flight Fights."

64. Interviews revealed that German and Spanish intelligence authorities also weighed in strongly.

65. The Five Eyes program, going back to the height of the Cold War, led the United States, the United Kingdom, Australia, Canada, and New Zealand to cooperate deeply on signals intelligence. Later, a second-tier program—the Nine Eyes—evolved, adding France, Netherlands, Denmark, and Norway. Then came the Fourteen Eyes—as a third tier—that included Germany, Belgium, Italy, Spain, and Sweden. The access to sensitive material varies by tier.

66. According to interviews by Amicelle.

67. A senior American official privy to these conversations shared this insight with us.

68. Jorg Monar, "The Rejection of the EU–US Swift Interim Agreement by the European Parliament: A Historic Vote and Its Implications," *European Foreign Affairs Review*, 15, 2010, pp. 143–151.

69. Germany may revise its strict privacy protections in the aftermath of the intentional crash in March 2015 of Germanwings Flight 9525 by its co-pilot. German privacy laws prevented his doctor from informing the airline directly that he was unfit to fly. See "German Privacy Laws Let Pilot 'Hide' His Illness from Employers," *Time*, March 27, 2015, accessed April 13, 2015, http://time.com/3761895/germanwings-privacy-law/. Similarly, Adam Segal notes that in the wake of the terrorist attacks on *Charlie Hebdo* weekly magazine, France considerably expanded its domestic spying.

70. The U.S. principal program is the Terrorist Finance Tracking Program. After 9/11, it began to subpoena SWIFT. The U.S. Treasury agreed to these safeguards. Leonard H. Schrank and Juan C. Zarate, "Data Mining, without Big Brother," *New York Times*, July 3, 2013, p. A23.

71. Amicelle ("The Great (Data) Band Robbery," 2011) summarizes the critiques nicely.

72. Barry Carter and Ryan Farha, "Overview and Operation of U.S. Financial Sanctions, Including the Example of Iran," *Georgia Journal of International Law*, 44 (2013): 903–913. Juan C. Zarate, *Treasury's War* (New York: Public Affairs Press, 2013).

73. Discussions with SWIFT executives and member institutions, Boston, September 2014.

74. "The Long Arm of the Law," *Sibos Issues* 8, September 29, 2014.

75. Aronson and Cowhey, *Managing the World Economy* (New York: Council on Foreign Relations, 1993), Chapter 5.

76. Quentin Hardy, "Amazon Opens a Data Center in Germany," *New York Times*, October 24, 2014, B2.

77. "IBM Adds Cloud Centers in Europe, Asia and the Americas," accessed January 4, 2015, http://www-03.ibm.com/press/us/en/pressrelease/45707.wss?lnk=ushpcs3.

78. Tom Mitchell, "Xiamomi Starts Shifting Data to Servers outside China," *Financial Times*, October 24, 2014, p. 14.

79. Chander and Le, "Breaking the Web," 2014, p. 32.

80. Another cloud service, Box, announced that it ultimately will encrypt all of its data to meet privacy concerns. Murad Ahmed, "Business Fears over U.S. Spying Prompt Amazon to Offer Web Hosting in Europe," *Financial Times*, October 14, 2014, p. 1.

81. "Breaking down Apple's iPhone Fight with the U.S. Government," *New York Times*, updated March 21, 2016, http://www.nytimes.com/interactive/2016/03/03/technology/apple-iphone-fbi-fight-explained.html.

82. The Bildt Commission presents an ambitious, but general blueprint for an MSO for the ICT space.

83. This summary is from the helpful exposition by Mark Webber, "A New ISO Standard for Cloud Computing," *The Privacy and Information Law Blog*, posted November 5, 2014.

84. Bojana Bellamy, "The Rise of Accountability from Policy to Practice and into the Cloud," *Privacy Perspectives*, posted December 10, 2014, https://privacyassociation.org/news/a/the-rise-of-accountability-from-policy-to-practice-and-into-the-cloud/.

85. "BCRs . . . provide a guarantee to the controller that a processor has a regime in place which adequately protects personal data when it is transferred outside the EU. This guarantee . . . can eliminate the need for reliance on other bases of transfer such as model contracts, thereby eliminating a significant administrative burden for companies engaging in frequent, large and complex international data transfers." Jan Doht, "Working Part Explains BCRs for Processors, The Privacy Advisor," posted June 1, 2013, https://privacyassociation. org/news/privacy-advisor. See also Taylor Wessing, "Binding Corporate Rules for Process," posted January 2013, http://www.taylorwessing.com/globaldatahub/article_binding_corporate_rules_processors.html.

86. Microsoft and Google sued the U.S. government under the Foreign Intelligence Surveillance Act for the right to increase the transparency of audits of the numbers and types of national security information warrants. Rory Carroll, "Microsoft and Google to Sue over U.S. surveillance requests," *The Guardian*, August 31, 2013.

87. *Litigation*, the journal of the section of litigation of the American Bar Association, published the results of the reports of Google, Facebook, and Twitter detailing government requests for information from January 1 through June 30, 2013, on the back cover of the magazine. It showed the U.S. government as the leading requester by far. Google had almost 11,000 U.S. government requests covering almost 22,000 users/accounts, of which 83% were honored with some data provided. India was second, with about 2,700 requests covering about 4,000 users/accounts and a 64% response rate. France followed with about 2,000 plus requests on about 2,500 accounts. Facebook and Twitter requests looked much the same in national rankings, but Twitter was much less frequently requested for data.

88. A lively blog on Indian policies is http://perry4law.com.

89. These are a subset of criteria advocated by a large group of experts' declaration International Principles on the Application of Human Rights to Communication Surveillance, cited in Schneier, pp. 168–169.

90. For example, industry associations are setting out templates for privacy contracts already extensively used in their industries.

91. For an example of a failed attempt to create an MSO code to protect students from having their test scores and quizzes posted publicly, despite bipartisan urging by Congressional members, see Stephanie Simon, "Big Tech Pledges Student Privacy; Critics Scoff—The Initiative Draws Only Lukewarm Reviews from Privacy Advocates," posted October 7, 2014, http://www.politico.com/story/2014/10/student-privacy-tech-companies-111645.html.

92. Imagine a dozen different default terms for privacy and their order of presentation to the user being rank ordered based on big data profiles of the user. Ariel Porat and Lior Jacob Strahilevitz, "Personalizing Default Rules and Disclosure with Big Data," *University of Michigan Law Review*, 112, no. 8 (2014): 1417–1478.

93. Acquisti et al., "What Is Privacy Worth?," 2013.

Possible Regime Principles

THE 1980 AND 2013 OECD PRINCIPLES AND 2011 APEC PRINCIPLES

1. Consent Principle: Personal data collection and use requires user consent

   A. **Collection Limitation:** (1980 OECD)
   There should be limits to the collection of personal data and any such data should be obtained by lawful and fair means and, where appropriate, with the knowledge or consent of the data subject.

   B. **Data Quality:** (1980 OECD)
   Personal data should be relevant to the purposes for which they are to be used, and, to the extent necessary for those purposes, should be accurate, complete, and kept up to date.

   C. **Purpose Specification:** (1980 OECD)
   The purposes for which personal data are collected should be specified not later than at the time of data collection and the subsequent use limited to the fulfillment of those purposes or such others as are not incompatible with those purposes and as are specified on each occasion of change of purpose.

   D. **Use Limitation:** (1980 OECD)
   Personal data should not be disclosed, made available, or otherwise used for purposes other than those specified in accordance with [the Paragraph on Purpose Specification] except:
   (a) With the consent of the data subject; or
   (b) By the authority of law.

2. Accountable Agent Principle: A primary agent accountable to users for implementation of protections, including a right of redress with transparent policies.

   A. **Accountability:** (1980 OECD)
   Data controllers should be accountable for complying with measures, which give effect to the above-stated principles.

   B. **Individual Participation:** (1980 OECD)
   An individual should have the right:
   (a) To obtain from a data controller, or otherwise, confirmation of whether the data controller has data relating to him;

    (b) To have communicated to him, data relating to him

      (i) Within a reasonable time;

      (ii) At a charge, if any, that is not excessive;

      (iii) In a reasonable manner; and

      (iv) In a form that is readily intelligible to him;

    (c) To be given reasons if a request made under subparagraphs (a) and (b) is denied and to be able to challenge such denial; and

    (d) To challenge data relating to him and, if the challenge is successful, to have the data erased, rectified, completed, or amended.

C. **Openness:** (1980 OECD)

There should be a general policy of openness about developments, practices, and policies with respect to personal data. Means should be readily available of establishing the existence and nature of personal data and the main purposes of their use, as well as the identity and usual residence of the data controller.

3. Appropriate Data Security Safeguards Principle: Users can expect reasonable protection of data based on rigorous risk assessment and reporting of security breaches.

A. **Security Safeguards:** (1980 OECD)

Personal data should be protected by reasonable security safeguards against such risks as loss or unauthorized access, destruction, use, modification, or disclosure of data.

B. **Protection Based on Risk Management:** (2013 OECD)

Appropriate safeguards based on privacy risk assessment are integrated into core corporate governance practices and internal oversight mechanisms.

C. **Review and Notification:** (2013 OECD)

There is a responsibility to cooperate with risk management authorities, including notification of data breaches to the authorities.

4. Government Privacy Capabilities Principle

A. **Government Capacity to Enforce Privacy Policies:** (2013 OECD)

This capacity includes consistent privacy policies with independent authorities responsible for their enforcement and an obligation to cooperate with international law enforcement efforts to protect privacy.[1]

B. **Agreed Criteria for Recognition of Privacy MSOs:** (APEC)

Competent national privacy authorities may recognize MSOs as agents for certifying compliance with privacy policies if they meet criteria specified in the APEC Principles.

C. **Cooperation Assistance among Countries in Enforcing Privacy Rules:** (APEC)

Countries should create a joint oversight panel for the rules and their implementation to advance mutual assistance on privacy protection.

5. Conditional Approval Of Transborder Data Flows Principle

A. **Data Flows Approved among Qualifying Countries**: (OECD 2013)
   "A [OECD] Member country should refrain from restricting transborder flows of personal data between itself and another country where (a) the other country substantially observes these Guidelines or (b) sufficient safeguards exist, including effective enforcement mechanisms and appropriate measures put in place by the data controller, to ensure a continuing level of protection consistent with these Guidelines."

B. **Proportionate Restrictions on Data Flows**: (2013 OECD)
   "Any restrictions to transborder flows of personal data should be proportionate to the risks presented, taking into account the sensitivity of the data, and the purpose and context of the processing."[2]

Notes

1. The language includes the following: "Member countries should: a. develop national privacy strategies that reflect a coordinated approach across governmental bodies; . . . c. establish and maintain privacy enforcement authorities with the governance, resources and technical expertise necessary to exercise these powers," OECD 2013, 19 a and c.

2. The text of the individual 1980 OECD Principles is verbatim, but our organizational scheme is different. We paraphrase the 2013 OECD and the APEC Principles. 6. A and B texts quoted from OECD Privacy 2013, paragraphs 17 and 18.

IV Conclusion

9   Creating an International Governance Regime for the Digital Economy

OUR STRATEGY FOR creating an international governance regime for the digital economy builds on a core "club" of nations that could champion new digital trade agreements to advance a trusted digital environment. This agreement would adapt to the information and production disruption by improving rules for digital market integration and would make it easier to forge significant pacts advancing the goals of improving privacy and cybersecurity while safeguarding against protectionist trade risks. These agreements establish a minimum common baseline of policy through the use of binding soft "soft rules" that allow significant variations in national policy trade-offs. Expert multistakeholder organizations drawn from civil society loom large in this scheme. If trade agreements prove unworkable as a starting point, such agreements could be anchored to other types of binding policy agreements. However, trade is the first best option for consideration.

Digital DNA enables IPDs that are powerful, ubiquitous, and global. These disruptions will scramble the boundary lines between industries, induce new business models, and promote new ways of innovating in both high-tech and traditional markets. These changes will open enormous opportunities even as they create political controversy and economic rivalry. The market alone will not resolve the inevitable disputes or enable the fullest leveraging of potential opportunities.

Skillful governance will be needed. Traditional negotiations and decision making by centralized intergovernmental bureaucracies, exemplified by the

International Telecommunications Union or the World Health Organization, will be too slow and too inflexible. The fluidity of the IPD market dynamics will require governance techniques that promote substantial learning, experimentation, and flexibility. Freelancing using unilateral actions will not suffice. There will be no neat "solution." Governments should emphasize principles and processes to create a sturdy beginning point and a fruitful way to improve and adapt over time. Governments should also rely on complementary governance systems where civil society—through MSOs and innovations arising from the marketplace—contributes prominently to problem solving. Civil society is close to the ground, has incomparable expertise, and has unique resources for pragmatic policy implementation. For example, governance innovations that work for one aspect of digital privacy may not work for all aspects. It is desirable to allow specialized, bottom-up problem solving. In short, MSOs should participate in international governance regimes that define problems, build consensus, find solutions, and support authoritative baselines of rules that can accommodate variations in national preferences. The makeup of MSOs will need to be customized to the policy context, however. Similarly, because implementation solutions emanating from civil society institutions such as MSOs are fallible, they must still be accountable to the mechanisms of democratic governance.

9.1. Choices to Guide the Creation of a New Governance Regime

9.1.1. A Design and Governance Philosophy

How can we arrive at a feasible international governance regime that will improve our ability to ride on the crest of the IPD? Chapter 5 suggested starting with a design philosophy that will improve problem solving. We dubbed this philosophy *FACE*: flexible mechanisms, accountable authority, complementary governance arrangements, and experimental problem solving. We also endorsed an approach to international economic governance that embraces the idea of "partial convergence" as the best fit for the design philosophy.

FACE's implementation requires a design with six important characteristics:

1. *A club of important core countries to overcome the threshold challenge for international action*: Wider membership is an ultimate goal, not a starting point.
2. *An umbrella of authoritative rules*, based on common principles and norms, whose scope varies according to the nature of market integration: A common framework allows more bottom-up problem solving.

3. *Quasi-convergence that emphasizes flexible mixes of binding hard and soft rules and policies* within a common governance regime: The governance mix features some specific hard policy rules; it relies mostly on binding agreements requiring the embrace of specific policy capabilities based on key principles that frame the parameters of specific national rules.[1]

4. *Expert, fragmented implementation* is needed, although decisions setting the rules are frequently interlinked: Horse-trading across a broader range of issues improves on the lowest common denominator for agreements. Grand plans, centrally administered, are a mistake. Ambitious partial solution strategies operationalized through multiple channels are more likely to evolve successfully.

5. *Transparency*: Substantial transparency is needed to operate in a world with strong civil society dynamics, including in policy implementation.

6. *Public accountability of governments and MSOs*: Both governments and MSOs are more credible if they are intertwined. Ultimately, governments bear the final measure of democratic accountability.

9.1.2. *Where Should the Reform of the Governance Process Begin?*

Any fresh effort must start somewhere. Laundry lists of initiatives are ubiquitous in governments because everyone wants a piece of an important policy game. But it is necessary to figure out where the cutting edge will be.

There is substantial consensus in theory and practice about many building blocks that might enhance a trusted digital environment. Thus, progress toward an authoritative baseline agreement of considerable merit seems possible. Therefore, we link a framework for a trusted digital environment to a broader international regime for market integration through trade and investment rules. The cross-linkage of issues provides an established, but not foolproof, way to deal with difficult trade-offs regarding national preferences. This approach also allows practical, detailed work to proceed in working groups nested within broad parameters set by the governance regime. This will better reconcile necessary regulations with more pragmatic measures for their implementation. Further, it provides substantial latitude to work out practical privacy and security measures that will be responsive to variations in national constitutional traditions.

There are four reasons why trade policy might contribute to building a trusted digital environment. First, although the political dynamics of elements of a trusted digital environment, such as privacy and security, are distinctive, many of the governance elements needed for a solution are analogous to issues tackled successfully in the WTO's 1997 BTA. As posited in Chapter 5, authoritative soft rules can anchor quasi-harmonization of national rules. Moreover, existing trade agreements already contain many rules that complement any new rules. For example, the parties could agree to implement the pact on the trusted digital environment in a manner consistent with basic trade obligations, such as nondiscrimination and least trade restrictive regulations.[2] This would lower the risks that coordination solutions (the preferred approach to handling rules on privacy and security) might be altered in ways that would lead to market manipulation schemes. Lowering these risks would make it easier to embrace stronger governance principles on the trusted digital environment.

Second, civil society practices show promise as a way to tackle complex technology dynamics. Some policy problems will atrophy in importance as a result of market innovations offering plausible fixes; others will require ongoing policy experimentation and adjustment. MSOs provide a way of harnessing invaluable bottom-up expertise. (MSOs usually emerge from bottom-up collective efforts.) Although the organization of MSOs varies depending on the nature of the particular issue, a common set of evaluative guidelines can identify whether they qualify as legitimate "players" in regard to implementing trade obligations. Such guidelines already exist, for example, in regard to standards-setting organizations.

Third, trade policy can foster the cross-linkage of issues. If security and privacy are treated separately while authoritative baseline rules are developed, the baselines are more likely to settle at the lowest common denominator. However, trade-offs introduce bargaining possibilities that make it easier to accommodate more ambitious deals. Hence, despite difficult political constraints, the politics shift to trade-offs when they are part of a larger trade package. At the same time, trade frameworks can delegate expert tasks to MSOs, which provide multiple overlapping routes to progress on individual challenges and nudge major players toward greater consensus over time. Furthermore, properly designed, the initial club can expand to a broader group of countries using a variety of governance mechanisms.

Fourth, trade rules have "enforcement" mechanisms that lend to their operational authority. As the work of human rights scholars, such as Emilie Hafner-Burton, has shown, the linkage of human rights planks to trade pacts is much more powerful than a traditional human rights agreement.[3]

The current political backlash against trade agreements in OECD countries may cripple the use of trade frameworks and make it difficult for the United States to spearhead a digital economy initiative. However, one positive response that would demonstrate international policy leadership by the United States would be for the president to initiate a comprehensive review of digital economy policies, both domestic and international, as a high-level, "whole of government" undertaking. This could extend beyond the issues explored in this book, such as human rights issues posed by the digital world or equity concerns about adjusting the social safety net to the new realities of digitally disrupted labor markets. Whatever the review's scope it would bring clarity to the American agenda both domestically and globally.

We also believe that our governance approach provides a possible antidote to a second criticism from civil society and many politicians about trade. Although we believe that trade negotiations cannot succeed unless reasonably confidential, which inevitably will raise complaints about transparency, our emphasis on MSOs could bring these critics into the tent on issues of implementation. Giving NGOs a larger consultative role during the negotiations of trade agreements might lead to a better balancing of the interests of diverse interests. This could make the negotiations messier; some civil society groups are deeply suspicious of the links between trade and commerce. But if the process succeeds, it would create greater trust among the private sector, civil society, and government.

If a serious initiative to roll back existing trade commitments emerges from a volatile mix of nationalism and populist protectionism, then our preferred approach stands little chance of succeeding. President Trump pulled the United States out of the TPP in his first week as president and made the approval of the TTIP unlikely in the short term. But other trade initiatives, forays into expanded transnational deals on regulatory cooperation or even other forms of specialized treaties could be building blocks for a new regime. Such agreements probably would "borrow" certain important rules and norms from the trade regime, which provide precedents for detailed oversight of global markets and contain examples of sanctioning mechanisms. For this reason, we focus on the trade option to sharpen and simplify our prescriptive analysis. But the format of the package that we envision is flexible. Even if the trade arena is not the main initial home for the agreements on a trusted digital environment, trade can still be a complementary vehicle at a later date, more propitious for a wider trade deal. At that time existing conventions could be converted into "additional commitments" in a trade deal on market integration. This precedent evolved in the TPP (especially in Chapter 20, which covers the environment), where adherence to the Convention on International Trade in Endangered Species of Wild Fauna and Flora became an additional commitment.[4]

If the first question is where to begin, the second question is with whom should we begin? Whatever the negotiating platform, a crucial consideration is that regimes always must overcome a threshold problem. Which elements of a coalition have enough at stake, significant influence on the world market, and sufficiently compatible interests to found a club to serve as the foundation for an effective regime? This club would need to address market access and competition issue—the classic domain of trade policy. The club also would need to deal with digital privacy and security issues involved in building a trusted digital environment.

If the FACE principles shape the approach to the negotiations, the prospects for a club to coalesce on a trusted digital environment are reasonable. Privacy speaks to constitutional rights and public passions about the workings of democracy, not just to market efficiencies. Significant policy variations are inevitable. We want to identify an authoritative international baseline for marketplace transactions and privacy protection that allows for a viable global market but accommodates different national traditions. Moreover, given the fluid technological context shaping privacy and security choices, it is prudent to negotiate flexible market governance rules. The best way is to move much of the governance "action" to MSOs while retaining an explicit role for the soft trade rules that frame the regime to complement hard trade rules. Some policy practices would be forbidden to reduce certain market risks for companies, such as the TPP rule forbidding a government from demanding a company's software source code as a condition for market entry. The soft trade rules give countries direction on how to achieve certain policy outcomes. Together, the hard and soft trade rules provide the framework of checks and balances that reduce the cooperation risks that can paralyze efforts at coordination. Various solutions may arise from coordination between national-level regulators and transnational MSOs within the checks and balances created by soft trade rules.

Finally, if new states accede to either pact, questions would arise about whether equivalency must be reaffirmed every time a new member joins the club. (We say yes.) This is a difficult task, but a good one. It is a positive sign if there is enough interest from other major players who might eventually promote a digital economy agenda (DEA). This could push countries to consider ways to expand it, for example, by creating WTO plurilateral agreements to bolster the DEA. Overall, soft rules about a trusted digital environment will require serious reconsideration of national policies by China, India, Indonesia, and other players.[5] That would be a welcome development.

9.2. An Overview of the DEA

Once political leadership gives its guidance, skilled negotiators need room to negotiate. This requires flexibility to sort out the most opportune forum and vehicle for each piece of the digital governance agenda. They also need discretion on the sequence of moves leading to the end game. Much of diplomacy is an ongoing process of continual discovery and adjustment as parties sort out the rigidities and flexibilities for action. Indeed, considerable time in economic negotiations is spent sorting out the same questions inside each country's political system. This is another benefit of the kind of whole-government review that we advocate President Trump undertake.

We will suggest likely options for negotiating vehicles to illustrate our thinking, but our goal is not to prescribe a narrow diplomatic roadmap. Instead, we lay out first principles, norms, rules, and institutional mechanisms (the building blocks of the international governance regime laid out in Chapter 5). We assess these items to show how they respond to the challenges of the IPD for governance and we explain our logic about their political economic feasibility. Critical to our thinking is that there are huge gains available from a coordination strategy globally, but it also requires careful management of cooperation risks outlined in Chapter 5.

We highlight our logic by suggesting a strategy anchored in trade policy that could cumulatively achieve what we call a DEA. We expect that the DEA will emerge through a variety of bilateral, regional, plurilateral, and global agreements. Our agenda does not encompass all of the important economic or political digital issues (such as human rights). But if we make progress on selective challenges in regard to the cloud, digital market integration, and the promotion of a trusted digital environment, we will launch a productive vector for future international governance choices.

How do we propose to pursue a strategy to link advancement of a regime for a trusted digital environment to trade agreements advancing the DEA? We lay out a set of classic trade policy issues in the next section that should be addressed to take full advantage of the IPD. This is a market integration agenda. The two sections that follow then link this agenda to proposals for building a trusted digital environment. But first, how do we solve the threshold problem?

We argued that global fragmentation makes it vital to create an initial club of supporters, which is deemed valuable to its members, even if the initial core membership never expands. In Chapter 4, we suggested that the OECD members plus TPP participants together constituted a large enough share of the world economy to be a credible club globally. This group covered the Pacific more extensively than the OECD countries alone. It also had a favorable set of initial incentives for members. In the IPD, more sophisticated economies had much at stake and strong incentives to explore better governance measures. Other TPP participants, like some small members, initially cared less about the IPD, but wanted to demonstrate that they were serious players who were eager to participate in the global innovation transition. Thus, if the TPP could have been paired with its U.S.–EU counterpart, the Transatlantic Trade and Investment Partnership (TTIP), a de facto club might have emerged. Even with the demise of the TPP and the likely demise of the TTIP (at least in its 2016 form) it is possible that bilateral and narrower regional pacts could still create a de facto club capable of luring latecomers over time. Whatever the negotiating vehicles, we favor building on provisions that emerged in the TPP and TTIP texts.

The WTO could anchor two additional DEA building blocks. First, the Information Technology Agreement (ITA), originally concluded in 1996, was updated in 2015 but still needs additional expansion to fully capture the IPD, as we will discuss shortly. The ITA's eighty-two members represented 97% of the world trade in IT products. The 2015 ITA Expansion added twenty-four members, including China, Chinese Taipei, Israel, and the OECD membership.[6] A third revision might cover additional items of a DEA.

The second candidate for a global plurilateral pact to extend the logic of the DEA would be the Trade in Services Agreement (TiSA), launched in 2013, which is being negotiated at the WTO. Twenty-three countries (including the EU) representing approximately 70% of the world's trade in services participate.[7] Because of its selective nature, TiSA is being treated as a plurilateral. But unlike the Basic Telecom Agreement, TiSA does not extend most-favored-nation benefits to WTO countries that do not participate in the agreement. This is crucial because large economies such as Brazil, India, Russia, and China—none of which participate in TiSA—should not benefit from a club in which they do not pay for admission and their performance is not assessed. This is especially true because a critical benefit would be to bring quasi-convergence to national regulatory practices. (We will discuss accession by later joiners shortly.)

To illustrate the options, OECD diplomats could focus on using bilateral or regional free trade agreements (FTAs) as building blocks for the Digital Economy accords for two reasons. They precisely target our initial core club without obligating the FTA members to extend similar market access and trusted digital environment benefits to nonmembers. These conditions reduce the fears of "free riding" by countries that seek market access without making commitments (a risk under the most-favored-nation rules of the WTO) and provide a basis to allow FTA groups to negotiate tailored accession conditions with countries that wish to join them later. (This was how China (2001), Saudi Arabia (2005), Vietnam (2007), and ultimately Russia (2012) negotiated to join the WTO.) In the case of TPP, for example, it was possible that Korea, Indonesia, and Colombia (or even the United Kingdom after Brexit) might have sought early accession. The larger question in the long term would have been the interest of China, Thailand, and others to meet the required terms.

Word-for-word replication of separate DEA agreements is unlikely, but as much similarity in terms as feasible is desirable.[8] This would reinforce the incentive for other future FTAs to take up the preferred regime measures, eventually coalescing around a broader, global "plurilateral" regime built on the precedents created by the FTAs.[9]

A plurilateral pact should feature what is known as "conditional most-favored-nation" clauses. This approach would confine the benefits of the plurilateral pact to the pact's signatories. Many of the key challenges for this regime will be in interpreting soft rules through the MSO process. Which companies can be involved and benefit? The answer is an important factor in charting the course forward. If Chinese firms (through, for example, a U.S. or Australian subsidiary) can benefit from privacy and security certifications without China being part of the club, this will complicate the politics and technocratic implementation of the soft rules. (The text of the TPP agreement went a long way toward establishing a precedent for such discretion).[10] With regard to the services component of the DEA, this is a possibility for TiSA because EU negotiators have settled privacy matters with the United States, which now suggests a path forward.[11] (If TiSA collapses, it may fall on agreements among national regulatory authorities to advance the DEA agenda.)

Although we envision multiple trade agreements, we proceed as if the discussion were about the template for a single DEA agreement. We focus primarily on privacy issues. Negotiations about security issues would face parallel, but not identical, negotiating problems. The structure of our proposed bargain for the DEA agreement has five parts.

1. Design market access commitments among DEA members to improve alignment between trade and the IPD, including the cloud ecosystem.
2. Create an agreement on the trusted digital environment that emphasizes soft rules that are consistent with existing OECD and APEC principles to create a minimum baseline for privacy protection that is cost-benefit effective.
3. Guarantee members of the digital economy agreement the right to establish additional privacy safeguards beyond the baseline, subject to safeguards set forth in the DEA trade framework.
4. Link the privacy agreement to the digital economy trade agreement to strengthen the privacy agreement and remove many of the reservations among countries on market liberalization unless there is a parallel commitment to bolstering privacy and security.
5. Empower third-party mechanisms to facilitate monitoring and verification of commitments made in other privacy agreements among DEA members, subject to security concerns.

9.3. Trade: Market Access Commitments

A major feature of trade negotiations is horse-trading over a wide range of issues that are of varying importance to different countries. This section lays out how new trade rules for market integration could better adjust the world economy to the opportunities made possible by the IPD. At the same time, it will be easier to get meaningful commitments on creating an authoritative baseline for a trusted digital environment in a multidimensional bargaining environment created by advancing market integration.

Any DEA on market integration might address the thirteen major issues that were summarized in Table 3.1. Some of these items are already on the negotiating agenda. However, even if the prospective trade agreements succeed, not all of these objectives will be achieved by 2020. These goals build on our analysis of significant governance challenges of the IPD in Chapters 3 and 6. This list is not exhaustive, but it illustrates the possibilities. To delve into somewhat greater detail, we next provide more analysis of these issues and how negotiators should proceed.[12]

1. *Expand the domestic regulatory framework for services set in the TPP to include both services and digital economy goods.* Make certain that administrative rule-making is transparent and uses timely, objective criteria. Nondiscrimination among member country firms based on national origin should prevail, policies should be technologically neutral, and a "least burdensome to trade" requirement should be adopted when designing a policy. Policies also should be designed to recognize the work of competent NGOs in some policy issues, including technical certifications and standards making.[13]

2. *Expand the ITAs to further cover innovation-intensive industries.* Since the IPD introduces more "technology-like" behavior even in traditional industries, every industry cannot be treated as high tech. However, even after the progress in the revision of the ITA in 2015, the pace of major innovation will further increase and the economics of innovation-intensive industries (such as network effects) will extend beyond IT. Wireless health is one industry to expand the list of products in an ITA.[14]

3. *Negotiate the highest standards of liberalization for products that cross the traditional boundaries between a good and a service.* Going forward, SMEs should be able to deliver specialized manufactured products produced by a 3D printer in its home office and then ship it abroad by DHL. Or, it could transmit a digital design of a product to a 3D printer at a subsidiary, directly to a customer, or to a DHL office in another country.[15] Do trade rules and market access obligations (such as service access or national tariff schedule commitments) make such decisions entirely about efficiency choices? Or are choices driven by incompatibilities between forms of market access?[16]

4. *Use "solutions packages" to liberalize the intermingling of goods and services.* Negotiators should work out accommodations of issues such as the growth of "smart fields" that combine elements of hardware, sensors, and

data analytics to guide planting and insurance packages and to deal with weather risks. Negotiators also should seek trade liberalization to better address the integration of services and goods. (A GPS unit unable to access geographic information services cannot function. This was a hindrance for Uber in China because its system relied on Google Maps that were blocked in China.) The closest thing to protection in current trade proposals is the attempt to build off the established principle of technology neutrality, so it will be a challenge to find ways to ensure that this principle is applied successfully.[17]

5. *Allow nonlinear distribution and supply of audiovisual (AV) content.* Once, most AV content was either mass entertainment or stodgy "educational" programs. As a result of WTO exceptions that permit countries to protect national suppliers in the name of cultural diversity, mass AV distributors such as Netflix may be permanently shut out of some markets, even if they manage to license rights for the content.[18] But non-mass AV suppliers such as YouTube mix combinations of amateur AV content, promotional content (of performers or companies), and excerpts from commercial AV content with elements of social media interaction.[19] These formats are morphing, opening new ways for artists to create and for teachers and professors to forge educational content. They are the stuff of corporate advertising and customer "how-to" support systems. Trade experts call these suppliers of content "nonlinear" AV providers. They are central to the future of the Internet and AV, but their coverage in trade policy initiatives remains a gray area.[20] The EU initiative on establishing a single digital market includes some intriguing proposals on this topic. The 2016 EU proposal for a single digital market emphasizes this priority, and thus the DEA could complement internal market objectives.[21] However, the package has many requirements for local European content that raised criticisms. Meanwhile, the TPP included a helpful provision that affirms the value of collective management societies for handling issues of payments for copyright use.[22]

6. *Clarify trade-related obligations on interoperability requirements.* Trade negotiators should explore how to deal with the trade implications of requirements that, for example, data should be portable among different services. This is a legitimate policy objective, but it is open to policy mischief. Some possible abuses might be curbed, say, by specifying that interoperability requirements must be least trade restrictive. Governments can legitimately regulate for valid reasons, including competition policy, but should do so in a way that does the least damage to market access obligations. Clarifying the

underlying principles in negotiating and assuring that they are least trade restrictive and nondiscriminatory would reduce risks. They also would set a foundation for letting MSOs assist in implementation.

7. *Clarify obligations of private firms to provide data for public-interest or competition purposes.*[23] As countries seek to mobilize Big Data for governance projects such as smart roads and smart cities, questions arise about when and how governments could require firms to share their big data holdings with public authorities. When and how should governments require firms to share their big data holdings with public authorities? There are precedents for requiring sharing in other fields, such as health, but this will be an important issue for the future of the IPD where international agreements could reduce potential cooperation risks. Similarly, if a firm is deemed to be dominant by a competition analysis and it controls Big Data that competitors cannot match, should it be required to make the data available to its rivals? Although competition remedies for potential harms by dominant firms with "essential facilities" can take many forms, the notion of requiring competitors' access to a firm's Big Data opens many difficult questions. Given the centrality of big data analytics to the IPD, getting ahead of these tough questions is desirable.

8. *Strengthen the intellectual property protection for certain forms of craft knowledge.*[24] The IPD opens the way to new "clusters" for innovation in traditional industries that have global market ambitions. Many of these clusters will marry IPD technologies to traditional craft knowledge. Trade agreements have extensive, sometimes controversial coverage of IP in the form of firmware, software, copyrights, and patents. However, craft knowledge may focus more on trade secrets, a domain long protected in national laws, but largely neglected by trade agreements. Negotiators should build on the TPP and develop additional approaches to deal with trade secrets for trade-related purposes and then ask how it fits into the logic of trade-related investment practices.[25] They could also build on the TPP's protection of industrial design secrets and soft laws calling for protection against theft of craft knowledge that is stored digitally.

9. *Affirm the use of international standards for encryption technology and recognize the right of any firm that qualifies as a "data controller" under the trusted digital environment* annex to the DE *to use encryption for commercial purposes.*[26] (This recognition would fall under the trusted digital environment annex to the DE that is discussed next.)

10. *Affirm freedom of cross-border information flows and the freedom to choose where infrastructure for the cloud ecosystem of services is located.*[27] (See

Chapter 6.) Further, negotiators should affirm the right of a foreign company to provide a service by accessing its own business data across national borders.

11. *Affirm the freedom to locate infrastructure wherever a supplier wishes. No local presence should be required.* The use of large global cloud hubs located in another country should be permitted. Discrimination against electronic delivery of services, including software, and quantitative limits on the number or volume of services delivered should be banned. As a corollary, cross-border payments for services, subject to prudential regulation, should be permissible.[28] When public policies block the ability to combine/experiment with the integration of payment systems with information services, this hinders market access for the basic service. International governance should target unduly restrictive regulatory barriers to flexible integration of payment systems.

12. *Affirm the right of customers to use extraterritorial suppliers of services via public telecommunications networks.* Government policy also should respect technological neutrality in the delivery and technical organization of a service and interoperability should be promoted as long as neutrality is respected.

13. *Develop an agenda of investment facilitation measures* for SMEs as an adjunct to trade facilitation measures targeted to benefit SMEs. The IPD both forces and allows SMEs to expand faster internationally. Some of this expansion will be by classic export strategies. But much of it will be by investments in foreign subsidiaries or joint ventures.

Together, these thirteen points constitute an ambitious agenda. As explained in Chapter 6, one obstacle will be the fear that a bold embrace of the IPD anchored by a trade framework could lock in American IT leadership for another twenty years. But with the emergence of digital platform clusters, the rapid changes in innovation will impact even traditional industries in poorer countries and regions, and it will bolster the prospects of smaller firms in world commerce in important ways. Our discussions with experts in many countries revealed a growing recognition that the IPD will be transformative and countries either will join in or suffer competitively. It will become evident that there is a shared interest in moving toward agreement on a more integrated, mutually acceptable framework of rules for trade and investment in the IPD. This is why a number of these individual points already surfaced by 2016 in the international economic agenda. Moreover, members of the club will share a common interest in the emergence of a coherent framework to use as a model in discussions with Brazil, China, India, and other countries. The toughest challenge will be to demonstrate that this type of deal would not jeopardize the trusted digital environment. We turn to that task next.

9.4. Privacy: Soft Rules as an Authoritative Baseline

Ideally, we would link soft rules about a trusted digital environment to the trade agreement on the digital economy. Here, we mainly focus on the privacy provisions. Negotiations to deal with security issues would face parallel, but not identical, negotiating problems. Still, we develop some examples of what security soft rules might embrace.

The needed soft rules resemble the WTO BTA obligations to create core regulatory capacities for telecommunications markets that still permit substantial discretion on the specifics of the rules. In brief, the soft rules in the DEA should be consistent with existing OECD and APEC principles to create a baseline for privacy protection with a light touch. DEA principles also should oblige members to develop the capacity to cooperate with other signatories on issues related to enforcement measures to promote a trusted digital environment. As part of the policy process, the soft-rule capabilities should include mechanisms to recognize and certify MSOs among the DEA signatories. (APEC is attempting to craft something similar.) Successful support for a system of certifications crossing national borders would greatly facilitate the IPD.

These rules should mandate the following:

1. Policy capabilities at the national level to safeguard privacy.
2. Cooperation on enforcement of privacy safeguards among DEA members.
3. Cooperation in the creation of a system for the certification of MSOs that is open to all member states that can assist in the implementation of privacy codes.[29]
4. A guarantee that members of the DEA have the right to establish additional privacy safeguards beyond the baseline so long as these safeguards are:
   a. Least trade restrictive and nondiscriminatory with regard to national origin for firms from members of the club,
   b. Consistent with trade practices regarding technology neutrality, and
   c. As transparent as possible within the constraints of national security policies.
5. Subject to security safeguards, require cooperation among club members to create third-party mechanisms that facilitate verification of commitments made in various privacy agreements among DEA members.[30]

9.5. Rules for a Trusted Digital Environment

How can an international governance regime for a trusted digital environment advance? We identified our preferred club. We now specify a set of principles and norms that can underpin an authoritative international baseline of hard and soft rules with regard to privacy and security for commercial transactions.[31] There is a substantial basis for such agreement yet difficult work remains.[32] Negotiators will need to experiment with practical solutions and negotiate the costs and benefits of alternative solutions. But there is substantial agreement on the definition of the problems and the range of practical responses. Thus, next we summarize the main consensus on principles and norms for privacy and provide an explanation of the vital role of MSOs.

To begin, for reasons explained in Chapters 7 and 8, digital privacy and security rules should be consistent with horizontal trade disciplines. To illustrate, Section 14.8 of the TPP agreement's section on electronic commerce did this even as it stipulated that each member country needed a privacy protection framework and should "take into account" principles and guidelines of relevant international bodies. The protections should be published and clear on how users can get redress and on how business can show compliance. This section was compatible with our emphasis on soft rules, but vague. Next, we show how the trade rules could be expanded to build confidence using established international precedents.

Policy makers also need to recognize that there are great advantages to advancing a trusted digital environment through trade if the trade pacts adhere initially to "conditional reciprocity." In common-sense terms, conditional reciprocity means that only the countries offering functionally equivalent concessions in a trade pact (in the judgment of member governments) receive those benefits. Conditional reciprocity in this policy context is especially useful because the provisions on the trusted digital environment come close to domestic provisions governing civil liberties, criminal justice, and security choices and require nuanced calls on major economic trade-offs. It is far easier to strike such agreements in a club dominated by, but not exclusive to, countries that share similar values, political orders, and market systems.[33] More important, the use of MSOs to build on soft rules requires building consensus mechanisms and mutual recognition of MSO certifications of behavior that will involve substantial experimentation and learning. In Chapter 5, we argued that international governance regimes work best when they provide paths for countries to build the "reputations" through trusted behavior that is costly to execute. Having a tent that is too universal too soon will drive the process to the lowest common denominator because trust and broader networks of international linkages will be lower. This will work against reputational dynamics being favorable. Thus, some form of conditional reciprocity must limit the club only to those willing to raise the bar for the agreement and its implementation by MSOs.

The TPP provisions on services suggested some useful starting points on conditionality (Articles 10.3 on national treatment and 10.4 on most-favored-nation treatment). They permitted TPP members to evolve a system for mutual recognition of MSO certifications of companies for privacy and security practices without granting most-favored-nation status to non-TPP countries for this certification system. The TPP also stipulated that a TPP company that was a shell for a non-TPP company could be denied these benefits. (For example, an Indian company with a subsidiary office in Tokyo could have been denied certification benefits because India did not belong to the TPP.) If the TiSA has provisions on a trusted digital environment, then it will have to make choices on how to handle this issue of selective benefits. For now, WTO experts agree that plurilateral agreements do not impose general MFN obligations. But a request for accession to the TiSA by China, for example, would raise important questions about what guarantees to require. The accession negotiation would impose some degree of conditionality on benefits.

What would be a set of principles to embrace? We suggest melding the OECD and APEC privacy principles. The EU endorsed the OECD principles because they are consistent with the problem-solving logic of the EU policies. (See Chapter 8.) The basic logic marries contract law to a set of consumer protections to address market problems created because personal information is nonrivalrous in its use and knowledge of its uses and value is asymmetrically distributed. The information service supplier (which includes services embedded in IoT physical products, like automobiles) knows more than the individual user.

There are nine central principles. They are somewhat more detailed on the processes than the OECD Principles.

1   A *"consent"* principle for personal data collection would require user consent. Some specific protections for the user are guaranteed because the supplier knows more about the information's potential value and uses. Consent will only include data collection that is legally permissible and is proportional to the purpose for which the user consents. In addition, once collected, the data must be accurate.

2. An identifiable *"accountable agent"* principle should specify who may deal with user questions and address (and redress) complaints about the data, including the security of the data. This data controller remains accountable even if the data are transferred to another party.

3 An *"appropriate data security protection"* principle should focus on risk management based on "risk assessment" as an auditable, core corporate function.

4 A *"transparency in governance practices"* principle should require actors that collect data to make their data collection and use policies transparent to users. The concept of *"review"* and *"notification"* of practices and problems by appropriate privacy enforcement and monitoring programs should be mandated, including for MSOs. Going beyond the OECD Principles, we endorse public disclosure of government requests for personal data, subject to aggregation (e.g., annual totals) and other techniques to safeguard security considerations.

5 A *"no restrictions on transborder data flows"* principle should require countries that host country data to observe the OECD Principles *or* that a data controller maintain appropriate protections.

6 An *"obligation to create appropriate national governance"* principle should require national authorities to act to enforce and protect privacy while cooperating with other countries.

7 An *"equal treatment of data privacy regardless of where it is stored"* principle should pledge, subject to security exceptions, that data receive the same standard of protection regardless of the medium (e.g., on a personal computer or in the cloud) or national location among the DE signatories.[34]

8 A *"privacy cross-border enforcement"* principle could commit governments to develop mechanisms for sharing information and assisting in investigation and enforcement actions designed to uphold privacy obligations.[35] This could be further specified in ways that we set out later.

9 A *"mutual recognition and certification of MSOs"* principle should promote cooperation in the creation of a transparent system that designates and certifies the MSOs of data controllers of all member states. This should include a commitment to work in club councils to coordinate the work of the data controllers and explicitly embrace sector-specific MSOs. Such a principle should be subject to challenge by a national regulator if it believed an MSO failed to fulfill its certification obligations. APEC already embraces this idea but the adherence to its framework is still weak. The TPP also enabled this framework.

These nine principles could serve as the basis for drafting soft rules as an annex of additional commitments on a trusted digital environment.[36] Such an annex would be analogous to the commitments on procompetitive regulatory principles for telecom markets that provided an additional commitment in the BTA.

Even if these nine commitments are adopted, states could still impose additional safeguards for privacy and security. However, such rules would need to be developed in accordance with the "horizontal trade disciplines." To illustrate the implications of the horizontal trade disciplines (the first item on our market integration agenda), it would be consistent with the disciplines to have EU-style requirements that compel an "opt-in" system whereby users must affirmatively consent to share personal data with an information service. Requiring data "portability" also would be legitimate, as would constitutionally mandated protections for privacy, such as the right to be forgotten. However, unless a country took an explicit exception in its initial market access commitments for a particular type of data, it would be illegitimate to require that information be retained in a country except for security or extraordinary privacy issues.[37] Chapter 10 of the TPP on "Cross-Border Trade in Service" authorizes regulation of cross-border data flows for legitimate public purposes (including requirement for storage in a local cloud facility). However, it noted that, as horizontal disciplines, these rules needed to be nondiscriminatory, contain no hidden trade barriers, and be proportional to the risk.

Soft rules also reinforce the trends toward operationalizing the governance of privacy and toward granting recognized roles to MSOs in crafting applications for industries or process requirements for operations by data controllers. (Chapter 8 discussed schemes accepted by the EU and APEC.) We propose that negotiators develop language that allows the FTC and other national privacy authorities to accept MSOs as auditors and reviewers of privacy guidelines. Soft rules should also outline conditions about membership. The guidelines will require thoughtful construction. The Bildt Commission, for example, urged a requirement that an MSO in Internet governance be open to all, but not dominated by any one faction. The WTO characterizes international standards organizations, one important form of MSO, as adhering to the following principles for developing standards: transparency, openness, impartiality and consensus, effectiveness and relevance, and coherence. An additional presumptive guideline for recognition could be that the MSO membership is expert and self-organizing, as was the case with the IETF. Such a guideline would be a safeguard against governments organizing the MSOs from the top down as a general rule. At the same time, it would recognize that the membership parameters of an MSO like SWIFT will necessarily differ substantially from that of other MSOs. It also reinforces the link between expertise and the willingness to delegate authority to an MSO. One illustrative effort to apply such criteria is playing out during the transition of ICANN's IANA from U.S. control to a more independent form of global MSO. The U.S. government participated in the negotiations and announced criteria by which it would judge the acceptability of the final proposal, but the MSO community took the lead.[38]

At the same time, exceptional formats will be needed for specific reasons. Chapter 7 outlined the process by which central banks, working through the BIS (itself a MSO), reviewed expectations for cross-border financial transactions organized by SWIFT (a commercial MSO) in partnership with primary oversight by the Belgian central bank. Another more complex variation occurred when the EU and the United States crafted the Privacy Shield. Under a set of joint principles, the EU announced a regulatory agreement to accept U.S. government guarantees of enforcement of corporate declarations of compliance with the principles. The EU has the option to withdraw acceptance if annual reviews reveal significant compliance issues.[39] Within this bilateral review mechanism, the long-term question is what systematic role MSOs will play in figuring out the practical meaning of the privacy guidelines. Table 9.1 summarizes the foregoing analytic narrative.

One of the most difficult challenges for privacy policy is the crossover to criminal and government surveillance and security issues. As a complement to the thirteen principles derived from the OECD and APEC, we outline four more principles to illustrate how the cybersecurity and surveillance issues might be addressed. We state them as anchor principles for trusted digital environment codes in trade agreements.

1. *Expand mutual legal assistance treaties to include "fast tracking" of responses to subpoenas by club members.* There would be agreed-on principles for when the international cloud facilities of a club member's company can fast track a response to subpoenas in regard to a criminal complaint by another club member.[40]

2. *Commit to a "proportionality" principle for government surveillance* that weighs the cost of loss to privacy against gains for security. The principle includes a commitment for a system supervised by an independent court taking account of due process safeguards and subject to transparency requirements. All rules governing surveillance should be transparent.[41]

3. All club members should *adhere to the Budapest Convention on Cybercrime* and "pursue a common criminal policy aimed at the protection of society against cybercrime."[42] The convention covers illegal access and interception, data and system interference, computer-related forgery and fraud, offenses related to child pornography and copyright, and misuse of devices. A later "Additional Protocol" makes the publication of racist and xenophobic propaganda via computer networks a criminal offense.

4. Each country should *create a cybersecurity capability* that includes the capacity to respond cooperatively on cybercrimes (including hacking or malicious software code) with other club members. This was in the TPP electronic commerce section. This capability could have been expanded to include recognition of MSO arrangements for certification of business adherence to cybersecurity best practices (much like we have envisioned for privacy).[43]

TABLE 9.1

Twelve Important Privacy Principles

Principles	Objective
Consent	Base personal data collection on the consent of the user
Identifiable accountable agent	Specify who deals with user questions and can address and redress data complaints
Appropriate data security protection	Base corporate risk management on risk assessment that can be audited
Transparency in governance practices	Data collectors must use policies that are transparent to users
No restrictions on transborder data flows	Countries that host data will observe OECD principles or have a data controller do so
Appropriate national governance	Members should pass, protect, and enforce national laws and cooperate with others
Equal treatment of data privacy	Data privacy should be maintained, regardless of medium and where it is stored
Privacy cross-border enforcement	Members should share information and assist in investigation and enforcement actions, including deference to mutual law enforcement procedures in most cases
Multistakeholder organizations are mutually recognized for certification	Embrace transparency and mutually accept findings of data controllers certified by other member states; includes guidelines for multistakeholder organization recognition
Develop collective review mechanisms for disputes over national certifications	Includes procedures for third-party monitoring by consent of parties
Commercial encryption for privacy	Accept commercial encryption by certified companies of member states
Affirm horizontal trade disciplines	Rule-making is transparent, nondiscriminatory by national origin, and least burdensome for trade

We expect that MSOs will emerge that incorporate and work with firms and NGOs across the member states. If that occurs, they should build transnational coalitions that engage in practical problem solving. We anticipate that learning and trust would develop over time. The MSOs also will enhance transparency and the reputational incentives for countries that reinforce international governance regimes. However, recall that MSOs cannot override national policies. A government agency could still reject their certifications or proposals, but would be obliged to publicly state their reasons for doing so.[44]

International governance is, in part, an exercise in capacity building. In support of this goal, we urge the creation of seminars and guidelines on best practices for MSO governance and accountability to government authorities in parallel with the trade negotiations. In building administrative capacity, development assistance will be useful for some countries. The case studies on cybersecurity and privacy also showed that MSOs could help enhance a trusted digital environment. They also demonstrated the need for careful, ongoing adjustments of the MSO membership structures, governance, and reporting to individual and multiple groups of relevant government agencies. Membership and governance can help build confidence that most important players are operating in critical MSOs and that governments and stakeholders want governance arrangements that reflect market realities. To be legitimate, MSOs must be composed of the "right" members. This may mean creating clear expectations about the role of NGOs from civil society.

It also would be valuable to hold parallel discussions to create safe harbors and other arrangements that complement governance mechanisms specified in trade obligations. These discussions could allow the member states to calculate how prospective trade rules would influence the dynamics for other governance arrangements. They also could build confidence among companies and NGOs about expected behavior in the emerging regime. The politics of international governance and the practicalities of effective implementation require such confidence building.

Normally, energetic endorsements of pure MSO governance arrangements for important global economic issues are empty rhetoric. Governments are accountable to their citizens (or should be!). They can, and should, delegate significant authority to expert MSOs to assist with key elements of governance. But MSOs and governments are more credible and more legitimate in their exercise of authority if there are clear ways in which accountability is defined. The regulatory review mechanism endorsed in the TPP exemplified one way in which trade pacts could increase transparency and encourage learning by government agencies.

In sum, club members would benefit from this pact in several ways. Above all, it would allow them to enable desired changes on market access and competition rules without endangering privacy to spur the innovation potential of the IPD. The soft rules would make it easier to create and implement interlocking bilateral or multilateral Safe Harbor or Privacy Shield agreements among members. The DEA would recognize the right of members to craft privacy and security rules (defense and public order) consistent with their national constitutions, subject to some traditional trade policy obligations that we specified. In addition, members still would be free to restrict their data from moving to nonclub members. Another important innovation would be a commitment to allow mutually acceptable verification of adherence to commitments made in Safe Harbor and other supplementary agreements.[45] This is where specialized MSOs could do much of the practical problem solving of balancing privacy with market practicality, including recognizing the value of innovation through experimentation. Such verification mechanisms exist and have earned substantial respect, even in the most sensitive areas of military security, as witnessed by the work of the inspectors of the International Atomic Energy Agency.

Among the thirteen core privacy principles, there would need to be some significant U.S. concessions. For a Trump presidency conceding the need for any new regulations will be difficult. None would be larger than a commitment to broaden the use of a mutual legal assistance framework. The United States would cooperate with other club members when requesting subpoenas of foreign nationals' private data for law enforcement purposes. A complementary concession would be to concede that the United States would respect encryption schemes used by data controllers who are certified by appropriate authorities in the club. The largest political asset for such proposals is the desire of the U.S. business community to forge a global framework with fewer prominent contradictions on privacy and security.

The largest EU concession would be its agreement to bind market access for the cloud ecosystem in trade obligations in return for getting others to adopt soft rules strengthening privacy enforcement among major trading partners. The EU would also obtain the guarantee that the trade commitment would not limit the EU from taking additional measures to protect privacy. Another appeal of this approach for the EU is that putting privacy and security inside a trade deal strengthens the commission's claim to competence, which provides a payoff to Eurocrats for compromising on their harder-edged demands.

9.6. Overview and Next Steps

To return to where we started, why does the digital DNA that promotes the IPD matter? Where will it drive innovation? And how can its robustness be promoted through global governance?

Part I explained how the post–World War II innovation systems evolved in three waves as the United States set the pace for leading-edge innovation. In the first wave, private, vertically integrated firms anchored America's innovation system. The second wave centered on the VC-driven "Silicon Valley model." Today, this second-wave innovation system is showing signs of age.

The IPD is transforming the innovation system. As a result, we expect major change.

1. New forms of innovation will make market entry easier and lead to previously undreamed-of hybrid innovations and business models.
2. Greater digital diversity will allow the intermingling of production and information and lead to more complicated divisions of labor and value divisions.
3. The IPD will disrupt even traditional markets such as agriculture and heavy manufacturing.
4. New, diverse, and often smaller regional startup clusters built on regional digital platforms will emerge, especially in nontraditional technology markets.
5. The IPD's productive reach will be global and will incentivize small firms in every country to go global earlier in their growth.
6. There will be increased demand for new public, private, and mixed governance solutions.

To illustrate these changes in more detail and show how they were redirecting the strategies of even established market leaders, we provided case studies of a traditional agricultural behemoth, Monsanto, and of an ICT leader, Qualcomm, as it moved into advanced medical markets.

Part II then tackled two interrelated tasks. It began by analyzing the international negotiating landscape to determine the possible building blocks of a refreshed approach to IPD governance. The bottom line was simple. Despite the diffusion of innovation and economic power, there was still a credible core club that could create governance innovations for the IPD. Its membership would have basically overlapped with the negotiating countries of the TPP and TTIP. But for reasons reflecting broader trends in global politics and economics, it is more difficult to sustain credible global governance arrangements without a larger role for civil society organizations. The most theoretical portion of digital DNA followed this. Building on the analytic literature on how to achieve global governance in a technologically volatile environment, we characterized the strategic bargaining problem as one requiring the management of both coordination and cooperation issues. We concluded that the most likely approach to succeed in crafting a new, flexible, and robust governance regime will require the active involvement of MSOs in a scheme combining a minimum authoritative baseline of hard and soft rules and substantial reliance on the quasi-convergence of national regulatory systems. This approach allows for diversity while providing enough of a common foundation to reduce risks and introduce global opportunities.

Part III focused on three hard cases for governance—the challenges that are emerging because of the global quasi-convergence resulting from the cloud, cybersecurity, and digital privacy. All three of these issues raised the challenge of creating major innovations in soft and hard rules while keeping governance flexible enough to adapt to a fluid technological and economic environment.

The cloud's global reach created political economic tensions over the control of this new information infrastructure and its sweeping disruption of business models in many sectors. This turbulence manifested itself in policy debates over cross-border flows of data, the right of commercial suppliers to choose their global supply architectures for delivering cloud services, and the issues pertaining to competition policy created by the information disruption.

Next, we considered cases involving cybersecurity in the highly sensitive financial arena. We explained how the functions of interlocking MSOs reduce the risk that foreign exchange transactions will be hijacked. SWIFT, the MSO created to provide cross-border payments messaging, is a tightly managed co-op of major financial institutions, subject to collective scrutiny by the central banks of major financial centers. This was because governments wanted to maintain tight control over financial payment systems to promote economic stability. Significantly, SWIFT was invented in a bottom-up action by financial institutions, and its control over time changed in response to the growing diffusion of global financial power. A second MSO, the BIS, essentially answers to the world's major central banks. The BIS also works with the Belgian central bank to monitor SWIFT, ensuring that it is accountable.

The second case considered the issues related to consumer protection and credit card fraud involved with systems run by Visa, MasterCard, American Express, and other domestic and international card issuers. The U.S. government and the EU independently worked with MSOs representing the credit card and merchant associations to determine a path to upgrading security. Parallel actions sufficed because the geographic markets were less tightly interdependent. No single global formula was required. But the common commercial participants in the two markets and informal consultations between the American and European regulatory authorities moved the two markets in sufficiently parallel manners to allow for compatible directions in their security upgrades. The horizontal disciplines of trade agreements reduced tensions over possible cooperation problems, thus making informal collaboration easier. These probes of cybersecurity in the sensitive financial sector makes clear that the form of international governance integration will vary depending on specific market needs. The way that MSO will function in governance also will vary.

The final discussion centered on efforts to identify an international baseline that can bridge the U.S.–EU data privacy debate and specify the role that MSOs might play in addressing this issue. Our analysis showed why it is difficult for government policy to deal with privacy challenges arising from political economic tensions over the competitive consequences of privacy regimes. Arduous negotiations hammered out some common understanding of what guidelines should apply to personal data in the Atlantic market. This precedent opens the possibility of creating an authoritative international baseline for privacy rules. Strikingly, the Atlantic privacy debate relied on a delegation of business data flows to sector-specific MSOs, but focused mainly on how the U.S. and EU governments would coordinate and hold each other accountable for personal data protection (through annual reviews with the right to withdraw from the Privacy Shield if performance was poor). The role of MSOs in implementing personal data protection standards was left to each government. In contrast, APEC privacy discussions began to sketch out a more comprehensive system for linking MSOs to privacy rules on a cross-border basis.

This chapter laid out a plan for creating a DEA for the global economy. It embraced building blocks in existing international governance mechanisms and then synthesized them within a new overall strategy. We do not try to solve every problem, but we argue that everyone would be better off if there were authoritative international baselines for governance involving hard and soft rules that could ease cooperation risks that imperil useful coordination of national governance strategies.

Establishing a stable baseline requires taking into account national and regional variations to accommodate various market and political traditions that reflect legitimate differences in preferences.[46] We emphasize the need for governments to set common governance baselines (involving binding obligations to achieve certain policy functions) without attempting total harmonization of policies. As the FACE principles articulated, in a turbulent technological and business model environment, it is extremely beneficial to harness the bottom-up expertise of civil society to develop implementation strategies that evolve flexibly to changing circumstances. This incorporation of MSOs also may increase the legitimacy of the governance strategies over time by spurring mutual learning among the participants. In addition, using MSOs to abet monitoring and transparency, it is possible for governments to focus more on observable efforts toward progress and less on determining a final detailed policy solution early in the problem-solving mode. As illustrated by the case studies, the structure of these MSOs will vary by the problem area. Still, the movement in international governance toward embracing the MSO process encourages us.

International negotiators prize flexibility when pursuing a policy strategy. Still, negotiators bet on what they feel are their best options. We argued that a strategy using trade agreements, especially those that stress soft rules, might serve as the foundation for the authoritative international baseline. We showed how a trade agreement could be linked to codes to advance a trusted digital environment addressing issues of digital privacy and cybersecurity. We also suggested that this trade strategy should embrace "conditional reciprocity" where the benefits of the trade agreement, including certifications for compliance with requirements on security and privacy protections, should be extended only to members of the trade agreement. We did so because the purpose of soft law is to create a common approach (not a uniform policy) for tackling key challenges for the IPD. It will be easier for a more decentralized, bottom-up approach to implementation to succeed if there is a common approach in the member governments. From our perspective, the OECD nations and a group of reasonably like-minded emerging economies are the prime candidates for an initial push for governance reform. They share some common beliefs about governance and the collective market power to make their coordinated choices influential for strategies for all other countries. Trade vehicles such as TPP, TTIP, and TiSA could have been convenient starting points for a club to propel this governance reform. However, more complicated paths are feasible. Regardless of the specific building blocks the goal should be the creation of an open club that expands over time if new members are willing to meet the governance standards. Creating a club will require heavy lifting and universal membership at the outset would work against making the hard choices and difficult commitments that could propel a club to success over time.

Our plan will certainly be wrong in the details, but our goal is to set governance on the right vector for reform. Our governance strategy advances as an approach to creating solutions to essential global issues to ensure that the IPD continues to spur innovation, growth, and jobs everywhere. As our colleague at the IDEA project and former chair of the Federal Communications Commission, Reed Hundt, says, "Plan beats no plan."

Notes

1. Chapter 5 explained that in the trade context, soft rules are binding obligations on countries to create particular capabilities, whether for making and enforcing rules or for creating rules to achieve certain agreed-on purposes. The specific mechanisms or policies are up to the individual nation so long as they fulfill the intent of the obligation. APEC Principles, in contrast, are not binding. For a similar approach on trade, see Chris Brummer, *Minilateralism*.

2. Least trade restrictive does not equate to weak regulation. It is a condition that governments can do what is necessary, but should be prepared to justify how the rules do not significantly harm market access for reasons unrelated to the purpose of the rules. Drug safety rules are both strong and consistent with trade policy obligations.

3. Hafner-Burton, *Forced to Be Good*, 2009.

4. The TPP built on such precedents as the Annex on Forest Sector Governance in the U.S.–Peru FTA. USTR argues that the Peru FTA "includes concrete steps the Parties will take to strengthen forest sector governance and combat illegal logging and illegal trade in timber and wildlife products."

5. This could be especially sensitive for China, which might have joined the TPP at a later date. Experts from Indonesia told us in August 2016 that an active conversation on how to conform its national laws to the TPP had begun.

6. World Trade Organization, "Briefing Note: The Expansion of Trade in Information Technology Products (ITA Expansion)," December 16, 2015.

7. Twenty-three WTO members are participating in the TiSA talks: Australia, Canada, Chile, Chinese Taipei, Colombia, Costa Rica, the EU, Hong Kong China, Iceland, Israel, Japan, Korea, Liechtenstein, Mauritius, Mexico, New Zealand, Norway, Pakistan, Panama, Peru, Switzerland, Turkey, and the United States.

8. Both the timing and the politics will make synchronization and approval of separate trade and regulatory pacts tricky. But the task may be feasible because countries usually prefer consistency across agreements.

9. There is precedent. The Trade-Related Investment Practices (TRIPs) agreement in the North American Free Trade Agreement borrowed language from the Uruguay Round agreement. Ironically, the North American Free Trade Agreement (NAFTA) was completed first.

10. We thank Don Abelson for his observations on most-favored-nation treatment.

11. Interviews, Brussels, July 2016.

12. See Deputy USTR Robert Holleyman's speech at the New Democratic Network, "The Digital Economy and Trade: A 21st Century Leadership Imperative." Video at http://ndn.org/videos/2015/05/video-amb-holleyman-speech-ndn-digital-economy-and-trade-21st-century-leadership-impe.

13. One endorsement of such horizontal disciplines is European Services Forum and Coalition of Service Industries Joint Statement, "Regulatory Cooperation Component in the Services Sectors to a EU–US Economic Agreement," released November 12, 2012, http://www.esf.be/new/wp-content/uploads/2012/11/ESF-CSI-Joint-Statement-on-Regulatory-Cooperation-Component-of-EU-US-Agreement-Final-12-Nov-2012.pdf.

14. This idea is from Michelle A. Wein and Stephen J. Ezell, "Concluding a High-Standard, Innovation-Maximizing TPP Agreement," Information Technology & Innovation Foundation, December 2013, and their "How to Craft an Innovation Maximizing T-TIP Agreement."

15. Initially, when fax machines were large and expensive, delivery services such as FedEx installed them in their offices so small businesses could get "instant delivery" of documents via a FedEx office fax. Today, firms like UPS run manufacturing support facilities near their transport hubs.

16. Other discrepancies in trade rules speak to these choices. For example, technical barriers to trade disciplines of the WTO only apply to goods, a major gap for the IPD.

17. A WTO dispute ruling endorsed the potential for overlap of goods and services obligations, but using a contingent, case-by-case approach. We seek a broader principle. WTO Appellate Body Report, European Communities Regime for the Importation, Sale and Distribution of Bananas, WT/DS27/AB/R (adopted September 25, 1997), https://www.wto.org/english/tratop_e/dispu_e/27abr.pdf.

18. There is a strong precedent. The only service industry mentioned in the original 1947 General Agreement on Tariffs and Trade articles was "Cinematograph Films." Under Article IV,

contracting parties were permitted to establish "or maintain internal quantitative regulations relating to exposed cinematograph films, such regulations shall take the form of screen quotas."

19. However, unlike Netflix, which has content rights issues, YouTube can be accessed, except in a few markets where it is explicitly blocked.

20. It also posed a variety of issues about intellectual property protection that are not treated here.

21. Communication from the Commission, A Digital Single Market Strategy for Europe {SWD(2015) 100 final}, June 2, 2015, http://eur-lex.europa.eu/legal-content/EN/TXT/?uri= celex%3A52015DC0192.

22. See TPP Chapter 18 on Intellectual Property, especially Article 18.74 on Civil and Administrative Procedures and Remedies. At https://ustr.gov/sites/default/files/TPP-Final-Text-Intellectual-Property.pdf. On a related matter of intellectual property protection obligations of Internet service providers, the Bildt Commission, p. 67, endorses the "Manila Principles." This might be the basis for MSO actions to implement this soft rule.

23. We have heard ruminations about this idea in several countries; most recently, we encountered this discussion in meetings with EU officials in Brussels in June 2016.

24. Competitiveness in information services (including hybrid combinations of goods and services) depends on flexible business models to monetize the service and their applications, like games that begin as "free" and then seek ways to earn revenues using "add ons" (e.g., money messaging services or the purchase of gaming resources). In contrast, ads depend on recycling data from interaction on users and then selling the analysis to help advertisers place ads. The policy implication is that when public policies block the ability to combine/experiment with the integration of payment systems with information services, this effectively hinders market access for the basic service. Any DEA should target regulatory barriers to flexible integration of payment systems.

25. Wein and Ezell make the recommendation on trade secrets. The logic linking this to the IPD is our responsibility. As noted in Chapter 2, piracy cases are likely to be less frequent with the advent of the cloud because content is more often downloaded directly from the cloud.

26. See TPP Chapter 8 on Technical Barriers to Trade, especially Annex 8B, Section A, on ICT Products that Use Cryptography, https://ustr.gov/sites/default/files/TPP-Final-Text-Technical-Barriers-to-Trade.pdf.

27. Chapter 6 spells out the specifics of this principle. It derives from a joint U.S.–EU position paper.

28. TPP countries could have "scheduled" this commitment with exceptions for specific services that could not be expanded once the agreement was ratified. Competitiveness in information services depends on flexible business models, such as games that begin as free and then seek ways to earn revenues by selling add ons (e.g., the purchase of gaming resources).

29. This is analogous to the role of standards organizations in regard to technical barriers to trade codes in trade pacts.

30. This is how the U.S.–EU dispute over SWIFT was resolved.

31. A principle is a causal theory that suggests how to solve a problem and a norm is the emergence of expected patterns of acceptable behavior.

32. The relevant security requirement concerns data pertaining to personal privacy.

33. A skilled analysis of WTO complexities and this theme is Chander, *The Electronic Silk Road*, Chaps. 6 to 8.

34. We believe that Rob Atkinson of the Information Technology and Innovation Foundation first suggested this principle.

35. The logic is similar to obligations in the Convention on Cybercrime. This might resemble the APEC Cooperation Arrangement for Cross-Border Privacy Enforcement.

36. The Bildt Commission also endorsed the OECD Principles.

37. For example, Australia limits health information to servers located in Australia for reasons of privacy protection. We question the efficacy or logic of this policy to secure privacy protection, but Australia could take a reservation on market access to protect the policy. It could not add exceptions as the political tides surge unless it demonstrated that it fit the exemptions.

38. For the U.S. criteria, see Lawrence E. Strickling, "Stakeholder Proposals to Come Together at ICANN Meeting in Argentina," June 16, 2015, http://www.ntia.doc.gov/blog/2015/stakeholder-proposals-come-together-icann-meeting-argentina.

39. The Privacy Shield featured far more government micromanagement at the front end than would meet our aspirations for flexibility and experimentation. But much of the implementation will, over time, come closer to that of the MSO model, especially because of sector-specific agreements on privacy management.

40. For example, imagine Amazon data in its German facility was asked for data by Japan. (The United States, Germany, and Japan are all members of the club in this example.) Amazon could respond expeditiously if Japan shows that it has a legitimate interest in a criminal (or security) activity that was subject to judicial review and the person in question is not a U.S. citizen. Jennifer Daskal and Andrew Woods, "Cross-Border Data Requests: A Proposed Framework," *Lawfare*, November 24, 2015. Also see Bildt Commission, p. 50.

41. This is a modified, much abbreviated version of the principles adopted by an international expert group that was endorsed by Bruce Schneier, pp. 167–169. There is considerable support for some principle along these lines in both proposed U.S. legislation and other international expert groups involving industry and civil society. See Bildt Commission, p. 50.

42. From the preamble of the Budapest Convention, http://www.coe.int/en/web/conventions/full-list/-/conventions/treaty/185.

43. An MSO for cybersecurity might examine whether a company meets the OECD and ISO provisions on cybersecurity by design. It might also include certification of independent laboratories (such as the Underwriters Laboratories in the United States) to test cybersecurity of new products and have capacity to be the middleman for cybersecurity updates for software.

44. Other organizations could propose ways to draft rules to promote a trusted digital environment. For example, auditing and certification are special responsibilities akin to those wielded by credit rating agencies, an MSO activity that is pervasive in international financial markets.

45. Chapter 8 explained that the United States and the EU worked out a mutually acceptable verification arrangement in the dispute over subpoenas on SWIFT.

46. See Dani Rodrik, "The False Economic Promise of Global Governance," August 11, 2016, https://www.project-syndicate.org/commentary/global-governance-false-economic-promise-by-dani-rodrik-2016-08.

Selected Citations

Abbott, Kenneth, and Duncan Snidal, "Hard and Soft Law in International Governance," *International Organization*, 54, no. 3 (Summer 2000): 421–456.

Acemoglu, Daron, David Autor, David Dorn, Gordon H. Hanson, and Brendan Price, "Return of the Solow Paradox? IT, Productivity and Employment in U.S. Manufacturing," *American Economic Review* Papers and Proceedings, 104, no. 5 (2014): 394–399.

Acquisti, Allesandro, Leslie John, and George Loewenstein, "What Is Privacy Worth?," *Journal of Legal Studies*, 42, no. 2 (2103): 249–274.

Adlung, Rudolf, and Aaditya Mattoo, "The GATS," in Aaditya Mattoo, Robert M. Stern, and Gianni Zanini, *A Handbook of International Trade in Services* (New York: Oxford University Press, 2007), pp. 48–83.

Aggarwal, Vinod, *Institutional Designs for a Complex World: Bargaining, Linkages, and Nesting* (Ithaca, NY: Cornell University Press, 1998).

Aghion, Philippe, and Jean Tirole, "Formal and Real Authority in Organizations," *Journal of Political Economy*, 105, no. 1 (February 1997): 1–29.

Akerloff, George A. "The Market for 'Lemons': Quality Uncertainty and the Market Mechanism," *The Quarterly Journal of Economics*, 84, no. 3 (1970): 488–500.

Alter, Karen, *The New Terrain of International Law: Courts, Politics, Rights* (Princeton, NJ: Princeton University Press, 2014).

Amicelle, Anthony, "The Great (Data) Bank Robbery: Terrorist Finance Tracking Program and the 'SWIFT Affair,'" May 2011, Sciences Po, Center for International Studies and Research.

Andrews, Matt, *The Limits of Institutional Reform in Development: Changing Rules for Realistic Solutions* (Cambridge: Cambridge University Press, 2013).

Armbrust, Michael, et al., "A View of Cloud Computing," *Communications of the ACM*, 53, no. 4 (April 2010): 50–58.

Aronson, Jonathan D., and Peter F. Cowhey, *Managing the World Economy: The Consequences of Corporate Alliances* (New York: Council on Foreign Relations, 1993).

Aronson, Jonathan David, *Money and Power: Banks and the World Monetary System* (Thousand Oaks, CA: Sage, 1978).

Arora, Ashish, Wesley M. Cohen, and John P. Walsh, "The Acquisition and Commercialization of Invention in American Manufacturing: Incidence and Impact," National Bureau of Economic Research Working Paper 20264, June 2014.

Arthur, W. Brian, *The Nature of Technology: What It Is and How It Evolves* (New York: Free Press, 2011).

Aspen Institute, "Project on International Digital Economy Accords, Toward a Single Global Digital Economy," April 24, 2012, http://csreports.aspeninstitute.org/documents/IDEA_Project_Toward_a_Single_Global_Digital_Economy.pdf.

Atkinson, Robert D., and Stephen J. Ezell, *Innovation Economics: The Race for Global Advantage* (New Haven, CT: Yale University Press, 2012).

Atkinson, Robert D., and Paul Hofheinz, "China's Dangerous Digital Agenda," Project Syndicate, February 23, 2015, https://www.project-syndicate.org/commentary/china-digital-agenda-by-robert-d--atkinson-and-paul-hofheinz-2015-02?barrier=true.

Auldt, Graeme, *Constructing Private Governance: The Rise and Evolution of Forest, Coffee, and Fisheries Certification* (New Haven, CT: Yale University Press, 2013).

Autor, David H., David Dorn, and Gordon H. Hanson, "The China Syndrome: Local Labor Market Effects of Import Competition in the United States," *American Economic Review*, 103, no. 6 (2013): 2121–2168.

Avant, Deborah D., Margaret Finnermore, and Susan K. Sell (eds.), *Who Governs the Globe?* (Cambridge: Cambridge University Press, 2010).

Azoulay, P., J. Graff-Zivin, and B. Sampat, "The Diffusion of Scientific Knowledge across Time and Space: Evidence from Professional Transitions for the Superstars of Medicine," in Josh Lerner and S. Stern (eds.), *The Rate and Direction of Inventive Activity: A New Agenda* (National Bureau of Economic Research, April 2012): 107–160.

Bauer, Matthias, Fredrik Erixon, Michal Krol, Hosuk Lee-Makiyama, and Bert Verschelde, *The Economic Importance of Getting Data Protection Right: Protecting Privacy, Transmitting Data, Moving Commerce* (Brussels: European Centre for International Political Economy, 2013).

Bauer, Mathias, Hosuk Lee-Makiyama, Erik van der Marel, and Bert Verschelde, *The Costs of Data Localization: Friendly Fire on Economic Recovery* (Brussels: European Centre for International Political Economy, Occasional Paper No. 3/2014).

Bergsten, C. Fred, *United States in the World Economy: Foreign Economic Policy in the Next Decade* (Washington, D.C.: Peterson Institute for International Economics, 2005).

Bildt, Carl and William Kennard, "Building a Transatlantic Digital Marketplace: Twenty Steps toward 2020," The Lisbon Council, April 4, 2016, http://www.lisboncouncil.net/news-a-events/688-building-a-transatlantic-digital-marketplace-twenty-steps-to-2020.html.

Bildt, Carl and William Kennard, "Obama and Merkel: A Chance to Make History in Hanover," Atlantic Council, April 23, 2016, http://www.politico.eu/article/barak-obama-and-angela-merkel-a-chance-to-make-history-in-hannover/.

Blank, Steve, and Bob Dorf, *The Startup Owner's Manual*, The Step-by-Step Guide for Building (Palo Alto, CA: K&S Ranch Press, 2012).

Botsman, Rachel, and Roo Rogers, *What's Mine Is Yours: The Rise of Collaborative Consumption* (New York: Harper Collins, 2010).

Bradford, Scott C., Paul L. E. Grieco, and Gary Clyde Hufbauer, "The Payoff to America from Global Integration," in C. Fred Bergsten, *United States in the World Economy: Foreign Economic Policy in the Next Decade* (Washington, D.C.: Peterson Institute for International Economics, 2005), pp. 65–109.

Branstetter, Lee G., Matej Drev, and Namho Kwon, "Get with the Program: Software Driven Innovation in Traditional Manufacturing," National Bureau of Economic Research Working Paper 21752, November 2015, http://www.nber.org/papers/w21752.

Bresnahan, Timothy F., and Pai-Ling Yin, "Standard Setting in Markets: The Browser War," in Shane Greenstein and Victor Stango (eds.), *Standards and Public Policy* (Cambridge: Cambridge University Press, 2012), pp. 18–59.

Breznitz, Dan, "Why Germany Dominates the U.S. in Innovation," *Harvard Business Review*, May 27, 2014, https://hbr.org/2014/05/why-germany-dominates-the-u-s-in-innovation/.

Breznitz, Dan, and Peter Cowhey, "America's Two Systems of Innovation: Innovation for Production in Fostering U.S. Growth," *Innovations*, 7, no. 3 (Summer 2012): 127–154.

Breznitz, Dan, and John Zysman (eds.), *The Third Globalization: Can Wealthy Nations Stay Rich in the Twenty-First Century?* (New York: Oxford University, 2013).

Brotman, Stuart N. "The European Union's Digital Single Market Strategy: A Conflict between Government's Desire for Certainty and Rapid Marketplace Innovation," Center for Technology Innovation, Brookings Institution, May 2016.

Brown, Ian, and Christopher T. Marsden, *Regulating Code: Good Governance and Better Regulation in the Information Age* (Cambridge, MA: MIT Press, 2013).

Broz, J. Lawrence, and Michael Brewster Hawes, "U.S. Domestic Politics and International Monetary Fund Policy," in Darren Hawkins, David A. Lake, Daniel Nielson, and Michael J. Tierney (eds.), *Delegation and Agency in International Organizations* (New York: Academic Press, 2006).

Brummer, Chris, *Minilateralism: How Trade Alliances, Soft Law and Financial Engineering are Redefining Economic Statecraft* (Cambridge: Cambridge University Press, 2014).

Brynjolfsson, Erik, and Andrew McAfee, *The Second Machine Age: Work, Progress, and Prosperity in a Time of Brilliant Technologies* (New York: Norton, 2014).

Brynjolfsson, Erik, and Adam Saunders, *Wired for Information: How Information Technology Is Reshaping the Economy* (Cambridge, MA: MIT Press, 2009).

Büthe, Tim, and Walter Mattli, *The New Global Rules: The Privatization of Regulation in the World Economy* (Princeton, NJ: Princeton University Press, 2011).

Calvert, Randall, "Leadership and Its Basis in Problems of Social Coordination," *International Political Science Review*, 13, no. 1 (January 1992): 7–24.

Camp, L. Jean, and S. Lewis (eds.), *Economics of Information Security* (New York: Kluwer, 2004).

Carlino, Gerald, and William R. Kerr, "Agglomeration and Innovation," Research Department, Federal Reserve Bank of Philadelphia, Working Paper 14–26, August 2014.

Carr, Nicholas, *The Big Switch: Rewiring the World, from Edison to Google* (New York: Norton, 2008).

Carter, Barry, and Ryan Farha, "Overview and Operation of U.S. Financial Sanctions, Including the Example of Iran," *Georgia Journal of International Law*, 44 (2013): 903–913.

Casper, Steven, "The University of California and the Evolution of the Biotechnology Industry in San Diego and the San Francisco Bay Area," in Martin Kenney and David C. Mowery (eds.), *Public Universities and Regional Growth: Insights from the University of California* (Palo Alto, CA: Stanford University Press, 2014), pp. 66–96.

Castells, Manuel, *Networks of Outrage and Hope: Social Movements in the Internet Age* (New York: Polity Press, 2012).

Castro, Daniel, "The False Promise of Data Nationalism," The Information Technology & Innovation Foundation," December 2013.

Castro, Daniel, and Alan McQuinn, "The Economic Costs of the European Union's Cookie Notification Policy," The Information Technology & Innovation Foundation, November 2014.

Castro, Daniel, and Joshua New, "10 Policy Principles for Unlocking the Potential of the Internet of Things," Center for Data Innovation, December 4, 2014.

Chandler, Alfred D., Jr. *The Visible Hand: The Managerial Revolution in American Business* (Cambridge, MA: Belknap Press of Harvard University Press, 1977).

Chander, Anupam, *The Electronic Silk Road* (New Haven, CT: Yale University Press, 2013).

Chander, Anupam, and Ulyen P. Le, "Breaking the Web: Data Localization vs. the Global Internet," April 2014, http://papers.ssrn.com/sol3/papers.cfm?abstract_id=2407858.

Cheung, Tai Ming (ed.), *Forging China's Military Might: A New Economic Framework for Assessing Science, Technology, and the Role of Innovation* (Baltimore: Johns Hopkins University Press, 2014).

Cheung, Tai Ming, and Bates Gill, "Trade versus Security: How Countries Balance Technology Transfers with China," *Journal of East Asian Studies*, 13, no. 3 (September–December 2013): 457–482.

Clark, David D., and Susan Landau, "Untangling Attribution," *Harvard National Security Journal*, 2, no. 2 (2011): 25–40.

Clarke, Richard A., with Robert K. Knake, *Cyber War: The Next Threat to National Security and What to Do about It* (New York: Ecco Press, 2010).

Cohen, Wesley M., Richard R. Nelson, and John P. Walsh, "Protecting Their Intellectual Assets: Appropriability Conditions and Why US Manufacturing Firms Patent (or Not)," National Bureau of Economic Research Working Paper No. 7552, February 2000, http://www.nber.org/papers/w7552.

Cole, David D., "Confronting the Wizard of Oz: National Security, Expertise, and Secrecy," *Connecticut Law Review*, 44 Rev. (2012): 1627–1635.

Cooper, Richard, *The Economics of Interdependence* (New York: Columbia University Press, 1968).

Cowen, Tyler, *The Great Stagnation: How America Ate All the Low-Hanging Fruit of Modern History, Got Sick, and Will (Eventually) Feel Better* (Boston: Dutton, 2011), pamphlet.

Cowhey, Peter F., "Crafting Trade Strategy in the Great Recession: The Obama Administration and the Changing Political Economy of the United States," in Miles Kahler and David Lake (eds.), *Politics in New Hard Times: The Great Recession in Comparative Perspectives* (Ithaca, NY: Cornell University Press, 2013).

Cowhey, Peter, "Domestic Institutions and the Credibility of International Commitments: The Cases of Japan and the United States," *International Organization*, 47, no. 2 (Spring 1993): 299–326.

Cowhey, Peter F., and Jonathan D. Aronson with D. Abelson, *Transforming Global Information and Communications Markets* (Cambridge, MA: MIT Press, 2009).

Cowhey, Peter, and Stephan Haggard, "The Information and Production Disruption: Implications for Innovation Policy." U.S.–Korea Business Council, 2014, http://www.uskoreacouncil.org/wp-content/uploads/2014/12/Innovation_WhitePaper_English_FINAL.pdf.

Cowhey, Peter, and Michael Kleeman, "Unlocking the Benefits of Cloud Computing for Emerging Economies—A Policy Overview," October 2012, https://www.researchgate.net/publication/256041798_Unlocking_the_Benefits_of_Cloud_Computing_for_Emerging_Economies--A_Policy_Overview.

Cowhey, Peter F., and Mathew D. McCubbins (eds.), *Structure and Policy in Japan and the United States: The Political Economy of Institutions and Decisions* (Cambridge: Cambridge University Press, 1995).

Cowhey, Peter, and Milton Mueller, "Delegation, Networks and Internet Governance," in Miles Kahler (ed.), *Networked Politics: Agency, Power and Governance* (Ithaca, NY: Cornell University Press, 2009).

Cowhey, Peter, and John Richards, "Dialing for Dollars: Institutional Designs for the Globalization of the Market for Basic Telecommunication Services," in Aseem Prakash and Jeffrey Hart (eds.), *Coping with Globalization* (New York: Routledge, 1999), pp. 148–169.

Cox, Gary, *The Efficient Secret: The Cabinet and the Development of Political Parties in Victorian England* (Cambridge: Cambridge University Press, 1987).

Cringley, Robert X. *The Decline and Fall of IBM—End of an American Icon?* (London: Mobi, Kindle edition, 2014).

Cukier, Kenneth, Viktor Mayer-Schönberger, and Lewis Branscomb, "Ensuring (and Insuring) Critical Information Infrastructure Protection," Kennedy School of Government, RWP05-055, October 2005, http://papers.ssrn.com/sol3/papers.cfm?abstract_id=832628.

Cutler, A. Claire, Virginia Haufler, and Tony Porter (eds.), *Private Authority and International Affairs* (New York: State University of New York Press, 1999).

Davis, Frederick T., "A U.S. Prosecutor's Access to Data Stored Abroad—Are There Limits," *The International Lawyer*, 49, no. 1 (Summer 2015): 1–20.

Deibert, Ronald J., *Black Code: Inside the Battle for Cyberspace* (New York: Random House, Canada, 2014).

Delgado, Mercedes, Michael E. Porter, and Scott Stern, "Defining Clusters of Related Industries," National Bureau of Economic Research Working Paper 20375, August 2014, http://www.nber.org/papers/w20375.

Demsetz, Harold, "Toward a Theory of Property Rights," *American Economic Review*, 57, no. 2 (May 1967): 347–359.

DeNardis, Laura, *The Global War for Internet Governance* (New Haven, CT: Yale University Press, 2014).

de Weck, Olivier L., and Darci Reed, "Trends in Advanced Manufacturing Technology Innovation," in Richard M. Locke and Rachel L. Wilhausen (eds.), *Production in the Innovation Economy* (Cambridge, MA: MIT Press, 2014), pp. 235–262.

Diffie, Whitfield, and Susan Landau, *Privacy on the Line: The Politics of Wiretapping and Encryption* (Cambridge, MA: MIT Press, 1999).

Dobson, Wendy, "Financial Services and International Trade Agreements," pp. 289–337, in A. Mattoo, R. M. Stern, and Gianni Zanini, *A Handbook of International Trade in Services* (New York: Oxford University Press, 2008).

Downes, Larry, and Paul Nunnes, *Big Bang Disruption* (New York: Portfolio/Penguin, 2014).

Downs, George W., David M. Rocke, and Peter N. Barsoom, "Is the Good News about Compliance Good News about Cooperation?," *International Organization*, 50, no. 3 (Summer 1996): 379–406.

Drake, William J., Vinton G. Cerf, and Wolfgang Kleinwächter, "Internet Fragmentation: An Overview," Future of the Internet Initiative White Paper (World Economic Forum, January 2016), http://www.academia.edu/20523166/Drake_William_J._Vinton_G._Cerf_and_Wolfgang_Kleinw%C3%A4chter._2016._Internet_Fragmentation_An_Overview._Geneva_The_World_Economic_Forum_January.

Drake, William J., and Monroe Price (eds.), "Beyond Netmundial: The Roadmap for Institutional Improvements to the Global Internet Governance Ecosystem," August 2014, http://www.global.asc.upenn.edu/app/uploads/2014/08/BeyondNETmundial_FINAL.pdf

Drezner, Daniel, "The Global Governance of the Internet: Bringing the State Back In," *Political Science Quarterly*, 119, no. 3 (Fall 2004): 477–498.

Drezner, Daniel W. "Globalization, Harmonization, and Competition: The Different Pathways to Policy Convergence," *Journal of European Public Policy*, 12, no. 5 (October 2004): 841–859.

Etro, Federico, "The Economic Impact of Cloud Computing on Business Creation, Employment and Output in Europe," *Review of Business and Economic Literature*, 54, no. 2 (2009): 179–209.

European Union, "The Directive on Security of Network and Information Systems (NIS Directive), July 6, 2016, https://ec.europa.eu/digital-single-market/en/network-and-information-security-nis-directive.

Evans, David, Andrei Hagiu, and Richard Schmalensee, *Invisible Engines: How Software Platforms Drive Innovation and Transform Industries* (Cambridge, MA: MIT Press, 2006).

Ezell, Stephen J., "Ensuring the Trans-Pacific Partnership Becomes a Gold-Standard Trade Agreement," The Information Technology & Innovation Foundation, August 2012, http://www2.itif.org/2012-ensuring-tpp-gold-standard-trade-agreement.pdf.

Fallows, James, *China Airborne* (New York: Pantheon for Random House, 2012).

Felsenfeld, Carl, and Genci Bilali, "The Role of the Bank for International Settlements in aping the World Financial System," *University of Pennsylvania Journal of International Economic Law*, 25 (2004): 945.

Florida, Richard, "The World's Leading Startup Cities," 2015, http://www.citylab.com/tech/2015/07/the-worlds-leading-startup-cities/399623/.

Ford, Martin, *Rise of the Robots: Technology and the Threat of a Jobless Future* (New York: Basic Books, 2015).

Fransman, Martin (ed.), *Global Broadband Wars: Why the U.S. and Europe Lag While Asia Leads* (Palo Alto, CA: Stanford Business Books, 2006).

Fratianni, Michele, and John Pattison, "An Assessment of the Bank of International Settlements," Paper for the International Financial Advisory Commission, December 26, 1999.

Gandal, Neil, David Salant, and Leonard Waverman, "Standards in Wireless Telephone Networks," *Telecommunications Policy*, 27, nos. 5–6 (June–July 2003): 325–332.

Gans, Joshua, *The Disruption Dilemma* (Cambridge, MA: MIT Press, 2016).

Gates, Bill, *The Road Ahead* (New York: Viking, 1997).

Gilbert, Richard, and Willard K. Tom, *Is Innovation King at the Antitrust Agencies? The Intellectual Property Guidelines Five Years Later*, *Antitrust Law Journal*, 69, no. 1 (2001): 43–86.

Global Commission on Internet Governance (The Bildt Commission), "One Internet," Final Report by the Centre for International Governance and the Royal Institute for International Affairs, 2016, http://ourinternet.org/report#chapter--preface.

Goodman, Ellen P. (Rapporteur), "The Atomic Age of Data: Policies for the Internet of Things," Report of the 29th Annual Aspen Institute Conference on Communications Policy, 2015.

Goodman, Marc, *Future Crimes* (New York: Knopf Doubleday, 2015).

Gordon, Robert J., *The Rise and Fall of American Growth: The U.S. Standard of Living since the Civil War*, The Princeton Economic History of the Western World (Princeton, NJ: Princeton University Press, 2016).

Gourevitch, Peter, David Lake, and Janice Gross Stein (eds.), *The Credibility of Transnational NGOs: When Virtue Is Not Enough* (Cambridge: Cambridge University Press, 2012).

Graef, Inge, Sih Yuliana Wahyuningtyas, and Peggy Valcke, "Assessing Data Access Issues in Online Platforms," *Telecommunication Policy*, 39, no. 5 (February 2015): 375–387.

Green, Jessica F., *Rethinking Private Authority, Agents and Entrepreneurs in Global Environmental Governance* (Princeton, NJ: Princeton University Press, 2014).

Grossman, Sanford J., and Oliver D. Hart, "The Costs and Benefits of Ownership: A Theory of Vertical and Lateral Integration," *The Journal of Political Economy*, 94, no. 4 (1986): 691–719.

Hafner-Burton, Emilie M. *Forced to Be Good: Why Trade Agreements Boost Human Rights* (Ithaca, NY: Cornell University Press, 2009).

Hafner-Burton, Emilie M., Brad L. LeVeck, David G. Victor, and James H. Fowler, "Decision Maker Preferences for International Legal Cooperation," *International Organization*, 68, no. 4 (Fall 2014): 845–876.

Hafner-Burton, Emilie M., Edwin Mansfield, and Jon Pevehouse, "Human Rights Institutions, Sovereignty Costs, and Democratization," *British Journal of Political Science*, 45, no. 1 (January 2015): 1–27.

Hagel, John, J. S. Brown, T. Samaloya, and M. Lui, "From Exponential Technologies to Exponential Innovation," Deloitte Edge Center, 2013.

Stephan Haggard, "Politics in Hard Times Revisited: The 2008–9 Financial Crisis in Emerging Markets," in Miles Kahler and David Lake (eds.), *Politics in New Hard Times: The Great Recession in Comparative Perspectives* (Ithaca, NY: Cornell University Press, 2013).

Harris, Seth D., and Alan B. Krueger, "A Proposal for Modernizing Labor Laws for the Twenty First Century: The 'Independent Worker,'" The Hamilton Project, Discussion Paper 2015-10, December 2015, http://www.hamiltonproject.org/assets/files/modernizing_labor_laws_for_twenty_first_century_work_krueger_harris.pdf.

Hart, David, *Forged Consensus: Science, Technology and Economic Policy the United States, 1921–1953* (Princeton, NJ: Princeton University Press, 1998).

Hawkins, Darren, David A. Lake, Daniel Nielson, and Michael J. Tierney (eds.), *Delegation and Agency in International Organizations* (New York: Academic Press, 2006).

Held, David, Anthony McGrew, David Goldblatt, and Jonathan Perraton, *Global Transformations: Politics, Economics and Culture* (Palo Alto, CA: Stanford University Press, 1999).

Helper, Susan, Timothy Krueger, and Howard Wial, *Locating American Manufacturing: Trends in the Geography of Production* (Washington, D.C.: Brookings Institution, 2012).

Henderson, Rebecca M., and Kim Clark, *Architectural Innovation: The Reconfiguration of Existing Technologies and the Failure of Established Firms,*" *Administrative Science Quarterly*, 35, no .1

(March 1990): 9–30, http://links.jstor.org/sici?sici=0001-8392%28199003%2935%3A1%3C9 %3AAITROE%3E2.0.CO%3B2-U.

Hill, Jonah Force, "Problematic Alternatives: MLAT Reform for the Digital Age," *Harvard National Security Journal*, January 28, 2015, http://harvardnsj.org/2015/01/problematic-alternatives-mlat-reform-for-the-digital-age/.

Hirt, Martin, and Paul Willmott, "Strategic Principles for Competing in the Digital Age," *McKinsey Quarterly*, May 2014.

Hofheinz, Paul, and Michael Mandel, "Bridging the Data Gap," Progressive Policy Institute, No. 15, 2014, http://www.progressivepolicy.org/wp-content/uploads/2014/04/LISBON_COUNCIL_PPI_Bridging_the_Data_Gap.pdf.

Hossain, Tanjim, and John Morgan, "Quality Beats First-Mover Advantage: The Quest for Qwerty," *American Economic Review: Papers and Proceedings*, 99, no. 2 (March 2009): 435–440.

Hossain, Tanjim, and John Morgan, "When Do Markets Tip? A Cognitive Hierarchy Approach," *Marketing Science*, 32, no. 3 (May–June 2013): 431–453.

Hunker, Jeffrey, "Global Leadership in Cybersecurity: Can the U.S. Provide It?" in Peter Shane and Jeffrey Hunker, *Cybersecurity: Shared Risks, Shared Responsibility* (Durham, NC: Carolina Academic Press, 2012).

Inkster, Nigel, *China's Cyber Power* (Washington, D.C.: Institute for International Strategic Studies, 2016.)

Janeway, William H., *Doing Capitalism in the Innovation Economy* (Cambridge: Cambridge University Press, 2012).

Kahler, Miles (ed.), *Networked Politics: Agency, Power and Governance* (Ithaca, NY: Cornell University Press, 2009).

Kahler, Miles, "Economic Crisis and Global Governance: The Stability of a Globalized World," in Miles Kahler and David A. Lake (eds.), *Politics in the New Hard Times: The Great Recession in Comparative Perspective* (Ithaca, NY: Cornell University Press, 2013), pp. 27–51.

Kahler, Miles, and David Lake (eds.), *Politics in New Hard Times: The Great Recession in Comparative Perspectives* (Ithaca, NY: Cornell University Press, 2013).

Kennedy, Scott, and Christopher K. Johnson, "Perfecting China, Inc. The 13th Five-Year Plan," A Report of the CSIS Freeman Chair in China Studies, CSIS, May 2016, https://csis-prod.s3.amazonaws.com/s3fs-public/publication/160521_Kennedy_PerfectingChinaInc_Web.pdf.

Kenney, Martin, and Richard Florida (eds.), *Locating Global Advantage: Industry Dynamics in the International Economy* (Palo Alto, CA: Stanford University Press, 2004).

Kenney, Martin, and David C. Mowery (eds.), *Public Universities and Regional Growth: Insights from the University of California* (Palo Alto, CA: Stanford University Press, 2014).

Kenney, Martin, and John Zysman, "The Rise of the Platform Economy," *Issues in Science and Technology*, 32, no. 3 (Spring 2016), http://issues.org/32-3/the-rise-of-the-platform-economy/.

Keohane. Robert O., and Joseph S. Nye, *Power and Interdependence* (Boston: Little, Brown, 1973).

Kindleberger, Charles P., *The World in Depression, 1929–1939* (Berkeley: University of California, 1973, 2013).

King, Gary, Jennifer Pan, and Margaret E. Roberts. "How Censorship in China Allows Government Criticism but Silences Collective Expression," *American Political Science Review*, 107, no. 2 (May 2013): 1–18.

Kirshner, Jonathan, *American Power after the Financial Crisis* (Ithaca, NY: Cornell University Press, 2014).

Klepper, Steven, *Experimental Capitalism: The Nanoeconomics of American High-Tech Industries* (Princeton, NJ: Princeton University Press, 2015).

Kose, M. Ayhan, and Eswar Prasad, *Emerging Markets: Resilience and Growth amid Global Turmoil* (Washington, D.C.: Brookings Institution, 2010).

Krasner, Stephen, "Regimes and the Limits of Realism: Regimes as Autonomous Variables," *International Organization*, 36, no. 2 (Spring 1982): 497–510.

Krasner, Stephen D. "Global Communication and National Power: Life on the Pareto Frontier," *World Politics*, 43, no. 3 (April 1991): 336–366.

Krugman, Paul (ed.), *Strategic Trade Policy and the New International Economics* (Cambridge, MA: MIT Press, 1986).

Lake, David, "Rightful Rules: Authority, Order, and the Foundations of Global Governance," *International Studies Quarterly*, 54, no. 3 (September 2010): 587–613.

Lake, David A., and Mathew McCubbins, "The logic of delegation to international organizations," in Darren Hawkins, David A. Lake, Daniel Nielson, and Michael J. Tierney (eds.), *Delegation and Agency in International Organizations* (New York: Academic Press, 2006).

Landau, Susan, *Surveillance or Security? The Risks Posed by New Wiretapping Technologies* (Cambridge, MA: MIT Press, 2013).

Lanz, Rainer, Sébastien Miroudot, and Hildegunn K. Nordås, "Trade in Tasks," OECD Trade Policy Working Papers, No. 117, 2011, http://dx.doi.org/10.1787/5kg6v2hkvmmw-en.

Lenoir, Noëlle, "Data Protection in Europe vs. the United States," *Politique Internationale*," No. 151 (Spring 2016): 77–83.

Lerner, Josh, and Scott Stern (eds.), *The Rate and Direction of Inventive Activity: A New Agenda* (National Bureau of Economic Research, April 2012).

Lerner, Joshua, *The Architecture of Innovation: The Economics of Creative Organizations* (Cambridge, MA: Harvard Business Press, 2012).

Lindblom, Charles, *Politics and Markets* (New York: Basic Books, 1977).

Litan, Robert E., and Carl J. Schramm, *Better Capitalism: Renewing the Entrepreneurial Strength of the American Economy* (New Haven, CT: Yale University Press, 2012).

Locke, Richard M., and Rachel L. Wilhausen (eds.), *Production in the Innovation Economy* (Cambridge, MA: MIT Press, 2014).

Lowenberg-DeBoer, Jess, "The Precision Agriculture Revolution—Making the Modern Farmer," *Foreign Affairs*, 95, no. 3 (May–June 2015): 105–112.

Lund, Jamie, "Property Rights to Information," *Northwestern Journal of Technology and Intellectual Property*, 10, no. 1 (Fall 2011), http://scholarlycommons.law.northwestern.edu/njtip/vol10/iss1/1.

Lynn, William J., III, "Defending a New Domain: The Pentagon's Cyberstrategy," *Foreign Affairs*, 89, no. 5 (September/October 2010): 97–108.

MacCarthy, Mark, "Government and Private Sector Roles in Providing Information Security in the U.S. Financial Services Industry," in Peter Shane and Jeffrey Hunker, *Cybersecurity: Shared Risks, Shared Responsibility* (Durham, NC: Carolina Academic Press, 2012).

Mahbubani, Kishore, *The Great Convergence: Asia, the West, and the Logic of One World* (New York: PublicAffairs, 2013).

Manyika, James, et al., "Big Data: The Next Frontier for Innovation, Competition and Productivity," McKinsey Global Institute, May 2011.

Mattli, Walter, and Ngaire Woods (eds.), *The Politics of Global Regulation* (Princeton, NJ: Princeton University Press, 2009).

Mattoo, Aaditya, Robert M. Stern, and Gianni Zanini, *A Handbook of International Trade in Services* (New York: Oxford University Press, 2007).

Mayer-Schönberger, Viktor, and Kenneth Cukier, *Big Data: A Revolution That Will Transform How We Live, Work, and Think* (Boston: Houghton, Mifflin Harcourt, 2013).

McAfee, Andrew, and Erik Brynjolfsson, "Big Data: The Management Revolution," *Harvard Business Review*, 90, no. 10 (October 2012): 60–66, 68.

McAllister, Lesley K. "Regulation by Third Party Verification," *Boston College Law Review*, 53, no. 1 (1-1-2012): 1–64.

McQuivey, James, *Digital Disruption: Unleashing the Next Wave of Innovation* (Amazon Publishing, 2013).

Meeker, Mary, *Internet Trends 2016—Code Conference*, Kleiner, Perkins, Caufield, Byers, June 1, 2016, http://www.recode.net/2016/6/1/11826256/mary-meeker-2016-internet-trends-report.

Meeker, Mary, *Internet Trends in 2014*, Kleiner, Perkins, Caufield, Byers, http://www.kpcb.com/internet-trends.

Meeker, Mary, "2015 Internet Report." Kleiner, Perkins, Caufield, Byers, http://kpcbweb2.s3.amazonaws.com/files/90/Internet_Trends_2015.pdf?1432854058.

Mell, Peter, and Tim Grance, "The Cloud Dividend—Part One: The Economic Benefits of Cloud Computing to Business and the Wider EMEA Economy," Center for Economics and Business Research, December 2010.

Mell, Peter, and Tim Grance, "The NIST Definition of Cloud Computing," U.S. National Institute of Science and Technology (NIST) Special Publication 800-145, September 2011.

Meltzer, Joshua, *Supporting the Internet as a Platform for International Trade Opportunities for Small and Medium Sized Enterprises and Developing Countries* (Washington, D.C.: Brookings Institution, February 2014).

Metter, Ann, and Anthony D. Williams, *Wired for Growth Innovation: How Digital Technologies Are Reshaping Small and Medium-Sized Businesses* (Brussels: Lisbon Council, 2012).

Miller, Charlie, "The Legitimate Vulnerability Market: Inside the Secretive World of 0-Day Exploit Sales," Workshop on the Economics of Information Security, 2007, http://weis2007.econinfosec.org/papers/29.pdf.

Milner, Helen V., and Andrew Moravcsik (eds.), *Power, Interdependence, and Nonstate Actors in World Politics* (Princeton, NJ: Princeton University Press, 2009).

Mollick. Ethan, "The Dynamics of Crowdfunding: Determinants of Success and Failure.," *Journal of Business Venturing*, 29, no. 1 (2014): 1–16.

Monar, Jorg, "The Rejection of the EU–US Swift Interim Agreement by the European Parliament: A Historic Vote and Its Implications," *European Foreign Affairs Review*, 15 (2010): 143–151.

Moore, Tyler, "The Economics of Cybersecurity: Principles and Policy Options." *International Journal of Critical Infrastructure Protection*, 3:3–4 (December 2010): 103–117.

Moore, Tyler, and Ross Anderson, "Economics and Internet Security: A Survey of Recent Analytical," in Martin Peitz and Joel Waldfogel (eds.), *The Oxford Handbook of the Digital Economy* (New York: Oxford University Press, 2012).

Mosley, Layna, "Regulating Globally, Implementing Locally: The Financial Codes and Standards Effort," *Review of International Political Economy*, 17, no. 4 (October 2010): 724–761.

Mueller, Milton L., *Network and States: The Global Politics of Global Internet Governance* (Cambridge, MA: MIT Press, 2010).

Mueller, Milton L., and Brenden Kuerbis, "Roadmap for Globalizing IANA: Four Principles and a Proposal for Reform," Internet Governance Project Working Paper, 3/2014.

Murphy, Craig, and Joanne Yates, *The International Organization for Standardization (ISO): Global Governance through Voluntary Consensus* (New York: Routledge, 2008).

Newman, Abraham L., *Protectors of Privacy: Regulating Personal Data in the Global Economy* (Ithaca, NY: Cornell University Press, 2008).

Newman, Abraham L., "Transatlantic Flight Fights: Multi-level Governance, Actor Entrepreneurship and International Anti-terrorism Cooperation," *Review of International Political Economy*, 18, no. 4 (2011): 481–505.

Nye, Joseph S., Jr., "Nuclear Lessons for Cyber Security," *Strategic Studies Quarterly*, (Winter 2011), https://citizenlab.org/cybernorms2012/nuclearlessons.pdf.

Obst, Lynda, *Sleepless in Hollywood: Tales from the New Abnormal in the Movie Business* (New York: Simon & Schuster, 2014).

Odlyzko, Andrew, "Privacy, Economics, and Price Discrimination on the Internet," in L. Jean Camp and S. Lewis (eds.), *Economics of Information Security* (New York: Kluwer, 2004), pp. 187–211.

OECD, "Exploring Data-Driven Innovation as a New Source of Growth: Mapping the Policy Issues Raised by "Big Data," January 30, 2012, http://www.oecd-ilibrary.org/science-and-technology/exploring-data-driven-innovation-as-a-new-source-of-growth_5k47zw3fcp43-en.

OECD, "The Impact of Internet in OECD Countries," OECD Digital Economy Papers, No. 200, OECD Publishing (2012), http://dx.doi.org/10.1787/5k962hhgpb5d-en.

OECD, "Cloud Computing: The Concept, Impacts and the Role of Government Policy," OECD (2014) Digital Economy Papers, No. 240, OECD Publishing, http://www.keepeek.com/Digital-Asset-Management/oecd/science-and-technology/cloud-computing-the-concept-impacts-and-the-role-of-government-policy_5jxzf4lcc7f5-en#.WFiBFqIrJBw.

Ostrom, Elinor, "Beyond Markets and States: Polycentric Governance of Complex Economic Systems," Nobel Prize lecture, December 8, 2009, video at http://www.youtube.com/watch?v=T6OgRki5SgM.

Packalen, Mikko, and Jay Bhattacharya, "New Ideas in Invention," National Bureau of Economic Research, Working Paper 20922, January 2012, http://www.nber.org/papers/w20922.

Parker, Geoffry G., Marshall W. Van Alstyne, and Sangeet Paul Choudary, *Platform Revolution: How Networked Markets Are Transforming the Economy—And How to Make Them Work* (New York: Norton, 2016).

Peitz, Martin, and Joel Waldfogel (eds.), *The Oxford Handbook of the Digital Economy* (New York: Oxford University Press, 2012).

Peltz-Steele, Richard J. "The Pond Betwixt: Differences in the US–EU Data Protection/Safe Harbor Negotiation," *Journal of Internet Law*, 19, no. 1 (July 2015), http://papers.ssrn.com/sol3/papers.cfm?abstract_id=2637010.

Perla, Jesse, Christopher Tonetti, and Michael E. Waugh, "Equilibrium Technology Diffusion, Trade, and Growth," National Bureau of Economic Research, Working Paper 20881, January 2015, http://www.nber.org/papers/w20881.

Polonetsky, Jules, and Omer Tene, "Privacy and Big Data: Making Ends Meet," 66 *Stanford Law Review On-Line*, September 3, 2013, pp. 25–33.

Polsby, Nelson W. "The Institutionalization of the U.S. House of Representatives," *American Political Science Review*, 62, no. 1 (March 1968): 144–168.

Porat, Ariel, and Lior Jacob Strahilevitz, "Personalizing Default Rules and Disclosure with Big Data," *University of Michigan Law Review*, 112, no. 8 (2014): 1417.

Prakash, Aseem, and Jeffrey Hart (eds.), *Coping with Globalization* (New York: Routledge, 1999).

Prakash, Aseem, and Matthew Potoski, "Global Private Regimes, Domestic Public Law: ISO14001 and Pollution Reduction," *Comparative Political Studies*, 47, no. 3 (March 2014): 369–394.

Prestowitz, Clyde, *The Betrayal of American Prosperity: Free Market Delusions, America's Decline, and How We Must Compete in the Post-Dollar Era* (New York: Simon & Schuster, 2010).

Rao, Arun, with Piero Scoratti, *A History of Silicon Valley*, 2nd ed. (Omniware Group, Kindle eBooks, 2013).

Raustiala, Kal, and Christopher Sprigman, *The Knockoff Economy: How Imitation Sparks Innovation* (New York: Oxford University Press, 2012).

Raustiala, Kal, and David G. Victor, "The Regime Complex for Plant Genetic Resources," *International Organization*, 58, no. 2 (Spring 2004): 277–309.

Rifkin, Jeremy, *The Zero Marginal Cost Society* (Basingstoke, UK: Palgrave Macmillan Trade, 2014).

Rodrik, Dani, *The Globalization Paradox: Democracy and the Future of the World Economy* (New York: Norton, 2012).

Rodrik, Dani, "The False Economic Promise of Global Governance," August 11, 2016, https://www.project-syndicate.org/commentary/global-governance-false-economic-promise-by-dani-rodrik-2016-08.

Ross, Alec, *The Industries of the Future* (New York: Simon & Schuster, 2016).

Russell, Andrew L., *Open Standards and the Digital Age—History, Ideology and Networks* (Cambridge: Cambridge University Press, 2014).

Sabel, Charles F., "Beyond Principal-Agent Governance: Experimentalist Organizations, Learning and Accountability," in Ewald Engelen and Monika Sie Dhian Ho (eds.), *De Staat van de Democratie. Democratie voorbij de Staat*, WRR Verkenning 3 (Amsterdam: Amsterdam University Press), pp. 173–195.

Sallet, Jonathan, Ed Paisley, and Justin Masterman, *The Geography of Innovation: The Federal Government and the Growth of Regional Innovation Clusters* (Science Progress, 2009).

Saxenian, AnnaLee, *Regional Advantage: Culture and Competition in Silicon Valley and Route 128* (Cambridge, MA: Harvard University Press, 1994).

Schaede, Ulrike, *Choose and Focus: Japanese Business Strategies for the 21st Century* (Ithaca, NY: Cornell University Press, 2008).

Scharfstein, David S., and Jeremy C. Stein, "The Dark Side of Internal Capital Markets: Division Rent-Seeking and Inefficient Investment," *Journal of Finance*, 55, no. 6 (December 2000): 2537–2564.

Schelling, Thomas C., *The Strategy of Conflict* (Cambridge, MA: Harvard University Press, 1960).

Schelling, Thomas C., *Micromotives and Macrobehavior* (New York: Norton, 1978).

Scheulke-Leech, Beth-Anne, "Volatility of Federal Funding of Energy R&D," *Energy Policy*, 67 (April 2014): 943–950.

Schneier, Bruce, *Data and Goliath: The Hidden Battles to Capture Your Data and Control Your World* (New York: Norton, 2015).

Scott, Susan V., and Markos Zachariadis, *The Society for Worldwide Interbank Financial Telecommunication (SWIFT)—Cooperative Governance for Network Innovation, Standards, and Community* (New York: Routledge, 2014).

Segal, Adam, *The Hacked World Order: How Nations Fight, Trade, Maneuver, and Manipulate in the Digital Age* (New York: PublicAffairs, 2016).

Shane, Peter, and Jeffrey Hunker, *Cybersecurity: Shared Risks, Shared Responsibility* (Durham, NC: Carolina Academic Press, 2012).

Sharma, Monica, Ashwani Mehra, Haresh Jola, Anand Kumar, Madhvendra Misra, and Tiwari Vijayshri, "Scope of Cloud Computing for SMEs in India," *Journal of Computing*, 2, no. 5 (May 2010): 144–149.

Shelanski, Howard A., "Information, Innovation, and Competition Policy for the Internet," *University of Pennsylvania Law Review*, 161 (2012): 1664–1706.

Shelp, Ron, "Trade in Services." *Foreign Policy*. Number 65 (1986–1987): 64–84.

Shroff, Gautam, *The Intelligent Web: Search, Smart Algorithms, and Big Data* (New York: Oxford University Press, 2014).

Sinclair, Timothy, *The New Masters of Capital: American Bond Rating Agencies and the Politics of Creditworthiness* (Ithaca, NY: Cornell University Press, 2008).

Singer, P. W., and Allan Friedman, *Cybersecurity and Cyberwar—What Everyone Needs to Know* (New York: Oxford University Press, 2014).

Smarr, Larry, "Quantifying Your Body," *Biotechnology Journal*, 7, no. 8 (August 2012): 980–991.

Snidal, Duncan, "Coordination versus Prisoners' Dilemma: Implications for International Cooperation and Regimes," *American Political Science Review*, 79, no. 4 (December, 1985): 923–942.

Stephenson, Neal, *Snow Crash* (New York: Bantam Spectra Book, 1992).

Stone, Brad, *The Everything Store: Jeff Bezos and the Age of Amazon* (Boston: Little, Brown, 2013).

Stone, Randall W., "Institutions, Power, and Interdependence," in Helen V. Milner and Andrew Moravcsik (eds.), *Power, Interdependence, and Nonstate Actors in World Politics* (Princeton, NJ: Princeton University Press, 2009), pp. 31–49.

Strahilevitz, Lior Jacob, "Towards a Positive Theory of Privacy Law," *Harvard Law Review* 126, no. 7 (2010 (2013)).

Subramanian, Arvind, and Martin Kessler, "The Hyperglobalization of Trade and Its Future," Peterson Institute for International Economics, Working Paper 13-6, July 2013, http://www.iie.com/publications/wp/wp13-6.pdf.

Tavares, Ricardo, "Rise of the Machines," *InterMEDIA*, 42, no. 3 (Autumn 2014): 26–30.

Taylor, Astra, *The People's Platform: Taking Back Power and Culture in the Digital Age* (New York: Metropolitan Books, 2014).

Tomz, Michael, *Reputation and International Cooperation: Sovereign Debt across Three Centuries* (Princeton, NJ: Princeton University Press, 2007).

Toobin, Jeffrey, "The Solace of Oblivion," *The New Yorker*, September 29, 2014, http://www.newyorker.com/magazine/2014/09/29/solace-oblivion.

UNCTAD, "Information Economy Report 2013: The Cloud Economy and Developing Countries," p. 20, http://unctad.org/en/PublicationsLibrary/ier2013_en.pdf.

UNCTAD, "Information Economy Report 2015: Unlocking the Potential of E-commerce for Developing Countries," http://unctad.org/en/PublicationsLibrary/ier2015_en.pdf.

U.S. International Trade Commission, *Digital Trade in the U.S. and Global Economies, Part 2*, Publication Number: 4485, Investigation Number 3332-540 (Washington, DC: USITC, August 2014), https://www.usitc.gov/publications/332/pub4485.pdf.

Vance, Ashlee, *Elon Musk, Tesla, SpaceX, and the Quest for a Fantastic Future* (New York: HarperCollins, 2015).

van der Meulin, Nicole, Eun Jo, and Stefan Soesanto, "Cybersecurity in the European Union and Beyond: Exploring the Threats and Policy Response" (RAND Corporation, 2015), http://www.rand.org/pubs/research_reports/RR1354.html.

Vatis, Michael, "The Council of Europe Convention on Cybercrime," Proceedings of a Workshop on Deterring Cyberattacks: Informing Strategies and Developing Options for US policy (Washington, D.C.: National Academies Press, 2010).

Victor, David, "Fragmented Carbon Markets and Reluctant Nations: Implications for the Design of Effective Architectures." in Joseph E. Aldy and Robert N. Stavins (eds.), *Architectures for Agreement: Addressing Global Climate Change in the Post-Kyoto World* (Cambridge: Cambridge University Press, 2007).

Vogel, David, "The Private Regulation of Global Corporate Conduct," in Walter Mattli and Ngaire Woods (eds.), *The Politics of Global Regulation* (Princeton, NJ: Princeton University Press, 2009), pp. 151–188.

Vogel, Steve, "Japan's Information Technology Challenge," in Dan Breznitz and John Zysman (eds.), *The Third Globalization: Can Wealthy Nations Stay Rich in the Twenty-First Century?* (New York: Oxford University Press, 2013).

von Hippel, Eric, *Democratizing Innovation* (Cambridge, MA: MIT Press, 2005).

Walshok, Mary Lindenstein, and Abraham J. Shragge, *Invention and Reinvention: The Evolution of San Diego's Innovation Economy* (Palo Alto, CA: Stanford University Press, 2013).

Wang, Yang, Pedro Giovanni Leon, Xiaoxuan Chen, Saranga Komanduri, Gregory Norcie, Kevin Scott, Alessandro Acquisti, Lorrie Faith Cranor, and Norman Sadeh, "From Facebook Regrets to Facebook Privacy Nudges," *Ohio State Law Journal*, 74, no. 6 (2013): 1307–1335.

Warsh, David, *Knowledge and the Wealth of Nations: A Story of Economy Discovery* (New York: Norton, 2006).

Waz, Joe, and Phil Weiser, "Internet Governance: The Role of Multistakeholder Organizations," *Journal of Telecommunications and High Technology Law*, 10, no. 2 (2013): 333–350.

Wein, Michelle A., and Stephen J. Ezell, "How to Craft an Innovation Maximizing T-TIP Agreement," Information Technology & Innovation Foundation, October 2013, http://www2.itif.org/2013-innovation-maximizing-ttip-agreement.pdf.

Weitzman, Martin, "Prices vs. Quantities," *Review of Economic Studies*, 41, no. 4 (October 1974): 477–491.

White, Lawrence, "The Credit Rating Industry—An Industrial Organization Analysis," NYU Center on Law and Business Working Paper 01-001, April 2001.

Wildavsky, Aaron, *Speaking Truth to Power: The Art and Craft of Policy Analysis* (Boston: Little, Brown, 1979).

Williamson, Oliver, *The Economic Institutions of Capitalism* (New York: Simon & Schuster: 1985).

Woll, Cornelia. *The Power of Inaction: Bank Bailouts in Comparison* (Ithaca, NY: Cornell University Press, 2014).

Wong, Wendy H., *Internal Affairs: How the Structure of NGOs Transforms Human Rights* (Ithaca, NY: Cornell University Press, 2012).

Wren, Anne (ed.), *The Political Economy of the Service Transition* (New York: Oxford University Press, 2013).

Wu, Irene S., *Forging Trust Communities: How Technology Changes Politics* (Baltimore: Johns Hopkins University Press, 2015).

Wu, Tim, *The Master Switch: The Rise and Fall of Information Empires* (New York: Knopf, 2010).

Zarate, Juan C., *Treasury's War* (New York: PublicAffairs, 2013).

Zysman, John, and Dan Breznitz (eds.), *The Third Globalization* (New York: Oxford University Press, 2013).

Index

Note: Page references followed by a "*t*" indicate table; "*f*" indicate figure.